CW00725264

# The Early Computer Industry

*Also by Anthony Gandy*

BANKING STRATEGIES BEYOND 2000

CUSTOMER RELATIONSHIP MANAGEMENT – PROFIT THROUGH KNOWLEDGE

ELECTRONIC BANK: Banking and IT in Partnership (*with C. Chapman*)

THE NETWORK BANK

# The Early Computer Industry

## Limitations of Scale and Scope

Anthony Gandy
*ifs School of Finance, UK*

© Anthony Gandy 2013

All rights reserved. No reproduction, copy or transmission of this publication may be made without written permission.

No portion of this publication may be reproduced, copied or transmitted save with written permission or in accordance with the provisions of the Copyright, Designs and Patents Act 1988, or under the terms of any licence permitting limited copying issued by the Copyright Licensing Agency, Saffron House, 6–10 Kirby Street, London EC1N 8TS.

Any person who does any unauthorized act in relation to this publication may be liable to criminal prosecution and civil claims for damages.

The author has asserted his right to be identified as the author of this work in accordance with the Copyright, Designs and Patents Act 1988.

First published 2013 by
PALGRAVE MACMILLAN

Palgrave Macmillan in the UK is an imprint of Macmillan Publishers Limited, registered in England, company number 785998, of Houndmills, Basingstoke, Hampshire RG21 6XS.

Palgrave Macmillan in the US is a division of St Martin's Press LLC, 175 Fifth Avenue, New York, NY 10010.

Palgrave Macmillan is the global academic imprint of the above companies and has companies and representatives throughout the world.

Palgrave® and Macmillan® are registered trademarks in the United States, the United Kingdom, Europe and other countries.

ISBN 978–0–230–38910–6

This book is printed on paper suitable for recycling and made from fully managed and sustained forest sources. Logging, pulping and manufacturing processes are expected to conform to the environmental regulations of the country of origin.

A catalogue record for this book is available from the British Library.

A catalog record for this book is available from the Library of Congress.

10  9  8  7  6  5  4  3  2  1
22  21  20  19  18  17  16  15  14  13

Printed and bound in Great Britain by
CPI Antony Rowe, Chippenham and Eastbourne

# Contents

# List of Figures

# List of Tables

# Preface

More than most books, this volume needs a preface because its gestation has been quite remarkably long. The original work behind this book was completed in the early 1990s as a PhD thesis at the London School of Economics and Political Science (LSE). It focused on the business histories of large-scale electronics companies as they tried to enter the computer sector in competition with business machines firms, which were extending their businesses from electromechanical calculators and tabulators to also cover the building and sale of computers.

Academic life and the development of business history case studies were then put to one side for twenty years, except for one gnawing concern; the global companies with which I worked seemed little aware of their histories and therefore had little understanding of how they had developed their capabilities. This lack of self-knowledge and the inability to relate an understanding of structure and capability to performance in the marketplace suggested that the spread of business education had failed to focus the mind on matching strategic decision making to operational capability and customer requirements. The case study is the tool which can illustrate to potential leaders of the future the link between theoretical management frameworks and the reality of building a winning strategy. What better way to learn but from those who have trodden the path before and have by good design, or indeed poor design, illustrated the success or failure of different strategies.

Given this general feeling that strategy and history were neglected, my old PhD musings, the ruminations of a person with little real-world business experience, started to seem relevant again.

Two events furthered this feeling. First, one of the industries I work with, banking, imploded. One of the key causes was a generation of bank leaders who had no understanding of the special circumstances created by the very function of being a financial intermediary, and who regarded lessons from the past as an irrelevancy. They deployed the capabilities, which were handed to them by past generations of more knowledgeable leaders, in a reckless manner, unheeding of the basics of bank strategy and value creation.

Second, as financial services declined, both in the US and the UK, the call went out to rebalance the economy and reintroduce manufacturing. This related to the other industry I have been involved with, information technology and the hardware therein. Politicians increasingly call for more emphasis on manufacturing, however, their interventions during the 1950s and 1960s in the UK computer industry prevented the logical allocation of resources to those firms which had the best capability compete in the emerging new industry and created artificial rivals through sponsorship of the wrong firms. This is a story common to the car industry, the shipbuilding industry and many other industries; the effort to preserve jobs and capabilities undermined the ability of those best suited to succeed. Governments pick badly.

In this context, it seemed all too sensible to express again the link between a firm's history and its capabilities, something that senior managers should know and government should appreciate when making decisions for the future. Studying the early computer industry gives us the opportunity to explore how firms compete and how their potential in a new and innovative industry is to a large extent predetermined. This may seem fatalistic, but maybe an understanding of why an enterprise is of the wrong model to succeed in a marketplace is surely the starting place to re-engineering it so it can work and the talents and capabilities within it will be deployed and enhanced in the right way.

The realisation that the past is useful for predicting the future seems now more important after years of neglect. Twenty years after completing my PhD, it seems like an excellent moment to explore the dynamics of an industry through in-depth case studies to provide evidence on how companies perform based on their historical capabilities and how, given the set of abilities which they have, they reach their strategic choices. Most importantly though, this is no longer the work only of a naive twenty-something, but a forty-something with two decades worth more experience, which scratches his head wondering why more people in business do not look at the fundamentals of their enterprises to better understand what they need to do and how they need to do it.

# Acknowledgements

Acknowledgements are complex because, of course, this is an 'inter-temporal' book, based as it is on two sets of work separated by twenty years.

Reworking of this book is in no small part down to the hard work of Alison Thomas Steer who has read each and every page, and many pages which did not make it in. Many thanks to Alison for her help.

Of course, historical research requires resources, primarily in the form of archives. Here, thanks have to go to two generations of people from the Charles Babbage Institute (CBI) of the University of Minnesota. In 1989–90, their generosity in awarding me the Erwin and Adelle Tomash Fellowship allowed me to go to the CBI and work in what must surely be the world's premier centre for the history of computing. Professor Arthur Norberg of the Charles Babbage institute greatly encouraged me in my work. Much of the archival work I have done was at the Babbage Institute; the stalwart help of the archivist Bruce Brummer and his assistant Pat Hennessey helped me to look at material not available in the UK. Again, the administrative staff, especially Judy Cilcain, were very helpful, particularly in overcoming the many difficulties in employing an overseas researcher. Again, in 2012, Susan Hoffman of the CBI helped me revisit the archive to check on references that did not seem quite right and to plough through the huge volume of new resources they have. The CBI is a truly impressive centre of excellence and I am grateful for their support.

My UK research was made possible by the very kind support of a number of people and organisations. Back in 1988–89, the archivists at the Institution of Electrical Engineers gave me invaluable help while I researched the documents of the National Research and Development Corporation, an archive now held by the National Archive for the History of Computing. Cliff Wimpenny helped me with material in the Ferranti Archive (now at the Manchester Museum of Science and Industry), while I also received valuable help in the Marconi Archive (now at the Bodleian Library in Oxford). An excellent source of material was made available to me by Professor John Hendry, who allowed me to use interview notes he had made while he was researching the computer industry; together with some letters and papers he had collected on the subject, these proved invaluable in my studies of Electric and Musical Industries.

Special thanks go to the National Archive for the History of Computing at the University of Manchester. Rather like those at the CBI, in 2012 the archivists there probably found it somewhat odd that a seemingly new researcher turned up and yet seemed to know the files inside out; that was very much down to the help and support in 1990–91 of Dr Geoff Tweedale when he ran the archive.

The PhD on which this was based was read through and enhanced by the comments and guidance of my supervisor, Professor Leslie Hannah, and this work is only possible because of his support and that of all the other people in the Department of Economic History and the Business History Unit at the London School of Economics.

Many people have helped me to develop my thinking in more recent times. Dr Roy Edwards of the University of Southampton helped enormously thanks to his wide reading of all things related to business history and business strategy. Work colleagues at the ifs have not put up a fuss when I have gone absent to visit archives or write a new chapters, and many academics, including Dr Francesca Carnevali and Professor Peter Scott have, probably unbeknownst to them, have given me a push into completing this work when I otherwise may not have, as indeed have the good folk at Palgrave MacMillan. Many family and friends have had to listen to me drone on about the topic of this book, maybe now I will stop which will, I am sure, be appreciated.

# A Note on Referencing Styles

Books, easily accessible academic papers and trade press articles are listed using the Harvard style. Full reference can be found in the References chapter. However, much of each case-study chapter is based on archival work. Archival sources and other papers, likely to be found in only one archive, are listed as endnotes at the end of the book and are not listed in general references (apart from a few trade press articles which may be available outside the archive where they were found).

References for archival material use the system then used in the archive at the time of research; however, some archives have been consolidated and the current whereabouts of the papers are listed.

A number of archival sources form the basic raw material of this book. The major British source used is the National Archive for the History of Computing's collection of the papers of the National Research and Development Corporation. However, the referencing used is that used at the Institution of Electrical Engineers which held these records when I read them and which still appear on the files. The format of these references is

NRDC 86/box number/file number.
i.e. NRDC/86/31/5.

Other papers from the National Archive use the appropriate collection number:
NAHC/collection reference/paper reference.
i.e. NAHC/Fer/b1.

The major source of material in the US half of the book is the Charles Babbage Institute's collection of the records from the anti-trust case, US vs. IBM. This material can also be found at the Hagley Museum and in Washington so I have chosen to use a number system which is transportable across all – that is the trial's own number system.

There are two major sources within this body of material. The first are the exhibits that were lodged with the court as supporting evidence. The format of the reference to this are

US vs. IBM, px*** or dx***.
px=plaintiff's exhibit: dx=defendants exhibit.
i.e.: US vs. IBM, px344 or US vs. IBM, dx3453.

The second source of material is the collection of the transcripts from the examination of witnesses. Here the format of the reference will include both the page number of the transcript and the name of the person giving evidence:

i.e.: <u>US vs. IBM</u>, tr2420, Beard.

Other collections used at the CBI are referenced using the collection name and the box/file number.

i.e.: CBI Auerbach Collection 4/10.

All endnote references include a description of the document involved, in detail on first reference; in short thereafter. This both helps readers understand the nature of the evidence and, as I have learnt myself, to help future generations of researchers if documents move to different archives and new referencing systems are applied.

The many other sources used are individually annotated.

# Part I
# Theory and Context

Part I
Theory and Origins

# 1
# Historiography

## Introduction

This book studies two phenomena. Both ask the same question – why did those seemingly best positioned to exploit a new and rapidly developing industry fail to become dominant in what would be economically and socially one of the greatest developments mankind has seen?

The book focuses on the structures and strategies adopted by large-scale integrated electronics firms as they competed for market share in the early commercial computer industry in the US and the UK. By commercial computers, we mean general purpose computers which were sold on a commercial basis to perform business data processing tasks and/or to perform scientific calculations. This is opposed to the special purpose computer market where systems were generally bespoke to a specific function, such as communications or process control.[1] This book covers the period from approximately 1950 to 1972. This period was chosen as it covers the time when the mainframe general purpose computer became commercialised and computing technology started to embed itself into all forms of large-scale enterprise and government operations. However, most importantly, it is by 1972 that we see the two phenomena studied in this book effectively reach their endgame.

The first, and main, phenomenon studied is how and why the giant electrical and electronics corporations in the US and the UK failed to take their chance to dominate the computer industry into the 1970s. Most of the big electronic corporates targeted this market and tried to deploy the technical and financial strengths that they had developed during the Second World War and Cold War. Yet by 1972 they had all effectively left the industry beaten by smaller corporations with seemingly less technical capability in electronics and systems development. This is the key focus of this book; it uses in-depth case studies to reveal how companies with what seemed like innately strong capabilities to enter this industry, in fact, had structural flaws making the deployment of their capabilities suboptimal.

From this a secondary focus of study draws on the case studies presented to consider how the UK, the only credible competitor to the US in computing technology throughout much of the 1950s and 1960s, failed to build a vibrant computer hardware industry. Success in the computing business is about planning for change, transitioning between generations of technology and spotting new opportunities and threats generated by these transitions. The UK had a preponderance of electrical and electronics firms which benefitted from government sponsorship; arguably these were the wrong firms to support and would eventually lead to government-sponsored consolidations which saddled potentially the only viable British company (a business machines form, not a broadly based electronics manufacturer) with a legacy that would undermine its competitiveness.

## The structure of this study

This study is about the enterprise, rather than the technologies of computing. However, as is described later in this chapter, it is the technology which drove everything that the businesses did. In an environment of technical change and innovation, those who might have been expected to have the greatest capability to deal with this change were often the least successful.

This book is based on case studies; together they form a description of the competition between two main groups of companies:

- Concentrically diversified electrical and electronics groups (firms which used their expertise and resources in electronics development and manufacturing as tools to enter the emerging market for commercial electronic data processing systems)
- Business machines companies, primarily from the punched card and accounting machines industries (which were seemingly less technically capable in electronics and with considerably fewer corporate resources)

The book concentrates on the failure of the concentrically diversified electronics companies, comparing them to International Business Machines (IBM) and International Computers and Tabulators (ICT), the leading business machines firms in the US and UK – and a number of other short case studies on smaller business machines survivors. Other firms were active in the market, but are only touched on in this book. What we are interested in are the largest corporate entities and how they locked horns in the computing industry, moving in from two differently related sectors, electronics and business machines.

The chapters are:

## Studying the electronics and computer industries

This book is a historical study, based on archival research. The aim is to understand the influences which determined the strategies of the enterprises involved. Many books have looked at the computer industry in its early phase, but have either focused on the personalities involved in innovation, or taken a broad view of the firms. Many of these works, a number of which are outlined later, provide incredible insight into the innovative atmosphere which dominated the sector. This book takes an enterprise view of the firm, focusing on capabilities and resources and the interaction between these and the environment in which the computer division was competing.

To achieve this goal, an insight into the internal operations of the firms is required.

<u>Sources: Electrical/Electronics Companies in the UK Computer Industry:</u>

The case study chapters do not pretend to be complete histories of the companies outlined. They focus on the interactions of the commercial computer division of each firm with the rest of the enterprise. This can be seen as the competitive advantage held by these firms in the sector; the huge technical and financial resources available to these firms were the leverage which would prise open the lid of success in the commercial computer sector.

Therefore, the cases slice through the vertical and horizontal structures of the firms and explain why the firms targeted the commercial computer industry and why their seemingly large corporate resources and capabilities did not deliver that success. Full histories of these firms are available in other studies.

As explained in the Preface, much of the research undertaken for this book began twenty-five years before the publication of this book. An awareness of the limits of a naïve PhD student's abilities was enough to stop turning a PhD thesis into a book before gaining any experience of business and strategic decision making in the real world.

In the intervening years many more papers and books on the sector have offered new knowledge, and this is to be applauded. However, in the UK, the inner workings of the companies involved in the sector are not quite so easy to find. It is the availability of a major source in the US that really gives us an insight into the strategy of the firms and provides enough information to understand the competitive model which the firms were aspiring towards.

The sources of information available in the UK and the US vary a great deal. In the UK, 20 years ago the information on the computer sector was dispersed and fragmentary, although the establishment of the National Archive for the History of Computing (NAHC) in Manchester University, set up just as the original research commenced has improved the situation. Since I originally researched there, it has now expanded to include more papers covering the period of this research.

The starting point for studying these companies was the company annual reports and the business and trade press, the aim being to ascertain which firms were active in the industry and what they were marketing. However, these sources only give an external view. Importantly, the NAHC has brought together material on a number of companies which at the time of the initial research were distributed around a number of locations and were only partially open because those firms were not keen to expose their less-than-successful activities in the computer industry. The NAHC now has papers from firms such as ICL, English Electric (EE), LEO and Ferranti. However, the inner strategic decision making cannot necessarily be seen, as the company archives, consisting of internal strategy notes, market research, senior management discussions and decision making records, are very limited in quantity and quality. Nevertheless, there is much there which gives a real insight into the success, and sadly the failure, of the industry.

The NAHC also holds a number of personal papers and memoirs. One that has been used substantially is a copy of a private paper written by the computer sales manager of Ferranti, a hugely interesting source. This forms a nearly complete history of the Ferranti computer department. However, this vital paper has to be treated with some caution as the Ferranti computer departments was riddled with schisms, and Swann was clearly aligned with one of the interest groups within that operation.[2]

However, the most important resource at the NAHC which is used in this book and which directly relates to two of the case studies, Ferranti and Electrical and Musical Industries (EMI), and to a lesser degree the other UK firms is the NAHC's holding of the archive of the National Research and Development

Corporation (NRDC). This was previously held by the Institution of Electrical Engineers, which is where I originally researched this resource.

The NRDC helped to fund many of the computer activities of the British electronics companies. Its aim was to underpin the UK's technological and industrial base by encouraging the development of new technology-based products. The NRDC's relationship with the companies that it funded, and its involvement with the industry, can be studied through these archives. This gives some insight into how the firms that were supported operated. An excellent history of the NRDC's involvement in the computer industry was written by John Hendry (1989).

The study of the Ferranti Company could be a full-time career, especially with the transfer of the Ferranti Archive to Manchester's Museum of Science and Industry (MoSI). This is a major change from when this research was started. At that time, the Ferranti Company still existed and was going through something of a renaissance – sadly Ferranti would, at the very time of this research, purchase International Signal in the US. The accounts of International Signal were fraudulent and this combined with a lack of effective due diligence would lead to the collapse of Ferranti.[3] Luckily the archive has been saved and these files are available in the MoSI collection.

Another interesting source is the collection of seminar papers held by the London School of Economics, from the Edwards and Townsend series of talks given by leading industrialists on the organisational history of their companies.[4] A number of electronics companies were included in this series. Useful information on specific points can also be gleaned from the archives of Ferranti and Marconi.

The final British electrical/electronics company studied is English Electric. The Bodleian Library has now acquired many papers from the Marconi archive. These do include papers on English Electric's computer operations, but they are limited and only through the eyes of the Marconi part of English Electric. These papers were originally researched at the offices of General Electric Company (GEC) in Chelmsford.

In addition to UK archives, the Charles Babbage Institute (CBI), at the University of Minnesota, greatly adds to our understanding of competition and strategy in the UK computer industry. Apart from many important sources of information on the US industry (see later), the CBI has a collection of product data on British computers. In common with the NAHC in Manchester, it has copies of the computer sales statistics compiled by Computer Consultants Ltd in the 1960s. It also has a collection of American investment appraisal documents that cover the computer industry. Of these, the biweekly publications of International Data Publishing (published from 1964)[5] prove a useful source of information on the UK as well as the US.

A real bonus in analysing the UK computer industry is the CBI's copy of a large and comprehensive evaluation document prepared by the London Branch of the United States Navy's Office of Naval Research.[6] This document seems to have been an assessment of the British industry carried out to evaluate competition to the US industry, though this is not explicitly stated.

<u>Sources: Electrical/Electronics Companies in the US Computer Industry:</u>

The US computer industry offers an opportunity to triangulate the UK research with both examples of larger-scale diversified electronics groups (in this study, General Electric (GE) and Radio Corporation of America (RCA)) and to companies which not only survived in the sector (NCR, Burroughs, Sperry Rand and Honeywell) but also prospered (IBM). Indeed the study of IBM is essential as it gives us insight into the firm which effectively created the competitive environment in which other firms operated. It is because of the availability of archival materials relating to these firms that insight into the strategy of the electrical/electronics combines can be really understood in the context of their competition against the ever present IBM.

Compared to the UK industry, the pulling together of various sources is not such a problem in the US. The CBI has been in existence for a number of years and has acquired a wide-ranging collection. The trade press, regularly published investment reviews, and product literature are all readily available. In addition to aforementioned IDC publications, Moody's industry appraisals are useful,[7] much more so than the standard trade press. The CBI also has a large oral history collection, which also covers the establishment of the UK's ICL.

However, the gem which the CBI had when the original research was conducted was its near-complete copy of the evidence and transcripts of the 1970s anti-trust case <u>US vs. IBM</u> which they hold as a part of their *Computer and Communications Industry Association Collection of Antitrust Records, ca. 1940–1980* collection. This is a vast body of information, some of which has already been drawn on by researchers of the case, and researchers studying the IBM company (Fisher, McKie and Mancke 1983; Fishman 1981; Malik 1975).

The case commenced in 1969 and was terminated in 1982. For historians it represents the creation of the world's greatest repository of business strategy papers on the early computer industry coupled with in-depth cross examinations of the authors of those documents. Employees of IBM's rivals may have regretted the failure of anti-trust; it may be of little comfort to them but the records created are a goldmine of information on the early computer market.

The evidence from this trial can be used in a number of ways. This book concentrates on the evidence and transcripts which were submitted during discussions of the roles played by the RCA and GE in the computer industry. A significant proportion of the business records of these companies were submitted to the court, both from the corporate level and the operational level. These records were used in the trial to argue that RCA and GE had been forced out of the computer industry by unfair competition from IBM.

This information allows a very detailed study of their history in the computer industry and substantially improves our ability to understand why broad-based electrical/electronics companies were inherently fragile in the computer market.

As in the UK, in the past twenty years more evidence has been added to key archives. The CBI has added enormous amounts of information to its collection. A fabulous extra resource at the CBI is the record of H. R. (Barney) Oldfield. He is a character that loomed large in the original research as a senior manager in the GE computer division. He submitted a number of boxes of material to the CBI which he collected covering GE's efforts to establish itself in the computer market and would himself write a history of the early efforts of GE to enter the computer industry (Oldfield 1996). However, this is only the tip of the iceberg. The CBI has in recent years added the personal collection of other GE stalwarts such as Borge M. Christensen and Charles W. Bachman.

Indeed there is so much information now available that it threatens to swamp the avid researcher. The CBI archive is a stunning resource which a researcher could get lost in.

# 2
# Scope, Scale, Concentric Diversification and the Black Box

## Economies of scope and the concentrically diversified enterprise

Dynamic capabilities literature and other academic research are working towards an understanding of how firms can develop and exploit managerial capabilities to create and support innovation in a firm. Lawson and Samson (2001) explore seven factors which, if in place, will make a firm 'innovation capable', these are

'Vision and strategy
Harnessing the competence base
Organisational intelligence
Creativity and idea management
Organisational structure & systems
Culture and climate
Management of technology' (Lawson and Samson 2001: 377).

However, while this book fully explores the innovation process in the firms outlined – it is really about whether there is a fundamental weakness in the economic model underpinning a certain type of large-scale enterprise. That is, a large-scale concentrically diversified (i.e., its diversification is centred around a common technology or a common market) company, which presented as having industrial logic, is fundamentally weak in a highly dynamic market due to strains caused by competition for resources.

The concept of economies of scope has been known for a number of years but was best described by Panzar and Willig (1975) and Baumol, Panzar and Willig (1982) and further explored by Porter (1985) and others. This concept has been valuable to analysts of corporate structure and strategy as it provided another dimension through which firms could be analysed, not just through understanding the scale of their resources, and also the scope of their capabilities. Chandler followed this theme in his book the *Scale and Scope* (1990).

The idea that the concentrically diversified firm offers competitive advantage relies on economies of scope existing. Firms that manage a number of different products based around a core market, technology or capability can gain economies from developing, making and selling a number of different products and services that together will deliver competitive advantage.

Initially, the focus of the theory was on disaggregating the benefits of economies of scope from the economies of scale, and it was therefore cost centred. For example, if a company produces two items, x and y, economies of scope exist if the cost of making x and y together is lower than building and selling those products separately:

$$C(x, y) < C(x) + C(y)$$

*where C is defined as the cost of production.*

Economies of scale presume that the greater the level of production, the lower the cost of inputs per unit of production. Economies of scope have often been applied to mean the benefits of co-production. They exist if the cost of producing two (or more) related products is less than producing those products separately. Clearly, this has resonance in many industries. An engineering firm able to build an electric engine should easily be able to build an electrical generator. As we will see, much of the strategy at Radio Corporation of America (RCA) and General Electric (GE) was based on this assumption, and there is also some evidence which shows that this shared capabilities view existed at Electrical and Musical Industries (EMI), Ferranti and, to a larger degree, at English Electric.

This cost and capability view is the competitive edge which the firms in this study had been striving for; at least those firms which looked at the computer market as a new way to exploit their technological capability.

However, there is another way of looking at economies of scope. When looking at the benefits of economies of scope in the banking sector, Berger, Hanweck and Humphrey (1987) focused on the revenue benefits of selling similar wares to same customer base.

Indeed, banking and finance has been an industry in which much work has been done on economies of scope. Financial services markets have a number of concentrically diversified enterprise forms. The three main models are the universal banking model where banks offer corporate clients an integrated range of banking products, the bancassurance model aimed at the retail customers selling both banking and insurance products to the same pool and the composite insurance model where insurance groups offer both life and general insurance services. However, while the arguments in favour of these structures are strong, in general such integrated groups have had mixed to poor records often reverting to more specialist forms when integration proves less beneficial than expected (see for example, Aguirre, Lee and Pantos 2008; Nagata, Maeda and Imahigashi 2004; and Vennet 2002). We see in this book that similar impediments to the economics of scope take place in the electronics manufacturing sector.

When we contrast the story of the electronics firms to International Business Machines (IBM) and the other business machines firms, we see that these firms concentrated on fewer markets and those markets tend to be linked by the type of customers and their requirements rather than linked through production logic. IBM used its relationship with business customers developed through its dominance of the market for tabulating and punched card systems (the electro mechanical data collation technology before the invention of the digital computer) and built on these customer relationships. The electrical/electronics companies on which this book focuses concentrated on gaining economies of scope based on their technical and productive resources, whereas IBM focused on cross-selling new product to a common customer – IBM won.

In this respect, IBM was exploiting not only intra-temporal, but also inter-temporal economies of scope (Helfat and Eisenhart 2004: 1217–32). IBM was able to carry over from its experience in the marketing, sale, distribution and service of tabulating machines for commercial data processing specialised resources and capabilities into the market for computer-based commercial data processing. This provided clearer advantage to IBM than the core technical competencies available to the electronics firms. More importantly IBM was able to use its prehistory in data processing to develop a better understanding of customer needs – its pre-entry resources and capabilities better suited the market needs (Helfat and Lieberman 2002: 725–60).

Yates (1993) has outlined how early tabulating firms and their entrepreneurs, primarily Herman Hollerith of IBM and James Rand of Remington Rand, interacted with the life assurance industry to developed the punched card tabulator to form a vital capability for the efficient processing of insurance information. The value of this co-evolution process is surely a key understanding which the business machines firms had and could exploit. Teece (1980: 226) notes that 'the marginal cost of employing knowhow in a different endeavour is likely to be much less than its average cost of production and dissemination (transfer)'. We see that for example RCA tried to achieve these economies through the sharing of technical capability. At IBM we see that, while technically IBM was less able to do this in the core technology of computing and had to 'produce' much of this knowhow from scratch it was nevertheless able to share knowledge of peripheral systems and the use of technology in data processing functions across time periods, and was able to couple these to pre-existent customer relationships which the electronics firms entering the computer industry did not have.

## Concentrically diversified enterprises in a rapidly innovating market – stretching capabilities and resources

Nevertheless, it seems wholly sensible that the big electrical/electronics firms would have had technical and resource advantages when entering the commercial computer market – having the ability to design and manufacture complex electronics systems was hardly a disadvantage. Their failure is therefore difficult to explain. In the case study chapters we consider both a resource-based view of the firm (Barney 2001) and also a relational view (Dyer and Singh 1998), with the latter we look specifically at the intracompany capabilities and how these were shared.

The ability of firms to collaborate within the institutional framework is core to this story. Much work has been done on cluster and linkages in the computer industry and the dynamic effect this can have on innovation (Swann and Baptista 1999). Here, however, we are looking at the ability of firms to exploit their internal cluster of technology and operational resources – though we do see moments where the big electronics companies are criticised for over reliance on internal capability and not exploiting a wider supply chain.

The firms we study show both good and bad practice in their ability to create internal clusters of expertise and resources. In the very early stages of development, we can find examples of internal rivalries and attempts to protect developments made in individual divisions from competition from other business units also trying to exploit the new digital computing technologies in the commercial data processing market. Some evidence of this can be found at GE, EMI and Sperry Rand. Such examples show that problems existed in exploiting the benefits of economies of scope. There were also some examples of 'not invented here' syndrome. This is usually applied to external capabilities being rejected (Katz and Allen, 1982 and Srivastava and Gnyawali 2011). In the story here we see similar rejection of capabilities which are available taking place within the firm. 'Not invented here', could mean 'invented on the other side of the corridor' and we will see continuous internal strife within the major electronics groups and a continuous struggle for resources with business units that could well have shared resources if better organised.

Most of the firms covered in the case studies tried to develop a more structured approach with the corporate head office trying to codify the relationships of rather disparate development teams into a unified commercial computer division. However, we will see, especially in the UK case studies, examples of internal competition continuing through the (often short) lives of their computer divisions.

Achieving the advantages predicted by industrial economics for the large vertically and concentrically diversified firm depends on getting the balance of operations and the internal structure of the firm right. Separating operational units too much can lead to the firm not achieving the advantages of synergy between closely related products: they can lose out on shared economies of scale and scope.

An underlying question about the electrical/electronics groups is whether they really were trying to exploit the economies of scale or were they really conglomerates only loosely linked by a common core technology?

Whether a firm offered multiple products or focused on a single product market has implications for the likely management structure it would choose. Derek Channon's (1973) work on British industry illustrates a difference between multi-product firms and single-product companies. Channon showed that the single-product firm was more likely to use a functional framework. However, firms with multiple products in multiple markets were more likely to adopt the 'M' form of organisational structure with decentralised product groups with their own allocated resources. The M-form structure is optimised when general management is isolated from the day-to-day operations of the company and confined to strategic decision making, but the amount of divisionalisation depends on the 'firm's size, functional separability, and the state of information technology' (Williamson 1975: 148–50). Following this line, the ultimate M-form organisation becomes an internal capital market, where the decision-makers have perfect knowledge of the operating divisions on which to base their investment judgements.

This structure reflects more the organisation of a conglomerate than a firm looking to exploit the economies of scale and scope, reflecting Chandler's concerns over 'conglomeratisation' in firms such as RCA (Chandler 2005). Chandler looked at the computing operations of both GE and at RCA. He identifies the 'curse' of the conglomerate in the way these firms extended themselves into other unrelated markets. Indeed, during the time period covered there was the rise of the diversified portfolio-based industrial enterprise, with firms such as International Telephone & Telegraph (ITT) being the leaders of the movement.

Chandler implies that some of the weaknesses of these firms were due to the impact of true conglomeratisation. However, in our case studies we see real evidence of these firms trying to exploit economies of scale and scope and looking to gain competitive advantage through linking vertical and horizontal technical and industrial tasks. These firms had strategies firmly based on 'industrial logic'.

The research finds that Chandler was correct about the negative impact that individual business units competing for resources within the firm could have on the overall company. However, the research here goes further and suggests this effect is magnified if the diversification is concentric – or based around a common core technology. We will see that the industrial logic of expanding from one use of electronic components to another could, in fact, create greater challenges than true diversification. Careful examination of the detailed case histories shows a misplaced faith in concentric diversification. The research suggests that, in an environment where rapid innovation in the underlying technology of interlinked diversified businesses is the norm, concentric diversification is more damaging than the curse of the conglomerate. At least the conglomerate will have the structural benefits of products which potentially act in a countercyclical manner. A well-structured conglomerate with geographical as well as horizontal and vertical reach should achieve a product set which creates counter cyclicality within the group. As one product reaches a low point in its life cycle or a market suffers from poor demand because of the local economic cycle, other products should be in growth markets.

What we see in the case studies here are business units all centred on common technologies and all demanding investment at the same time, magnifying the problems associated with poorly constructed conglomerate business forms.

## The life cycle of market entry – getting into the early computer industry

Having pointed to the weaknesses of the concentrically diversified model, there were advantages to concentric diversification and we see them most profoundly in the first stages of market entry, even if we also see some examples of internal competition and even interdivisional jealousies occurring at this stage.

In the case study chapters of this book, which focus on the individual computer operations of each firm, three phases of development are outlined:

- Experimental phase;
- The structured market entry phase;
- The consolidation phase – coping with continuous innovation.

Of course, clearly while each of the companies studied managed to enter the industry and most came up with a strategy for long-term competitive survival, if not advantage, a number of firms fell out of the industry at each stage. Some never really managed to do more than develop computers as low-production volume electronic capital goods. More managed to launch a structured approach to the market. However, the rapidity of change and the need to survive the many transitions of the industry was often something they had not really planned for, or, more to the point, they predicted a timetable for change which others, primarily IBM, did not stick to.

Looking at these three stages of development of firms in the computer industry clearly fits with a life cycle view of products and of firms (Porter 1980: Chapter 8). Such views argue that the factors causing change in an industry alter as that technology develops. The hypothesis suggests that change in an industry is initially driven by product innovation and that competition is based on the properties of the product itself. As the technology develops and the market expands, emphasis shifts to process innovations, the target being to produce the product more efficiently. Abernathy and Utterback (1978) concluded that innovation in an industry shifts from a fluid period to a static period. In the initial stages of a new industry when the product is not completely settled on, there is room for further improvements to it. At this stage there may not even be a single view on what is the best format for the product. Competition and further innovation improves the product and shakes out the less successful product ideas, eventually reaching a point of near standardisation. This is the start of the static stage where technical competition is primarily focused on the efficient production of a known commodity, leading to greater emphasis on process innovation and the growing importance of scale economies. Examples include the semiconductor industry (Tilton 1971) and the automobile industry (Abernathy 1978).

### Experimental stage

In the first stage of development, we see a number of experimental and often ad hoc steps into the new commercial data processing market. Often the projects were high technology, but hand-built with small-scale development projects. Some were planned as the first stage of a formal entry into the industry; some were simply fulfilling one-off contracts for capital electronics equipment that could be further developed at a later stage. At this stage we can characterise the concentrically diversified electrical/electronics firms as mainly successful in exploiting their internal capabilities to develop the core technologies needed for commercial data processing systems. A number of the rival business machines firms had to look outside of their structures for the technology – though this is not the case with IBM which had its own electronics capability but, as we will see, there was not a totally harmonised strategy even at IBM during this period of their development.

The building of computers was an extension of the electronics firms' horizontal and vertical scope, an extension of the way in which they exploited their core capability – electronic engineering. There is some discussion in each case study chapter of where and how the product champions for computing developed within the firm in this 'internal corporate venturing process' (see, for example, the work of Burgelman 1988). The position of the product champion is an important issue and greatly affects the political standing of divisions within a company, which in itself influences the likelihood of successful diversification (Rothwell et al. 1974 – This research project looked at paired examples of successful and unsuccessful company innovators which included study of the internal entrepreneurs.) It is important to establish whether the product champions of a new activity in the electronics firms, in this case those championing the building of commercial computers, had as much influence as those representing older activities. This is vital in determining who had the most say in how corporate resources were allocated between different divisions. The single most important theme of this book is how the electronics companies handled this process of allocating limited resources between their many potential growth paths. This process of decision making is greatly affected by the political standing of the various divisions in each company; this political issue will be considered in each of the case studies and in the Conclusion. Some of the initial start-ups were often ad hoc. Some of the internal product champions not only lacked corporate authority to start the development of commercial computers but even used sleight of hand to cover up what they were really doing – as in the case of GE. Other firms found that development of commercial computers began in multiple divisions creating competing teams (EMI, and to some degree, GE) or only entered the business to fulfil a one-off development contract or series of development contracts with little regard for staying in the market thereafter (Ferranti, RCA and again, to some degree, EMI and GE). This may sound negative, however it shows the ability of these firms to understand and complete capital electronics development programmes using the internal resources they had. In the early phases of the computer industry (see the outline of the computer generations later in this chapter), they were not alone in not knowing whether this was a sector of the capital electronics market or another market altogether.

It would soon be obvious that it was another market and the firms involved had to create a formal structure and strategy for delivering commercial computers for data processing work.

**Structured market entry**

While initial developments tended to be ad hoc in nature, there was a second stage to truly entering the market – creating a second generation of systems aimed at solidifying early developments and providing a more robust product strategy for winning market share. For those firms that achieved this stage, it was a move away from viewing and producing computers as a series of one-off capital electronics projects to series production and wide and comprehensive support for those systems in the marketplace. These more structured approaches to the computer industry were only possible as the technology developed and as market need developed (for some firms this second effort was based on the first-generation computer technologies while some waited until the second generation of technology to develop this structured approach).

In nearly all cases, we see the concentrically diversified companies exploit the real benefits of their enterprise form as they drew in internal resources, exploited their capabilities in digital design, electronic engineering, production engineering while drawing on financial support from the centre of the enterprise. These tended to be larger-scale developments and the resources of the enterprise were important to building a robust challenge in the commercial Electronic Data Processing (EDP) market. This was certainly the lesson of both the US and British.

However, the productisation of the computer was only one element in this process. The move from producing systems as capital electronics goods, usually purchased by the government for very advanced technical users meant competing in the commercial data processing market a market which had been developed using punched card technology. It required software support so less technically advanced clients could exploit systems, it meant reliability and service capabilities beyond what had already been offered and, most importantly, it meant fitting into the economic model for that market. This economic model was based on the leasing of systems not the purchase of systems. IBM had for many decades leased its systems and provided a package of support as a part of that lease arrangement. To make the transfer from interesting technical innovation to batch produced, widely marketed and distributed office equipment, firms had to be able to support leases. The computer industry was fast growing and profitable, at least for the leader, however, other firms had to balance the cost of development, production of leased systems 'and their' cost of capital, many would find that this reduced the pace they could grow and their ability to produce in large numbers. Producing in smaller numbers reduced capital costs because few leases needed financing, and it also meant development costs were spread over fewer systems.

### Consolidation phase – coping with continuous innovation

Once firms had established a presence in the market, with a generation of systems that were credible and for which a customer base had been found, firms could expect to move into what Abernathy and Utterback (1978) called the static phase. In this market, effort was focused on consolidating and exploiting the earlier development and market position through the delivery of a generation of new systems which were based on a more standardised approach to commercial data processing. Some firms tried to create a universe in which their customers would operate in a standardised environment which the firm itself created; others (RCA and English Electric) would try to piggyback another firm's standardised environment – namely by providing some compatibility with the IBM third-generation family, System/360 (Takahashi 2005 describes some of the efforts of other firms in achieving 360 compatibility).

It is at this stage where we see whether the largest concentrically diversified electronics firms sampled, RCA, GE and English Electric, really gained any long-term advantage from their corporate structure. However, despite the logic of their strategy and the mutually supportive capabilities of their related product groups, none of the main firms studied here managed to survive this phase. The problem they faced was that there was never really a period in which they could exploit the investments that they had made because the market and the technology would simply not stand still. For these firms, with a common core technology across many different product sets, resources were always needed to introduce the latest techniques, not just to the commercial EDP market but to all the other associated products that these firms were involved with as well.

As we will see – in the computer industry there really was no static period. Many firms hoped for such a period to arrive, and indeed many of them aimed to get their products to the point of standardisation before the other firms in the industry (we will see that there was a race to third-generation computing which IBM managed to win by putting customer requirements ahead of technological achievement).

This focus on enterprise structure is clearly redolent of the work of Chandler (1977 and 1990) in business history and uses history to shed light on the decision making and capabilities of different enterprise forms. Studying enterprise must surely mean taking not only snapshots of a firm's performance but seeing decisions being made through their life cycle. Did the decisions these firms were making succeed or fail? Did they deploy their resources effectively or not? It is not surprising, therefore, that this book uses Business History as the core technique to explore the reasons for the failure of certain enterprise forms in this market. The aim is to understand the institutional structures and historical developments that 'affect the nature of competition and innovation in industries' (Jones and Wadhwani 2006).

## The early computer market

Given the weakness of concentrically diversified firms in rapidly innovating, ever-changing markets, we must consider whether the computer industry was such a market and whether the scale of the operations were so large that market participants would require complex design, productive and marketing capabilities to maintain a position in the market. If computers were hand-made and sold to only a handful of customers in low numbers, then large firms, no matter what their structure, should have been able to cope, although the appeal of such a market would be somewhat questionable. Indeed many of the firms in the study did stay major players in the electronics sector after they left computing (and other businesses), but concentrated on defence electronics, which very much showed the traits of low-production quantities, hand craftsmanship and bespoke low-volume engineering.

The commercial computer market is usually divided up into generations, the first three main generations being defined by the core componentry being used (see Figure 2.1). It is the first three generations of computing with which this book is concerned, although, of course, the computer had a prehistory before the commercialisation phase began.

### First-generation computing part 1: experimentation

Clearly, the first builders of computing technology are heroes to the modern twenty-first-century person – our world is one of digital computing capability embedded into nearly everything we do. This book is about the enterprises which commercialised computing, so only the briefest of outlines of early computing is given here – however, in each case study we explore in the details how each firm entered the industry and what capabilities the

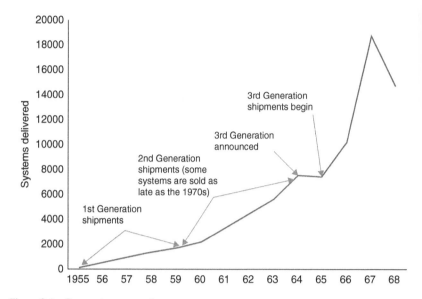

*Figure 2.1*   Computer generations
*Source*: Phister 1979: 247, compiled from IDC data – Annotations, Gandy.

firm had to achieve this. There are many comprehensive works on early developments in computing already covering developments in both the UK and the US (examples include Ceruzzi, 1983; Flamm 1988, Hodges 1983; Lavington 1980; Metropolis, Howlett and Rota 1980). This is a period when developments in universities and government research labs were tentatively turned into computers which could be sold, but the complexity was high, the reliability low and the nature of the demand not really understood. This covered the period of approximately 1949–54.

Studies of this early phase show that the UK was on a par with the US in what could be termed the pre-competitive phase of the industry: the period when computer technology was confined to small groups of pioneering scientists and entrepreneurs. Developments at the Universities of Manchester and Cambridge and at the National Physical Laboratories were extremely important to the progress of early computer technology, as indeed was the earlier work undertaken at Bletchley Park in code-breaking during the Second World War.

However, there was quite an early demand for university and research centre work to be commercialised, if only for organisations that had a similar profile. Only a few laboratories and universities had the financial resources, skills or interest necessary to develop these complex and intricate machines for their own use. Yet many other laboratories had a requirement for increased calculating speed, created by the growing complexity of science and technology, especially in the nuclear and aeronautical fields. It was this science community which created the first demand for computers.

The British electronics company Ferranti was the first firm to offer fully functional computers for commercial sale, based on the work it had carried out with Manchester University, with the Manchester Mark 1 operating from 1949 (see Chapter 5). The Manchester team had developed the first computer with a stored program and Random Access Memory (RAM), making it the first computer offering all the functions of what we would recognise as a computer – though it is hardly recognisable to us as a computer! Ferranti sold its first computer to the University and installed it by 1951 and thereafter began domestic and even international sales of the Ferranti Mark 1 and 1* computers. Other British electrical/electronics concerns would rapidly follow Ferranti, including English Electric, using technology from the National Physical Laboratories (see Chapter 7), and Elliott Brothers, in part based on their work in naval fire control computers (Lavington 2011). Later, with the development of the transistor, other firms also entered the market, including EMI which used the new componentry as a launch pad into the market.

The UK would have some 'odd-ball' entrants into the computer sector. Chief among these were the Lyons Electronic Office (LEO) computers made by the tea-rooms company J. Lyon and Co. This development was based on the Electronic Delay Storage Automatic Calculator (EDSAC) computer developed in 1949 in Cambridge and would be squarely aimed at commercial data processing from day one – rather than sales to laboratories and engineering enterprises which was the launch strategy for most other firms. Developed as a one-off system, Lyons decided to commercialise its new capability, and in 1954 launched LEO II with first installations taking place in 1957 (see, Caminer 2003 and Hendry 1988). LEO would be absorbed into English Electric in 1964 to bolster their commercial computing operation, although this turned out to be a forlorn hope.

In the US, the initial technical interest in computers resided in similar institutions; universities and government laboratories. However, early US systems for use in scientific-driven computation were developed by companies which were significantly different from the early companies in the UK market. The two most important early producers were small entrepreneurial organisations, Eckert–Mauchly Computer Corporation with the universal automatic computer (UNIVAC) machines (See Stern 1981) and Engineering Research Associates with the ERA 1101 (Cohen and Tomash, 1979). In contrast to the UK, the first firms to make computers available for sale on a commercial basis were start-up enterprises, although these were again exploiting developments made in universities and research centres (Eckert and Mauchly at the University of Pennsylvania (Lundstrom 1987) and Engineering Research Associates (ERA) less directly, exploiting connections and capabilities made by the founders while working on US Navy cryptology projects in the Second World War).

Both UNIVAC and ERA were to become part of the UNIVAC Division of the business machines firm Remington Rand, which in turn became a part of Sperry-Rand.

Other entrepreneurial enterprises building early computers were also snapped up by business machine firms. ElectroData was taken over by the business machines firm Burroughs and the Computer Research Corp. was absorbed into National Cash Registers (NCR).

The final strand to development was IBM who would begin to develop fully digitised stored memory computers slightly after the Remington Rand stable of bought-in development teams (Bashe et al. 1986, gives a good description of IBM's early computer developments). However, it had been heavily involved in both the development of electromechanical systems for code breaking in the Second World War and was blessed with something the smaller firms did not have – in-depth relationships with business users of data processing systems based on punched cards and tabulators, where it was well ahead of Remington Rand and smaller players such as NCR and Burroughs. IBM would soon begin experimenting with computers exploiting the Williams Tube, designed for the Manchester and Ferranti computers and providing an early form of random access machine memory.

The role of the electronics giants in the US industry was on the whole limited to components and technical assistance; their major push into the market came somewhat later in what we could call the first-generation computing part 2: commercialisation.

### First-generation computing part 2: Commercialisation

The world's stock of computers grew rapidly from the mid-1950s onwards. From the production of a handful of computers for scientists, machines that were viewed almost as science fiction mysteries and which looked somewhat Heath-Robinson due to their complexity, the mainframe computer became a commonplace tool in large-scale enterprises and government departments.

The defining feature of the first-generation systems was the use of the vacuum tube as the underlying component technology: tubes were used for all logical functions. This made the machines large, power hungry and initially very unreliable. Memory was simple, initially based on cathode ray tubes (the Manchester development, which allowed Ferranti to be the first to market and was also used by IBM in the 701 system, mercury delay lines (used by nearly all firms) or the much slower magnetic drums (which would carry on as a data storage device after they had been replaced as main memory). These systems were capable of storing only limited amounts of data, capacities which now seem tiny. The 'electro-static' store in the Manchester Mark 1 (built by the University and which would be the blueprint for the Ferranti Mark 1) was just 256 words long. Interaction with these early machines ranged from programs being wired in using patch cables and switches or the faster, but still incredibly slow, punched hole paper tape. Programmers would type their program onto the tape and feed this into the machine, the machine would run the program (assuming the tubes did not break) and the machine would output the findings – again very slowly. All this is assuming that there were no errors in the paper tape which could lead to re-keying. This may have worked in engineering laboratories, but was not the basis for high input-output tasks required by commercial customers.

However, during the second phase of the first generation of computers a number of incremental improvements began to create wider use of computers, which then created larger production runs, in turn leading to better engineering of the systems and a growing pool of people able to use them.

Innovations included the more reliable, lower power, mini-valve, magnetic core memory instead of delay lines, magnetic drums or cathode ray storage, and the introduction of magnetic tape and magnetic disk storage. Magnetic cores became the most important computer program memory until the 1970s when microchips began to take over (there were rival technologies in bubble memory and thin-film memory, but magnetic cores dominated). Magnetic core memories were first found in large-scale computers following development based on the Whirlwind Project at MIT, which became the most widely used RAM and, through IBM's involvement with defence projects developed from the Whirlwind project, would give IBM early access to this technology (see Pugh 1984). For data storage and retrieval the magnetic tape began to rival and then take over (in later generations) from punched cards. In addition however, in 1956, IBM announced the RAMAC 305, in which IBM introduced the magnetic disk drive allowing a larger pool of storage to sit behind the system's core memory and taking over as secondary random access data from the older drum memory. This innovation would revolutionise the access to large amounts of random access data and program storage and would eventually see the near wholesale replacement of sequential memory (punched cards and tape) with RAM for real-time and multi-tasking systems. As these improvements were incorporated, and as prices were reduced through better manufacturing techniques, new functions for computers were developed, leading to computers becoming more than just scientific calculators.

As these developments took place, first-generation computers began to be used for business processes, accounts, sales control, payroll, stock control and many other functions. The LEO and Ferranti machines would find a small role in these markets, effectively markets which rivalled the more traditional punched card systems then available. Yet again, however, it was IBM's small first-generation computer – the IBM 650 – which really made a market for tasks previously carried out by tabulating and punched card equipment.

Commercial data processing (accounts, payroll, customer records, insurance records and, towards the end of this generation of systems, bank records), a source of demand that rapidly outstripped the scientific market.

Not surprisingly these new demands led to tabulating and punched card systems being the key input and output devices for this second phase of first-generation computing. Office automation based on punched cards was well established with the leaders being IBM and Remington Rand. As computing developed, input-output would become critical as processor speeds increased. As we will see, IBM built its dominance, in part, on its underlying strengths in electro-mechanical systems vital to computer input-output devices (see Chapter 8).

When analysing the dominance of IBM in the computer industry, the focus of attention is usually on how IBM dominated the third generation of computers. However, IBM sold over one thousand 650s (see Chapter 8). The next commercial data processing to come out of IBM was the first generation RAMAC 305. With its early disk drive technology, it would also sell close to one thousand systems. Output by the other firms in the computer sector was a rounding error compared to IBM even by the end of the first generation of computing.

IBM was clearly already the market leader in business systems. It was able to build on this using other developments to bolster its technology and its manufacturing capability. Following IBM's collaboration with Project Whirlwind project at MIT, IBM was selected to build the large-scale AN/FSQ-7 computers used to manage air defence in the system known as the Semi-Automatic Ground Environment or SAGE (Redmond and Smith 1980). This was a truly massive system which could guide aircraft to intercept targets and even fire their weapons, though the success of the latter was not good. IBM built 56 AN/FSQ-7 systems which provided a technological launch platform for its range of large-scale first-generation scientific systems, as well as providing it with advances in manufacturing practice (Usselman 2011).

In the UK, the rapid acceleration of demand which IBM was able to exploit in the US was more muted. First-generation computers were not built on such a large scale: only a few systems sold more than 20 and demand was spread out among nearly as many firms as existed in the US. Nevertheless, UK systems advanced rapidly as well with Ferranti managing to produce a number of first-generation systems to build on the start it had made with the Mark 1 systems. However, the UK did not manage to produce systems anywhere near the same scale as IBM.

## Second generation computing, late 1950s-mid 1965

Following the dissemination of the new transistor technology within the electronics world, a number of solid-state computers started to emerge in the late 1950s. William Shockley, Walter Brattain and John Bardeen developed the transistor in 1947 (Riordan and Hoddeson 1998) at the Bell Telephone Laboratories and announced it in 1948. The first fully transistorised computers were the Philco TRANSAC S-2000 (Rosen 2004 – a firm outside of this study as it only had a limited impact on the commercial computer market) and, in Europe, the first commercially available system was the EMI 1100 built by that firm's Computing Services Division. It also built another early and larger-scale solid state system, the EMIDEC 2400, built by another team in EMI using different solid-state technologies, namely a transistor-diode arrangement, including a small solid-state diode-capacitor high-speed data store as well as core memory (see Chapter 6).

Such machines offered great advantages over their predecessors. Transistors greatly reduced size and power consumption, were reliable and easy to package and made much greater calculation speeds possible.

Second generation computers also had better peripherals, incremental improvements which greatly enhanced the throughput of the computer. Magnetic tape drives improved, as did printers, allowing greater speeds at both ends of the computational process, though the punched card was still the main input-output device for large amounts of data, but the tape was catching up. In the area of random access, second generation machines greatly surpassed the first systems. Disk drive technology was hugely enhanced, with IBM producing ever faster and larger disk storage systems for random access mass storage (though not on a scale which could replace magnetic tape). Second, magnetic core main memory came down in price. This made large capacity memory on computers possible, greatly increasing the complexity of the tasks that they could handle.

Improved technology and the falling price meant that computers could be applied to many new tasks. Computer languages such as Formula Translating (FORTRAN), written by IBM for engineering and Common Business-Oriented Language (COBOL), a common language for business applications developed by an industry and government-led committee. These greatly improved programming productivity and libraries of code expanded rapidly. Computers were given the ability to perform multiple tasks, such as printing out the results from one program while calculating another – though true multi-tasking was yet to come. This ability, together with the availability of large random access stores, led to a number of new real-time applications, where computers performed tasks as required, rather than processing tasks in strict batch order. Above all, the large user base that was being built up was leading to new application ideas, which were developed for one user then attracted others.

At the end of the first generation of computing and during the second generation, there was great momentum behind the computer. By the end of the second generation of computing, all the business machines firms had turned their attention to building small systems to complement their old tabulating machines. The computer started to become a significant product for American business machines firms, rapidly becoming their main product line as the punched card was slowly reduced to an input-output device for computers which took over the role of tabulators and calculators. Likewise International Computers and Tabulators (ICT), the UK's incumbent punched card and business machines manufacturer, was also investing in and acquiring technology to supplement its business by adding computer technology. Its acquisition of Ferranti's computer division midway through the second generation of computing would somewhat fortuitously give it a computer architecture it could rely on for twenty-five years. For these firms there was little choice: the computer was replacing the old electromechanical punched card technology.

It was at the cusp between the first generation of computers and the introduction of the second that many of the large-scale electrical/electronics companies entered the new industry, those firms that are the focus of this study. While Ferranti and English Electric were already involved, others had waited. By 1956–57 it was becoming clear that the computer market was going to be significant. Three of the major case-study companies, EMI, RCA and GE, entered at this time, as did the more successful Honeywell Company. English Electric would use this phase to greatly increase its effort in the computer industry. A number of other electronics firms also made short-lived forays into the early second generation computer market, including the UK's other two electrical/electronic giants, General Electric Company (GEC) and Associated Electrical Industries (AEI), as did two of America's electronics and systems specialists Philco and Bendix.

In the case-study chapters it will be seen that electronics companies hoped to use their knowledge of electronics, especially their early experience of the transistor, to lever their way into the forming market. They were deliberately targeting this industry with an overt strategy of using developing capabilities and extending their product ranges to exploit economies of scope and scale. Philco in the US and EMI in Europe both managed to market the first large-scale solid-state computers. Interestingly most of these companies targeted the commercial, rather than the scientific, computer market for their forays: this had become the largest part of the market with the greatest potential for growth.

Notably, it was during this generation of computing that two of the most significant start-up computer companies were founded: Control Data Corp. and Digital Equipment Corp., both of which became major players in the world market supplanting the big electronics companies as rivals to IBM.

However, the most notable second generation machines once again came from IBM. The 1401 was the first computer to exceed 10,000 installations, an installed base in an order of magnitude larger than the machines it replaced and nearly two magnitudes greater than its greatest rivals. The 1401 became the workhorse of the commercial computing world. The second notable series of machines were the various IBM 70** series computers. These were large commercial and scientific machines which were also the workhorses of their fields, the 7070/2/4 in large-scale commercial computing and the 7090/94 in scientific computing. Both of these lines sold many hundreds of machines.

Chapter 8 shows that it was IBM's ability to control the second generation of computers that was the key to its continued dominance of the market. It was at this stage that the electronics companies, a number of which were much larger than IBM, had a potentially significant competitive advantage by applying their electronic technology to the computer market. IBM's better market knowledge and marketing techniques saw off this potential threat.

### Third generation, mid-1960s onwards

This represents the period in which computer technology became more formalised, but far from static. The core change in technology was the move from the discrete transistor as the logic component (there were other forms of solid-state technology, though these were short-lived), to the integrated circuit (IC). These combined a number of transistors, together with other solid-state components such as diodes and resistors, onto a single piece of silicon or germanium. Since this time, much effort has gone into striving for an ever greater density of circuits on the 'chip'.

However, the third generation of computing was heralded by the IBM System/360 family: a system which did not use these integrated components (Usselman 2011). IBM instead used a hybrid technology, thick films which it branded as Solid Technology Logic units, similar to circuit boards with resistors and other passive components built directly into the film but with transistors soldered on. This and the launch of the later System/370 took rivals by surprise. Rivals, especially the electronics firms, based their product strategies on component changes; IBM did not wait, they built the capability customers wanted – the latest components could be integrated later, though as Usselman (2011) notes it was often to the frustration of management that the latest generation of components or technologies could not always be used.

The UK's business machine/computing company took a similar approach with the most successful British third-generation computer, the ICT 1900 family. It used transistors in the first iterations, not using ICs until the 1969 1900A midlife update. ICT and IBM knew that third-generation computing was not really about the components. The components could be made transparent to users, bar the machines being slightly larger and slightly slower than if the latest component was used in their core. But there were other features which were not transparent to users and which greatly improved the usability of computing.

What really distinguished the third generation of machines was the adoption of a more advanced architecture, the introduction of the first real operating systems, and compatibility between whole families of computers. Before this time, computers were optimised for the scale of calculation they were meant to undertake and they varied greatly because rapid technical change meant that models entering the market at just one or two year intervals were very different. The use of new operating systems isolated the development of user code from the functioning of the machine itself and allowed the wider use of more advanced programming languages. Productivity in development was increased by the spread of these languages while operational productivity increased because of the improved input-output capabilities of disk drives and better printer technology.

In addition, it was at this stage that firms began to develop hardware and operating systems which made timesharing possible, allowing systems to not only batch process data processing tasks (by far the dominant form of processing), but also to allow multiple users to undertake multiple tasks simultaneously on one system in real-time. This was however difficult to achieve and delivering this capability became a source of bitter rivalry between firms with only a few systems truly delivering it. Ferranti (Atlas) and Burroughs (B5000) had begun the introduction of virtual memory, vital for timesharing multitasking. However, it would be GE which would become most associated with multitasking operating systems, through its ambitious Multics project developed in conjunction with MIT. Delays to this and the very large cost of systems able to handle hundreds of simulations transactions left one unexpected legacy – the frustration of waiting led other scientists at Bell Labs (which pulled out of the Multics partnership in 1969) to start the development of the Unix system aimed at decentralising rather than centralising computing power. IBM's efforts in multitasking was the 360/67 and its inability to deliver key elements of the operating system would not be corrected until virtual memory was announced for the follow up 370 family of computer – and even then this announcement came a year after the original 370 announcement. Nevertheless, timesharing agencies using IBM 360/67, GE, Burroughs and other kit began to offer the ability for multiple users to access different tasks on the same computer at the same time.

These changes to the organisation of computer ranges were additional to the usual cycle of using faster components and lowering manufacturing costs, producing better price:performance ratios and greater functionality.

The IBM 360 was a range of computers which offered all these features. Users of the range could opt for a small system with punched card input-output, or a very large computer capable of the most complex tasks and controlling banks of disk and tape drives. These systems were compatible throughout. For a large user company, this meant that computer and software standards would be the same throughout the company and that development could take place on small systems but run on larger production systems when in the field. For smaller firms hoping to grow, expansion to larger systems would not create headaches of reprogramming applications and arranging complex data swapping, a common problem before this concept.

All the competitors in the market would follow this approach to some degree, though not all as completely as IBM. However, a number of novel tactics were adopted to take advantage of the change to the new generation.

Honeywell, and to a lesser degree GE, made their new machines backward compatible with old IBM computers in the hope that users would upgrade to their systems rather than the new IBM range which actually required more reprogramming and change than if the customer choose the Honeywell or GE route.

RCA's strategy centred on the RCA Spectra 70 series, which instead of being made compatible with older IBM systems, was made compatible with the new IBM 360 range, a tactic which was aimed at making RCA the standard second source for IBM architecture machines. RCA also hoped that it would benefit from its more advanced component technology; it was the first major range to exploit integrated components techniques and hoped this would give it an advantage over all rivals, including IBM.

The 360 was a worthy successor to IBM's second generation of computers. Figure 2.1 showed a stall in computer sales in 1964 following the announcement of the IBM 360. This was followed by a boom in installations, due, in the main, to the thousands of 360 family machines produced. By this time computer technology was becoming commonplace, employing hundreds of thousands in both building the machines and operating them.

**Fourth generation, early 1970s onwards**

The final stage of this story is the introduction of fourth generation computers. However, even more than the third generation, the fourth generation core components (very or ultra large ICs (VLSI/ULSI) and ultimately microprocessors, large-scale disk arrays and IC memory) were not really the issue. In many ways it is harder to define the fourth generation as it was a period which began with the use of large-scale ICs in mainframes and would lead to microprocessors powering everything from mainframes to desktop systems. It was a period of diversity, but this diversity centred on improving the capability of individuals to interact with computing systems in a more useable manner.

This was a generation of computers which used the greater capability of very large-scale circuits and IC memory (as opposed to the older core memory systems) to deliver cost-efficient large-scale timesharing capabilities to make real-time and multi-tasking computing. Ironically, it would be the generation of computing which also allowed the development of first mini then microcomputers able to give us personalised computing wherever we needed it.

As we will see, none of the firms in the major case studies, RCA, GE, English Electric, Ferranti and EMI would survive the change to this generation of computers, even though some of them led the way with the technology. The business machines firms would survive.

Certainly, RCA, GE and English Electric were still players as the replacements to the early third generation systems were being planned; they expected to be in the market. However, EE's third-generation computer

strategy ended its involvement in the industry (selling its computer operations to ICT to create International Computers Limited in 1968 in an ill-
thought-out state-sponsored merger). For GE and RCA the final nail in the
coffin came with IBM's early announcement of the System/370 on 30 June
1970, an incremental improvement over the 360 offering customer-centric
improvements if not, yet again, the latest components.

Was it IBM that created the environments in which they failed? – Yes. Was
it IBM which caused them to fail in their strategy? – this book argues no,
it was the weakness of their corporate structures which undermined their
efforts to compete and which led them to adopt strategies which were not
capable of defeating their rival. Other companies did manage to survive.

This was the dynamic market in which the electronics firms were trying to
establish a presence. What follows is a study of the strategies adopted by firms
wishing to exploit technical knowledge and market power, derived from a
broad base of other electronics activities, to win a share of this new industry.

## Intercepting IBM's strategy

Of course, anyone with any feeling for the computer industry of this period
will know that IBM became a computing behemoth and really represented
the business environment around which all others eventually had to fit.
This is especially true from the early 1960s and the most interesting strategic
issue was how its rivals were going to compete against it.

While IBM was the incumbent leader from the middle of the first generation of computing, it was clear to all the players that the computing market
was going to change across a number of dimensions:

- Technology – fundamental shifts in the core technology. Components,
  storage systems, input-output systems etc, could be fairly well predicted,
  especially changes in the core componentry;
- Function – New applications, coupled to lower costs, allowed the spread
  of computing into new functions and to add new value propositions;
- Scale – as technology improved, costs would fall allowing the market to
  grow in size;
- Scope – as applications developed, the technology cheapened and new
  functions opened up to computers, so did the scope of the industry, no
  longer limited to the scientific-aligned engineering functions or to traditional data processing functions.

This was not a static environment, IBM had established leadership in the
early computer industry which will be described in Chapter 8, but rivals were
fully aware of the dynamic nature of the technology and the market. There
were opportunities for growth within an expanding pot, and opportunities
to move faster than the incumbent to reach new customers before they did.

Studying the strategies of firms looking to intercept the strategy of an incumbent rival is important to this book. However, the very nature of the predictability of change meant rivals to IBM were often locked into a strategy which was determined by what they saw as the logical path IBM should take, and failed to predict what IBM would actually do as a competitor trying to maintain its competitive advantage over rivals. Work by Craven et al. (2009) describes the difficulties that firms in an industry face in thinking outside a conventional wisdom. Firms get locked into a 'competitive box' (Craven, Piercy and Baldauf 2009: 38) where conventional strategy based on known competitors and known business models. The challenge in such an environment is for the strategist to be able to look outside and recognise new models, new competitors and new technologies.

What happens when firms look at a major market incumbent and see it as being the heart of the 'competitive box' and think that circumventing and moving ahead of its strategy is the goal? This is fine if the incumbent is set on a predicable pathway using predictable technology and with an established business model. However, if that firm in the box is not on the pathway predicted by rival firms then the strategies of its competitors could be fatally flawed. In such a circumstance, the 'alternative' path competitors could end up arriving at the same point at the same time, or even later than the incumbent supplier. If the incumbent can achieve this leapfrogging, it can bring with it the economies of scale and depth of market presence that goes with its established position.

GE, RCA and English Electric had each planned to get to a point ahead of IBM, but failed to do so. They then had to adapt their strategies to cope with the swift footedness of their successful rival. This is not a story of David and Goliath: while IBM had won the leading position in the early computer market, rapid change in the technology of computing, the technical capabilities of its rivals (GE, RCA and English Electric were large technology-driven companies) and the rapid evolution in the use of general purpose computing certainly meant that its position was not assured. No, IBM had real threats.

It was being challenged by firms, which while relatively ineffective competitors during the second generation of computing, were nevertheless technological power houses. Could they deploy their technical resources to get to the future generations of computing first, or exploit other competitive advantages to create new alternative business models?

It was clear there was going to be changes in the core technology used for building the computer: this book concentrates on three significant change moments: the migration from first- to second generation computing, the transition from second- to third-generation computing and then shift to early fourth-generation computing. However, in reality the key strategic decisions being made are related to how its rivals perceived the strategy and timetable of IBM in these generational shifts. IBM is the 'competitive box'against which its rivals benchmarked their strategies.

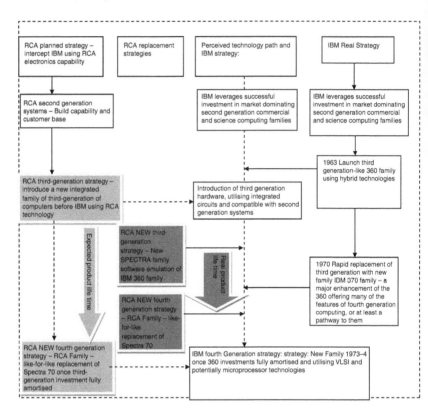

*Figure 2.2*   RCA product strategy based on perceptions of IBM's strategy vs. IBM's real product development strategy
*Source*: Gandy 2012.

Figure 2.2 collates RCA's strategy and how their strategy related to what they perceived would be IBM's strategy. The flowchart shows that RCA's efforts to intercept IBM failed because IBM was not willing to wait for either new components or for old capital investments to be depreciated at the rate rivals wanted.

An important feature of the computer market was not simply that there were high capital costs in developing the machines, requiring quite long time periods and production runs to fully cover the initial development costs, but that the systems were leased. IBM moved to from second to third to fourth generations quicker than RCA expected. This seriously reduced the timeframe in which RCA, and the other firms in the industry had to spread development costs across a long enough production run of second- and third-generation systems, and also reduced the time the systems were in the field. RCA's expectation was that they could depreciate what were primarily leased systems over an eight-year period. Its reaction to the 360 was to change its own third-generation system and refocus it as IBM 360 compatible – which took time. This had a calamitous effect on RCA (see Chapter 3 for more details) as the gap between the launching of new systems became shortened with dire resource and financial consequences. IBM changed systems generations much faster than RCA's plans allowed for meaning they failed to fully amortise the either its development costs nor the costs of the systems it delivered customers under lease agreements. All IBM's competitors suffered from this faster-than-expected development pace, though RCA's like-for-like strategy with systems pitched directly at intercepting the IBM 360 and 370 series illustrates the case the best.

Was this fair? It is a good question. In the case of the mainstream offerings of GE, RCA, English Electric, Ferranti and EMI, IBM consistently moved ahead of them and delivered ahead of them, that is competition. These firms had a timetable in mind, determined by technology. The firm which created the environment in which the other firms operated did not keep to that timetable. These firms could not see into the IBM black box and their guesses at its strategy were as much self-serving as they were guesses aimed at making their own strategies work. IBM was not going to play that game. It was not IBM's doing that some of these firms offered to replace third-generation systems with fourth-generation systems on a like-for-like basis as soon as they were available – that was a disastrous policy the firms created themselves (especially in the case of RCA), however the pace at which change took place was very much set by IBM.

There has, of course, been real criticism of IBM. In the area of supercomputing and multitasking systems, it announced new capabilities for its 360 and 370 series computers well ahead of its ability to deliver those capabilities. Buyers of these systems wanted IBM kit because software developed for IBM multitasking and supercomputers could be developed with lower-cost systems and migrated to the bigger production systems once developed. It is argued that IBM, unlike with their mainstream offering, failed to deliver these enhanced capabilities on time. This 'vapourware', it is argued, damaged rivals looking to beat IBM by offering these fairly specific capabilities. This allegation led to the US vs. IBM antitrust case. Supercomputer manufacturer Control Data Corporation (CDC) also started anti-trust actions against IBM, alleging that it announced the supercomputer in the 1960s, which it knew it could not deliver in a reasonable timeframe, but which prevented the sale of CDC systems.

However, the research presented here focuses on competition between IBM and the large-scale electrical/electronics companies. Here the 'vapourware issue' is not a major factor of the failure of these large powerful firms leaving the sector. Instead, it was a combination of a poor concentrically diversified structure which magnified the problem of internal concentration for resources as business units reached major investment points at the same time further exacerbated by their major rival, IBM continuously shortening development cycles as it moved ahead of them in introducing new systems capability while ignoring the logical path based on the availability of new componentry.

## Failure in the British computer hardware industry

The secondary focus of this study is to ask whether the UK was correct to sponsor the development of computer industry by providing support to large-scale electrical/electronics groups. For an established industrial power like the UK, maintaining its economic standing in the world depends on either preserving its competitive advantage in established industries, or using its economic power to develop new industries and markets. In traditional industries the UK has been losing market share for many decades. Even in the early part of the twentieth century, declining world market share was the trend in many industries including coal mining, shipbuilding and textiles, to name but the classic examples. Since then, relative decline has spread to most of the UK's older manufacturing industries.

In itself, this does not matter to the overall manufacturing strength of a country. Past profits from the older sectors could have been invested in new industries. The pace of technological change in the twentieth century has been astounding. This has meant that the leading industries have changed. Many of the world's top companies now come from the ranks of the automobile, electronics, pharmaceuticals, and aerospace industries, industries that barely existed before the 1914–18 First World War. Leadership in these industries would more than make up for relative decline in older sectors. Sadly, in most of these newer sector, the UK is now also a bit player.

One of the purposes of this book is to take one of these sectors, and to examine its internal structure to see if there was any deficiency which could explain the lack of success. The broad area chosen is the electronics industry and within that the manufacture of early generations of commercial computer systems. The conclusion is that the electrical/electronics concentrically diversified conglomerates which, bar one firm, dominated the UK computer market were ill-structured to survive in an industry with the features of the early computer industry – a lesson we also find common to the US electrical/electronics groups.

Before 1939, the UK was able to compete with the US in most areas of electronics. After the war, the UK was the USA's only serious competitor in electronics. Indeed, many of the most important electronics innovations had been developed in the UK to aid the war effort. From this position of relative strength, the UK's position slipped, which is not surprising as other countries were bound to catch up.

However, the UK's overall loss of competitiveness in this market is quite astonishing. In 1963, the UK had a positive balance of trade in electronics and associated electrical equipment, amounting to £105.7m. Twenty years later (1982) this had become a negative balance of £-1402m (Soete and Dosi 1986: 67). By 1982, the UK was losing its position in computing and office automation systems, and had all but abandoned the consumer electronics market (Arnold 1982). The only significant areas where the UK held on to a positive balance of trade were those sectors dominated by military electronics. Even here, a wave of firms would disappear in the 1990s, including Racal, Ferranti, Plessey and even the mighty GEC.

Soete and Dosi's figures (1986) show that the decline in mainframe commercial computer trade was a major contributor to the UK's fading position as an exporter of electronics equipment. In 1963, the UK was in approximate balance with a tiny trade surplus of £0.5m in computers; by 1982 this had become a negative trade balance of £-554m, second only to consumer electronics (£-922m) in explaining the UK's failure to build a sustainable position in electronic manufacturing.

The UK's decline in smaller-scale computing, mini computers, was equally notable. The electrical and electronics companies stayed in this business once they had disposed of their commercial data processing (mainframe) operations (Hamilton 1996: 81–104). However, the likes of GEC and Ferranti were no match for the US start-ups in this field and found application only in military and industrial control primarily in the UK, a market always destined to decline and end. Their lack of interest in the use of such systems in commercial application doomed them to being marginalised and losing the critical scale needed to continue development.

However, this prognosis of gloom for yet another failed British manufacturing sector needs to be tempered – there is ongoing and clear success continuing in this area. For example, much of this book has been written on the train to and from work, using an Android-powered tablet computer, containing, at the centre of it, an ARM designed chip, a British company whose intellectual property is at the centre of nearly all mobile devices, at least as of 2012. Does ARM make microprocessors? No, but 15 billion mobile devices have been made using central processor units based on its intellectual property (ARM, company Profile as at 30/11/2011) and its architecture is beginning to be adopted in the desktop and even supercomputer markets. In addition, the UK runs trade surpluses in areas such as business services (Oxford Economics, 2010: 28) and financial services, itself a high technology industry.[1]

While the implementation and the exploitation of technology is alive and well in the business services and financial sectors, the UK ecosystem for electronics manufacture and the related area of computing hardware has all but collapsed, barring some islands of capability.

Focusing on the period of study – the 1950s through the early 1970s – nothing illustrates this collapse more strongly than Figures 2.3 and 2.4. From having positive balance of trades in most electronic trade categories, by the early 1970s the UK was a net importer of everything from computers

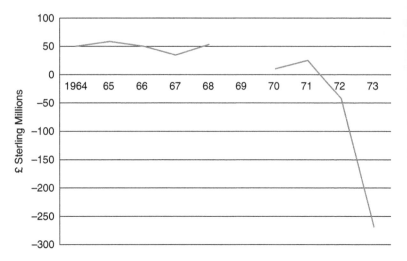

*Figure 2.3* UK balance of trade in electronics: capital goods, components, consumer goods and computers
*Source*: National Economic Development Office (NEDO), Committee for the Electronic Industry, Statistics and Sources, 1968 and NEDO Annual Report 1973.

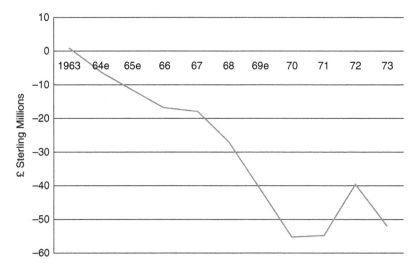

*Figure 2.4* UK balance of trade in electronic digital computers
*Source*: National Economic Development Office (NEDO) Committee for the Electronics Industry (EDC), Electronics Industry Statistics and Sources 1968 and NEDO Electronics EDC Economics Assessment 1974.

to components, with only areas such as electronic capital equipment, an area related to the activities of defence electronics, remaining in the black.

It is wholly reasonable at this stage to conclude that this book follows a predictable pattern, one played out many times. The British story in computing is one of successful innovation followed by a failure to maintain its position in a globalising market, a story which has been told in many manufacturing sectors.

Many theses have been put forward to explain the relative decline of UK manufacturing. Explanations range from the neo-Marxist to the neo-Schumpeterian and beyond. For example, Williams, Dennis and Williams (1983) blamed, among other things, the over-financialisation of decision making in the UK industry. Sir Geoffrey Owen (1999), on the other hand, finds, among many other factors, that government policy of nationalistic protection of industry prevented change and the building of competitive enterprises. You can quite happily add another few dozen books following this theme.

This book does not pursue the theme of general decline in UK manufacturing. Indeed the implicit assumption that manufacturing jobs are somehow more valuable than service jobs clearly does not hold much sway in this sector. Jobs which implement and exploit information systems technology are quite valuable enough in a modern society. What the book does do, however, is to focus on the failure of one specific entrepreneurial form, the concentrically diversified electrical/electronics combine and the failure of that business model in the computer market. The story of the failure of this form of enterprise is common to the UK and to the US.

# Part II
# US Electronics Companies in the Computer Sector 1950–72

# 3
# RCA

## Early RCA

RCA's roots were back in the early telecommunications market. It started life as the American Marconi Company (Graham 1986: 21; Sobel 1986: 33; Warner 1957: 3–6[1]), the US subsidiary of the world's leading telecommunications company, Marconi. According to General James G. Harbord, RCA President (1928[2]), during and after the First World War the US government, especially the US Navy, started to put pressure on Marconi to sell its American operations. Marconi was seen as having a monopolistic hold over radio communications, a situation made worse by its foreign ownership. Under this government pressure, Marconi was forced to sell its American subsidiary to a US consortium led by General Electric. The US government encouraged further consolidation of the radio industry, leading to the assets of GE, Westinghouse and AT&T being pooled to form the Radio Corporation of America (RCA). This meant that the USA had a firm that had control over all the patents needed to produce every aspect of radio equipment.

Initially the firm was little more than the embodiment of a cartel, nicknamed the 'radio ring'. Much of the capital equipment it used, and all the consumer sets it sold, were produced by GE and the other shareholders. The National Broadcasting Company and the marine communications network were the main operations that RCA controlled. However, during the 1920s and 1930s, RCA became more independent. There were two reasons for this. First, the 'radio ring' risked coming under anti-trust scrutiny. Second, RCA became annoyed with the sluggishness of the producer companies to make consumer sets that were in line with market demand, as well as having to give its suppliers a 20% margin on all the sets it sold (Graham, 1986:39). In 1929, it acquired the consumer electronics company, Victor, to which it added the vacuum tube operations of GE and Westinghouse to form the RCA Victor Company and RCA Radiotron. At this stage the company became independent. It was the supplier of the largest public broadcasting system, NBC, had an international telecommunications business, and was now a vertically integrated electronics company: within a few years electronics accounted for the majority of its activities.

There are three aspects of RCA's early history that are particularly important, all of which are linked. First, the company's growth was guided by one central character, General David Sarnoff. Sarnoff became the president of RCA in 1930 having established his reputation through building the company's assault on the commercial radio industry. Second, this central autocrat reinforced the formal organisation of the firm with the strength of his own authority. Finally, Sarnoff ensured that research had a central role in the company:

> More than 1000 engineers engaged in radio research express the efforts of the Radio Corporation and its associates to develop this art and industry. Millions of dollars are spent annually by the Corporation and its associated interests in these efforts. We are, therefore, inevitably in possession of many valuable patent rights, the fruits of intensive, continuous and costly research. But we doubt whether any other corporation in the industrial history of the country, possessing patented inventions, has ever licensed so many of its competitors and at so early a stage in the development of a new art.
>
> (Sarnoff 1928: 97–113 – from the same seminar series at which Harbord also spoke)

Later the firm's research assets were pooled into one of the world's largest laboratories, the Sarnoff Research Centre.

RCA had a crucial role as a provider of technology to the world. In the mid-1930s, the company was faced with a squeeze in its domestic electronics markets, caused on the one hand by the Depression, on the other by a surfeit of suppliers. It reacted by cutting back overseas operations, the idea being to sell off these operations, such as EMI and JVC, and use the monies raised to bolster the domestic operations. After this RCA no longer operated directly overseas, it was not a large exporter nor did it own many overseas operations; instead it sold technology rights to its old subsidiaries or to new partners. It used its patent ownership to earn overseas income from licences. It also sold some of its output to overseas firms to re-market.

Given RCA's strong technical base and the attitude of Sarnoff to public service, it is not surprising that RCA fared well out of the 1939–45 war:

> From a $100m corporation in 1938, RCA soared to the billion dollar corporate rank in 1955.
>
> (Engstrom 1958. (Senior executive VP, RCA))[3]

## RCA's post-war expansion

Demand for all the company's products grew greatly after the war. NBC led the expansion of broadcast radio and television. This in turn led to big demand for the company's consumer electronics equipment. RCA and EMI had developed broadcast quality television, and it was RCA which after the war started to drive towards colour transmission. In response to a mechanical colour system under development at CBS, RCA initiated a huge development project to produce an electronic colour system (Layton 1972: 119). Colour television would have a major impact on RCA and on its computer operation, pulling cash away from the computer developments.

Not only were the broadcast and consumer operations in rapid growth, but so also were RCA's component and capital electronics businesses. After the war, RCA had the opportunity to sell these new developments into both the military market, especially when revived by the Korean and Cold Wars, and in the civil market.

RCA's returns were excellent compared to its UK equivalents. The rapid expansion of television in the US and the huge demand from the US government for capital electronics to support its Cold War efforts meant incredible returns for this company. The following charts show RCA's growing sales and profit (see Figure 3.1) and excellent return on equity (see Figure 3.2)

However, expectations were very different and it could not deliver the expected returns while carrying out expansions on all fronts. There were

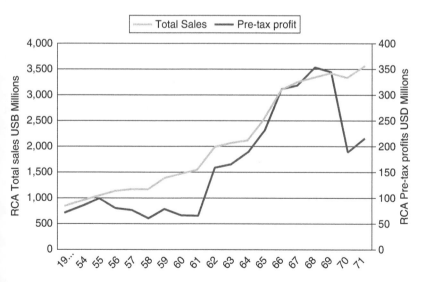

*Figure 3.1*   RCA basic financials, sales and profits
*Source*: RCA Annual Reports 1962 and 1971.

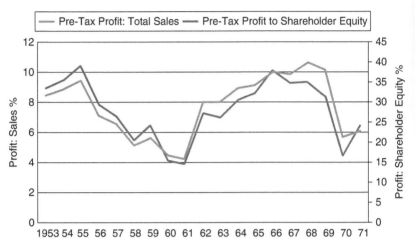

*Figure 3.2*   RCA basic financials, profit ratios
Source: RCA Annual Reports 1962 and 1971.

two distinct troughs in performance; both of these were associated with high development costs of some major RCA projects. The first trough, in the 1950s, caused in part by the cost of putting colour television on the market, greatly damaged the computer operation as both divisions (and indeed other divisions) were competing for the same pool of resources. The second, during 1969–72, was caused by crisis at both the computer division and in the Hertz car rental company which it owned. Both were problems associated with the way rental valuations and depreciation were calculated. RCA disposed of Hertz (one of a number of true conglomerate diversifications it attempted) and sold its computer operations to Sperry Rand.

In common with most companies, RCA entered the 1950s with a functional structure, with functions such as manufacture and sales being unaligned with specific product groups. However, RCA was acutely aware that as the diversity of products increased such an organisation was ineffective. RCA itself outlined the problems in its own journal:

> Product leadership was divided. Coordinating a product was proving difficult. There was a high administrative load. Profit responsibility was difficult to delegate. The outlook was for further growth and diversification.
> (Mastran, 1956, RCA Administrator of Organisational Planning)[4]

RCA followed the example of other firms and adopted a multi-divisional, decentralised profit-centre organisation which was the fashion of the time:

> Basically, the organisation changes taking place are the outcome of RCA's adoption of the philosophy of decentralizing the responsibility

for operations. This philosophy may be further defined as the delegation of responsibility and authority to individuals for the profitable conduct of the business operations of integrated units within the Corporation. By integrated unit is meant one having all of its own functions, such as engineering, purchasing, manufacturing, marketing, and any others necessary to manage a particular product line or lines. Such a unit becomes the responsibility of one person.

(Mastran 1956)[5]

After a temporary arrangement where the whole of the electronics operation was under one organisation the company was divided into four operational groups:

- Defence Electronic Products
- Commercial (later Industrial) Electronic Products
- Radio Marine Communications
- National Broadcast Company.

The Defence and Commercial groups are the most important groups in this study. The CEP group controlled the Computer Systems Division, the focus of this case study.

## RCA and computers

### Part 1: The experimental phase

In the late 1940s and early 1950s, RCA was busy fulfilling the demand for consumer electronics, developing its television business and supplying advanced electronics for the US armed forces. RCA had only a limited involvement in the genesis of the computer. At the firm's Princeton laboratories a small team built a large analogue computer, the Typhoon,[6] for the US Navy aeronautical research,[7] but this did not lead to further developments.

Of more importance was RCA's early work with computer storage techniques. As the leading electronics firm, RCA was consulted on potential memory techniques for a number of early computer developments, such as the US Army sponsored ENIAC, and the JOHNNIAC built by the Rand Corporation (Gruenberger, 1979). For these projects, RCA developed the SELECTRON tube.[8] This was an advanced and highly complex electron tube memory device. However, the Williams Tube from Manchester proved much simpler, cheaper, and became available much earlier. Eventually all the machines adopted other techniques, except the JOHNNIAC and its precursor system. RCA produced 2000 of the tubes for various projects (Rajchman, 1980).

In the early 1950s RCA developed a second, and much more important, memory technique. This was the magnetic ferrite core which could store information in a matrix of magnetised rings. This became the standard computer memory system through to the mid-1970s (Rajchman, 1980). There was controversy about who developed this technique as it was simultaneously developed by Jay Forrester of the Massachusetts Institute of Technology. Forrester's device was used in the SAGE air-defence project which proved to be a crucial stepping stone for IBM in its development of its own computer capabilities.

### The Advanced Development Group (ADG)

In 1950, the company formed a special team of engineers, the ADG.[9] During its eight years of existence it was charged with the task of spreading the use of new digital and computer techniques to all parts of the company:

> At that time, in the development of RCA's Camden organisation, we were the only advanced development group and we had been supporting in that activity both military and commercial type endeavours. So it was quite natural for this group to be given the responsibility of looking at digital technology for both commercial and military uses
> (Beard, Chief Engineer RCA Computer Systems Division)[10]

During its first four years, much of the ADG's effort was focused on commercial applications. From 1954 onwards, it became increasingly involved in military work, eventually becoming a part of the West Coast Missile and Surface Radar Division in 1958.[11]

ADG is the finest example of how electronics firms used their core capabilities to generate product development and economies of scope. ADG was an embodiment of economies of scope in action.

(1)  ADG and the BIZMAC commercial computer.

The ADG's first project was the foundation of RCA's Computer Systems Division. In 1950, ADG started the development of the BIZMAC. This was a computer designed especially for sorting through large databases. It used the new magnetic core storage developed by RCA plus a random access drum memory. However, its main function was to access data held on hundreds of low cost magnetic tape drives which held the database. Photographs of the machine show that it was truly impressive. It weighed 250 tonnes and took up 18,000 sq.ft., almost every part of it made by RCA itself.[12]

It was built under contract to the US Army's Ordnance Corps, and used for keeping control of the tank spares in its armament depots and factories:

> contract was negotiated in 1951 with the Army Ordnance Corps for equipping one of their large supply depots (Letterkenney, Pa.) with the RCA BIZMAC electronic processing system. In 1952, the Ordnance Corps requested enlargement of the contract to cover the inventory control at one of their largest stock control points, the Ordnance Tank-Automotive Command. Delivery of the complete system was set for 1955.
> (Leas 1956)[13]

The contract was worth $4.5m. RCA remained a major supplier of computers to the US armed forces for logistic control purposes.

In 1954, the Commercial Electronic Products Group took over responsibility for the BIZMAC and decided to sell the system on a commercial basis.[14] However, the machine did not sell in great numbers: somewhere in the region of 6 were made. Users included a large mail order firm and two large personal insurance companies in New York, users with big database problems. However, not surprisingly for such a giant early generation computer, BIZMAC was dogged by problems of unreliability. The low-level of sales has led some to the conclusion that the product was a failure.[15]

However, it was a large and expensive system which generated revenue of between $10–20m during 1955-1958. It also allowed RCA to develop a working knowledge of the commercial market place. It was a launch pad and few other companies can truly say their first computer was any more successful.

The ADG had a staff of just 30 when they developed BIZMAC, which was too small to cope with such a large system. To further its development, the Commercial Electronic Products group formed the BIZMAC Engineering Group, consisting of 100 engineers, which took over responsibility for the system.[16] This group was then expanded to form the Electronic Data Processing Division which would later become the Computer Systems Division (CSD), and finally the Information Systems Group (ISG).

With the BIZMAC Engineering Group continuing work on that machine, the ADG was freed for other projects. Initially it would develop a number of defence systems, but would later return to support the nascent computer operations within RCA and design the firm's first second generation system, the RCA 501 system.

## (2) ADG and military computer projects

Before looking at the rest of RCA's commercial computer operations, it is worthwhile outlining its activities in defence computers, as these directly affected the economics and organisation of the early commercial products. ADG worked on a number of minor military developments. These included a magnetic logic computer, bomb-aiming systems and encryption techniques.[17]

However, the most notable early work of the ADG was in the use of solid state transistorised electronics in large military systems: this ability was used by the ADG to design the 501 transistorised computer for the Commercial Electronic Products Group. In 1958, the ADG abandoned its dual commercial and defence role and became solely involved in the military side of the company, the Defence Electronic Products group (DEP):

There were two events which I think bore on this [the absorption into DEP]. One was that the Commercial Computer Group had grown considerably and was capable of doing [its] own advanced development work as well as product design. And, second, the Missile Group had recently won an award for the Ballistic Missile Early Warning System (BMEWS) system, which entailed a considerable amount of digital technology.

(Beard)[18]

The BMEWS was one of the major strategic control mechanisms developed in the 1950s. It was probably second only to the huge Semi-Automatic Ground Environment, SAGE system. BMEWS was a computer-controlled warning system covering the US, Canada and Great Britain. As prime contractor, RCA was not only in charge of the sub-contractor's efforts, but also had to integrate all the systems into one. IBM was chosen as the supplier of the major central computer, and the system is famous for enabling IBM to develop the capability to build large scale scientific processors and real time systems as well as develop packing techniques it would use in the third generation 360 system. However, despite the fame IBM achieved in this project, RCA was the lead contractor which would itself supply three computer types of its own; the Communications Data Processor (CPD), RADCON and DIP systems.[19] All three developments used a common architecture and packaging and were used for various roles in processing radar data, transmitting the data and then displaying the end result at the NORAD command bunker in Colorado.

Following BMEWS, RCA received another large contract, this time for a communications network for the US Air Force. This was ComLogNet (later known as Autodin 1), which was to transmit logistics information around the world to ensure the availability of parts of US Airforce planes. This built on RCA's strength in logistics work developed during the BIZMAC programme. This system used the CPD computer developed for BMEWS communications to buffer and switch high speed data transfers through microwave and high capacity cable links.[20] The prime contractor for ComLogNet was Western Union, a firm well used to such communications systems.

Initially, the CPD was not handled by the Defence Electronic Products Group. It was closely related to normal computer activity and was based in the commercial operation. It was expected that the CDP computer would be built in conjunction with the large scale 601 commercial computer being constructed by the EDP Division, again for use in communications systems as well as large scale data processing. However, in 1960, a separate Communications and Controls Division was formed to take over this work, see Figure 3.3.

In 1962, the communications operation was transferred to the Defence Electronic Products division[21] and the links between the CDP and 601 systems were completely severed. It will be seen that this had a serious effect on the 601 project.

## Part 2: Structured entry

BIZMAC was only a partial entry into the market. However, it gave RCA a chance to build up a team of engineers, and gave it a base for future work.

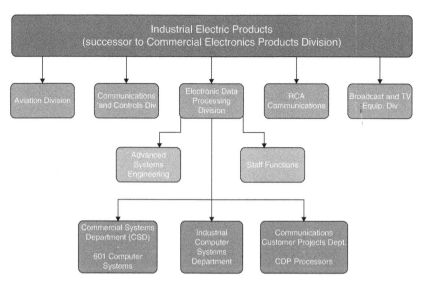

*Figure 3.3*  IEP major reorganisation
*Source*: University of Minnesota Library. RCA Engineer, August/Sept 1960: 38.

In the second generation of computers, like its offspring EMI, RCA made a drive to become an important player in the market.

*The 501 computer*

With the BIZMAC engineering team taking over responsibility for that system, ADG was not only freed to do its defence work, but also to prepare the logical design for RCA's first second generation system, the 501. Design of this system was quickly assimilated into the EDP Division. There were three significant factors in the market positioning of this machine:

1. It used fully transistorized logic, building on the developments of the Semiconductor and Materials Division, which had worked on transistors for military products.[22]
2. It was a purely commercial system, with little provision for scientific application. The system was one of the first to offer the business language COBOL, but it was not initially provided with the IBM FORTRAN language which was the staple language for engineering.[23]
3. The system was targeted at a perceived gap in the market for medium capacity machines.[24]

The RCA 501 was a very deliberately targeted. A gap in the market was identified which straddled the gap between the larger and small machines then available. As Figure 3.4 shows, the 501 was divided into three sub-categories (the 503 best covering the original 501 space) and was a medium scale system, a larger system than IBM's hugely popular 1401 but under its large scale 7070-1401 combination. RCA hoped to exploit a gap that it perceived in the market for middle size computers.

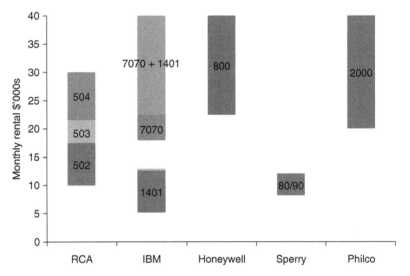

*Figure 3.4*    RCA established product positioning
*Source*: Charles Babbage Institute, University of Minnesota, Collection 13. <u>US vs. IBM</u>, px114, RCA, 1/12/59. 'Business Review of the Electronic Data Processing Division'.

The 501 and its siblings formed RCA's real market entry, based not only on the BIZMAC experience, but also the design work of the semi-military ADG and the developments of the Semiconductor Division, again based on its military work.

The 501 was delivered quickly: the first internal installation was April 1959, and the first customer delivery was that June, to the Bureau of Weapons.[25] By November 1959 three had been delivered, twenty one were on order and fourteen letters of intent had been received. Eventually in the region of 100 were installed.[26] Of these, the military used 29.[27] Most of the military sales were used by the US Army for logistics work. Overall, the marketing staff concluded that the system was competitive apart from some minor flaws in peripherals:

It is my understanding that the 501 was a competitive system; that it was well designed by the standards of the time. It had architectural features which were considered to be excellent. It was somewhat weak in some of its peripheral equipment ... such as the card reader and punching equipment ... and the line printer, with which we had considerable trouble, but, as a central system, the 501 was considered a good design and competitive with other equipment in the market place.

> (McCollister, ex-Marketing Vice President of the
> Computer Systems Division)[28]

As will be seen, RCA's first competitive, mid-tier, second generation system sold in numbers way beyond its British peers at Ferranti, EMI and English Electric.

### The big push – the 301 and 601 systems

However, the 501 could only cover the medium scale market. The firm was concerned that this would mean it would miss out on large sales elsewhere. The division estimated that both the large scale and small scale markets would grow in size as outlined in Table 3.1.

*Table 3.1*  Future demand for computers, and RCA's projected market share

| Target market | Large Scale Systems | Small Scale Systems |
| --- | --- | --- |
| 6000 firms with 100+ clerical employees | 2000 | 4000 |
| 8000 firms with 50–99 clerical employees | 0 | 4000 |
| total market | 2000 | 8000 |
| RCA's planned share | 416 (20%) | 615 (8%) |

*Source*: Charles Babbage Institute, University of Minnesota, Collection 13. US vs. IBM, px114, RCA, 1/12/59. 'Business Review of the Electronic Data Processing Division'.

It could not achieve these levels of sales with the 501, it needed to also provide both larger scale and smaller scale systems.

The division planned to cover the smaller scale market with a new system called the 301 and also to introduce the large scale 601 based on the work it had been doing on the CDP system. This strategy was expected to give RCA very broad market coverage (see Figure 3.5). It was now planning to offer computers across the broad, greatly expanding the market that the 501 series of computers had covered and creating a strategy to compete with the second iteration of its major rivals' second generation systems:

Thus, RCA was offering one of the most comprehensive ranges on the market, second only to IBM. Table 3.2 shows the engineering resources and marketing expenditures that were planned to support the second generation systems:

These are fascinating figures to contrast with the spending at the UK firms, where technology was centre stage. In the US, even a technology-orientated

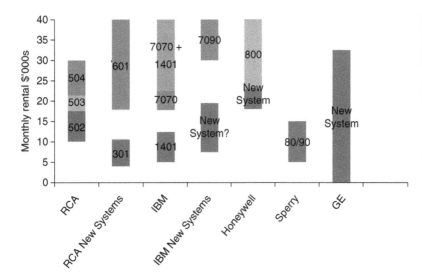

*Figure 3.5*　RCA expected product positioning
*Source*: Charles Babbage Institute, University of Minnesota, Collection 13. US vs. IBM, px114, RCA, 1/12/59. 'Business Review of the Electronic Data Processing Division'.

*Table 3.2*　Forecast engineering and marketing costs

| $Million | '60 | '61 | '62 | '63 | '64 | '65 | Total |
|---|---|---|---|---|---|---|---|
| General Engineering | 9.3 | 9.1 | 8.3 | 8.4 | 8.7 | 9.1 | 52.9 |
| Marketing | 9.2 | 12.5 | 16.0 | 18.6 | 20.9 | 22.8 | 100.0 |

*Source*: Charles Babbage Institute, University of Minnesota, Collection 13. US vs. IBM px114, RCA, 1/12/59.

firm like RCA was spending two dollars on marketing for every one dollar spent on development and production engineering.

With these resources, RCA expected to start shipping machines quickly. However, it expected that income would lag behind expenditures. The reason for this was that, like all the other firms in the industry, RCA had to follow IBM's example and place most of its machines onto the market under leasing arrangements, so it expected to take a number of years for receipts to match the value of the systems shipped out; a profit was not expected until 1964:

*The 301*

The 301 and 601 were announced together in April 1960.[29] The 301 was the less ambitious machine, primarily aimed at the commercial market.

It was pitched in a much more price-sensitive part of the market than the larger scale 501 and 601: RCA did its best to tightly "value engineer' the system

*Table 3.3*   Financial forecast for the RCA computer division

| $Millions | 1960 | 61 | 62 | 63 | 64 | 65 | Total |
|---|---|---|---|---|---|---|---|
| Net Value Shipped | 37.8 | 73.9 | 109.3 | 132.2 | 165.7 | 351.2 | 870.1 |
| Net sales | 12.6 | 47.7 | 55.8 | 78.5 | 114.2 | 196.5 | 505.3 |
| Profit or Loss | −10.2 | −8.2 | −5.4 | −1.1 | 8.8 | 24.1 | 8 |

*Source*: Charles Babbage Institute, University of Minnesota, Collection 13. US vs. IBM px114, RCA, 1/12/59.

to keep the price down. It was also in a higher volume part of the market. The firm built a new plant in Palm Beach, Florida, to produce the 301.[30] Of the $9.3m spent on engineering in 1960, the largest single item was the development of this system. RCA committed itself to a large marketing campaign and a policy of accepting large losses on its computer operations, so as to establish the 301's market share (Table 3.3). By doing this it was hoped that the installed 301s would bring in good rental revenues in the future as most systems were being leased – this would be a key feature of later RCA strategies which would go horrendously wrong.

Nevertheless, the company took steps to ensure that it did not spend too much on the 301 project. It learnt from the problems that it had encountered with the peripherals on the 501 system and contracted third party companies to supply peripherals, especially punched card equipment and printers. There was a secondary reason for this. RCA was competing for an order in excess of 30 machines to be used at USAF bases for logistics work, probably connected to the ComLogNet programme. To use the existing USAF data, IBM compatible punched card peripherals were needed.[31]

Initially, these peripherals were obtained from IBM; later, RCA would use its technology licence partners for these systems; ICT of the UK and Bull of France provided punched card equipment. Printers came from Anelex and optical character readers, for cheque processing etc, from Farrington. Random access disk drives, rapidly becoming the most important peripheral of all, came from Bryant.

Unfortunately, the Bryant disk drives proved unreliable and difficult to service.[32] They also proved unsuitable for real-time, on-line data processing. These problems later forced RCA to restart its peripheral development, and to try to provide itself with better disks. However:

... when RCA decided to redevelop its products, it had lost the continuity of the engineering effort that had been going on in such things as printers and essentially had to re-establish its engineering skills and manufacturing skills in those areas. So in a sense time was lost by the early decision to abandon these peripheral developments.

(Beard)[33]

One peripheral project did remain a key part of RCA's strategy. The RACE was RCA's alternative to the disk drive. RACE was meant to leapfrog the current disk drive technology, but proved to be a major product failure, and put RCA further behind in storage techniques. The inadequacies of RACE are studied below.

Another problem with the 301 was that, like the 501, it was not initially offered with a FORTRAN compiler for scientific.[34] The problem was that, during the 1960s, most firms wanted to use their computers for both commercial and scientific work. Therefore, RCA transferred Arthur Beard from the DEP group to the EDP Division: he was briefed with developing arithmetic co-processors for the 501 and 301 computers, to improve their usefulness as scientific machines.[35] At the same time a FORTRAN compiler was provided for both systems.

Despite the weakness in peripherals and the lateness of support for advanced science and engineering work, the 301 was a success. IBM credited it as such:

> RCA, in the past, had been one of the most successful of the IBM competitors with the RCA 301 selling some 620 systems.
> (IBM Competitive Environment 1966)[36]

The first 301 was delivered in February 1961, with the last being delivered in 1967. In 1965, the US government was using 95 of them, most for logistics work, some for civil administration.[37] The rest of the sales were spread widely throughout the rest of the EDP industry. It seems to have been the right scale system for the rapidly growing market, though its sales were only some 5–6% of the equivalent IBM system, the 1401.

## The 601

This was the largest machine in RCA's range and was marketed as the flagship system. Unfortunately, it sank.

It was a large scale computer designed to handle large amounts of data. It came in two versions: the basic 603 for general purpose data processing, and the 604 which was enhanced for scientific work,[38] using a similar co-processor unit to the 301. The basic price was around $1.5m or rental of $31–34,000 per month.

It was designed to run a number of programs at once, and used the so-called Omni-channel input-output system to control up to 64 peripherals simultaneously.[39] It was also meant to offer 'unprecedented compatibility with RCA data processing and communications equipment and other processors'. It used so-called modular packaging to enable it to be easily enhanced. However, the system eventually offered neither of these advanced features. The packaging technique used led to great difficulty, and it was completely incompatible with any RCA or other system. RCA had a vision of what the next generation of computers would be – compatible families of systems spanning very small to very large computing – the 301, 501, 601 range, comprehensively failed to deliver compatibility.

A number of further problems came from the broken relationship between the 601 and the military CDP computer. With the EDP Division fully occupied with producing the 501 and 301, it was decided that the 601 would be built at the military operation in Camden.[40] This was logical as it was envisaged that the 601 and the CDP computer, to be used in ComLogNet, would be close relatives. RCA believed that the 601 would benefit from this link, and planned to sell the 601 to the telecommunications industry. It was estimated that the New Jersey Bell Telephone Company alone would have a requirement for 100-150 of these systems.[41]

A number of difficulties arose with this arrangement. First, it has already been seen that the computer communications operation became a separate unit of the Industrial Electronic Products Group, and then joined the Defence Electronic Products Group. This meant that the CDP and 601 design teams became separated and the designs diverged massively. Second, there was a lack of communications between the EDP Division and the Camden manufacturing site.

The 601 had been costed in the expectation that it would benefit from sharing many components with the CDP. McCollister, Marketing Vice President of the Computer Systems Division, saw this as the root of the project's cost problems:

> from what I learned of it, I would say it [the cost errors of the 601 project] was probably errors in judgement as to what costs were likely to be to accomplish the functions that had been specified, but there was also one organisational action that may have contributed to this.
>
> There was a parallel machine called the CDP or Communication Data Processor, which was the processor in the ComLogNet, later called Autodin Communication System, for the Federal government, and originally it had been expected that the 601 and the CDP would be one and the same machine, but for perhaps several reasons, this turned out not to be so.
>
> For one reason because what had been in one organisation was subsequently put into two organisations and to a certain extent each pursued its own independent way.[42]
>
> (McCollister)

The divorce from the CDP was only one of its problems. RCA also failed to deliver the performance and functions promised and costs were multiplied by its unique packaging problem:

> Also, there was difficulty in providing some of the functional capabilities that had originally been announced ... for one thing, the 601 system was intended to be an on-line type of system and a multi-programming type of system, and the cost of some of the controllers to put these capabilities on line, so to speak, with the central processor, were so far out of line that this was economically just a totally impractical thing to do.

... Finally ... to achieve the performance that had been specified in the central processor, they had to go to the extensive use of coaxial cable in the back frame of the system, and there were so many of these wires, and they were so bulky ... that it was virtually a physical impossibility to interconnect all of the points on the back side of the machine that had to be interconnected.

So, just in summary, there were severe technical problems, both in a functional and in a manufacturing sense, and there were also severe financial problems, so much so that the company began to look for a way out of the programme.

(McCollister)[43]

In early 1962, the company stopped offering the 601 for sale.[44] It was only sold for just over a year and RCA accepted around five orders for the system.

### Managerial changes and financial restrictions

By 1962, while having the most advanced strategy in the industry to combat IBM, the EDP Division also had a number of difficulties. Its top-of-the-range 601 had become a very public failure and the resources that could have been used to build another system had been wasted. The 501 was getting old and needed replacing, its sales were slowing up dramatically, and the firm needed to improve its peripheral equipment. Interviewed in 1962, McCollister estimated RCA had invested $100m in the computer department (Bergstein, H. 1962),[45] but had not seen any profit from this investment, and there was little expectation of an imminent return, despite the clear success of the 501 and 301.

A number of new personnel were brought in to deal with the cost and technical problems. Beard was bought in to head up engineering in 1961 and McCollister was poached from Burroughs and took over marketing. In 1962, a new Vice President, Art Malcarney,[46] took control of the operation, and he appointed Arnold Weber, another long term RCA employee, as General Manager of the EDP Division.

Interestingly, Malcarney came from the defence side of the business and had previously been in charge of the Camden plant which had produced the 601 and had been very critical of the running of the EDP Division.[47]

At the corporate level, Dr Elmer W. Engstrom became president of RCA. He ordered the computer operation to cut its losses and to break-even:

... instructions from the corporation, from the Chairman and the President, were to reduce our losses [by] half [each] year from the end of 1961 ... and to achieve a break-even by the end of 1964.

(McCollister)[48]

RCA was undergoing a profits squeeze in the early 1960s, as was seen in Figure 3.2. It wasn't just computers which were damaging RCA's usually stellar returns. The firm was undertaking a number of other expensive development projects. The largest of these, and the one that drew heavily on the company treasury, was the cost of bringing colour television to the market. This meant not only preparing facilities for the mass production of domestic sets, but also the building of capital equipment to give NBC and third party television stations the ability to transmit in colour. Television was seen as central to RCA's operations and many hundreds of millions of dollars were sunk into it. Beard believed that the effort in television was larger than the company's efforts in computers:

> ... I believe that there was some greater total effort in television from the engineering point of view than there was in the computer.
>
> (Beard)[49]

To pay for these developments the company had to rein back on losses elsewhere, so the computer operation was ordered to cut its cloth to fit into the wider plans.

While the development of colour television was undoubtedly the main reason for RCA suspending its efforts to increase market share in the computer industry, there were other RCA developments that impacted on the computer operation. For example, Beard noted that, from 1959, the DEP was expanded substantially.[50] Its main area of growth was the Astro Electronics Division. This was RCA's space and ballistic missiles operation which became involved in many aspects of the space and nuclear weapons programme. Its most public role was as the prime contractor for the electronics for the lunar lander. In 1965, the Astro Division employed 3202 qualified engineers and scientists;[51] the EDP division employed only 217. Many other military projects needed the skills of computer engineers, a further draw on RCA's limited pool of experts.

> Overall RCA had a policy of expanding its defence operations: Defence electronics is a consistently broadening field and it is manifestly impossible to have a representation in all areas. It is our policy to develop pre-eminence in selected technical areas.
>
> (Malcarney 1961)[52]

While most of these developments were paid for by government contracts, and therefore did not drain the firm of funds (indeed rather the opposite), it did mean that RCA's skills had to be spread thinly.

It is argued later that these cuts and competition for skills undermined RCA's third generation computers, as it was during this period of cuts that these systems were being designed.

Overall, during 1962 to 1965, the computer operation missed a beat and sales were flat, by this stage only the 301 was selling in numbers, the 601 had failed and the 501 was too old. Cutting expansion meant reduced losses, this allowed the Computer Systems Division to crawl towards break-even. However, from 1966–67, when profits from colour television started to flow in, the computer operation was again allowed to expand and build up large losses in its efforts to gain market share (see Figure 3.6)

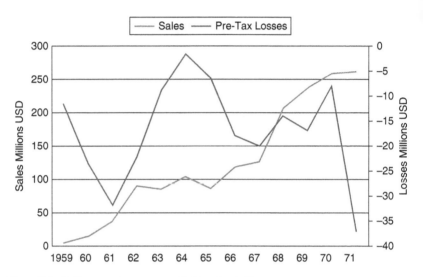

*Figure 3.6*   RCA computer systems division basic finances
*Source*: Charles Babbage Institute, University of Minnesota, Collection 13. US vs. IBM px242, RCA 1971 'EDP Five Year Plan 1963–1967' and dX952, RCA 'Business Plan II'.

### Keeping the second generation product line alive

The new edict to move towards break-even was not to be carried out at all costs. The computer operations were aiming at cutting losses by 50 per cent per annum while the colour television expansion ran its course, and was to be carried out without damaging RCA's market position. This boiled down to a three-point strategy for the computer operation:

- Protect its current revenue and present customer position, both domestic and foreign.
- Become a profit contributor to RCA.
- Maintain growth which is at least comparable to that of the industry as a whole.[53]

The plan was to reduce the number of new systems placed on the market. This would allow rental income to catch-up with capital expenditure on new leases. At this time RCA believed it was number two in the market, at least in terms of systems being shipped, if not in terms of an established user base (see Table 3.4).

Table 3.4   RCA's internal estimate of market share

| Market share by value of new computers shipped. | |
| --- | --- |
| IBM | 78.7 |
| RCA | 4 |
| RemRand/UNIVAC | 3.5 |
| NCR | 3.2 |
| GE | 3.2 |
| Honeywell | 2.4 |
| CDC | 2.1 |
| Burroughs | 1.1 |
| Others | 1.8 |

Source: Charles Babbage Institute, University of Minnesota, Collection 13. US vs. IBM, px242, RCA CSD 'RCA EDP Five Year Plan 1963–1967'.

To ensure that its systems stayed competitive enough to maintain its position in the market, it had to undertake a programme of improvements to its product line, while not draining company funds. This led to a number of small enhancement projects.

1. The enhanced 501 and 3301
   Beard's first task on officially joining what was now the Computer Systems Division (CSD) was to design a "speed pack" for the 501.[54] This unit improved the speed of the 501 by 30%, helping to keep the system alive for a few years. However, this was seen as only a temporary measure. Similar packs were provided for other RCA machines to allow them to carry out a secondary scientific role – the previously mentioned arithmetic co-processors.
2. The 3301
   The 501 was inherently old and needed replacement, RCA decided to introduce an improved and larger scale cousin to the 301. The 3301 was launched in August 1963 and was designed to utilise more advanced disk drives, and had the now usual RCA arithmetic co-processor, now referred to as the PINE unit. However, the peripheral which the 3301 would be most associated with was the RACE storage system (see on the next page), and it was this that it hoped would give it a competitive edge. It was intended that the 3301 would give 301 users a way of increasing their computer power without having to swap their data to a new architecture. However, RCA had relatively low expectations of the system:

   > It was not a new design. It wasn't intended to be the foundation of a future line of products; rather, it was a product that we could develop

relatively quickly, at relatively low engineering expense, that would give us an additional offering to take the place of the 601, and that in a sense would give us time to get on with a complete new product program in the long range future.

(McCollister)[55]

However, rather than being in the 601 scale it was in the same price region as the 501. McCollister estimated it cost just $2m to develop the 3301.[56] One significant improvement over the 301 was its ability to operate as an on-line real-time computer and as a communications machine. It was given the marketing title of the 3301 REALCOM, to underline its communications abilities. It benefited from some of the 601 research, using the same very fast memory.

Using all these cost saving tactics, it was estimated that only 50 3301s needed to be sold to break-even: Beard estimated that 80 were sold.[57] It has been argued that these relatively low sales, and the fact that it was quickly eclipsed by the third generation Spectra series, meant that the machine was a failure (Fisher et al. 1983: 202–3). However, given the stop-gap nature of the machine and that Beard testified that so few needed to be sold to recover costs, it must be counted as one of RCA's successful products.

## Peripheral failure; the RACE system

Peripherals, systems based primarily on electro-mechanical engineering rather than pure electronics, were a continuing problem for RCA, as they would be for all the electronics firms. The inadequacies of RCA's own printers and punched card units on the 501 led to it purchasing these devices from elsewhere. It had to do the same with disk drives. It has been seen that the Bryant disk drive proved unreliable and was not a match for IBM systems. It was not really until the late 1960s, and the establishment of a number of so called 'plug compatible' manufacturers who produced copies of IBM kit, that an adequate source of IBM type disk drives became available for purchase. Beard outlined the perceived strengths and weaknesses of the firm:

We felt that the electronic capability of RCA was very strong ... We realized that RCA was not particularly strong in the mechanical or electro-mechanical areas, but this capability could be achieved either inside the company or obtained outside the company as was necessary. So, in the earlier years, I believe we looked on it primarily as a technological challenge which we felt very optimistic about.

(Beard)[58]

With the failure to secure adequate devices from third parties, RCA concentrated its efforts on producing a peripheral system that would leap-frog the current technology. This was the RACE, which was heavily marketed with the 3301 and, for a while, with the third generation Spectra 70 series. Like NCR's CRAM, RACE used magnetic cards/effectively short strips of tape.[59] The cards were held in a robotic magazine, which, when selected, mechanically transported the cards to a rotating drum. The card was attached to the spinning drum and read by magnetic heads and would then be returned to the magazine. RACE could hold a massive 250 million bits of information. RCA hoped to deliver the system by 1965.

This 250mb random access data store was meant to leapfrog other technologies, although in reality it was either a very very slow disk drive or a very fast tape drive, depending on how you looked at it; of course, it was a system which would have fitted very neatly with its old BIZMAC machine which had been a fairly efficient way of accessing databases in functions such as stores management. Sadly for RCA, this much publicised system was a failure for a number of reasons. First, such a complex mechanism proved expensive and unreliable. The cards wore out quickly, and had to be regularly copied to protect the data; there was no way of telling which cards were wearing out so they all had to be copied (there are legion stories of RACE systems simply spending all day backing up data and then backing it up again in an endless loop).

It also took a long time to access the data. Worse still was the fact that, in 1964 and 1965, IBM introduced the 2311 and 2314 disk drives. These offered massive improvements over old disk systems.[60] The 2311 was cheap, while 2314s could be daisy chained together to give nearly as much storage as the RACE while allowing much faster access times. RACE could not compete with these systems. It also diverted RCA's limited electromagnetic and electromechanical design resources and delayed RCA's efforts to develop better disk drives for its computers.

It wasn't all bad news; RCA was more successful in supplying communications peripherals for its computers. Linked to this was a project to provide its computers with the ability to control industrial processes remotely, but this development was abandoned in an attempt to save money.

## Part 3: Consolidation phase

*RCA's overseas partners, and plans for third-generation systems*

RCA had some success in selling its second generation designs abroad, a business which had some impact on RCA's plans for third generation computers.

RCA's first overseas computer collaboration was with English Electric (see Chapter 7). English Electric took the 501 design and produced the 'anglicised' KDP 10[77] which it sold in small numbers. However, as English Electric became fully occupied with its own development and with those of its newly acquired LEO systems, it decided not to licence the 301. This proved a boon for ICT, English Electric's main UK rival. ICT had been sluggish in computers, and it needed an up-to-date small-medium scale computer that could fill the needs of larger tabulator users who wanted to trade up to the new technology. Machines Bull of France had a similar requirement. Both companies ordered a number of 301s to resell, generating cash sales for RCA, which meant it avoided the need to fund leases on these machines. ICT sold over 80 301s as the ICT 1500 and Bull sold more than 95. A few were also shipped to Hitachi. RCA also bought some punched card peripherals from ICT and Bull.

This was big business for the RCA EDP Division with $15m of overseas sales in 1962 and an expected $25m in 1963[61] and yet this was business which used little capital – ideal for the company as it struggled to maintain its high returns on equity. RCA actively strove to preserve its position in this market. It believed that it had to develop machines that were technically ahead of the systems that its partner/customers could create themselves, while also ensuring that they also matched the marketing plans of these customers.

In the early 1960s, RCA was considering how to replace its second generation systems. It decided that it should offer a compatible range of computers from the small scale to very large computers. Initially, it was planning a series called the Ultra, though this was rapidly replaced by the Vanguard series.[62]

Vanguard was planned to be RCA's main computer family, but the firm also decided to start developing a smaller system called the Poplar. This system was targeted at helping the tabulator companies to upgrade their users to computers, but it was very cautious about using the system in its domestic American market:

> At the present time, we are actively at work with ICT in the logical design of this system, and expect to produce the unit, with the first deliveries beginning in early 1965. While the machine may prove to be attractive in the domestic market, it must be sold on a carefully conceived marketing plan if we are to avoid the unusually high marketing costs which would be attendant with a machine of such small average dollar rental. Nevertheless, we expect POPLAR to make a contribution toward future domestic revenue.
>
> (RCA)[63]

By 1963, the EDP division employed 926 personnel in marketing, nearly 40% of its total staff of 2471. Given the policy of reducing losses, a machine that would add disproportionately to this staff was not seen as a good prospect. As it was, while the marketing team was growing continually, the engineering staff had been cut back from 755 to 579 to save costs.[64]

The POPLAR plan fell to pieces. First, ICT acquired Ferranti's computer operation, giving it the engineering skills necessary to develop its own third generation system. Second, Bull had been in crisis for many years, struggling to cope with the migration from punched cards to computers.

The continual crisis had become too much for the French government, who sold it to General Electric (see Chapter 4). GE did not want to continue to buy RCA equipment. Finally, IBM's announcement of the 360 family scuppered all RCA's third generation plans, as the 360 was introduced earlier than had been expected and RCA, like others were stuck with half-engineered plans, in part driven by an overseas strategy which no longer existed.

All was not lost though – it would find overseas partners for its radical third generation strategy and RCA had returned to old allies to sell its computers abroad. English Electric decided to follow RCA's third generation strategy, and produced another anglicised RCA system, the System 4, though we have seen what a disaster this was. Siemens and Hitachi produced parts for the new RCA range and imported the rest. All three tied themselves into RCA's third generation strategy.

*Spectra 70*

IBM's announcement of the System/360 family of computers radically changed the market, though technically the system was only a culmination of a number of trends. IBM introduced a unified line of commercial and scientific computers and made obsolete most second generation systems. The 360 was announced much earlier than other firms expected and was backed by IBM on a scale that took the industry by storm. Every other firm had to offer something to compete with the new IBM range. RCA dropped its plans for the Vanguard and Poplar systems, to concentrate on a new range. While RCA had been working on the small scale Poplar, the main family, Vanguard, was a long way from production. RCA had to take quick action if it wanted to announce a new range that was competitive with the 360.

In April 1964, within two or three weeks of the 360 announcement, RCA's planning staff received Art Malcarney's permission to cease the Vanguard programme and to start work on a radical new strategy.[65] The Five-Year Plan of June 1964[66] outlined a new range, called at the time the New Product Line, NPL, which would be known as the Spectra 70. There were two main elements behind the design of the Spectra, the first of these was the choice of advanced components:

> The new RCA product line ... will have total capabilities which will be at least a match for those offered by IBM System 360. Furthermore, several, if not all, of the systems in the product line will be built with truly integrated circuits rather than the semi-integrated circuits which IBM plans to use in its system. This should represent a significant 'first' for RCA. We expect the new product line to provide us with the future product capability to enable us to meet the goals which are shown in the plan.
>
> (RCA CSD 1964)[67]

For IBM, it was more important to get a third generation family on the market, rather than wait a year or two for third generation components (integrated circuits) to be made available. RCA, using its knowledge as a builder of military systems and component maker, hoped that its technical prowess could overcome finding itself behind IBM's conceptual leap forward. Eventually, the upper half of the Spectra range introduced real third generation components to the commercial computer world. The lower half of the range used second generation components. This was because integrated circuits were still expensive, and would have made the smaller machines too expensive, as semiconductors make up a larger proportion of the cost of smaller systems.

However, this was only half of the plan and the market strategy for the machine was very radical for the time. The product planners decided that the new family should be made program-compatible with the new IBM 360.[68] While such compatibility now seems common, at the time it was a huge statement by RCA and would mean it pitching its systems like-for-like against IBM. It needed scale to be successful at this.

There was, however, one major problem with such a strategy; there were no 360 machines available to copy at that time. Beard's team of engineers 'reverse engineered' the systems using the 'privileged instruction set' of the 360.[69] In effect, they produced a completely different machine, but one which could run 360 programs. RCA's architecture was unique, based in part on the Vanguard, but to the user it was similar to the 360.

Clearly this would create some difficulties. IBM delayed giving RCA details of the 360's input-output protocols.[70] This meant that the Spectra had to have its own operating system, and that its peripherals were not completely plug compatible with IBM's. However, users had a real choice: they could run the same software, and use the same data, on either the new RCA or IBM ranges, even if they could not mix and match the kit as later generations of plug compatible systems would allow.

RCA believed there were a number of advantages in being (nearly) compatible with the new IBM range. RCA wanted to become the natural second source of computers to large corporations.[71] A large firm could decide to adopt the IBM 360, but would have the safety of having a second source of software compatible systems. It also meant that RCA could benefit from the huge amount of software that was expected to be written for the 360.

This latter point was one of the reasons for rejecting some of the other strategies that were put forward. Beard believed that a natural tactic would have been to produce a third generation family compatible with the old 301 and 3301.[72] This would have allowed RCA to keep its old users locked into its unique architecture and exploit the software that had been written for these machines. However, the 301 architecture was not as advanced as the 360 and would not have offered RCA the chance to exploit new hardware and software ideas.

Other firms tried to exploit IBM's decision to produce a new system not based on the old IBM machines. The most successful of these was Honeywell's 200 family of computers which were based on the IBM 1401, which had a user base of over 10,000. It was Honeywell's hope that users of these machines would upgrade to its more advanced, but still compatible, machines (see Chapter 9). GE also hoped to benefit from IBM's move to the 360. Its large 600 series was close to compatible with the scientific IBM 7090/94 computers and it hoped to upgrade this market (see Chapter 4), though this strategy of near compatibility was nowhere near as the successful Honeywell concept.

However, RCA saw greater potential in leaving behind second generation architectures, and adopting the new policy of making a technically advanced 360 look-alike. RCA expected the market for the Spectra to fall into two phases. The first phase was envisioned to consist of RCA competing to install the first, third generation machine in a customer's computer room. In the second phase, during the late 1960s, it was expected that the main trade would be in replacement systems.[73] RCA expected there to be a move to large systems: users who started with a medium sized system such as an IBM 360/40 would require a larger system. This was not just because data processing needs always increase, but also because RCA expected there to be a change in the way computers were used. It believed that computers would become part of 'large integrated management systems'.[74] They would become increasingly a part of information providing networks. To this end, RCA hoped that the RACE would provide the huge data store that would be needed in such a role, and that terminals being developed as part of military programmes could be attached to these systems, to provide managers with access to this information system. A number of companies had this vision of a centralised interactive computer information system. However, it seems that RCA was not that committed to it. RCA was not in the forefront of developments in the field of time-sharing, the method by which many people can use a computer at once, which was a core feature of such a system. RCA did try to develop such timesharing systems but, like IBM, found that vast resources were required to develop such an operating system, and therefore RCA would struggle to deliver this capability.

Within the strategy of IBM compatibility, RCA had to ensure that users would be willing to look to RCA as the second supplier of data processing equipment. RCA hoped that its newer technology would offer certain advantages:

> We felt that we could not underprice IBM product for product because it is very difficult to take out cost in a computer system, but it is not so difficult to put in added performance. So, therefore, the philosophy that we adopted was to provide equipment, a processor in this case, at about the same price as IBM, in fact almost exactly on it, plus or minus a few

per cent ... but to be able to have anywhere from 35 to 45 per cent greater performance or greater computational ability than the corresponding IBM system. So we were holding at the same price but emphasizing performance.

(McCollister)[75]

IBM had very high profits built into its prices: it was by far the most profitable computer company (see Chapter 8). RCA could compete with IBM's scale by foregoing a large amount of this profit. It also planned to avoid parts of the market that required disproportionately high marketing and support expenses. Reflecting its earlier lack of enthusiasm for the small Poplar machine, RCA planned:

> To become the primary second supplier to major U.S. corporations. To concentrate marketing effort on multiple systems sales or $10,000 monthly rental systems.

(RCA CSD 1966)[76]

RCA hoped that the Spectra, and the targeting of large scale users, would make RCA the number two computer company by the end of the 1960s. RCA wanted to achieve a 10% market share, a target which it believed was the level at which the division would become self-sufficient.[77]

*Spectra, an under-engineered system*

This direct assault on IBM's new family had to be done within the terms of the edict that the Computer Systems Division (CSD) had to halve its losses each year. This was reflected in the engineering budget available to the division during the years 1964–66, the years of peak Spectra 70 development. Table 3.5 shows what was available. It should be noted that this includes engineering support for the older machines that still were in the field:

*Table 3.5*   RCA EDP engineering expenditures

|                      | 1959 | 60   | 61   | 62   | 63   | 64    | 65    | 66** | 67** | 68** |
|----------------------|------|------|------|------|------|-------|-------|-------|-------|-------|
| Advanced Development |      | 1.62 | 1.8  | 1.57 | 0.99 | 0.47  | 0.3   | 0.3   | 0.5   | 0.75  |
| Design and Development | 5.29 | 7.82 | 9.29 | 5.87 | 7.57 | 9.95  | 16.76 | 12.75 | 15.11 | 16.31 |
| Net engineering costs | 5.29 | 9.44 | 11.1 | 7.44 | 8.56 | 10.43 | 17.06 | 13.05 | 15.61 | 17.06 |
| % of sale revenues   | 115  | 64.8 | 29.3 | 8.3  | 9.9  | 10.6  | 21.1  | 15.5  | 13.7  | 11.5  |

*Source*: Charles Babbage Institute, University of Minnesota, Collection 13. US vs. IBM, px245, RCA CSD '1966 Five Year Plan'.

There are various estimates of what IBM spent on the 360, Tom Watson Jr wrote that IBM spent $750m on 360 series research and development and a total of $4.5bn when including the cost of new production facilities and launch marketing (Watson 1990: 347). What is sure is that the IBM computer operations were in scale well over an order of magnitude larger than the scale of RCA's Computer Systems Division.

This lack of resources would show through in the end product. The Spectra was less well engineered: Spectras were physically larger, power hungry, needed massive air-conditioning and were less reliable. RCA's field engineers were all too aware of some very poor comparisons between their systems and IBM, especially on the level of availability:

(1) RCA equipment apparently requires larger amounts of dedicated preventive maintenance time than that of our main competitor, IBM. Customers that have both our equipment and IBM equipment are aware of this, and this works to our detriment in the market place.
(2) RCA equipment is apparently more sensitive to environmental fluctuations than that of competition, particularly IBM. This makes our customers somewhat sensitive to the difference [between] our maintenance policy and theirs. I am told, for example, that 360/30's can be left without any maintenance whatsoever for weeks on end. Yet, most of our systems require that we take the system from the customer for periods of time every day.

(Rooney, RCA memo 26/6/69)[78]

On top of this, RCA's decision to stop development of electro-mechanical peripherals led to continuing problems, problems which persisted even after the loss cutting order ended. While Spectra was initially marketed with RACE and bought in disk drives, RCA eventually decided to restart peripheral design. At the end of 1967, 18 months after the first Spectra deliveries, RCA could supply an equivalent to IBM's 2311 disk drive.[79] Before this RCA had lost patience with Bryant and had changed supplier buying disk subsystems from super computer start up CDC, and even purchased some drives from IBM itself.[80] What concerned RCA was that peripherals, especially storage devices, were becoming a very significant part of a machine's rental income.

However, by the time RCA started offering its own 2311 equivalent, IBM had added the 2314 to its range; a system which offered massive storage capacity for large users, the type of users RCA wanted to sell to and who RCA envisaged would use RACE. RACE was clearly a dead-end, so they needed to produce an equivalent to the IBM 2314 quickly, but again its peripheral plans were thrown into confusion. First, Jim Linnel, who had headed the development of the 2311 clone, left the company with his engineers to form his own company, Linnel Electronics. He developed and sold IBM plug compatible peripherals.[81] Second, the whole peripheral operation was moved, which seems to have caused a lot of operational and production problems. This disruption meant that RCA could not supply its own 2314 equipment until 1970, five years after IBM. During 1968–69, RCA accepted that RACE would never be competitive and decided to buy 2314-type equipment from Memorex.[82] When RCA eventually managed to produce these disk drives itself, IBM instantly released the revolutionary 3330 Merlin drive, once again putting RCA at a disadvantage. RCA was always a generation behind in random access storage systems.

Given RCA's small R&D budget, it is not surprising that its software development was also inadequate. While the policy of being 360 compatible limited the amount of software work RCA had to do, RCA still needed to develop operating systems for its kit which could emulate the IBM operating environment – operating systems were one of the biggest challenges of 1960s computing. The standard operating system, TDOS, was adequate to start with but rapidly aged, it needed updating by the end of the decade.[83] A second problem was that the two smallest Spectras, the 70/15 and the 70/25, only offered sub-sets of the instruction set and were not offered with COBOL compilers. COBOL was the main business language so this damaged sales and the small machines were not particularly successful.

The reason TDOS was not updated was because RCA was working on a new time-sharing, virtual memory operating system, the TSOS-VMOS. This was RCA's largest software project. Two machines, the 70/46 and 70/61, were specially developed in the late 1960s to offer large scale interactive computing. However, TSOS-VMOS took much longer to develop than was expected, not only affecting these two machines, but also greatly damaging RCA's next family of machines which was designed to use TSOS-VMOS as their main operating system.

There was one final, and rather surprising, weakness in the Spectra 70 range. Despite the fact that RCA's Memory Products Division was a reasonably large supplier of memories to the computer and capital electronics industries, it consistently failed to provide memory of good enough reliability and functional advantage to the Computer Systems Division. In 1968, this came to a head when the then Information Systems Division informed the corporate management that it had to place an order for $35m worth of memory for a proposed addition to the Spectra series, the 70/49, with a third party supplier. ISD wrote to Bob Sarnoff (Gen. Sarnoff's son, Robert, had taken over the company on his father's retirement), informing him that the division of the two operations was illogical and that they should be merged:

> Development processes must involve more than theoretical analysis and its immediate physical embodiment. A thorough understanding and consideration of mechanical design, reliability, manufacturability, and maintainability of a complete memory system is required. Nothing less can

meet competition today. Economical and functional trade-offs between hardware and software must be optimized.

The present structure within RCA is not conducive to efficient operation or to meet these requirements.

(Bradburn CSD General Manager memo to CEO 18/12/68[84] (note at this stage some managers still referred to CSD, others to ISD))

RCA failed to deal with the problem. After RCA had sold its computer operation, it then sold its memory manufacturing facilities to DEC. What is clear is that, in the eyes of the computer division, the decentralised structure was an unnecessary disjoint between development work in the two operations.

*Spectra 70: sales growth and the Accrued Equity Contract*

Despite the restricted resources available to develop the Spectra, it fared moderately well in the market. By the end of 1965 there were over 100 orders.[85] While not a great number, this was in line with the slow growth RCA wanted for CSD at the time. Most systems were leased so a slow build up to deliveries would reduce capital demands as RCA got through the hump in investment required to exploit its colour TV and other developments.

The most successful machine was the 70/45, the smallest of the full scale machines. With the success of this system, RCA introduced a smaller, but fully functional system, below the 70/45, called the 70/35. Unlike the other small machines it used IC components and had the full instruction set. It was in effect a value engineered 70/45, and became the real base level machine. The 70/35 was also offered with an emulator for the old IBM 1401 machine, then the largest user base in the world[86] giving RCA an intercept strategy for both the IBM 360 and the Honeywell 200 which was directly aimed at the large 1401 user base.

IBM was very aware of the Spectra range and strategy and believed that RCA's systems had a number of advantages:

- Higher internal speed in comparison with comparable IBM System/360 models.
- One-third higher speed magnetic tape drives at equivalent rentals compared to IBM.
- High speed printing is provided at $300 to $600 below our prices.
- Availability of magnetic tapes on the Model 15 gives them a magnetic tape system in a price range where we have no current entry.

(Fizzel, 11/12/64 IBM memo to CEO)[87]

Nevertheless, IBM was not worried, noting that RCA's marketing was very conservative. Though IBM did not know it, this was because of the order to reduce losses to pay for colour television development. However, conditions at RCA were changing rapidly. IBM noted that, in 1966, two of RCA's major investments were starting to generate returns and that the RCA company was again performing very well:

> RCA is performing very well as a corporation. Its colour television program is highly successful and it has been doing very well in government and defense business. The data processing portion of RCA has not been doing very well for the last two years.
>
> This is significant on the basis that in the early '60s RCA undertook two major programs – colour television and data processing.
>
> (IBM 7/11/66)[88]

IBM staff were not sure how this new profitability would affect the computer operations and clearly did not realise the shoestring on which elements of the Spectra development relied. IBM thought RCA would take one of two courses of action: using the television profits to reinvest in the computer department, or abandoning general purpose computers and concentrating on communications systems. The capital released by the latter course, together with the television profits, could be used for other areas of expansion. RCA choose to split its resources; it backed the computer operation further, while also expanding in other directions as well.

In 1966, the computer division proposed to the corporation that it be allowed to run up large new losses, in an attempt to achieve a higher market share:

> This was fully accepted, by the corporation, and the reason is that they felt we were making good progress and they felt that this was a worthwhile investment in the future of the business.
>
> I think they felt, as they had felt earlier, that it was an industry that had significant growth potential for the RCA Corporation and that at some point in the future had a significant profit potential.
>
> In fact, the profitability of the television business had become quite strong a year or two prior to that.
>
> I think the overall profit position of the corporation made it possible for them to support the Division at the level recommended by Division management, but obviously they would not have done this if they did not feel that the Division had a potential in the future for becoming an important part of the total overall RCA operation.
>
> (McCollister)[89]

From 1966, CSD was given permission to place machines on the market, without the need to balance the books. At the same time the company took on a number of new staff to support its expansion. Of these new staff, the key player seems to have been Chase Morsey, who took over as Vice President for Marketing. In the late 1960s, he bought in a number of IBM marketing staff and made market share the key goal (Sobel 1986: 195), and RCA again tried to establish itself firmly as the number two in the computer industry. McCollister believed this form of market share targeting was a function of Chase Morsey's history in the marketing function at Ford:

> he was very conscious of market share statistics and he was also influential, and this caused the division to give increasing recognition to share of the market.
> I think it was a legacy from his experience in the automobile Industry.
>
> (McCollister)[90]

McCollister did not think that this was a good influence:

> [B]ecause it tended to place the emphasis upon increasing market share and relatively deemphasized control of expenses and achieving profit, and the end result is that the expenses in the RCA Computer Division mounted to the point where they contributed significantly to RCA's withdrawal from the business.
>
> (McCollister)[91]

Given freedom to lose money, RCA was able to increase its market share.

RCA's own estimates of its market share shows a big jump in 1970 as it began to deliver more systems free from previous restrictions (see Table 3.6).

*Table 3.6*  RCA market share, 1968–71

| Year | 1968 | 1969 | 1970 | 1971 plan |
|---|---|---|---|---|
| Domestic market share | 4.10% | 3.70% | 7.50% | 5.80% |

*Source*: Charles Babbage Institute, University of Minnesota, Collection 13. US vs. IBM, dx952, RCA '1971 Business Plan II'.

This was achieved by offering large discounts on newly leased systems. A much favoured tactic was to offer a potential customer a larger machine for the same rental as a smaller one.[92]

However, the most important method of increasing sales was the use of a new lease agreement called the Accrued Equity Contract. Users were offered machines on a six year lease basis. At the end of six years, the user owned the machine and no more payments were required.[93] However, so that the user could still benefit from the advantages of leasing, they had the option of swapping to a lease contract at any time in the six years and upgrade to a new machine.

This proved a disaster for RCA. RCA was in the habit of depreciating its leased computers over six years, which was reflected in the Accrued Equity Contract. However, IBM, with its much lower cost base, could afford to depreciate over four years and could write-off leased machines quicker, meaning that they could afford to replace a generation of leased machines must faster.[94]

The effect of this was two-fold. First RCA's drive to expand Spectra's market base happened a long time into the third generation of computing, with a surge in deliveries in 1970/71. By this time a significant percentage of IBM 360s had been fully depreciated and IBM, much to the surprise of the rest of the industry, was preparing to introduce the next range, the 370. Second, the division's accountants had counted the accrued contracts as firm sales which made its balance sheet much stronger. However, when the IBM 370 was released, and RCA was forced to react by introducing the RCA-Series of computers, users swapped accrued equity contracts for leases so as to get the new, more powerful systems. Financial disaster ensued, as is described below.

However, before considering the accounting practices which would lead to RCA exiting the computer sector, it is worth considering how else RCA used the profits it began to see flow in from its success with colour television and other programmes. The firm undertook a wide range of acquisition aimed at broadening the income base of RCA and creating a truly diversified feel to the company, not just a concentrically diversified operational structure.

In the late 1960s it was not just the CSD management that changed, so did the corporate leadership. Bob Sarnoff gradually took over from his father as head of RCA, eventually becoming Chairman, President, and CEO. IBM lawyers in the US vs. IBM anti-trust case made great play of RCA's change of emphasis at this time. The early 1960s Annual Reports talked of RCA's full commitment to 'computers, control and communications' the '3 Cs'. This changed to a policy of diversification; RCA started to spread its risk. Table 3.7 shows its major acquisitions.

*Table 3.7*   RCA acquisitions, 1966–71

| Date | Company | Method of payment | Value |
|------|---------|-------------------|-------|
| 05/19/66 | Random House (publishing) | Common stock | $40.1m |
| 05/11/67 | Hertz Corp. (car rental) | Preferred and common Stock | $248.4m |
| 03/31/70 | Banquet Foods | Common stock | $116.5m |
| 10/14/70 | Cushman & Wakefield Inc. | Common Stock | $30.0m |
| 02/24/71 | Coronet Inds. | Common Stock | $183.9m |
|  |  |  | $618.9m |

*Source*: Charles Babbage Institute, University of Minnesota, Collection 13. US vs. IBM, dx965 and 966, IBM attorneys compiled this list from RCA annual reports.

IBM made the point that RCA's commitment to its electronics activities was becoming less at this time, and this was one of the reasons it abandoned computers in the early 1970s.

In reality, some of these diversifications, which were aimed at reducing risk, would in reality increase the variability of RCA returns on capital, not reduce the fluctuations. The diversification which did the most damage was the purchase of Hertz. In the early 1970s recession, it proved impossible for Hertz to sell its ex-lease gas guzzling cars; a disaster for its finances. This directly affected the computer operation.

The overall failure of the diversification programme had a quick impact on the management of the firm. In 1971, Anthony L. Conrad took over the presidency and CEO roles at RCA, reflecting the failure of Bob Sarnoff's dual policy of diversification and computer expansion. Sarnoff would remain chairman until being forced out in 1975, rapidly followed by Conrad (Conrad being forced out following a scandal about not paying income tax, Chandler 2005: 42–5). Chandler described this as the curse of diversification, however, as has been seen, the non-conglomerate version of RCA in previous years had its own weaknesses and the failure of the RCA Computer Systems Division was as much to do with strategic and governance issues as it was to do with competition for resources from non-core businesses.

## Exit from the computer sector

### The RCA Series

RCA knew that IBM's next series was going to be announced in 1970 and installed in 1971. RCA's long term project for new systems had started in 1966. RCA had long before set out a general strategy for replacing the Spectra, even if it supplied little resource to develop such a system:

> Compatibility with Spectra 70 and, where possible, with IBM is a ground rule. This policy will permit maximum growth in a replacement market and retention of our own customers.
>
> (RCA CSD 1966)[95]

Beard had developed a concept for a replacement system called system 'X', which was meant to fulfil the above criteria, however, this was cancelled in 1969.[96] This was because it was expected to take too long to get to the market, and had a number of architectural problems. The next system plan became known as the New Technology Series; it faced the same problem, it would take too long to get to market.

RCA commissioned F. Withington, of the consultants A.D. Little, to consider their forthcoming need for a new systems. He informed RCA's staff that, in his opinion, the advanced concepts of the NTS could not be brought to the market until 1973, while RCA needed something to take to customers in 1970–71. This forced the firm to put the NTS on the back burner as a long term project for a future concept of computing. Within RCA there was division about what the next system should achieve:

> I think that in looking at the next family or generation of equipment beyond Spectra, there was a lengthy debate between people responsible for programming systems, that is, the so called software organisation, and the people responsible for hardware or equipment specifications, and perhaps the engineering organisation as well, as to exactly what the nature of this product should be.
>
> (McCollister)[97]

A. D. Little told the company that it needed a new system earlier than 1973 to maintain its broad line strategy, which A.D. Little considered the only way of achieving the company's goal of being the industry's number two:

> When I first got to RCA Arthur D. Little had been hired to review the marketing strategies of the RCA Corporation and product strategy. At a meeting I attended they presented the concept that you had to have a broad product line because you could not possibly sell enough share of any particular product category to achieve this goal [of being number 2 to IBM] and that strategy was accepted as being valid.
>
> (Rooney)[98]

To cover its short-term need to compete with IBM's new 370 series, RCA resorted to relaunching what was essentially the same product:

> The RCA Series was an attempt to bring out what was seemingly a new product line for whatever psychological influence it might have on the marketplace.
>   But it was a restyled product line. There was a new set of covers, the frames were the same, and it was essentially a cosmetic treatment of the existing Spectra 70 Series with new model numbers and new pricing.
>
> (McCollister)[99]

> They were not precisely the same processors. Architecturally they were the same.
>
> (Rooney)[100]

The main difference was that new manufacturing techniques and components would be used which would make the hardware cheaper to produce, and the memory was speeded up.[101]

Half of the new RCA Series was to use the old TDOS operating system, these were the RCA 2 and 6. The other half, the RCA 3 and 7, were to be offered with the time-sharing VMOS 4 operating system. It was on VMOS that RCA focused its main marketing effort. However, the development of VMOS remained a significant problem. In late 1970, it was 6–9 months behind schedule.[102] It was estimated that this would lead to a loss of 17-20 RCA3 orders and 20-22 RCA7 orders. This represented $2.14m of monthly rental income, and was described as being close to a disaster.[103]

### The RCA Series and the market environment

The RCA Series was launched at a difficult time for the computer industry. The divisional Vice President for Marketing, Rooney, noted that

> The economic situation for the computer business in 1970 was quite bad. As I recall, the shipments that year were down some 20% from the previous year. In 1971 that situation persisted, at least as long as we were in business.
>
> (Rooney)[104]

This was a difficult environment for the new RCA Series.

A second problem was the competitive stance IBM was taking. The IBM 370/155 and 165 were announced in June 1970 and the smaller 135 and 145 in September 1970.[105] However, importantly, the 135 and 145 were to offer virtual memory and time-sharing operating systems. The original system, the 155 and 165, were then quickly replaced by the 158 and 168 which offered the same functions. They used integrated components and semiconductor memory, rather than magnetic core memory. The combination was faster, more powerful, while being comparatively lower cost machines (though IBM well knew that adding the peripherals needed to make use of time sharing would greatly increase revenues). Within the IBM range, the system that most concerned RCA was the 370/145, which fell right into RCA's most successful class of machine.

Because of the staging of IBM's announcements, the smaller 370s were announced after the RCA Series. This was to cause RCA to believe that it was a direct swipe at their plans:

> Well, the 370/45 was announced within days after we had announced the RCA 6 ... it was our opinion that IBM had priced the 145 out of its normal relationship to [the] other ... systems that they had announced. We felt that there was a good probability that an alteration had been made in pricing the system as a direct response to the announcement of the RCA 6.

In addition to that, we felt that their delivery pattern, as it would relate to the larger memories in the 145, was not consistent with the other patterns of deliveries on the other newly announced machines, and we felt that it was, in effect, a retaliation [against] the announcement of the RCA 6.

(Wright – joined RCA from IBM as head of government marketing)[106]

RCA made some representations to IBM that the 145 was 'priced selectively' to attack RCA.[107] RCA believed that the 145 was announced specifically to hit RCA, as it had a delivery time of 18 months rather than IBM's usual 12 months. RCA argued that it was announced ahead of schedule in order to hit RCA 6 sales. It was also argued that the pricing of the semiconductor memory was artificially low. IBM responded that the delay in delivery was due to the time it took to build up yields of memory chips, and that the price was set to reflect the cost that was expected to be achieved as IBM advanced down the learning curve of producing these devices. These are standard practices in the semiconductor industry where initial yields of useable components are low, but the pricing is set to reflect the likely outcome of yields in the future: RCA did not pursue these complaints.

The real problem was that the 145 was being offered with time-sharing, which required large amounts of fast memory which RCA could not match at the price. However, RCA believed that its representations to IBM kept it conscious of the fact that it was under anti-trust scrutiny.

A second problem IBM created for RCA concerned peripherals. Not only did IBM introduce the new 370 computers, but also at more or less the same time it introduced the very advanced 3330 Merlin disk drive, and the ASPEN tape drive:

Their announcement of the 3330 disk with the 370 family we felt was very significant, very profound, and would have a great impact on RCA if we were to compete against IBM in this market place.

(Rooney)[108]

At this time RCA had only just managed to produce the 2314 drive that IBM had introduced in the mid-1960s. RCA wrote to IBM asking for details of the new systems just after they were announced.[109] However, the material IBM sent RCA did not contain enough information to enable it to start copying the systems.[110]

In August 1971, RCA eventually received a reference manual on the Merlin, the same month it was delivered. Memorex and ISS, the two leading plug compatible manufactures, had managed to get this information much earlier, but RCA wanted to develop this vital equipment itself.

## Strategy failure: the RCA Series and the Spectra 70 demise

In reality, the RCA Series was a marketing ploy, an attempt to re-launch the old range with some evolutionary improvements. In support of this, RCA came up with a strategy to 'intercept' the IBM range:

> There was a very elaborate strategy at the time as to where these units of the RCA series would fall against the IBM [range], either as it was announced or was expected to be announced ...in this elaborate strategy the RCA series would fall at certain point[s] within the IBM product line spectrum and that IBM would be unwilling to disturb the equilibrium of that product spectrum and, therefore, negate the rationale of the RCA product concept.
>
> (McCollister)[111]

The RCA Series machines were planned to be positioned at the mid-point between IBM machines in terms of scale. The hope was that as a user decided that they wanted to trade up to a larger machine, they would be attracted to the RCA system rather than the IBM, which would often be too big a jump. This plan fell to pieces as it was realised that the part of the range that was to use VMOS would be late. A second problem was that the potentially largest selling of RCA's normal machines, the RCA 6, was pitched directly against the IBM 370/145, which was not only keenly priced, but was also planned to offer full time-sharing facilities.

While the RCA failed to intercept the 370, it did manage to affect the old Spectra range. McCollister described the RCA Series as 'blowing the Spectra out of the water'.[112] In the late 1960s, up to and including 1970, the Spectra had gone through a veritable boom despite the computer recession:

> This investment has already resulted in a more rapid growth rate for RCA than for the domestic industry as a whole. In 1970, the value of RCA's net domestic shipments rose by more than 50 per cent while that of the industry fell by more than 20 per cent.
>
> (RCA 1970 Annual Report)[113]

However, the RCA Series offered much improved price/performance ratios, so users of the Spectra exercised the options they had in their leases and Accrued Equity Contracts to exchange their old Spectra 70s for the equivalent new machines.

In the first seven months of 1971, 78 Spectra 70 computers had been returned, and another 137 were already booked in for return, all to be replaced by RCA Series machines,[114] but with no extra revenues accruing from these replacements. The following table (Table 3.8) breaks down the causes of these returns, and upgrading to new systems accounts for the great majority:

*Table 3.8*    Reasons for returning RCA computers

| | System | Losses to competition | Losses other than competition | Upgraded |
|---|---|---|---|---|
| Second generation | 301 | 2 | 7 | 9 |
| | 501 | | 1 | |
| | 3301 | 5 | 1 | |
| Third generation | 70/15 | 2 | 1 | |
| | 70/25 | | 1 | |
| | 70/35 | 10 | 5 | 30 |
| | 70/45 | 20 | 8 | 81 |
| | 70/46 | 1 | 2 | 18 |
| | 70/55 | | | 5 |
| | 70/60 | | | 4 |
| | RCA 2 | | 2 | |
| | | 40 | 26 | 149 |

*Source:* Charles Babbage Institute, University of Minnesota, Collection 13. US vs. IBM, dx872. RCA 4/8/71 'Returns Presentation'.

IBM's earlier than expected upgrade to the 370 was clearly having a major impact on RCA because of the strategy of offering RCA Series replacements to keep pace with IBM in the race for new sales, but of course the impact was being felt where it hurt most – the currently installed leases. RCA would not be the only ones to suffer damage. Industry estimates of the residual value of computers on lease were somewhat optimistic. The Auerbach Corporation had estimated the expected value of IBM 360/30s and /40s leased by General Acceptance Corporation.[115] GAC was in a strong position compared to RCA – at least they were leasing 'real' IBM 360s to clients. However, their estimates that an IBM 360/30 leased in June 1965 would still have a residual value of 52 per cent of its original value in June 1971[116] would seem somewhat optimistic given the early arrival of the IBM 370 (though if GAC could keep the systems which were compatible with the new series out on lease the problem of falling values hardly arose). Auerbach estimated that if IBM released an 'integrated circuit' version of the 360 residual values would fall by only 5 per cent.[117] The impact on RCA was substantially greater than this as Spectra 70s flooded back with no place to go!

Another problem was that the economic downturn and the consequential "computer recession" affected which machines upgraders would choose. In the past, in price terms, users traded for equivalent or better systems. For example, when companies traded in their second generation systems for third they would at least spend the same amount of money, which would normally give them a more advanced and powerful machine. Such a change gave the user greater power for the same money, but as any change was a big decision operationally, many would take the chance to build in more head room and get a larger system. This time it was different. Spectra 70/45s were traded up to 'low yield' RCA's. This was effectively the same computer power for fewer dollars.[118]

RCA's investment in computers via leases and the Accrued Equity Contracts was being wasted. Machines were being returned much earlier than the depreciation policy had allowed. This forced the Information Systems Division (as the unit was now called, though it was almost always still referred to as CDS) to update its December 1970 plan, and in April 1971 the 'Business Plan II' was launched which cut the profit expectations for the Information Systems Division.[119] Revenue for 1971 was expected to fall from $323m to $261m, even though it the unit was producing ever greater numbers of computers. This was because, while gross shipments were increasing, net shipments were falling (see Table 3.9)

*Table 3.9*  Effect of returned computers on RCA's net computer shipments

| ($m) | Business Plan II | Business Plan I |
|---|---|---|
| Gross Shipments | | |
| RCA | 171 | 118 |
| Spectra | 170 | 202 |
| Total Gross | **341** | **320** |
| Minus value of returned | | |
| Spectra computers | 155 | 90 |
| Net Shipments | | |
| RCA | 171 | 118 |
| Spectra | 15 | 112 |
| Total Net | **186** | **230** |

*Source*: Charles Babbage Institute, University of Minnesota, Collection 13. US vs. IBM, dx952 RCA 1971, 'Business Plan II'.

The outcome was an expected loss of $37m in 1970: worse still was a large increase in the 'cash run-off' (see Table 3.10). This was the cash outflow to pay for the new RCA machines being built and put out on lease.

*Table 3.10*  RCA ISD negative cash flow

| $m | 1968 | 1969 | 1970 | 1971 BPII |
|---|---|---|---|---|
| Cash Run-off | −75 | −45 | −89 | −126 |

*Source*: Charles Babbage Institute, University of Minnesota, Collection 13. US vs. IBM, dx952, RCA 1971, 'Business Plan II' – RCA Investment Summary 1968–1971'.

### RCA's reassessment of its costs and financial position

The real situation was even worse than the new business plan showed. Chase Morsey started to take a dim view of the situation in the computer division, and its effects on the rest of the company. He became concerned that even the new plan, predicting a loss of $37m for 1970, was way off target, as the division's accounting procedures were so irregular.[120] Concerns were being raised about how revenues had been booked against leases and the Accrued Equity Contracts, especially the latter where their treatment was most unusual. The division had been counting 70 per cent of the expected revenue from an Accrued Equity plan in year one. It was treating these contracts as certain sales, and writing 70 per cent of their value into the books immediately.[121] It became evident that to be able to upgrade to the new RCA Series, Accrued Equity customers were exercising the right to convert these contracts into leases and were then free to return old Spectra machines to RCA for an upgrade. Accrued Equity Contracts were far from certain sales.

These criticisms of these accounting practices and the way sales were easily converted back into leases were later reinforced by a report in the policies used by the Accounting Principles Board.[122]

The problems at the computer division came at an inauspicious moment. The general economic downturn and specific problems with achieving value from gas-guzzling cars meant that both the Hertz and NBC divisions of RCA were suffering from a downturn in consumer demand. Figure 3.2 showed that RCA's profits collapsed in 1970 and returns were half of what had been occurring only three years earlier. Morsey informed Conrad and Sarnoff of the increased trading loss at the computer division, and the large increase in the division's net assets,[123] net assets with little earning power compared to prior expectations. The company saw a rapid move into negative cash flows of $315m, of which computers accounted for $140m.

For the coming decade, Morsey believed that the company's cash requirement had risen from $700m to $1bn; in the first half of the decade he expected that it would be the computer operation which would be the main drain on cash.

> As a result of these changes, it is clearly necessary to reassess RCA's cash requirements and new funding capability over the next six years.
>
> (Morsey 1971)[124]

Morsey then went on to make a telling point by comparing RCA's financial status with that of other electrical/electronic and computer companies. First, he showed that RCA's ratio of earnings to fixed charges was lower than the average for the electrical and computer industries, and was falling the quickest (see Table 3.11).

*Table 3.11*   RCA ratio of earnings to fixed charges compared to key rivals

|  | 67 | 68 | 69 | 70 | total change in cover % |
|---|---|---|---|---|---|
| RCA | 10.3 | 9.1 | 7.8 | 3.5 | −66 |
| GE | 11.9 | 10.5 | 7.5 | 6.4 | −46 |
| ITT | 3.4 | 4.5 | 4.6 | 4.5 | +31 |
| Westinghouse | 15.9 | 11.8 | 10.6 | 5.5 | −64 |
| **Average** | **10.4** | **8.9** | **7.6** | **5.5** | **−47** |
| Burroughs | 7.2 | 6.8 | 5.5 | 3.9 | −46 |
| Honeywell | 6.2 | 6.9 | 6 | 3.2 | −48 |
| IBM | 35.7 | 46.7 | 57.8 | 41.6 | +17 |
| NCR | 4.7 | 4.2 | 4.1 | 2.5 | −48 |
| Sperry Rand | 9.9 | 10.6 | 6.3 | 4.7 | −52 |
| **Average** | **12.7** | **15** | **15.9** | **11.1** | **−12** |

*Source*: Charles Babbage Institute, University of Minnesota, Collection 13. <u>US vs. IBM</u>, px201. RCA internal report, Chase Morsey to Sarnoff and Conrad 27/8/71.

Morsey believed that this was the ratio on which investment bankers made their decisions. RCA's low and falling status severely limited the amount of new borrowing RCA could raise.

As it was, RCA already had a very poor debt/equity position compared to a number of the other companies listed. Morsey was very concerned about the high gearing of the firm (see Table 3.12).

*Table 3.12*   RCA and rivals' gearing ratios

|  | '67 | '68 | '69 | '70 |
|---|---|---|---|---|
| RCA | 0.79 | 0.79 | 0.77 | 0.88 |
| GE | 0.32 | 0.3 | 0.27 | 0.22 |
| ITT | 0.69 | 0.56 | 0.55 | 0.52 |
| Westinghouse | 0.36 | 0.32 | 0.28 | 0.44 |
| <u>Average</u> | <u>0.46</u> | <u>0.39</u> | <u>0.37</u> | <u>0.39</u> |
| Burroughs | 0.48 | 0.74 | 0.57 | 0.6 |
| Honeywell | 0.59 | 0.61 | 0.56 | 0.87 |
| IBM | 0.14 | 0.12 | 0.11 | 0.1 |
| NCR | 0.69 | 0.42 | 0.61 | 0.82 |
| <u>Average</u> | <u>0.44</u> | <u>0.44</u> | <u>0.44</u> | <u>0.51</u> |

*Source*: Charles Babbage Institute, University of Minnesota, Collection 13 <u>US vs. IBM</u>, px201. RCA internal report, Chase Morsey to Sarnoff and Conrad 27/8/71.

Morsey guessed that the ratio would have to rise to between 1.25–1.80 by 1976, believing that RCA would not be able to raise finance after it passed a ratio of 1.23. Even plans to sell the radio network and stop development of the highly expensive Video Disc system would not reduce cash demands enough to prevent new funding being required.

When the revised 1971 computer business plan arrived on Sarnoff's desk it was accompanied by a note from the Finance Department's H.L.Letts.[125] He concluded that

> Unless the substantial cash requirements of Computer Systems can be improved it may prevent us from making investments in other areas of RCA with better and more immediate returns on capital.
>
> (Letts 1971)[126]

His main concern was that costs at CSD[127] had got out of hand. The Head of Government Marketing, V.O. Wright, who had joined RCA from IBM, believed that this had been a major problem and that fundamentally RCA could not be price competitive with IBM. What he saw made him believe that the numbers were wrong and the reality was that expenses were much greater per system shipped.

> It stemmed from several sources. One was the fact that the manufacturing process in RCA was not as fully automated as I had seen it automated in IBM manufacturing. RCA was not devoting sufficient attention to engineering a product to the matter of cost. They tended to engineer the product to get it built, but ignore what it might cost to build it after it was engineered.
>
> There was no value engineering work going on after the product was developed to reduce cost within the manufacturing organisation ... The cost, as I recall it, when I first got involved ... early in 1971 ... was running at ... about 42% of revenue. That is, the cost of the product was about 42% of revenue ...
>
> I was aware of IBM's manufacturing cost, as I had remembered from my days with IBM, would have run something on the order of 14 to 15% of revenue.
>
> (Wright)[128]

Wright went on to estimate that Sperry Rand's manufacturing cost was 24% of revenue and at Burroughs it was 21%. Morsey's arguments won the day. In July 1971, Conrad recorded a videotaped message for the workers of the computer operation to scotch rumours that RCA was about to sell out.[129]

However, in August 1971 such a plan was under consideration. On the 16th of September, the senior management came to the decision that the commercial computer division had to be sold off to protect developments in the rest of the company.[130] On the 17th of September, Conrad invited Morsey to present the proposal to the Board:

> As a result of the factors outlined in the forgoing analysis of CSD and its impact on RCA, the conclusion has been reached that the additional investment required in CSD no longer appears to be a prudent financial risk. The major reasons for this conclusion are as follows:
>
> The further delay in the achievement of sustained profitability at CSD to the middle or late 1970s, as opposed to the early 1970s, could jeopardize the ability of the Corporation to finance its capital requirements.
>
> The many healthy and vital parts of the rest of RCA could be hindered in the event of a down turn in the economy in the mid-1970s because of the high level of outside financing required to support the growth of CSD (as well as the other parts of RCA) .....
>
> It should be recognized that RCA does have strengths in certain special and more narrowly defined computer-related businesses and these opportunities can be pursued on a prudent basis without risking large amounts of capital.
>
> Beyond these factors, the dominant presence of IBM in the computer industry contributes to the difficulty of achieving a viable computer business for RCA. The manpower and financial resources of IBM, including the size and strength of the marketing, research and development organisations, are such that achieving market share growth as well as acceptable profitability, is extremely [unlikely].
>
> (Morsey proposal 1971)[131]

After negotiations with a number of companies, Sperry Rand (which was still associated with the brand name UNIVAC following aquisitions of early computer companies) bought RCA's commercial computer operation for $137m. In September of 1971, RCA set up a reserve of $490m to cover the losses it had sustained on the operations of the computer division.[132]

Later the company was able to reduce this reserve by $78m as the disposal was less financially damaging than had been expected because Sperry managed to get a better than expected return from the RCA operation. Initially, Sperry paid RCA $70.5m with the rest paid over five years according to the revenue generated by the RCA systems in the field. Under the sales arrangement, a part of the price was linked to the Computer Systems Division's performance under Sperry management in their first few years of control.

RCA estimated in 1971 that total payments would be from $100.5m to $130.5m. As Sperry did relatively well at keeping the RCA installed base the payments were at the top of the range. In August 1972, Sperry commissioned a report from the Auerbach corporation regarding what was now called the

Series 70 range, the names used by Sperry's Univac division for the RCA systems. It concluded that it was a major opportunity for Sperry to permanently increase its user base. What customers had left since the end of RCA ownership tended to be for reasons prior to the sell off. The real problems lay with providing confidence to customers that the series would be supported and had a growth path, and that it was a very price sensitive segment of the market because customers could fairly easily switch to IBM.[133]

The RCA computers fitted in well with Sperry's range, a range which included some partially IBM compatible machines. The RCA systems improved this ability and Sperry maintained a reasonably large business in pseudo-IBM compatible systems.

There were a number of reactions to RCA's abandonment of computers. Datamation led with a headline 'In Breach of Ten Thousand Promises'.[134] A number of 'autopsy' articles ensued.[135] In general, RCA was seen as letting down its customers. On the other hand, financial, rather than industry, journals saw the RCA move as very acceptable:

> RCA's recent announcement to leave the computer mainframe business, even though it has resulted in a $250m [after tax write downs]non-recurring write-off, eliminates an area of continuing earnings loss, one which has demanded a great amount of management time and attention, and also returns the company to being predominantly a consumer goods company.
>
> (*Wall Street Journal* 8/11/71)[136]

The same article went on to predict an upswing in consumer demand, and that with a 14.4 price:earnings ratio the company was well under the price of similar organisations. The recommendation was to buy; RCA's main concern was the financial market's view not the computer market's view of it.

## Conclusions

An enormous number of lessons can be drawn from the case study. Some key areas of importance to strategic decision making include:

- While concentric concentration can help enter an industry, it can also later create conflicts between business units requiring ever greater resources as those business grow in step with each other;
- When estimating the pathway which the "black box" competitor is on (the competitor that determines the nature of the competitive market place) expectations of this competitor's strategy should not be assumed to be a strategy convenient for supporting in-house business plans – that competitor is trying to win the market, plans need to be made assuming that the black box competitor will be as aggressive as it possibly can;

- There is equal danger in investing too much at the wrong point in a product's life cycle as there is in investing too little at other points;
- Conglomerate investments should not be random, but should be actively designed purchases aimed at creating true counter cyclicality;
- That investing in the core technology of a product, in this case digital technologies in the central processors of mainframes, needs to be matched by investment in the other technologies which make a product useful to customers – in this case peripherals and software;
- Accounting practices matter!

This case study is the clearest case of a firm using its capability to try to enter a new market as a concentric diversification. RCA's incredible technical strengths allowed it to exploit a central core of digital engineers, the Advanced Development Group, across a number of different product groups where digital technologies could be exploited. It attempted to continue shared capability thereafter, such as in its efforts to co-produce the 601 and CPD computers but, like other firms, found that there were great dissimilarities between military and commercial production and markets.

Nevertheless, the very structured approach RCA had to the market following the introduction of the 501, then the 301/3301 and the Spectra, did not show the kind of infighting within the computer division which can be seen in the later UK case studies. Leading computer industry consultant Irwin Auerbach vistied RCA in April 1960.[137] He and his company expressed concern about the structure of the organisation. They portrayed IBM as an integrated monolith able to make strategic plans and execute them. While Auerbach noted that the unity of IBM may not have been as great as RCA portrayed, he made some damning notes on the feedback he got from the RCA management:

> There appears to be too much fuzziness and lack of single-purposeless within RCA, whereby the political activity of managers and on down into the engineering ranks tends to be the order of the day rather than the accomplishment of technical programs or economic or profit goals.
>
> (Auerbach 1960)[138]

Competition for resources was clearly an issue even for the mighty RCA. Its return on equity was quite frankly astonishing compared to its UK equivalents, however, multiple high-technology, concentrically diversified operations were a problem and the RCA computer drive had to take second place to other concerns.

In the mid-1960s, colour television and defence work had received a higher priority when investment funds were squeezed by the number of hi-tech opportunities the firm was pursuing. This seems to have been where the real damage to the computer operation was done. If RCA had attempted its big market push at an earlier stage, it would have been in a position where a much larger proportion of Spectra 70 machines would have been fully depreciated and would thus have earned a bottom line profit when the IBM 370 was launched.

One of the computer division's great weaknesses was that it was forced to work out of sequence with the market, but it wasn't just the lack of funds at crucial stages, it was also the injection of funds at the wrong time which would cause its crisis. Being able to grow substantially in the late 1960s, meant that it was selling the wrong computers at the wrong time. It exacerbated the whole sequence by its reclothing of the Spectra as the RCA Series. However, this was unavoidable. RCA was in a catch-22 position: it had to introduce a new range to prevent IBM's new series replacing a substantial number of the IBM-compatible Spectras. Compatibility was not an advantage at this time. At this stage it was concern about IBM poaching RCA customers which drove RCA to launch its new range, despite the fact that it destroyed its old installed base.

Above all, RCA's computer division had to cope with a higher cost base than IBM. When the emphasis changed from cutting losses to buying market share, it seems that controlling costs took second place. This was a fatal error given its direct competition with the low cost, high output IBM. Even the company's role as a broad-based electronic firm was of ambiguous advantage. Certainly, the Advanced Development Group greatly aided market entry. The division was also helped by RCA's expertise in integrated circuits, allowing it to lead the market with this kind of technology.

However, the decentralised organisation led to problems. The divorce of the CDP and the 601 helped to scupper the flagship of the RCA range. Equally, the Computer Systems Division received little help from the Memory Systems Division, indeed it proved something of a handicap. However, the real battle was not between the technical capabilities of divisions it was to secure precious capital within an organisation that was, until the end, superb at finding uses for that capital.

RCA was not forced out of the market by specific anti-competitive actions by IBM. Indeed, at the beginning of the story, RCA was much larger than IBM and could wield a lot of market power. However, IBM's day to day strategies, its low cost base, high absolute level of R&D focused on one business, and its established position in the business machines market, all overwhelmed RCA's half-hearted efforts which were subject to the needs of the rest of the company. RCA missed its opportunity to succeed in the computer market when it decided to support colour television development to the hilt, though this certainly proved a profitable option. When it did decide to back its computer diversification, again the timing was out of step with the product cycle; increasing deliveries of the Spectra 70 at the end of the product cycle and the drive for market share at this stage was an expensive mistake.

By the end of the period studied, RCA preferred to support diversifications away from the risky, though potentially profitable, electronic engineering sector. The purchase of car rental firms and food companies was an attempt to stabilise its income, and was, fundamentally a defensive diversification. It had used more of its enormous profits from colour television for this purpose than for developing its computer division. The fact that these truly conglomerate-style purchases would, in fact, exacerbate RCA's financial cycle increased the pressure on it to rein back on its computer operations where its lack of understanding of the market cycle had caused such large losses.

# 4
# General Electric

Competition for funds and the availability of capital within the corporation played an important role throughout the life of RCA's Computer Systems Division. General Electric's (GE) history in the industry is similar, though it is a more complex story. GE suffered from numerous poor management decisions which exacerbated its problems, and stopped it from taking advantage of the strengths that the firm undoubtedly had. It was forced out of the industry in similar circumstances to RCA, having to cope with the same kind of internal pressures on its finances. However, it also displayed some of the intra-computer division schisms which firms in the UK, especially Ferranti and EMI, displayed.

## The post-war General Electric

Like English Electric and Ferranti, GE was born in the heavy electrical industry (Chandler 1990: 212–21). It produced everything electrical and became one of the largest corporations in the world, and easily the largest in the electrical industry. During the war, the company expanded very rapidly and in many new directions. In 1939, sales were $300m; during the war they broke the $1bn mark. By 1955, it was the fourth largest company in the US and had the third largest work force (Harris 1955: 110 – based on an interview with GE's CEO, Ralph J. Cordiner). By 1960, it had sales of $4.4bn and 250,000 employees.[1]

Until the Second World War, GE, as with so many successful companies, was run by a tight central autocracy. The leading figures were the Chief Executive Officers: Charles A. Coffin; Edwin Rice; and Gerard Swope (Harris 1955).

These people made GE highly successful: GE was in the fastest growing industry in the world and was twice the size of its nearest rival, Westinghouse.

Controlling such expansion and the wide range of new products generated by their war time work was a challenge. New CEO, R. J. Cordiner, was concerned that the autocratic centralised model needed changing as centralised decision making was a handicap for the rapidly diversifying company:

> The basic problem, he [Cordiner] had discovered was not GE's gigantic size but its fantastic diversity. He had to figure out how to make decision making flexible at the operational level where minutes count.
>
> (Harris 1955)

Under Cordiner, GE started a process of decentralisation. The aim was to break the company into operating departments which would have day-to-day management responsibility. The centre was to be reduced to corporate planning and coordinating inter-divisional activities; all central functional control was to end. During 1948–49, these plans were tested out in a number of affiliated firms, such as the white goods company, Hotpoint (Harris 1955). During the early 1950s, Cordiner extended decentralisation to the rest of the company. The reorganisation caused a great deal of disruption and for a while led to a downturn in profit ratios. However, Cordiner hoped that in the long term these changes would lead to better control over the company. The results of this case study cast doubt on whether this was achieved.

The changes implemented would become the stuff of business school case studies and created a model for other firms creating new methods of managing via decentralised target setting and establishing internal management consultancy groups to manage change and monitor performance. It would be the model for both true conglomerates and for the multi-divisional, concentrically diversified firms covered in this study. Just about every electrical and electronics company would establish something akin to this system of hands-off control within a target-setting culture. The UK case studies suggest such an approach was not always successful.

The company's basic operating unit became the department. By 1955, there were 100 independent operating departments, organised into 22 Divisions, which in turn made up the four Operating Groups. The breakdown of GE's activities was (see Table 4.1).

*Table 4.1*　GE group sales

| | |
|---|---|
| Apparatus (mostly electrical capital goods) | 30% |
| Industrial Products and Lamps (capital goods and consumer non-durables) | 28% |
| Appliances and Electronics (durables and capital goods) | 27% |
| Atomic Energy and Defence Products | 15% |

*Source*: Charles Babbage Institute, University of Minnesota, Auerbach Collection 4/10. Auerbach Corporation for RCA 6/1960 'A Corporate Business Strategy for Information Processing', Chapter IV.

This structure was quickly changed with the formation of an Electronic and Flight Systems Group. This new group contained the Defence Electronics

Division,[2] which in turn controlled the Heavy and Light Military Electronics Departments, both of which had interests in computer technology. However, when the Computer Department was formed it was a part of the Industrial Electronics Division of the Industrial Group.

The company tried to develop organisational structures intended to ensure that the operating units worked in the same direction, and that there was an adequate flow of information within the company. The earlier experiments with the decentralised structure showed that there was one major problem; the interests of the decentralised affiliates were not always the same as GE's overall corporate interests. Cordiner wanted to allow a degree of decentralised operational responsibility yet also to have central control over long-term planning. To do this, GE set up the Office of the President, supported by the Services Division (Harris 1955). There were 4,000 staff in the Services Division. Of these, 3,300 were in the central research laboratories, but many of the rest were involved in the Management Consultation Service. This operation was involved in managerial research, advising departments on management matters, and coordinating inter-department activities. The Management Consultation Service supplemented the ten functional Vice Presidents who were there to ensure that new methods of management were disseminated to the operational departments and that monitoring standards were maintained. The ultimate control was the President's Office. This consisted of Cordiner and six other Vice Presidents. The main role of the President's Office was to continually 'needle' operational units, not just with regard to immediate profitability, but also to ensure that planning was adequately carried out and that departmental plans fitted into the overall corporate scheme.

## GE in the computer market

### Part 1: The experimental phase

Like RCA, GE entered the computer industry on the back of a single large contract. It also joined at the same time as RCA, EMI, Philco, and a number of other electronics firms, which, following the Korean War, extended their range of electronics activities into computers. At this stage it was becoming obvious that the computer was going to be the basis of a big industry and offered an opportunity for electronics firms to utilise their know-how. These firms all made their bids to enter the industry at the cusp of the transition from valve-based computers to solid state systems.

The general manager of the Electronics Division's Commercial and Government Equipment Department, George Metcalf, wrote a report in 1954 on the computer industry; he believed it was a market on the brink of a boom (Snively 1988: 74–8. George Snively joined G.E. in 1952, as the supervisor of Accounting at G.E. Electronics Laboratories and later worked in GE's Computer Division). GE's early computer work was somewhat undirected, being undertaken at the time that the firm was reorganising itself into decentralised profit centres. There was a lack of direction at this time, and indeed it will be argued that this was the perennial problem for GE's computer operations.

Before the company started commercial computer work, it became involved in some early computer development projects. Its first computer work started in 1948 with a research programme on computer guidance for the anti-missile Thumper, but this was cancelled in 1950. In 1951, the firm started to develop a mid-course guidance computer for the Hermes missile.[3] However, the most important pre-commercial development that GE undertook was the one-off ORAC computer which it produced for the US Air Force's Wright Field Development Centre (Snively, 1988), a centre for aeronautical research. ORAC was developed by GE's Electronic Laboratory and was completed in 1954. The successful production of ORAC led to a number of business plans recommending that GE enter the production of computers as a commercial enterprise. These were all rejected by Cordiner who explained in March 1956 to Clair Lasher, an author of one of these proposals and who later became head of the Computer Division, that

> Under no circumstances will the General Electric Company go into the business machine business. However, sometime in the future, in support of our historic businesses it may be necessary for us to go into the process computer business.
>
> (Snively 1988)

It was ironic that it was at about the same time that GE became the first company in the world to install a computer for commercial work. In 1954, a UNIVAC 1 was installed at GE's newly constructed Appliance Park (Fisher et al. 1983: 9).

Indeed, GE's internal market for computers was large, which is unsurprising given that it produced so many high technology products. Later, GE's own Computer Department established the Internal Sales Section to market computers within the firm.[4] By the late 1960s, GE alone represented 0.3 per cent of US computer demand.[5]

## ERMA

Lasher may have been told that commercial computers were not part of GE's strategic plans, but in the decentralised company, there were other paths to pursue. Lasher asked the head of the Microwave Laboratory in Palo Alto, Homer R. (Barney) Oldfield, to investigate a computer being designed for the Bank of America (Snively 1988).

This system was the Electronic Recording Machine, Accounting, 'ERMA', being designed by the Stanford Research Institute under contract to the

Bank of America (Flamm 1988: 125). The design of this computer started in 1951, a remarkably early stage for a purely commercial design. ERMA was to be used to automate the record-keeping on customer accounts. Oldfield's small laboratory started an assessment of the machine in April 1956.[6] According to Snively (1988), Oldfield was a great believer in computers, and unilaterally started negotiations with the Bank of America to produce the design for the bank, SRI not really being able to develop such a system into production, let alone build 40 in series. Armed with a $30m letter of intent for 40 machines, Oldfield flew to the East Coast and met Dr Walter Baker, the General Manager of the Electronics Division. Baker had been planning to start a computer laboratory at Syracuse based on the ORAC development staff, but he gave the ERMA project permission to go ahead. Cordiner's diktat that the firm would not produce commercial computers was ignored and the team argued that ERMA was a form of process automation, and process automation was a core activity for GE. However, the contract was designed in such a way as to allow GE to sell systems to other buyers and contained a number of clauses covering royalty payments to the bank if GE sold the system to other users, as can be seen in the copy of the original bid documentation held by the Charles Babbage Institute.[7]

ERMA was a fairly advanced system: SRI designed it as a first-generation system, GE and SRI redesigned it to use transistors and core memory wherever possible – a kind of generation 1.5 machine. By luck, or judgement, GE was using the same window of opportunity to enter the computer market as other electronics companies: the cusp between the first and second generations of computers.

Significantly a number of the ERMA personnel had worked on semiconductors elsewhere in GE.[8] The system included magnetic tape drives from Ampex and peripherals for the magnetic encoding and reading of cheques, making GE clear leaders in the processing of bank cheques, a market which would become substantial, though would become a sector dominated by business machines firms Burroughs, IBM and NCR. The first ERMA was delivered in late 1958 and, after debugging, was in service by late 1959.

However, the grand unveiling of the first machine was not a happy moment for Barney Oldfield. Cordiner, invited to the ceremony as CEO of GE, saw that it was a cover operation for business computers and Oldfield left GE (Snively 1988). Lasher was placed in charge of reorienting the operation to the area of industrial control computers once the ERMA deal was over. By this stage the contract was worth $40m. For a commercial capital electronics project this was quite a sucess and the ERMA team had taken the opportunity to market the system as the GE 100 (Oldfield 1996: 65) and two other banks had ordered ERMA systems.[9] The ERMA system would later be branded the ERMA 210 to give it a veneer of membership to the later GE200 series and to avoid confusion with what would become the GE100 range of small scale general purpose systems created initially by the company's Italian associates (see later).

*NCR/GE 304*

The second vital contract that GE won came from the National Cash Register company. By the late 1950s, NCR was in a difficult position. Second generation computers were starting to replace traditional business machines, but NCR had little background in this area. NCR reacted to this, like other business machine firms, by setting out to purchase the skills needed to produce computers. NCR's first move was to acquire a small start-up company, the Computer Research Corporation, to develop computers for the firm.[10]

However, progress by CRC was slow and its first-generation machine system development was soon overtaken by the new solid state computers being developed (Datamation 1958: 12–14).[11] NCR had to offer a second generation machine to its clients, so it contracted GE to design and produce the electronic sections of a new machine, the NCR 304. This work commenced early in 1957.[12]

GE estimated that, if this order led to GE building 40 systems, it would be worth $15m;[13] NCR was hoping to sell 100 of these machines. GE was given the right to market the system as the GE304 within the company, and it built four for internal use.[14]

NCR missed its sales target substantially and only sold 33 NCR 304s. Nevertheless, this still helped GE establish its computer operation.

*Other early computer developments*

Most of GE's computer engineering activity in 1957 was devoted to the two main contracts, ERMA and the NCR 304. GE had a large resource at its disposal, including 220 engineers and, ironically, an IBM 704 for design work.[15] The resource was held in the Technical Products Department, later called the Industrial Computer Department which was a part of the Industrial Electronics Division.

The only further development of a commercial-orientated system was the 'paper processor', a small drum memory computer, designed in conjunction with the ERMA.[16] It was for processing accounts in smaller bank branches and GE hoped to sell them to ERMA users. It was not offered to a wider market.

However, not all the Industrial Electronics Division's computer work was dedicated to the commercial market; some developments did follow corporate orders and concentrated on industrial systems. A control computer called the Tin Processor was designed to control the tin-making process. There were similar contracts to make computers to control electricity generation plants. A monitoring computer was also produced for the testing of jet engines at the Aircraft Gas Turbine Division. Lasher expected these types of systems to be worth $10-20m to GE over the first five years of operations.[17]

**Part 2: Structured entry**

At the beginning Oldfield had become adept at staying below the corporate radar. Oldfield and the computer section manufacturing operation moved from Palo Alto to Phoenix, Arizona, though the ERMA developers stayed on the West Coast. It was a good location to attract the skilled staff needed, and it also had the added advantage of being a long way from GE's main centres in the North East (Oldfield 1996: 79). This reflected the back door method by which he had started to produce commercial computers. However, the Palo Alto team there was deep concern. They were committed to the ERMA project not to GE and it was California which was rapidly becoming the epicentre of the burgeoning electronics industry (Oldfield 1996: 79).

From an early stage, the computer operation within GE's Industrial Electronics Division was using stationery marked 'Computer Department'. According to Snively, this was mostly due to Oldfield's efforts to get the ERMA contract (Snively 1988). This was premature. In 1956, the divisional general manager for the Industrial Electronics Division, Harold Strickland, insisted it be called the Industrial Computer Department as he was all too aware of the corporate edict not to enter the commercial computer market. Formally the organisation was set up in 1956 as a section of the Technical Products Department.

However, in January 1957, this section was raised to the level of a department.[18] At this stage the (Industrial) Computer Department became involved in a new planning mechanism; a Product Scope Review meeting. It was the first new department to undergo this process, which was intended to ensure that the new organisation fitted into the overall company scheme and did not impinge on any other department's authority.[19] The review group sent out a statement outlining the department's role to 161 various departments and other operations in the company. Most departments had no product conflict with the new department. However, three operating departments felt they overlapped significantly with the new operation. This led to a review meeting held over a three-day period in October 1957.

The conflict of interests were with the following departments:

Heavy Military Electronics,
Light Military Electronics,
Industrial Controls.

Also present at the review meeting were representatives from: Aircraft Nuclear Propulsion,[20] Aircraft Accessory Turbines, Missile and Ordnance Systems, and Apparatus Sales. These probably attended as large users of computers. These operational departments were joined by the head of the Industrial Electronics Division, Strickland, together with a number of consultants from the Management Consultation Service.[21]

The conclusion of the conference was that the two military electronics departments had an interest in the computer-like elements of their tactical systems. It was concluded, however, that the Computer Department should be in charge of sales of industrial, business and scientific computers to the military. It was recognized that a number of slow data logging and small control systems were the responsibility of Industrial Controls, but that larger scale control systems were the responsibility of the computer operation. By the mid-1960s almost all industrial systems were the responsibility of the Industrial Controls Division – the computer department was busy enough by that stage.

The most interesting aspect of the meeting was the presentations made by each department, especially the plans presented by the Computer Department. It amounted to a formal business plan and a justification of the need for a separate computer operation; the department still felt it needed to justify itself. Its business plan still emphasized industrial systems, and while it was willing to build systems of all types for industrial companies, it downplayed commercial computers, even though almost all the computers it was selling were going to banks. The official product plan was to take part in four parts of the market:

1. *Industrial*, and here we recognize two categories of product- *computing for control* and *business and scientific computing*. Because of the technological similarities, manufacturing economies, and ultimate system integration, we claim that these products are within the product scope of the Computer Department.
2. *Business*, and here we definitely restrict ourselves to definite markets where we can demonstrate to Company management that such participation will be profitable.
3. *Military*, not as contractors for complete tactical systems employing data processing, but only as contractors for computers and advanced computer developments purchased separately by the military, and
4. *Applications* of computers to the solution of industrial, business and military problems which fall within our scope of interest.'[22]

Oldfield then presented a number of tables and graphs showing how the business machines, ERMA and 304, were laying the foundation for work more in line with Cordiner's views. First (Table 4.2) he outlined a belief that general purpose computers were the core of the computer market and that while control systems were going to grow in importance this market would not be as large.

This was a conservative estimate for the growth of the general and business computer market. Oldfield had already noted that in the previous three years the computer market had tripled.

The plan also predicted that the divide between control and general purpose computers would diminish. Having identified the importance of the general purpose computer, Oldfield then outlined the kind of economies

*Table 4.2*   Computer market size: estimates for 1957 and 1967

|  | 1957 $m | 1967 $m |
| --- | --- | --- |
| Industry: General Purpose (business & scientific) | 166.6 | 530 |
| Industry: Special Purpose (control, data logging etc) | 10.5 | 150 |
| Business | 85.5 | 245 |
| Government | 291.0 | 475 |
| **Total** | **553.6** | **1400** |

*Source*: Charles Babbage Institute, University of Minnesota, Jacobi Papers, Collection 41, 'Barney' Oldfield, October 1957 'Opening presentation, Product Scope Review Meeting'. Slide 5.

of scale that could be achieved from producing all types of computers. To show this he listed the common components, and the numbers used, in each of the machines that the department planned to make (see Table 4.3).

*Table 4.3*   GE estimated production of common components

|  | Flip Flops | Registers Cores | Memory cores | Drums | Tape Units | Predicted Sales |
| --- | --- | --- | --- | --- | --- | --- |
| ERMA | 875 | 7 | 130 | 0 | 8 | 95 |
| Paper Processor | 200 | 5 | 0 | 1 | 1 | 47 |
| NCR 304 | 660 | 27 | 132 | 0 | 10 | 52 |
| Machine Tool Director | 600 | 3 | 0 | 1 | 0 | 8 |
| Tin Line Data Processor | 1500 | 3 | 0 | 0 | 1 | 15 |
| Total | 154145 | 2928 | 19214 | 55 | 1335 | 217 |

*Source*: Charles Babbage Institute, University of Minnesota, Jacobi Papers, Collection 41, 'Barney' Oldfield, October 1957, 'Opening presentation Product Scope Review Meeting', Slide 6.

To reduce the cost of producing process control computers, the manufacture and sale of general purpose machines would allow increased scale economies. Therefore, the Computer Department argued that it should continue to produce commercial computers to reduce the cost of making industrial control systems. To placate senior management the department's sales plan emphasised increasingly large, non-commercial activities. Figure 4.1 shows the department's predictions for future sales, which clearly shows an increasing emphasis on non-commercial computers, a plan which they did not adhere to.

The Computer Department told GE management that its main development project was for an industrial controls computer.[23] However, Oldfield always had a plan to replace the electro-mechanical memory of the industrial

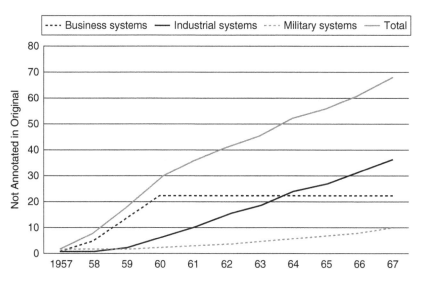

*Figure 4.1*   GE planned build-up of computer sales
*Source*: Charles Babbage Institute, University of Minnesota, Jacobi Papers, Collection 41, 'Barney' Oldfield, October 1957, 'Opening presentation Product Scope Review Meeting', Slide 6.

control machine under development, with a magnetic core memory, a change which would make it suitable for commercial use (Snively 1988). Lasher later prepared another product plan and persuaded the company that, given GE's work on the ERMA and 304 computers and the boom expected in the market, business machines were a worthwhile activity for GE. The process machine which was being developed was given its magnetic core memory and became the GE200 series of computers. This was the first range of commercial systems based entirely on GE's own work and which it could market freely. Lasher managed to halt the uncertainty surrounding the department stopped. He was more of a company man and got permission to market the 200 series to commercial users, belatedly allowing the department to exploit the start made with the ERMA and 304.

## Second generation computers: taking on IBM 1960–65

### US-developed hardware

GE's major push into commercial computing came in the form of a number of late second generation systems. Together they represented a major drive to become a serious competitor to IBM and to challenge RCA's target of becoming the number two in the industry. This acceleration of activity took place on two fronts, one in hardware development and the other in software where GE was an early developer of very large timesharing systems.

By the mid-1960s, GE's Computer Systems Department had four US-based computer engineering groups at work. These covered the four main hardware products: the 200, 400 and 600 computer ranges plus a fourth group covering peripherals. This decentralised approach to engineering led to a number of problems, not least of which was lack of compatibility between systems, which was unfortunate at a time when others were pushing towards whole families of small to large systems. GE would make plans to overcome this weakness, but its ambitious plans, at least equivalent to RCA's plans, would not find the support they needed in the company as they competed against other departments for huge injections of resources. In addition, the group had a number of other development groups, some covering the major software area of timesharing systems and also major hardware development groups in France and Italy through connections it formed with Machine Bull and Olivetti.

For a firm which was dubious about commercial computers it suddenly had a lot going on.

### The 200 series

Following the development of the early banking systems, GE turned to general purpose systems, applicable to both scientific calculation and business use. The first computer for which GE had sole responsibility was the GE225 (Snively 1988). The 225 was based on the 312 process control computer with magnetic core memory replacing the original magnetic drum (Datamation 1959:18); a plan that Oldfield had had before he left the operation.

The 225 was seen by Datamation (1960: 11–12)[24] as GE's long-awaited, true entry into the general computer market. No longer was it just making special purpose machines or sub-contracted systems. Further, it was expected that GE would use the 225 to reduce the $12m rental bill that GE paid IBM each year for its leased computers (Datamation 1960). Initially, the 225 was sold for scientific duty, which was also the function most valuable to GE internally.[25] However, the development of the commercial application programming language, GECOM, led to it also being heavily sold for commercial application as well.[26]

The 225 was the most successful of GE's early machines. It was announced in June 1960 and first delivered in April 1961.[27] Initially, it was in the

*Table 4.4*    Sales of the GE 200 series up to 1966

|     | Installed | On order |
| --- | --- | --- |
| 205 | 42 | 10 |
| 215 | 53 | 3 |
| 225 | 139 | 2 |
| 235 | 60 | 8 |

*Source*: Charles Babbage Institute, University of Minnesota, Collection 13. <u>US vs. IBM</u>, px4462, IBM 1966 'Competitive Environment'.

small to medium scale class. However, its success meant that the range was extended and, by 1966, it had become a small family of systems including a number of smaller and larger variations (see Table 4.4).

The 215 and 235 were updated machines introducing better components, an improved arithmetic unit for scientific use and better peripherals for the business user.[28]

The engineering group that was in charge of the 200 machines was also placed in charge of supporting ERMA, and the follow up to ERMA became known as the 210,[29] of which 53 were sold from 1959 to the mid-1960s.[30] It also looked after development of the Datanet 30 communications processor, which will be discussed later. By 1963, the 200 range had given GE 2 per cent of the computer market.[31] The 200 was to remain important to the Computer Department for the rest of its existence, as it was one of the principal machines in GE's time-sharing and service operations; a key reason it would outlast most other computers from its generation.

## The 400 series

At the same time as the small and medium scale 200s were being updated, another GE engineering group was bringing the medium scale 400 series to the market. The range was announced as the 425, 435, 455 and 465,[32] and in advertising the range was nick-named 'the compatibles'.[33] This is remarkable in that the 200 series, or at least the 215, 225 and 235 members, were also being marketed as 'the compatibles'.[34]

During this period IBM believed that GE was making a direct assault on its market.[35] From 1963 to 1966, IBM judged that GE was fully committed to establish a strong position in the computer market. IBM saw this as a major threat because of GE's huge financial resources. The 400 led this drive, being the most comparable range to IBM's 360 family,[36] though its design predated the 360.

Despite IBM's concerns, the 400 series never fulfilled the expectations held for it, a number of the family members were never delivered and, while the 400s were compatible within the family, they were not compatible with any other part of the GE range. By calling the range 'the compatibles,' GE was really emphasising the advantage that the IBM 360 family had when it was announced in April 1964.

The larger members of the 400 family were not delivered. While IBM decided to cover as much of the computer market as possible with the 360, GE dropped the larger 400 series machines for a wholly unconnected series. It was not competition from IBM which killed the larger members of the 400 series; it was competition from within GE:

> The machine reached the point where a prototype existed on the manufacturing floor, I believe that continued business examination, plus continued competition for resources in the Computer Department by

the other computer lines – specifically the 600 – eventually came to the point where the development of this second [larger] member of the 400 family was abandoned.

(Weil)[37]

Instead of extending the range up, this second generation system was given a smaller cousin, the 415.[38] The 400s were general purpose machines, though they were seen as particularly relevant to the business user.

Despite IBM's concern that the 400 range and GE's resources represented a major competitive combination; the initial marketing of the 400 was not a great success. By 1966, only 255 were installed and 137 were on order, respectable compared to its previous systems, but orders of magnitude behind IBM.[39] GE had reacted to this lack of sales and the announcement of the IBM 360 family by cutting prices, but sales were still limited. Much of the problem was the lack of compatibility between the GE ranges of computers. The 400 was not compatible with the older 200 range (which was still selling in small numbers), nor with the larger 600 series. Further, it would also be incompatible with the small scale 115 range that was delivered later in the decade. This was completely out of step with the growing compatibility within other firms' ranges, no matter what its advertising might have said, and this incompatibility also impacted the level of economies of scale that GE could achieve.

Nevertheless, the 400 did contribute to a slow rise in GE's market share and it did outsell previous products. All the same, sales were not high enough to achieve a goal that GE had set itself of capturing 10 per cent of the computer market. The 400 had been the main hope for achieving this target but was capturing substantially less of the market.[40]

## The 600

The third of the four engineering groups within the domestic Computer Department was headed by J.W. Weil. Its role was to develop a system that was a larger, multi-processor computer designed for scientific work. Again, it had the title 'Compatible', yet it was not compatible with any other GE system. Like the 400 series, it was largely designed before the IBM 360 and was basically a second generation system.[41] It had, however, an advanced architecture with a number of features that made it uniquely attractive in a number of applications.

The 600 range had two lineages. The first line of development was the M-236, a computer developed by the Heavy Military Electronics Department.[42] The M-236 was produced for the control of large strategic radar systems using 'wired logic' and had facilities for the real-time control of such a system.

Responsibility for the project was transferred from Syracuse to Phoenix and Weil's engineering group. The 600 series reflected the architecture and component design of the M-236. One area of overlap was the memory organisation, which not only allowed for real-time applications but also helped in developing the so-called 'time-shared computers'.[43] The 600s were to become the cornerstone of GE's time-sharing and service bureau developments, which is discussed below.[44]

The second branch of its ancestry came from GE's aim of replacing the large number of IBM large scale 7090/7094 scientific computers then in use:

> the 'machine was basically a scientific machine derived from the 7090/7094.
>
> (Weil)[45]

> what we were doing was trying to displace equipment of the 7090 family that was already installed.
>
> (Weil)[46]

GE had targeted a market for which it was a major customer itself; it had a large internal demand for scientific computing power. The design of the most successful operating system for the GE 600, GECOS, was 'based heavily on the knowledge we had as users of IBM 7090 and 7094 scale equipment'.[47]

The 600 may not have been compatible with other GE systems, but it was nearly program compatible with IBM 7090 machines, and was given something of a boost when it became clear that the 360 was not backwardly compatible with old IBM systems. It was not as easy to transfer from a 7090/94 to a 360 as it was to move from an IBM 7090/94 to the GE 600. GE's plan was to offer 7090 users a better price:performance ratio than their current machines, while avoiding the large reprogramming task needed to upgrade to the IBM 360 family. A GE 635 offered 4–5 times the performance of the IBM 7090, at only 80 per cent of the cost.[48]

Honeywell received a similar windfall for its 200 range which was compatible with IBM's main second generation business computer, the IBM 1401.

This strategy was successful as 'the initial acceptance' of the 600 series was good.[49] The first members of the range, the 625 and 635, were joined by the smaller 605 and 615. However, the flagship system, the large scale time-sharing system running the MULTICS operating system, the 645, was never sold commercially.

A further problem for GE was that IBM learnt quickly. Initially, sales of the larger members of the IBM 360 family were comparatively weak, one reason being the incompatibility with the 7090/94. IBM reacted to this by announcing 12 hardware emulators for older systems. IBM was able to do this because one of the great advantages of the 360 was that it could use Read Only Memory (ROM) and this could be used to emulate other systems fairly efficiently. This undermined some of the 600 series' early advantage.

Apart from the failure to market the 645, there were other less successful aspects of the 600 project. Despite the fact that GE had its own components division, it could not produce the memory sub-systems of the 600. The Oklahoma City-based Memory Equipment Department supplied ferrite cores for the 200 and 400 series, but was not able to supply the faster memories required for the high performance 600. These had to be were bought from Fabritek, Lockheed, and Ampex.[50]

The biggest crisis for the 600 series was its suspension from the market during 1966/7.[51] There were two reasons for this. First, 600 computers proved very difficult to maintain in the field, with a lot of down-time being experienced. Second, the installed machines were failing to deliver the computing power that had been advertised for them.[52] The 615, 625 and 635 delivery schedules were suspended to sort out the problems. The suspension led to a number of redundancies at the Phoenix factories and undermined morale in the organisation. The 600 series had been very much the flagship of GE's range so its failure was a big blow to the firm. It also had a negative effect on the profitability of the computer operation.[53]

Problems with the 600 series were well known in the marketplace making the marketing system somewhat difficult. In 1968, GE's Large Systems Department in Phoenix commissioned the Auerbach Corporation to look into the issues facing the system in the market. When it came to the hardware, image was a real problem:

> General Electric personnel realize that the industry's image of the 600 Series hardware is such that it poses a major problem in marketing. Although the 600 Series is currently operable, it has taken a considerable amount of time to reach this point and now verges on being 'out of style'.
>
> (Auerbach)[54]

By 1968, the system's performance now lagged behind large scale systems from its rivals and was facing new competition from third-generation systems.

### Peripherals

The fourth of the Computer Department's engineering groups had responsibility for developing peripheral equipment. Despite the existence of this unit, GE, like RCA, had problems supplying electro-mechanical peripherals. One of the major problems was mass storage disc drives, a critical element in a mainframe system. For a number of years Burroughs, and to a lesser extent CDC, supplied these devices to GE.[55] In 1968, GE finally started to supply its own IBM 2311-compatible disc drives. These drives were sold both to users of GE equipment by GE and were also sold to the leasing company Greyhound, which marketed them to IBM 360 users.[56] However, by the time these 2311- drives were supplied, IBM was releasing new drives. GE was behind on drives and other peripherals a story very familiar at RCA as well – as we will see UK manufacturers greatly lagged behind in peripherals.

## Time-sharing equipment and services

One of the brightest spots in GE's computer portfolio was the advances it made to interactive, time-shared computer systems which came through GE's involvement in two of the premier conceptual developments in computing in the 1960s.

In the 1960s, batch processing was the most common form of performing large-scale tasks; it was a form of processing which required programs and data had to be entered sequentially on magnetic tape or punched cards. It allowed rapid processing of common tasks and even to this day is a common way of performing updates to bank accounts, running large payroll jobs and processing government payments.

However, batch processing was a particular handicap for engineers and program developers who had to wait a long time to find out whether programs worked, making debugging a slow process. The scientific community wanted an interactive form of computing to overcome these problems. At the time, putting an individual computer on to each person's desk was not practical. Centralised time-shared computers were seen as the answer. It was not thought that distributed resources in the form of minicomputers were an economic solution; only later in the 1960s did Digital Equipment Corporation (DEC) and Scientific Data Systems (SDS) start to prove that, in fact, the minicomputer was a viable option.

Time sharing has been variously described. It can simply refer to a machine able to switch between different programmes protected from each other in memory, so that different resources of the computer can be kept utilised as different programmes require different resources. This is almost like multiple batch processes running simultaneously and is a precursor to the form of time sharing we are discussing here. The next stage of time-sharing is to allow multiple users to use a mainframe computer in real-time, running their own programs and getting results, without ever knowing that other users were simultaneously on the system.

### The Dartmouth system

The simpler, but commercially more successful, of GE's time-sharing systems was developed from work done at Dartmouth College, New Hampshire.[57] In the early 1960s, the college developed a language and operating system called Dartmouth Time Sharing System with the closely associated BASIC, probably the most famous computer language ever. It was produced using a GE 225 and was picked up by GE's Valley Forge Missile and Space Division for its own engineering design work.[58] The Missile and Space Division started to offer time on its system to other companies in its area. With the success of this ad-hoc service bureau, the Computer Division started marketing a fully-engineered version to outside users and started to develop a computer bureau service itself.[59] The machine it was selling and operating was known as the 265. This was basically a second generation 235 computer, coupled with GE's communications computer, the DataNet 30, which handled all the input-output routines. By 1968, the system could handle 40 simultaneous users and had a library of 400 programs. This development kept the second generation GE200 in operation for a lot longer than would otherwise have been the case. Even in 1968 there was still a small demand for these units.

The same system was also implemented on the 420 and 635. The main marketing emphasis was placed on the GE635 which could interact with 120 users simultaneously. They offered the same suite of programs as the 265. Indeed both systems were used in GE's internal computer bureaux network; the user did not know which system they were using, except that there was a larger charge for using the faster 635.[60]

### MULTICS system

The second time-sharing development was also a windfall from outside. It was a highly prestigious venture, though it led to few commercial sales. In 1964, the Massachusetts Institute of Technology (MIT) was the USA's leading centre for real-time computing and was, arguably, the leading academic computing hub. MIT's labs had developed many important computer systems, especially in the area of air defence systems, including the Whirlwind and SAGE systems.

SAGE was the huge computerized North American continental air defence environment, by far the largest computer project in the 1950s and 1960s. MIT was interested in improving the efficiency of engineers working on such projects. One method of doing this was to use a time-shared computer. MIT established a programme called Project MAC to develop the MULTICS operating system. This was an effort to produce a highly complex operating system, to give engineers the most sophisticated operating environment to work in. The project was funded by the Advanced Research Projects Agency. (ARPA) had been formed to coordinate and fund basic research for all the US armed forces, and thus was also very interested in improving scientific productivity. AT&T would become the other major institution involved with the MULTICS development as its massive Bell Labs faced the same kind of challenges as MIT in trying to improve development productivity.

A number of companies competed to supply the hardware for this project as it would mean not only a valuable and highly prestigious sale, but that the MULTICS operating system would be also available for their kit. The contract went to GE. This was an immense shock to IBM which had worked so closely with MIT on the SAGE.

MULTICS called for huge processing power and a number of hardware refinements, especially in the area of memory. To get its 635 and DataNet equipment chosen, GE had to fight off strong challenges, notably from IBM,

DEC and CDC. GE could offer a more suitable system: the 635 which, thanks to its military lineage and supporting DataNet 30, offered more of the necessary features in terms of communications and memory management.[61]

GE announced the combination of the 635 and DataNet 30, together with the many modifications and enhancements required by MIT, as the 645.[62] The first and only sale of the system outside of MIT and GE was the sale to AT&T's Bell Laboratories, which was the world's leading commercial research centre. Bell Labs was also interested in improving efficiency and the way in which computers worked with engineers. IBM was worried that there was a snowball effect behind these prestigious orders and that GE was a threat.[63] So concerned was IBM that it had lost the bid for the MULTICS hardware and then the related sale to the Bell Labs, that a copy of an article from the Wall Street Journal (18/11/1964) on the replacement of IBM computers with GE systems at AT&T's Bell Labs was sent to IBM's top executives with a memo recommending that it be kept on their desks until IBM had captured the lead in time sharing.[64]

However, MULTICS was a research project and the 645 system was not commercially marketed.[65] The complexity of the system proved to be enormous. MULTICS was not delivered until after GE had sold its computer operation to Honeywell, and then it only had a few users. Bell Laboratories recognised just how large and complex MULTICS was turning out to be, and withdrew its engineers from the project, setting them to work producing a stripped down operating system called UNIX, which became the dominant scientific and minicomputer operating environment until the development of the related open-source, Linux operating system.

The only real benefit of MULTICS to GE was that the 645 gave prestige to GE and gave it an image as the leaders in time-sharing technology which it could leverage when selling time-sharing computers based on the less sophisticated, but immediately workable, Dartmouth system.

*Sales of time-sharing computers and services*

In 1968, an IBM report noted the rapid growth in time-share systems sales.[66] It was estimated that in 1965 there were only 6 such machines, 12 in 1966 and 100 at the end of 1968, 50 of which were delivered in the first 6 months of 1968. IBM estimated that GE had installed just over half of the total. On top of this, GE was the leader in time-sharing bureau services. These services offered customers a terminal in their premises which allowed them to communicate with a remote time-shared computer. GE had 3000 terminals in the field, 800 within GE and 2200 with outside clients.

Revenue growth from the bureau service had been spectacular. In 1965, GE was expecting to sell $10m worth of bureau services, and expected this to grow to over $40m by 1970.[67] However, IBM estimated GE was well ahead of this target, believing that they had achieved annual sales of $30m in 1967, 60 per cent of the total market.

Another estimate suggested there were 112 computers used for commercial time-sharing generating revenue of $70m per annum; GE's share was estimated at 40 per cent.[68]

### International expansion

As well as strength in time-shared computing systems, in the mid-1960s GE also developed another potential area of rapid expansion through an aggressive expansion into overseas markets. The strategy was much more direct than the approach taken by RCA, though ultimately it failed to deliver profits.

Outside the USA, IBM identified GE and UK's ICT/L as its main competitors. Unlike RCA, which used licensees to sell its equipment abroad, GE bought foreign computer companies as a way of directly entering overseas markets. The two operations that it controlled were the computer arm of the Italian firm, Olivetti, and a 66 per cent holding in French firm Bull.[69] These two acquisitions greatly decreased GE's reliance on the US computer market (see Table 4.5)

*Table 4.5*   GE's share of national computer markets

| Country | Total size of national market in 000s points (1) | % of world computer market | GE's share of national market | % of GE's total computer activity |
|---|---|---|---|---|
| US | 128,166 | 62.1 | 6.2 | 37.2 |
| France | 10,977 | 5.3 | 45.3 | 23.4 |
| Italy | 3 435 | 1.7 | 62.8 | 10.2 |
| Germany | 8,336 | 4.0 | 17.2 | 6.7 |
| Netherlands | 1 979 | 1.0 | 31.2 | 2.9 |
| Belgium | 1 161 | 0.6 | 52.1 | 2.8 |
| Switzerland | 2,516 | 1.2 | 18.8 | 2.2 |
| UK | 18,463 | 8.9 | 1.9 | 1.7 |
| Sweden | 1,845 | 0.9 | 19.0 | 1.6 |
| Spain | 1,061 | 0.5 | 31.4 | 1.6 |
| Canada | 3,992 | 1.9 | 5.9 | 1.1 |
| Mexico | 527 | 0.3 | 44.2 | 1.1 |
| Austria | 481 | 0.2 | 42.6 | 1.0 |
| Japan | 13,605 | 6.6 | 1.4 | 0.9 |
| Australia | 2,192 | 1.1 | 8.4 | 0.9 |
| Argentina | 414 | 0.2 | 44.2 | 0.9 |
| Others (2) | 7,281 | 3.5 | 11.2 | 3.8 |
| Total | 206,431 | 100.0 | 10.33 | 100.0 |

(1) IBM measured market share in points, 1 point was the equivalent to $1 of monthly income received if all equipment installed was leased.

(2) 16 countries none over 150,000 points.

(3) IBM's estimate that GE had 10.3 per cent of the world market seems too high compared to other evidence, GE's own estimates never put them above 5 per cent of worldwide shipments.

*Source*: Charles Babbage Institute, University of Minnesota, Collection 13. US vs. IBM, px3222, IBM, 1968 'A company history of the General Electric Corporation'.

Bull and Olivetti brought more than just local market share to GE. Bull had a large range of systems called GAMMA computers; the smaller systems in this range had sold reasonably well in Europe (Datamation 1961: 30–3).[70] Bull also had expertise in punched card and printer devices which could have strengthened GE's peripheral activities. Later, both Bull and Olivetti would design computers which were added to GE's worldwide range. These were Olivetti's successful small computer, the GEll5,[71] and the even smaller Bull-built GE 50.

However, there were also problems, especially at Bull. Bull had completely lost control of costs. It produced a large range of computer and punched card equipment; however, costs of maintaining such a wide range had got out of hand while development resources had been wasted. For example, Bull made the situation worse by undertaking an abortive super-computer project; meanwhile the mainstream ranges of systems offered by Bull were old and sales were slowing down. Replacements were not that impressive and even new designs were outmoded: for example the GAMMA 300 system, released in 1961, still relied on drum memory (Datamation 1961b: 47).[72]

However, it was the cost issue which was the real problem and GE had a great deal of trouble in cutting Bull's high cost base. Bull employed 11,500 compared to GE's own Computer Department which employed 9,500 and yet produced more than twice the total output of Bull. It was difficult to cut staff as the French state put pressure on GE not to make cuts; costs at Bull therefore remained a continual problem for GE; one that they failed to solve.[73]

GE also had little success in integrating its overseas acquisitions with its four US-based computer engineering groups. Each part of GE was engaged in its own development and production work, with little coordination. Failure to integrate these activities meant that it was not achieving the economies of scale that were possible. By 1968, IBM estimated that GE had invested $100m in its overseas affiliates,[74] but due to its incompetent management and rigidity in its local affiliates it had failed to achieve a profit from these assets.

*Failure to unify the product range*

Undoubtedly, GE had an interesting computer portfolio. Not only did it have the usual hardware and software organisations, but it also had the second largest international presence and the innovative time-sharing and bureau activities. During the mid-1960s, GE undertook its first major restructuring programme since the decentralisation policy of the early 1950s. As a part of these changes it attempted, but failed, to pull its disparate computer activities together.

GE restructured its corporate activities increasing the number of operating groups from five to ten, one of which was the Information Systems Group (ISG), the structure of which is shown below in Figure 4.2.

One slight oddity clearly stands out – ISG reported to a director in charge of both computing (ISG) and aero engines – on the face of it an unusual mix. However, it reflected the fact that GE was expanding on many fronts, both

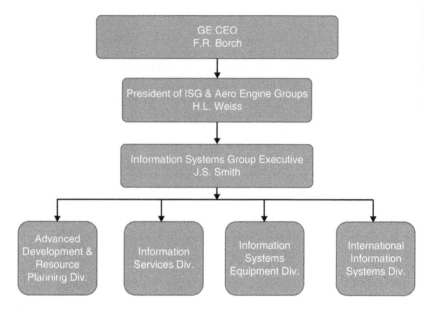

*Figure 4.2*    Information systems group structure
*Source*: GE 1967 Annual Report.

exploiting its capability in light electrical and electronics systems, such as
in computing, and heavy electrical – where turbines were essential technology. GE was attempting to build on its knowledge of turbines by expanding
into turbo fan jet engines; this is the logic of technology-led concentric
diversification. Computers and jet engines were high technology and very
expensive to develop. Weiss had both under his control. As will be seen, GE
was forced to make a choice between these developments and a number of
other developments it was also pursuing.

While ISG's structure seems logical on paper, the reality was very different: this was only a paper organisation. GE completely failed to integrate the
operations of its various arms. Responsibility for hardware was split between
the US Information Systems Equipment Division and the International
Information Systems Division, and the reality was that there were many more
sub-divisions that were not working together. The real challenge this created
for GE was in developing a truly unified third-generation computer family.
This was essential to GE not only in product and market terms, but also to
unify the hardware architecture to cut development costs and to achieve scale
economies from producing common components. Table 4.6 shows the many
different products it was supporting across its three international locations.

In general, large and medium scale systems were the responsibility of the
US operations, while Europe looked after the small machines. However, Bull

*Table 4.6*  GE products; breakdown by nation

| Domestic: | Large scale | 600-sold and manufactured |
|---|---|---|
|  | Medium scale | 400-sold and manufactured |
|  | Medium scale | 200-support for installed machines |
|  | Small scale | 115-marketing only |
|  | Small scale | 50-marketing only |
| France: | Large scale | 600-marketing only |
|  | Medium scale | 400-marketing (and manufacturing?) |
|  | Small scale | 50-sold and manufactured |
|  | Small scale | Gamma 10-sold and manufactured |
|  | Small scale | Gamma 55-sold and manufactured |
|  |  | Unit Record Accounting Machine |
|  |  | Punched card machinery |
| Italy: | Large scale | 600-marketing only |
|  | Medium scale | 400-marketing only |
|  | Small scale | 115-sold and manufactured |
|  |  | 130-sold and manufactured |

*Source*: Charles Babbage Institute, University of Minnesota, Collection 13. US vs. IBM, px3222, IBM, 1968. 'A company study of GE'.

had to also support its established base of medium scale GAMMA users and at one time France was given responsibility for developing medium-sized computers.[75]

GE started at least three programmes to replace the whole of its range with a single compatible family. In fact the first plan for a single range of machines to cover the whole of the computer market predated the 400 and 600 lines. In 1962, a team in Phoenix studied a series of machines dubbed the WXYZ range.[76] Of these only the middle ones, the X and Y, were seriously studied. The X machine became the 400 series, but the Y was cancelled in favour of the 600 project, based as it was on military work.

The idea of the unified WXYZ series was ahead of the rest of the market, but only just. Decentralisation of development into four separate development groups seems to have worked against the idea of a unified range and created real problems for the future.

After the purchase of the European firms and following the announcement of the IBM 360 family, GE once again turned its attention to producing an integrated range of computers. During 1964-66 general manager Lou Raeder proposed a programme to develop a single, worldwide, range of systems.[77] It was christened the 100 Line and was to build on the perceived strengths GE's disparate computer teams:

The 100 line had a series of processors. They were to some extent oriented in the same directions that the IBM 360 had been oriented. It was an eight bit byte machine and consisted primarily of three sets of processors, the smallest of which were to be manufactured in Italy, the medium scale ones were to be manufactured in France, and the larger scale ones were to be designed and manufactured in the US, in Phoenix.[78]

(Weil)

The Computer Department hoped that such a range could increase its share of the market from 3[79] to 10 per cent.[80]

IBM also developed a system by which design responsibility could be divided internationally. However, this was done within a framework of tight central control over basic architecture and design protocols to ensure complete compatibility. Nothing was said about how this was to be achieved within GE.

The whole concept of the 100 line came into question in 1966 when Hershner Cross took over the operation.[81] His first act was to put the 600 series into hibernation until its problems had been sorted out. His second act was to call for an assessment of the 100 plan:

> a study was called at Crononville, New York, at GE'S installation there, the worldwide marketing and engineering and general management [were] involved.
>
> We broke up into work groups, studied the 100 line versus the then existing 400 lines, and we were asked to recommend should we continue with our existing lines worldwide or should we actually go ahead with the 100 line.
>
> All the study groups recommended we go ahead with the 100 line ... Hershner Cross overruled all the study groups and decided that the 100 line would be abandoned, I assume for resource reasons.
>
> (Weil)[82]

The Italian operation ignored this edict and went ahead with its small machine, the GE115. Weil believes that this was because the Italian operation had a strong general manager who was willing to take personal responsibility. The Italian developed 115 was marketed worldwide and greatly bolstered GE's otherwise weak low-end machines. It was the only GE computer to sell over one thousand systems.[83] Nevertheless, despite the great sales of the 115, its market penetration was small. The rival IBM 360/20 had a 90 per cent market share and the Honeywell 120/125 held 5 per cent, the rest scrabbled for the remains.[84]

By the time the 100 line was cancelled (bar the Italian development), the French unit had already secured 15 orders for its medium scale 140 and 145. A corporate edict declared that these orders should be cancelled and emphasis in Europe placed on marketing the old GE400.[85] This action was known to market commentators such as IDC and was reported in a way reflecting poorly on GE and would have damaged customer confidence.

Following the failure to establish the 100 line as the worldwide GE architecture, another study, Project Charley, was initiated in France.[86] A number
of meetings in Paris led to no decisive action beyond a few specifications.

The next effort at developing a more advanced family of modular systems
came in the form of the E.R.W. study, named after the project manager
Eugene R. White. The project was initiated by John Haanstra who had been
appointed as Head of Development in the US in 1966 and, of note to IBM,
had been recruited from IBM.[87] Again it was a similar plan to the 100 Line
and Project Charley. It also came to a dead end, mainly because Haanstra
became Head of the Information Systems Division, with its emphasis on the
GE600 and the related hardware developments for large scale time sharing.

After all these false starts, plans for an integrated family of systems were
then dropped until the Advanced Product Line scheme.[88] The story of the
APL is tied up with the story of GE's departure from the industry and will
be considered later.

## The policy of retrenchment

From 1966 the disarray in the product line started to materially affect the
position of the Information Systems Group; losses mounted. In late 1966,
J.S. Smith took over ISG and cost cutting was started; further undermining
customer confidence.[89] The industry analysts IDC estimated that by 1967
GE lost $400m on its computer operations.[90] The dropping of the 140 and
145 and the suspension of 600 series sales, allowed for a programme of
cutbacks in France, though these achieved little. These moves also allowed
for cuts in the US. Engineering, software development and marketing
departments were cut back, leading to the loss of several hundred jobs. In
Phoenix, 500 were laid off from manufacturing positions. Additionally, the
Computer Research Laboratory, which dealt with fundamental research, was
shut down altogether.

Another method of retrenchment was to concentrate on fewer vertical
markets. One of the major markets that GE chose to remain focused on was
banking. GE had remained stronger in this sector than other sectors thanks
to ERMA. It hoped to win business from banks by upgrading ERMA and 200
series systems.[91] However, by this stage it now trailed a long way behind IBM
and Burroughs in the banking sector.

Despite the lay-offs and other cost cutting measures, IBM thought that GE
still had cost problems, especially in France,[92] pressure from the French government had restricted the number of redundancies which could be made.
IBM believed that GE had not dealt with the duplication of research facilities
across the US and had been inept in its handling of its excellent opportunity
in the international market.[93]

By 1968, cost problems and falling sales caused by a lack of modern
systems had further damaged ISG's bottom line performance. Despite the

efficiency drive, GE's market share was declining. IBM gauged that in 1967–68 GE's US operation actually saw a fall in sales of 3 per cent, while its international sales grew by only 11 per cent, against an average market growth rate of 25 per cent.[94]

Despite all these problems, IBM concluded that in 1968 GE was not going to leave the industry: rather the opposite, it expected GE to try to justify the $400m it had already lost by investing in a new internationally competitive system. The new head of ISG, Smith, was seen by IBM as one of GE's most successful managers, having already turned the Outdoor Lighting Department around. He bought in new managers, managers that had expertise in computers, such as R.M. Bloch from Honeywell and Haanstra from IBM. The oft-quoted GE adage, 'A good manager, no matter what his background, can manage anything',[95] seems to have been wearing thin.

## Part 3: Consolidation phase

During 1968–71 two reports were written within GE which determined the future of both GE's Information Systems Division and the corporation as a whole. The rest of this chapter will look at the background to these two documents. These reports focused on a key problem, not only for GE, but for the other electronics firms involved in the computer industry – competition for resources.

### The Advanced Product Line Master Plan

In 1968, Bloch, the new head of the Advanced Development and Resource Planning Division, started work on the 'APL Master Plan'.[96] The APL (sometimes referred to as the GE700 range) plan aimed to take the company into a strong number two position in the computer industry.[97] It called for GE to attack IBM directly.

Before the APL plan was finalised there was an extensive consultation period. In April 1969, Bloch's Division presented to the Information Systems Strategy Board, calling for GE finally to launch a unified computer range and to try to achieve a 10 per cent market share, seen as the minimum scale needed to compete with IBM.[98]

The scale of such a project was immense. Total lifetime revenue was expected to be $8.2bn; pre-tax profit was expected to be $2.3bn.[99] The full APL plan showed that this would require a very big improvement in its market performance, which had been in decline (Table 4.7).

Although rental income from the installed Current Product Line (CPL) was expected to pay for some of the APL development, the plan still called for a massive injection of funds into the ISG. Profits would take years to build; in the meantime cash flow would be negative until the mid-1970s. The large amount of cash and capital needed were not only to cover developing, building and selling the range; GE also had to fund a big increase in leases if it was to reach a 10 per cent market share – most systems were rented in the commercial sector. The income from the CPL was not likely to cover much of this cost.

Figure 4.3 shows that the APL was expected to generate very large revenues, but would not show a profit until 1974 and that cumulative cash flow was expected to be negative until 1977.

The Advanced Development and Resource Planning Division presented a number of alternative strategies to ISG aimed at reducing the financial burden of the APL, or at least aimed at reducing initial cash outflows. These ranged from delaying the launch of either the small or large members of family, to only selling not leasing the systems. All these plans had very little

*Table 4.7*   GE's share of the computer market, 1964–69

| % of shipments | 1964 | 65 | 66 | 67 | 68 | 69 |
|---|---|---|---|---|---|---|
| Worldwide | 2.1 | 2.5 | 5.0 | 4.2 | 3.6 | 3.9 |
| US only | | 4.2 | 2.5 | 2.9 | | |

*Note*: How much smaller the shares are compared to IBM's estimates.
*Source*: Charles Babbage Institute, University of Minnesota, Collection 13. US vs. IBM, px353, GE 1/1/70. 'APL Master Plan'.

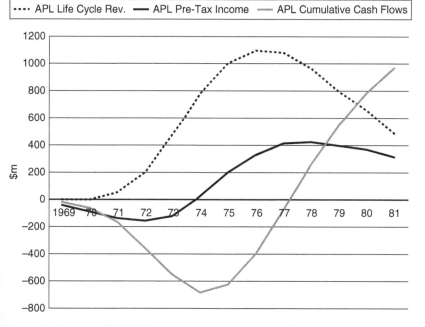

*Figure 4.3*   Forecast GE700/APL revenues, cumulative cash flows and pre-tax profit
*Source*: Charles Babbage Institute, University of Minnesota, Collection 13. US vs IBM, px322. GE 15/4/69 'Alternative Business Strategies – Base Strategy'.

effect. The final alternative was to replace the 400 and 600 ranges with like for like compatible models – again the impact was limited. Fundamentally – it was APL or nothing!

*Decision Day 2 – the Ventures Task Force and the decision to exit*

The newly branded Information Systems Group had been a continuing drain on the corporation, but it represented only a small fraction of GE's vast electrical/electronics empire and GE could easily cope with ISG as it was in the mid-1960s. However, the APL plan called for a much larger commitment. ISG was calling for the corporation to earmark computers as one of its 'Venture Activities', alongside GE's activities in civil nuclear power and civil aero-engines. All three were seen as markets that would grow much faster than the general economy and as such would be allowed massive injections of capital to enable GE to capture significant stakes in these industries.

Together the cost of supporting all the three venture activities was huge, forcing GE to reassess whether it could support all three of them. This reassessment was carried out by the Ventures Task Force. The Task Force was headed by R.H. Jones, a long-time employee of GE, who later became CEO and Chairman, undoubtedly helped by his work on these reports.[100]

The Task Force presented a number of reports to the board intended to assist them 'in evaluating the business proposition advanced by [the] Information Systems Group'.[101] The aim was to put the APL plan into the context of the wider company. The Task Force began work in November 1969. It started by interviewing a number of ISG staff to establish what the position of the Advanced Product Line was. It also took advice from outside the company, notably the computer industry consultants, A.D. Little and Diebold. Jones wanted to get an idea of where GE stood in the market and where the industry was going.[102] While most discussions centred directly on the likely outcome of the APL plan, this was done against a background of great concern about the ability of GE to fund any further major projects. There was a growing view in the company that GE's financial performance was not good. Over the period 1965–69, earnings per share had fallen by nearly 25 per cent[103] and as a consequence the company's share price had under-performed the rest of the market and, more significantly against one of its major rivals, Westinghouse (see Table 4.8)

*Table 4.8*   GE stock performance

| | |
|---|---|
| GE stock price 1965–69 | –26% |
| Dow-Jones Average | –17% |
| Westinghouse | –7% |

*Source*: Charles Babbage Institute, University of Minnesota, Collection 13 <u>US vs. IBM</u>, px225, GE Ventures Task Force, Undated. 'Preliminary report on [the] computer business'.

Overall, the GE Corporation had seen turnover continue to increase, but profit growth had been uninspiring in the late 1960s. Figure 4.4 shows that while GE was successful at growing the business, the high cost of so many of its product developments was causing erratic earnings:

*Figure 4.4*   GE revenues and net income 1961–70
*Source*: Charles Babbage Institute, University of Minnesota Collection 13. <u>US vs. IBM</u>, dx555, GE Annual Report 1970.

Against this background of variable profit performance, GE was faced with the prospect of funding three very large developments in the early 1970s. Even without the APL plan, GE was expecting greatly to increase its gearing ratio to pay for the other projects. The critical concern was the negative cash flow that the APL would cause. The other two venture activities were also expected to be cash hungry.

The first of the competitor developments was turbo jet engines. In jet engines GE had been fairly successful, especially in winning the contract to supply engines for the military C5A Galaxy transporter, but expected to lose money on this operation for many years.[104] To improve its position in the civil market it was developing two new engines. One was for the new generation of 'airbuses' – not 'Airbus Industries' the firm, which was not yet on the horizon – but a new generation of wide-bodied, medium-haul aircraft. The second development was for an engine to be used in supersonic passenger aircraft. IBM estimated that GE would not show a profit on its substantial engine investment until the mid-1970s.

The second major investment was in nuclear power. GE had a backlog of orders in 1968 worth $2bn.[105] By 1970, GE had completed or had on order an incredible 54 nuclear plants.[106] In 1970 alone, 7 plants were completed. To cope with this demand GE had invested an extra $250m.[107]

Such a massive order book one would think was a sign of great and immediate success. However, there was an issue. GE was suffering from large losses in nuclear power due to major cost overruns on 'turnkey' contracts.[108] These contracts were for complete power plants, for which GE was supplying the generating equipment and managing the civil engineering. The construction costs on these plants had been much higher than expected, leading to losses on the contracts and forcing GE to use an outside construction company for future work. There were long delays on delivery and therefore long delays in revenues.

However, both nuclear power and civil jet engines were seen as areas of massive potential, at least matching that of computers. The Task Force concluded that

> Beset with mounting pressures for immediate growth in earnings, carrying an inordinate load of losses from major risk ventures that have not sequentially offset each other's financial impacts as originally planned, and facing increasing financial demands from its core businesses, [the] General Electric Company cannot undertake any half-billion dollar venture that produces substantial immediate net income losses.
>
> (GE Venture Task Force)[109]

This conclusion was reached before any of the weaknesses of the APL plan were considered.

When it came to the APL plan itself, the Task Force appears to have been more impressed with the niche strategies of other firms. Examples included Burroughs in banking (an area GE had once led), NCR in banking and retail and CDC in the scientific market. However, the Task Force recognised that ISG could not follow this path as its current user base was already highly dispersed: there was no niche strategy for GE – it was either a large player or nothing. It concluded that the target of 10 per cent of the market could only be achieved by an across-the-board approach, or it risked losing its current user base.

The Task Force was also concerned that the APL plan did not take into account possible IBM reactions to being challenged by such a huge company across its whole product line.

Another problem identified was ensuring that the APL offered significant price/performance advantages over IBM. If it could not do this it would be difficult to get customers to swap suppliers. ISG was looking for a 20 per cent performance/price advantage over IBM to stand any chance of customers moving to GE. However, this seems to have been an impossible target. It was noted that in 1969 47 per cent of ISG's costs were manufacturing costs, this compared to 20 per cent at IBM.[110] If IBM reduced its very high profit margins by even a small amount GE would be squeezed out.

The Ventures Task Force also believed that the plan made too many assumptions. The plan envisaged that by 1975 IBM's market share would have fallen from 66 per cent to 59 per cent, but this depended on vigorous anti-trust actions against IBM – clipping IBM's wings through the courts was a rather risky assumption. The plan was also very optimistic about the efficiency of the sales force it needed to build:

> To reach our market position objective in [the] U.S.A. by 1975 [we] must increase [our] sales force 60-70% per year in size and must develop sales-men who are <u>twice</u> as productive [as] those of IBM.[111]
>
> (Ventures Task Force)

Outside views were equally as damning. Industry consultants Auerbach Corporation reported to Salomon Brothers that GE 600, beset with prob-lems as it was, still represented 68 per cent of its shipments (presumably by value) in the US.[112] The key problem was the mid-range 400 system '...suf-fers from a lack of adequate support, peripheral equipment and applications software'.[113] Maybe most damning was the comment that:

> General Electric does not have a business oriented marketing force. It has attempted to develop the small business computer market but has not really been successful. In the short run, the lack of an adequate business marketing force will severely curtail its computer activities, since the scientific market has been the hardest hit by cutbacks in the government spending.
>
> (Auerbach)[114]

The Task Force did not hesitate to recommend the sale of ISG. It recommended that the best potential buyer would be another generalist company, but one which had complementary strengths: Honeywell was recommended.[115]

The Honeywell H200 was strong in the market for medium scale systems, while the GE400 was weak and aging. However, in the area of large scale systems Honeywell was weak, and while the GE 600 had had its problems, it was back on sale and was a relatively advanced machine because of its time-sharing capabilities. It was only in the area of small scale systems in which the two firms really competed on an equal footing, thanks to GE's Olivetti operation going its own way and launching the GE115.

Importantly both firms were in need of a new range of machines: it would be cheaper to develop one system for both companies.

The decision to leave the industry was taken soon after the Task Force's recommendation. Honeywell and GE merged their computer interests into a new company called Honeywell Information Systems, which instantly had a work force of 50,000. Honeywell had a stake of 81.5 per cent and GE 18.5 per cent, which it soon sold to Honeywell.

GE did not abandon computers altogether. It had long detached its control and industrial computer operations from the business machines area. It also retained its computer bureau operation and computer communications network, both of which supplied a constant cash flow and were useful for its own operations. GE Information Systems, GEIS, remains a significant business for many years.

## Conclusions

The reasons for GE leaving the market were similar to those of RCA. They were a combination of fear that supporting multiple growth paths would drain corporate funds to a critical point, and an inability to match IBM's low costs and successful marketing strategy. RCA's decision was made following the crisis caused by displacement of Spectra 70 computers by newer RCA Series machines before the former had been fully depreciated. While GE had already lost money on some aspects of its computer operations, the crucial factor was the large sums that would have been required to complete the APL plan; without the APL product line GE's executives did not see any scope for the company in the computer industry. The corporate staff did not believe that GE could undertake such a large investment, feeling that funds could be better used elsewhere. In these circumstances, GE was willing to give up the chance of being a player in a market that it acknowledged would continue to be one of the major growth sectors of the economy. It opted instead to provide funds for other projects – projects which were closer to its traditional fields of excellence. From 1970 to 1974, GE raised $600m in long-term debt to fund its operations: much of this debt was used to finance the aero engine and nuclear power diversifications.[116]

This book argues that competition for funds weakened the ability of the electronics firms to invest in their computer operations at crucial stages in the development of the industry. Nevertheless, the fact that it was the computer department which was sacrificed when finances were tight has to be explained. It was, after all, the fastest growing market around. In GE's case the reasons were its inability to compete with IBM, numerous poor management decisions, and a failure to integrate the computer operations into one effective division – which in turn meant that it failed to produce an integrated family when it had the opportunity. It failed to produce such a family, the obvious missed opportunity was the 400 series, on which it could have developed a full range in roughly the same time period that third-generation families were being launched.

GE's lack of a single product range meant that it could not exploit the economies of scale that other firms were achieving. It also meant that it was duplicating its engineering activities across its many designs, and duplicating this effort in three countries. GE also managed to waste resources on dead end projects.

Bloch believed that GE's policy of decentralisation was the problem; ISG was not able to operate as a coherent organisation.[117] Even within the operating unit there was little coordination. In his eyes, it was this excessive decentralisation which prevented the firm from creating a single product line before the APL plan. Bloch believed that, if such a range had been built, a 10 per cent market share could have been achieved in the early 1960s.

Barney Oldfield argued that the production of control computers went hand in hand with business machines. However, GE's policy of decentralisation meant that this operation was soon moved into a separate profit centre, the Industrial Controls Division. One of the few machines that seems to have benefited from cross fertilisation of ideas within GE was the 600 series which drew on the development of the military M-236 computer built by the Light Military Electronics Division. However, these systems were not built together, negating any production advantages.

One area in which GE did actively try to take advantage of its scope was in the field of basic components. IBM noted that GE had a policy of sourcing components internally. However, IBM went on to note that GE had lost market share in the semiconductor industry, and saw this policy as tying the Information Systems Group to one of the less successful component sources.[118] The Semiconductor Products Department had been a late mover in developing integrated circuits – potentially one reason GE was late with third-generation systems, launching two very late second generation families, the 400 and 600 ranges. It did not invest large sums in the design of ICs until 1967. GE never really had a third-generation computer system. There seems to be a connection between this and GE's weakness in the area of ICs.

Business machines companies had to focus resources on computing as computers replaced older punched card tabulating systems, and, once they had acquired the relevant technology, they tended to take a more integrated approach to products and marketing. To a firm like GE, it was a new market which was very different to its old product lines. It failed to gain sustainable advantage from the exploitation of economies of scale and scope, suffered the disadvantages of supporting multiple growth paths, struggled with the potential weaknesses of decentralisation and lacked focus on individual markets.

# Part III
# UK Electronics Companies in the Computer Sector 1950–68

# 5
# The Ferranti Company

## Development of the company

As essentially a family-owned firm, Ferranti is unique among the companies studied in this thesis. The other companies we will be looking at, RCA, IBM and English Electric all had powerful autocrats leading them who passed control of the firm to their sons. However, the actions of these father-son dynasties were tempered by the need to satisfy external sources of capital, and by the non-family board members. Ferranti was less bound by this issue. Because of this ownership structure, Ferranti was a firm carrying an unusually large historical legacy. It is important to understand the history of Ferranti so that the strategy it adopted in the computer industry can be seen in proper context.

The company was formed in 1882 by Sebastian Ziani de Ferranti (born in the UK with Anglo-Italian heritage) and two backers, Alfred Thompson and Francis Ince (Rendell 1946). Sebastian worked at the forefront of technology in the rapidly expanding electrical industry and the firm's initial heritage was as a heavy electrical company. His achievements included the first alternating current power plant, high voltage distribution cables, electric current meters, and advances in electrical transformer technology (Ferranti International Signal 1989).[1]

Sebastian and the company also made some important developments in the lighter end of the electrical equipment market. Sebastian developed the most common form of domestic electric fire, the common bar fire with reflective metal behind the element bars to radiate heat. The firm also produced domestic electronic products such as early radio kits, and, in the late 1930s, television sets. However, like so much of its business, domestic electrical and electronics goods were only a short-lived activity; both were abandoned by the end of the 1950s as competition increased. Ferranti sold its failing radio and television business to E. K. Cole Ltd (Ekco) for £300,000 in 1956.

Indeed, this exit from the light electrical and consumer electronics industry is prescient of repeat behaviour which Ferranti would exhibit over time. The company suffered a number of setbacks before the 1914–18 war, due to growing competition from larger electrical firms, and because of the costs associated with Sebastian's many innovations. For a period, the firm was placed in administration (Wilson 1988 and 2007). However, restructuring and disposal of important business units, such as the switch-gear department kept the company in Ferranti's hands (Ferranti 1955).[2] It was a rigidly private company committed to limiting outside investment and unwilling to take on substantial long-term debt.

Ferranti was a company that relished technology. However, many of the new products that it became involved with were only of passing interest to the company: it was a willing developer of new technology but was innately conservative when faced with a competitive market. It would enter into a new industry, develop clear technical capability but would not be willing to invest in the business to help it reach minimum economic scale and to market its wares globally. These business units would be sold to fund the next high technology venture.

## Building a capital electronics capability

The firm's most important pre-war electronics activity was radio components. It produced a range of components, including the AF3 transformer, which greatly improved the quality of radio reception (Wilson 1988: 137–8). In 1935, the Moston Radio Works was opened to take over production of all parts for the lighter side of the Ferranti business including the Radio, Valve and Domestic Appliance Departments. The valve and component operations would outlast the domestic appliances business and led to Ferranti's large post-war electronic components business. The second major element in Ferranti's electronic development was the Instruments Department. This was Ferranti's capital electronics engineering operation. Some of its first products were electro-mechanical aircraft instruments, which proved useful in the war:

> Out of this, it [the Instruments Department] eventually became almost a development laboratory for government contracts.
> (The Electrical Manufacturer 1958: 22–5)

Such a background made the firm vital to the war effort and meant that Ferranti transformed into one of the leading electronics manufacturers in the UK, just as the world was about to enter a period of explosive growth in electronic technologies.

## The imperative to find a new market

The Second World War had a great effect on the Ferranti Company, as it did the rest of the electronics industry. The fundamental change was the growth of the high technology capital electronics markets. To deal with military work, Ferranti built up a significant electronics capability, with large development and manufacturing facilities being dedicated to capital electronic equipment.

The transformation into peace time manufacture was not an easy one for the company to make. Ferranti was not a recognised force in capital electronics before the war (Marconi hardly noted it as a pre-war competitor[3]), but it now had a very large commitment to this market. After the war, it was faced with a collapse in its order books.

This was not unique to Ferranti, the end of war meant a collapse in the order book for all electronics companies: most companies expected there to be a delay between the end of war related orders and a commensurate rise in commercial work. This is illustrated in Figure 5.1 which shows what the leading company in the electronics market, Marconi, expected to happen to its sales after the War:[4]

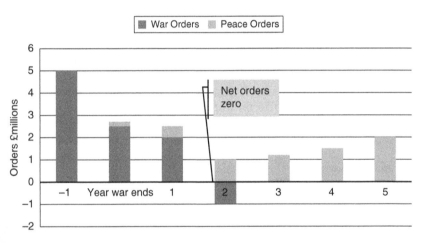

*Figure 5.1*  Projected effect of War ending on Marconi order book
*Source*: Bodleian Library Marconi Archive Shelf Mark 405. Bangay, R.D. (Marconi) 10/5/44b. 'Report on post-war problems in relation to sales policy'.

The reality was clearly every bit as bad. In 46/47 UK defence spending declined by 62.8 per cent (Chalmers 1985). The firms were not in a position to know that the falling out of the Western and Eastern Allies would lead to a cold war in which defence expenditure would rise sharply again, with capital electronics at the heart of the new arms race.

This was the situation faced by Ferranti's Instruments Department, it was facing a bleak immediate outlook, however, other parts of the company benefited from peace. A good example was the electrical side of the company which would gain from the post-war re-equipment and expansion of the nationalised electricity industry.

On the face of it, this temporary downturn in the demand for capital electronics would not seem to have been much of a problem. Ferranti wanted to maintain an interest in the new electronic technologies, and it had profits from the electrical side of the business to tide it through the period in which civil products were being developed. However, such cross subsidisation was not a part of the company ethos; the Instruments Division had to find its own work and gain new revenues quickly.

## Ferranti and the computer industry

### Part 1: The experimental phase

The business needed to find a new purpose and to do it quickly. Computers were one potential option for the company. It was the head of Ferranti's Instrument Department, Eric Grundy, who became interested in the possibilities which computers held. His initial interest was in industrial control systems and the role his department could play in making and selling these systems.[5] Interestingly, industrial control computers would become a business which would survive within Ferranti until the firm's demise. In the world of Ferranti, Grundy would have little recourse to the company to fund his department, so it was up to him to find a way of exploiting the skills they had developed.

One of the key influences on him was a paper given at the Institution of Electrical Engineers in 1947. It was from Professor Arthur Porter (Porter was Professor of Instrument Technology at the Royal Military College of Science: Cobbold, 2010), who would briefly work for Ferranti setting up a research department in Canada, and who acted a consultant to the firm in the critical period. Porter outlined three advantages electronic equipment could offer industry:

- First, electronic equipment is extremely flexible. The controlled member can be remote and the same controller may be used for more than one purpose;
- Second, a vast amount of experience in electronic techniques had been developed during the past six years; and
- Third, the non-technical point that in the US the design and application of automatic controller equipment was ahead of the UK, but with the coming of modern electronic techniques there was no reason why we should not achieve parity.

(Swann 1975)[6]

On the recommendation of Professor Porter, Grundy employed a servo-mechanism expert, Dietrich Prinz[7] (Prinz was a key character in the development of early computers and even developed the first chess computer programme). After being interned as a German national, Prinz was released and served under Porter on the Ministry of Supply's Servo Panel. Grundy planned to use Prinz, and his assistant, to develop electronic control systems, but this plan to start developing computerised control systems was usurped by more immediate opportunities to win contracts:

> Grundy asked Sir Vincent de Ferranti to sponsor a study of automatic control from general company funds, but this was refused, and Prinz was employed on a study of radar display for the Ministry of War.
>
> (Swann 1975)[8]

Sir Vincent Sebastian Ziani's successor had good reasons to divert the talented Prinz to radar work. First, the Berlin blockade increased the urgency of radar developments. Second, Ferranti had learnt lessons from its past and was formalising its policy of operating autonomous departments (Drath 1973: 4–12 – based on an interview with Grundy), a policy in keeping with the general Ferranti way of operating. Radar looked like a more immediate way of achieving self-funding for this flagship department during the postwar order slump. Prinz could come on board, but the resources for computing would have to wait a while.

In the summer of 1948, Prinz was again available to Grundy, the radar display having been completed. Grundy dispatched Prinz to study computer developments in the US (Young 1958a: 18–20). With the aid of Porter, Prinz managed to look at a number of the key developments in America.[9] Grundy's instructions to Prinz still exist in a telegram sent to him in 1948:

> Will you please consider the preparation of a complete report on digital computing as you have seen it Stop I would like to submit this to Hitch's superiors as a lever to persuade them to finance our developments for their use Stop.
>
> (Grundy 1948)[10]

One thing is clear, while many of the scientists remain legends in the history of computing, Grundy deserves a footnote for providing a corporate entity willing to take scientific inventions and turn them into fully developed products.

### The Mark 1 Computer development

It appears that one of Prinz's main conclusions from his trip was that the UK had as good a position in the new technology as the US. One of the UK's centres of excellence was developing at Manchester University (Young 1958a), the company's home town. The University's computer activity was centred in the Electrical Engineering Department and was led by Professor F.C. Williams and would later be led by Professor Tom Kilburn. Williams and Kilburn had been working at the Telecommunications Research Establishment during the war years. In 1946, they moved to Manchester and continued their work on electronic storage techniques (Lavington 1980). Williams' most famous contribution to computer hardware development was the Williams Tube. This was a cathode-ray-tube that was used to store digital information. It was one of the few early methods of storing data for use by a computer. This device was not only used in early Ferranti machines, but was also used by IBM in its first electronic computers (Bashe, et al. 1986). It was one of the many storage systems of the time that seem a little Heath Robinson these days. Effectively using a TV-like screen to store data, it used the photo static capability of the screen to store dots representing 0 and 1. The screen would 'remember' the image of the dot for a fraction of a second, long enough to read and rewrite the dot as the program running on the computer demanded. It was a rival to the more common delay line memory where data was stored as a sound wave in a loop of mercury!

In June 1948, Williams had completed the 'baby Mark I' which is generally accepted to be the world's first stored-program computer (Lavington 1980). Most of the funding for the early Manchester work came from the Royal Society, but this was a finite source. Grundy saw this early machine and clearly it fitted with his aspiration and the work he hired Prinz to do. However, his Instrument Department did not have the financial resources to develop the test bed into a full-scale computer. In any case, the whole field was completely unknown to the company, and there was little idea of who would be the customers for such machines.

While Grundy was interested in the system, Ferranti's first involvement came through the Radio Department. Williams was an advisor to the Radio Department and in return it provided some hardware to the university project (Hendry 1989: 49). Later there was a certain amount of conflict between the Radio and Instruments departments as to which should have responsibility for developing Williams' design. The Instruments Department won the battle but the team that worked on computers was drawn from both operations. The Radio Department developed the circuits, while the Instruments Department provided the precision engineering side, especially the magnetic drum which acted as a large backing store to the faster Williams Tubes (Young 1958a).

While the Instruments Department had no resources to develop Williams' inventions, Government, the only likely short-term purchaser of computers, was becoming interested. Professor P.M.S. Blackett, of Manchester University's Physics Department, discussed the situation with the government's Chief Scientist at the Ministry of Supply, Sir Ben Lockspeiser (Drath 1973). Lockspeiser immediately sent Ferranti a letter of intent to purchase a larger version of the Baby. This would become the Mark 1 computer and was installed in the University, a machine known also known as Manchester Automatic Digital Machine MADM – this was an era where every individual computer was so rare that it had its own name.

The contract was not placed through the Contracts Department of the MoS, and was not open to tender; Ferranti would build the computer for the university. This seemed appropriate as Ferranti had already contributed components and engineering to the Baby project and was close to the Manchester development team. However, Hendry (1989) relates that Williams himself would have preferred to work with EMI which he saw as the premier electronics company in the country. As will be seen later, EMI, were one of the premier systems engineering company following its work on developing electronic television and soon became interested in computers itself.

*Producing and selling Mark 1 computers: MADM and FERUT computers*

Ferranti were in the computer game. From 1949 to July 1951, the Ferranti Instruments Department was constructing MADM. The Ministry of Supply provided £120,000 to develop and produce one machine, an engineered version of the original computer to be delivered to the university. The question that occupied the minds of a number of interested bodies was what would happen next?

Ferranti then achieved something quite extraordinary: it managed to win the first export order for a mainframe computer. Ferranti sold a Mark 1 to the University of Toronto – a machine known as the FERUT. This sale owed much to the personal contacts of Professor Arthur Porter and the efforts of Ferranti's first computer sales representative, Vivian (later Lord) Bowden.

FERUT was purchased to help in the construction of the joint US/Canadian St Lawrence Seaway. Canada wanted to ensure that it matched the contribution of the USA in the construction of this canal. One way in which it did this was to provide the design calculations: this was where the computer came in.

FERUT was an ambitious project. Problems were caused by a number of factors. First, it was one of the world's first computers, and the first to be exported three thousand miles. Another cause of the problems was that Ferranti was not willing to bear the total cost of building the machine nor was the Canadian government willing to pay for it ahead of delivery. The result was that, as each sub-assembly of the machine was manufactured, it was exported to Toronto and paid for by the Canadian government. The computer was not therefore first assembled and tested in Manchester. Nevertheless, the University, Ferranti and others managed to get the machine working for the 1952 Toronto Computer Conference. The Seaway calculations were also finished in record time.

*Government efforts to structure a competitive industry*

With the MADM being built, Lockspeiser at the Ministry of Supply tried to keep the momentum going to ensure the UK had a source of computer capability. He initiated the Brunt Committee which was chaired by the eminent meteorologist Sir David Brunt.[11] This committee brought together leading academics and the relevant government departments and was intended to advise government on computers. He also tried to persuade Sir Henry Tizard of the Advisory Council on Scientific Policy to authorise the purchase of three Mark 1 machines. This was refused, with Tizard suggesting that the appropriate sponsoring body was the Department of Scientific and Industrial Research. Late in 1951, Lockspeiser took charge of the DSIR.

A meeting was held in January 1951 between Lockspeiser, Brunt, Williams and the head of the Ministry of Supply, Brigadier G.H. Hinds, where it was agreed that the MoS contract needed to be renewed to keep the Manchester and Ferranti team together.[12] This was only for continued research and was a DSIR contract administered through MoS.[13] However, production was what was needed. Brigadier Hinds let it be known that MoS wanted a Mark 1 computer for atomic weapons research at the Fort Halstead research establishment. However, he could not award the contract. First, the cost of the system would be above his expenditure authorisation; second, he could not just award a contract to Ferranti, as the MoS had competitive tender policies. Nevertheless, he and others wanted Ferranti, with the most advanced computer production capability in the UK, to be supported until a real market could develop.

The answer came through a new body, the National Research and Development Corporation. The NRDC was not mandated to employ inventions for military work but to ensure that new innovations (often based on investments made by the British government for military work) were exploited for the benefit of the British economy (Hendry 1989). The NRDC was a public Corporation set up by the Board of Trade under the Development of Inventions Act, 1948. The act was amended by the Development of Inventions Act, 1954, which somewhat broadened the Corporation's functions, which was necessary given the much more interventionist role that it played. Finance was provided by the Treasury in the form of loans, the outstanding amount of which, initially, would not exceed £5 million at any one time (Bard 1955).

The NRDC's main assets were the patent rights it took over from other government departments. It was expected to make a commercial return from exploiting these patent rights. Following the War, this was a rich vein to mine, though to achieve a return on these assets, the NRDC would first have to invest large amounts of public funds into ventures to exploit these new inventions. Among these patents were included the rights to the Williams' computer inventions.

Discussions between Ferranti and the NRDC can be divided into two distinct conversations. One set of plans concerned the direct support of the computer operations at Ferranti. Another, less formal, set of talks related to the efforts of the NRDC to bring the nascent UK industry together, to combine the capabilities of a computer company and a business machines company.

The talks on creating an integrated computing and business machines champion were based on a desire to ensure that the UK had a competitor to IBM (Hendry 1989: 60–73), a cause the managing director of the NRDC (John Giffard, 3rd Earl of Halsbury) would try to pursue. In 1950, IBM was dominant in computers, but had already taken out a license from the NRDC for the Williams Tube, indeed this proved to be a good source of funds for the Corporation. Halsbury saw a major threat posed by IBM building computers as an extension to its tabulator business. He believed that there was a major threat of IBM cornering the world market for computers.

His initial efforts in arranging round table talks between the electronics and the business machine companies to develop a strategy for computer production came to nought. However, Halsbury made a second effort to produce a British competitor when he learnt that IBM was trying to form a partnership with British Tabulator Machines, which had previously been the licensee of IBM technology in the UK, but now facing competition from IBM as it entered the UK market directly.

Halsbury could see a situation where Manchester/Ferranti's electronic technology innovations would effectively be sold back to the UK via IBM systems using the Williams Tube. Halsbury did manage to promote some initial plans for Ferranti and BTM to work together but they came to nothing as BTM had neither the time to work in this area and was concerned at what the arrangement might mean should they take up the offer.

BTM was fully occupied trying to compete with IBM in the field of tabulators and had little time for an unproven technology. BTM was also concerned that if it formed a partnership with Ferranti, IBM could get hold of any technology that it might develop under contract with the NRDC through IBM buying a licence from the NRDC.

The NRDC later attempted to develop a link between Ferranti and the other British business machines firm, Powers-Samas, this also came to little and indeed may have damaged Ferranti's efforts to market its computer systems.

The early effort by the NRDC to structure a UK competitor was forward looking. If Ferranti could develop the main 'computer' and the stored program memory, others with more experience in electro-mechanical systems could work on the input (punched cards and tabulators) and output (punched cards and printers). Sadly it was not to be.

### Ferranti Mark 1* and NRDC funding

Having failed to influence the structure of the embryonic industry, the NRDC was left with little choice but to support and encourage Ferranti in the exploitation of the Mark 1 computer. This proved difficult to arrange, and at least ten months were wasted in pursuing a plan that would be unacceptable to the senior Ferranti management. In February 1951, W.G. Bass, now the director in charge of Ferranti's computer operations within the

Instruments Department, wrote to Halsbury with a plan of action. It consisted of four areas of activity:[14]

a. Fundamental research;
b  Commercial sale of fully engineered Mark 1 computers;
c. Production of specialist business versions of the Mark 1, to be produced in conjunction with users; and
d. Development of a business-orientated computer to replace the existing types of business machines.

Bass wanted the NRDC to support sections (c) and (d) of this scheme. Ferranti estimated that expenditure on these areas would amount to £100,000 over three years. Bass suggested that the NRDC contribute 50 per cent of the cost of these long-term developments. The NRDC was unhappy at this proposal as it was more interested in Mark 1 sales. It was these patents that the NRDC was administering as was noted in an internal comment by the NRDC's Patent Manager, Dennis Hennessey;[15] selling Mark 1 computers was the immediate concern of the NRDC and, it believed the best way of establishing a computer industry in the short term.

The NRDC suggested an alternative. Instead of an equity stake in future development, it would instead make a loan against a development and production agreement for the Mark 1.

Bass and Grundy made a counter proposal, suggesting the NRDC make a direct investment in Ferranti's computer operation.[16] The NRDC chairman, Sir Percy Mills, was cool to the idea, as he believed that it would show too much bias in favour of Ferranti. The NRDC was not there to support Ferranti, but to act as a patents pool, enabling British firms to get access to all possible technology.

On 9 November 1951, Halsbury wrote to Bass with a firm proposal based on Bass's earlier idea.[17] The NRDC was prepared to loan the company £50,000 at an interest rate of 5 per cent. It was to be repaid by a simple 5 per cent levy on sales of all computer equipment made by Ferranti. Further, it was proposed the NRDC to receive the rights to any Ferranti invention made under the arrangement until 50 per cent of the loan had been repaid, and thereafter, Ferranti would retain UK rights and the NRDC overseas rights, or vice versa.

It seems possible that up to this stage the Instruments Department management had been negotiating on its own behalf, looking to put a firm proposal in front of the Chairman of the Board, Vincent de Ferranti. The NRDC loan proposal was indeed put forward, but the reaction was negative. The computer manager Bass reply to the NRDC proposal showed that Vincent de Ferranti was not well disposed to such schemes:

> My chairman has given some thought to your kind letter of November 9, but has come to the conclusion that he does not want to borrow money

from anyone except the bank, particularly as there are no conditions with regard to licences attached to money lent us by the bank, and they have no charge on our business.

(Bass 22/11/51 letter to Halsbury)[18]

Vincent had a counter proposal which Bass quotes at length:

I understand that the function of the NRDC is to encourage the rapid application of inventions to industry.

The only way I can see that the NRDC could help us to do this in the case of computers, would be to order computers from us which we would keep in stock for sale against firm orders. As a sale took place, we would pay them [the NRDC] the cost of the machine, plus an agreed profit, say 10 per cent, and get what price we could for it. This, in fact, would be similar in its action to a rocket launching apparatus - once in the air we can fly - and I suggest is the most appropriate use of their venture capital.

(Bass 22/11/51)

Vincent wanted sales, not subsidy and loans. Sales would not only ensure the engineering and design teams could be kept together, but that manufacturing facilities would be assured work. The proposal was simply for the NRDC to buy machines on spec and then get their money back when Ferranti or, indeed, the NRDC managed to sell these systems from stock to a real customer.

Halsbury, contacted the Brunt Committee and S.A. Dakin, the Assistant Secretary of the Board of Trade,[19] to see if they would be in agreement with this plan. At the 27th NRDC board meeting (27/11/51) it was reported that the Board of Trade would approve of NRDC funds being spent in such an arrangement.[20] However, the NRDC wanted to turn the plan around so that it was Ferranti that received a fixed percentage profit and the NRDC any profit above this. It was proposed that the NRDC should buy four machines and then act as the sole stockist of Ferranti computers. Ferranti would then be appointed as selling agents, and would receive a fixed percentage reward for each sale that it made.

After the drawn out negotiations on a loan, the talks on the purchase agreement seem to have gone very smoothly. The Instruments Department was getting to the stage where more contracts were needed for its computer operation, while the NRDC was desperate to retain momentum in the UK computer industry; so desperate that it was willing to invest large sums on becoming the world's first computer wholesaler.

Halsbury met Vincent de Ferranti in December 1951, and reported to the next board meeting that the proposed arrangement was substantially agreed on; Ferranti was to receive cost +7.5 per cent to build the computers and then would receive another 5 per cent for completing a successful sale.[21] It is quite astonishing to think that the company and the NRDC thought the cost of marketing and selling such complicated pieces of equipment could be incentivised by a 5 per cent sales commission; however, as one of the few sources of such systems in the world, and with a tiny community of early adopters primarily from government research laboratories, the complexity of sales would be much less than in later years.

The new NRDC machines were to be called the Mark 1*. The name change reflected improvements suggested after experience with the MADM and FERUT Mark 1 computers. These suggestions were in part based on recommendations from NRDC consultant Christopher Strachey who prepared plans for detailed testing of future machines aimed at avoiding the problems encountered with the poor project planning and testing strategy used for the FERUT.[22]

The notional cost of stocking four machines was £220,000 based on manufacturing costs of £55,000 and the customer price would be £83,000 for the base machine installed (see Table 5.1)

*Table 5.1*   Cost and price break-down of the Ferranti Mark 1*

| Manufacturing cost | 50,550 |
| --- | --- |
| Ferranti 7.5% profit | 3,787 |
| | 54,337 |
| Computer ex works cost roughly | 55,000 |
| Installation at site | 10,000 |
| 6% royalty on NRDC patents | 4,925 |
| Notional 20% NRDC profit | 11,000 |
| Selling commission to Ferranti | 2,075 |
| **Customer price** | **83,000** |

*Source*: National Archive for the History of Computing. NRDC 86/10/2: NRDC, 28/5/52. 'Managing Directors report to the 33rd NRDC board meeting'. Reproduced by courtesy of the University Librarian and Director, The John Rylands Library, The University of Manchester.

The export price was £103,000 to cover the extra costs involved. If the customer wanted the provision of high-speed input-output devices (at this stage third party punched card systems), the home price would increase to £100,000 (approaching £3 million in 2012 prices) and overseas buyers would pay £115,000.

Eventually 7 Mark 1*'s were produced, 6 were stocked by the NRDC plus one sold to the Ministry of Supply; it is uncertain whether this machine was stocked by the NRDC or bought directly by MoS. The customers and sponsors for all the Mark1 and 1*'s follows are shown in Table 5.2.

The final machines were purchased despite some resistance from the Board of Trade, which was worried that the on-going contract was *ultra vires*, and was in reality a form of venture capital. The NRDC's function was

*Table 5.2*   Ferranti Mark 1 and 1* sales

| Code No. | Type | Sponsor | Customer/User | Installed |
|---|---|---|---|---|
| DC1 | Mark 1 | MoS/DSIR | Manchester University and MoS | 1951 |
| DC2 | Mark 1 | National Development Council of Canada | University of Toronto | 1952 |
| DC3 | Mark 1* | MoS or NRDC | MoS | 1953 |
| DC4 | Mark 1* | NRDC | Shell labs. Holland | 1954 |
| DC5 | Mark 1* | NRDC | National Inst. for the Application of Mathematics, Rome. | 1955 |
| DC6 | Mark 1* | NRDC | AWRE, Aldermaston | 1954 |
| DC7 | Mark 1* | NRDC | MoS | 1955 |
| DC8 | Mark 1* | NRDC | A. V. Roe & Co. | 1954 |
| DC9 | Mark 1* | NRDC | Armstrong Siddley Motors | 1957 |

*Source*: NAHC Swann, 1975. Reproduced by courtesy of the University Librarian and Director, The John Rylands Library, The University of Manchester.

primarily to exploit patents owned by the government and were tasked with exploiting these for a royalty. However, the issue was rather moot as by the time the last machines were being delivered the Mark 1* was quite clearly outdated and was receiving little new interest from potential buyers.

*Ferranti a reluctant computer company*

Organisationally, Ferranti nominally operated a strict decentralised structure, as evidenced by the refusal to use profits from electrical engineering to fund the Instruments Department. However, it was still at heart a family business and the chairman, Vincent de Ferranti, was heavily involved in decision making in the divisions and was less than vigorous in strict adherence to nominal managerial structures. Lord Halsbury experienced a number of problems arising from Sir Vincent's attitude:

> [Sir Vincent] is in the French sense of the word 'le patron' and, whatever managerial structure may be adopted on a paper chart, everybody in the organisation is in reality working for Sir Vincent.

> One of his concerns of course is to know what is going on everywhere, and from this point of view I do not think he has any great objection to members of his team being at sixes and sevens among themselves. It means that in the end they come to him with their stories and this enables him to keep his ear to the ground. The elder members of the Ferranti family frequently

quarrel among themselves, and one of Sir Vincent's main preoccupations seems to be to keep anyone else out of his personal family enclosure, now reserved for himself and his sons Sebastian and Basil.

(Lord Halsbury, 15/2/57)[23]

The Instruments Department went ahead with detailed talks with the NRDC and negotiated with them a number of possible scenarios only to have the favoured one, a loan, ruled out by Vincent despite some considerable time on the negotiations. Bass' idea of the NRDC taking a stake in the Department would undoubtedly have been abhorrent to Vincent.

Vincent's overall attitude to the computer venture seems to have been negative from its inception. This is seen not only by the initial reticence to fund the expansion into computing, but also by continued displays of doubts about the advisability of being in this market. The NRDC made this clear to the Board of Trade when it requested permission to fund the Mark 1* project:

I would be grateful for your earliest indication that the BoT will approve this transaction in principle. You are sufficiently acquainted with the history of this matter to be aware that we have gone to endless trouble to persuade Ferranti to show some initiative in the development of computers. They are, however, extremely reluctant to invest any financial stake in their development notwithstanding the fact that the project has been, so far, financed from the public purse. In these circumstances it seems to me that we are fully justified in trading in these machines as a means of securing their development and exploitation at a faster rate than will take place if the matter is left in Ferranti's hands. If the latter were the case then in my opinion our computer inventions would be currently 'insufficiently developed and exploited' within the meaning of section 1 of the Development of Inventions Act.

(NRDC, 27/12/51)[24]

Of the next two computer systems developed by Ferranti, the NRDC would sponsor one and was in active discussion about supporting the second. Despite the success of the Mark 1* and the fact that the next machines were expected to sell in greater numbers, the company continued to show reticence about taking the responsibility of investing in this growing line of products.

In March 1953, Halsbury discussed with Sir Vincent how the NRDC could speed up the development of the UK computer industry.[25] Halsbury suggested that the NRDC take over the responsibility for marketing the machines that it was purchasing. Vincent was against this idea as he expected that this would lead to duplication of effort, and that, in any case, marketing was the natural forte of the private enterprise. He argued that Ferranti was progressing at a sustainable rate, and that the slow expansion of the computer operation was the prudent course.[26]

Halsbury believed that much of Ferranti's conservatism was due to a longer than average company memory, not surprising given its family nature:

> A contributory factor towards this state of affairs may be that his [Sir Vincent's] father pretty well broke the firm through indebtedness to the banks in the early days, and Sir Vincent's one determination is never again to get into a mess. As his outlook is dominated by the twin factors of a desire for complete independence and a super-cautious attitude to risk taking, he has avoided the worst forms of hubris and the firm is merely overdrawn £4 million.
>
> (Halsbury, 15/2/57)[27]

Given this conservatism, Sir Vincent was against Ferranti bearing the risk of assuming the role of a computer manufacturer. Sir Vincent would make this abundantly clear to the NRDC in a meeting in 1954. Halsbury noted:

> If Sir Vincent were looking for a new enterprise to invest Ferranti money in, he would not himself pick computers. He has, however, no objection to a Government agency picking computers for him provided that he is fully compensated for the use of Ferranti facilities. He expects 100% compensation in the first instance and the right to be the sole ultimately interested party in whatever comes of the project.
>
> (Halsbury, 23/3/54)[28]

Sir Vincent offered a graphical representation of how he expected costs and profit to develop as the Computer Department matured. He only expected profits after an initially large outlay of money for R&D. If the government was willing to pay for him to reach the breakeven point (E in figure 5.2) he was willing to build computers, otherwise not.

Vincent proposed that whoever sponsored what was to become the Computer Department they would receive all the profit up to time F, with area D providing repayment and some profit. From this point the whole operation would be Ferranti's responsibility. He described this as the 'launching' point for the new department.

This plan was outlined during negotiations over the Mark II Mercury computer, the Mark 1* successor (see below). It is worth noting that even when Sir Vincent decided that Ferranti should develop the Mercury without NRDC support, it was made clear that this decision was made with considerable unease. One of Ferranti's staff put Vincent's agreement to this in terms of his own sky rocket analogy:

> Sir Vincent has accepted our view that you [the NRDC] have in fact launched us and that we can now fly. He did not come round to this without a lot of heart-searching ... We on our side are under the suspicion

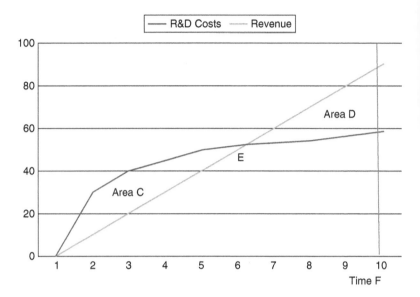

*Figure 5.2*   Vincent de Ferranti's plan for subsidising the Ferranti Computer Department
*Source*: NAHC. NRDC 86/29/7: Halsbury, 23/3/54. 'Note on meeting with Ferranti Ltd'. Reproduced by courtesy of the University Librarian and Director, The John Rylands Library, The University of Manchester

of wanting to run the computer business at no profit or a loss by subsidising it out of the rest of the Ferranti enterprises.

(Halsbury quoting Ferranti staff member)[29]

Many of the weaknesses of the Ferranti Computer Department were sown early, discord would be rife, a situation which may not have been helped by the lack of commitment from the senior management. They viewed the operation, at least in the early stages as a series of one-off contracts with government acting as buyer – this mind state barely shifted.

### Part 2: Structured entry

As with other firms which launched into the computer industry, Ferranti would go from an experimental phase, where one-off developments in an interested department (in this case the Instruments Department) would be built upon in a more formal attempt to master the computer market.

This second phase of the Ferranti story has three main elements:

- the establishment of a formal Computer Department created to build a strategy for the sector;
- the development of a system aimed at a wider market – the Ferranti Packaged Computer 1 or the Pegasus;

- the development of a large scale system to follow up on the Mark 1* –
a computer that would be known as the Mercury.

Even before any of these plans for the two new systems were completed, things were already going wrong, with division growing within the Computer Department, in part caused by the introduction of new resources sponsored by the NRDC.

### Restructuring – the creation the Computer Department

Halsbury was concerned that the building of computers was a marginal activity for the company.[30] He suggested that Ferranti's managerial commitment drew unfavourable comparison to the situation at IBM, where computers were receiving the highest attention.

Sir Vincent stated that he believed his top team in the Instruments Department, Grundy, Toothill and Carter, were quite capable of running wholly independent companies and were, therefore, capable of running a single department. However, Halsbury pointed out that these three men were all involved in the running of the whole of the instruments operation. In fact, the first people who were solely involved in computers were Bowden and Swann in sales and marketing and Brian Pollard in design and manufacturing. They did not report to a single person with complete responsibility for computers, but to Grundy who had multiple operations to run.

In a July 1953 visit to the company, Halsbury learnt of a major shake-up in the organisation.[31] The shake-up had been precipitated by a revolt by Pollard who headed design and manufacturing for computers. He was apparently tired of 'government by committee' and had demanded a better structure. To force this through he handed in his notice. The company responded by restructuring the computer operation into a full department: it was given the same organisation and status as the other departments in the company and Pollard was persuaded to stay.

Pollard became the overall manager (Young 1958a), though Grundy of the Instruments Department remained the senior director in charge. At the time this satisfied Halsbury – not only were the NRDC buying most of the Ferranti output, but they were doing so in the hope that the business developed could be self-sustaining. However, it soon became clear that there were huge rifts within the department, which eventually proved costly for the NRDC. These rifts were caused, in part, by the NRDC which sponsored the development of a second computer team at Ferranti, a team based in London and which developed the Pegasus computer, while the Manchester team would develop the large scale Mercury as a replacement for the Mark1* and using Ferranti investment resources.

### Pegasus

As early as 1952 some NRDC board members were enthusiastic to see Ferranti working on a smaller and cheaper system, which they hoped would find a larger user base than the complex Mark l*.[32] NRDC advisor Professor Blackett suggested that such a computer would be useful both to smaller scientific users and in some commercial roles, especially in PAYE calculations. At this meeting the NRDC's Hennessey noted that two smaller systems were already being developed in the UK. However, neither of these developments were primarily aimed at commercial work.

First, there was the English Electric version of the National Physical Laboratories Pilot ACE machine aimed at smaller scale scientific calculations. The NRDC had little knowledge of the Pilot Ace project, and was not particularly interested in a machine geared to scientific research. The second system was being supported by the NRDC. It was a design project within the military and instruments firm, Elliott Brothers.

The relationship between the NRDC and Elliott Brothers was not a great success, at least on the part of the NRDC, though it did benefit Ferranti. Two NRDC representatives, John Crawley and Dennis Hennessey, visited Elliott Brothers in 1950 to look at its computer developments. They saw a computer system which had been developed for a Royal Navy fire control system.[33] The NRDC was impressed by the packaging of the machine, which used interchangeable printed circuit boards, greatly easing the maintenance problem associated with earlier machines (for more on history of Elliott Brothers/ Elliott Automation in the computer industry see: Lavington S. 2011).

The NRDC team were also impressed by the computer development group at Elliott's, especially its head, W. S. Elliott, who was an ex-employee of the Ministry of Supply and an important figure in wartime radar developments. Finally, the Managing Director of Elliott Brothers, Sir Leon Bagrit, had plans that appealed to Lord Halsbury. Bagrit talked about building a small machine at a cost of £20–25000, for sale in the vast US market.[34] Bagrit would later develop a plan to link up with the small French accounting machine firm, Logabax, in which Bagrit had a holding.[35] Such an arrangement would give Elliott access to the business machines market and was thinking clearly aligned to Halbury's own wishes.

The NRDC provided sponsorship to Elliott Brothers to exploit the patents and technologies developed for the Royal Navy. This led to the prototype 401 computer completed in 1953,[36] which was eventually installed at Cambridge University.[37] Cambridge was given use of the machine in return for fine-tuning it. However, they discovered that it was a flawed system that needed a good deal of work done on it to make it a useful system.[38]

In the meantime, the main members of Elliott's computer team, including W.S. Elliott and H.G. Carpenter, decided to leave Elliott Brothers. To overcome the problems with the 401 the NRDC employed the ex-Elliott team to work with the university. W.S. Elliott then left NRDC employment and started work at Ferranti.[39] Despite the issues with the 401 Elliot W.S. was well regarded.

Grundy, of the Ferranti Instrument's Department, had already put in a bid to replace Elliott Brothers as the main contractor for the 401 project.[40]

Initially, the NRDC could see no reason for this change of allegiance. Two months later, the NRDC and Ferranti were actively negotiating around this proposal.[41] The concept of the 401 was interesting because it would give Ferranti a way of developing a smaller and more reliable system than the Mark 1*. The NRDC agreed, telling Ferranti that it did not want a 'Chinese copy of the 401', but a machine based on the design's strong points.

*Developing and building the Pegasus – internal competition*

The sales team at Ferranti were excited about having a smaller more reliable system to sell. Swann, of the Ferranti sales team, wrote to the NRDC stating the belief that there would be strong demand for such a system.[42] He noted that the initial markets would be industries that required advanced scientific calculations, and, of these, the aerospace industry was the largest. It was planned to later add magnetic tape drives to the system, which would make the machine suitable for more input-output intensive tasks, associated with commercial and administrative duties. He concluded that commercial applications would prove to be a much larger market. The computer was expected to sell for £16,000–22,000, putting it within reach of large scale commercial users.

In early 1954, Halsbury (2/2/54) wrote to Ferranti ordering 10 Ferranti Packaged Computer 1 computers (later Pegasus), in a similar arrangement to the Mark 1* contract.[43]

The Corporation expected the purchase of ten machines to cost £220,000. Of this total, the development costs were to amount to £70,000, to be recovered at a rate of £7000 on each machine. Like the Mark 1* the contract was cost plus; Ferranti was to receive a fixed percentage profit for producing the machines and then a commission for selling them. For the NRDC this would prove a major error.

The Pegasus would use standardised electronics 'packages' which improved reliability and maintenance, an idea borrowed from the Elliott 401. It would use a nickel delay line for high speed memory, instead of the older Williams Tube and also used a secondary memory source a slower but larger drum memory (a spinning drum mechanism similar but hugely less efficient than the modern disk drive). This hardware architecture was becoming the standard set-up for later first-generation machines.

Pegasus was designed by W.S. Elliott in a new centre in Portland Place, London. It consisted of the London Computer Laboratory, a number of personnel from a new Computing Research Group plus the Computer Sales Department (Young 1958b). However, production of the Pegasus was to be at the Moston plant in Manchester, under the control of Pollard. Simultaneously, the Moston operation was developing a new scientific computer, the Mercury. The London centre marketed all the computers made by Ferranti.

This arrangement created much infighting, with the Moston and London operations in competition for supremacy. Grundy hired W.S. Elliott to design the new smaller system. According to both Swann and Halsbury's,[44]

Elliott had once turned Pollard (the head of manufacturing for Ferranti Computers) down for a job. Pollard was not pleased that Grundy had hired Elliott, nor that he was being given his own operation in London, although Pollard would be Elliott's superior.

Swann seems to have sided with W.S. Elliott in future conflicts, and his recollections tend to support the views held by the London half of the Computer Department. He thought the Pegasus was the more saleable machine compared to the scientific orientated and larger Mercury developed in Manchester. He believed that competition between Elliott and Pollard led to empire building. Elliott wanted to build the first two or three Pegasus computers in London: it was argued that building the first machines near the development team would be beneficial. Once all the problems had been ironed out, full production could be moved to Moston. Swann, claims that Pollard instead decided to rush into the production of Pegasus, in order to secure the pre-eminent position in the project.[45] Swann believed that this was one of a number of ways in which Pollard tried to frustrate the London operation. The outcome was huge cost over-runs and delays in deliveries, caused by going into production too quickly.

*Pegasus crisis – the NRDC view*

Pegasus was meant to be the great success – a medium-sized system at an attractive price able to penetrate the engineering and the commercial markets. As the project ran into multiple problems, the NRDC view of what was going wrong contrasted to the view of Swann. The NRDC apportioned blame more widely, but less on Pollard and the team in Manchester, proven builders of computers, and more on Elliott and the London team. It would also level blame at the Sales Department and Ferranti's Costing Department.

One of the consequences of the conflicts between manufacturing and the London team was the failure of the London departments to keep Pollard informed that the cost of the Pegasus was getting out of hand; this was critical because the Pegasus was meant to be a relatively low-cost system. The Cost Department likewise failed to inform Pollard and the Manchester management.

The cost calculations used for planning the project, were based on direct manufacturing labour and materials costing 20 per cent of the total production costs, overheads were to be 60 per cent, plus a 20 per cent margin.[46]

In addition to the costs of making the systems, a key factor was the expected £70,000 development costs which were to be spread across the ten systems ordered by the NRDC. This seemed a reasonable estimate at development costs as the machine was partly based on the 401 which had cost £60,000 for the design and prototype.

By 1954, the NRDC estimated that overheads had risen to 900 per cent of direct costs because of development overspend.[47] By autumn 1956, the NRDC had bills amounting to £444,500 with the likelihood of the total being over

£500,000. Manchester did not know that costs were already out of control even before the contract with the NRDC had been signed. Indeed, the NRDC noted that Pollard originally considered a fixed price contract with the NRDC not a cost plus contract, clearly unaware of the issues of cost over-run.

The NRDC believed that some of the blame came from the splitting of responsibilities, and the geographical separation of design and manufacture. This was compounded by the decision to go straight into production without a prototype. This was similar to the views of Swann in 1975, who argued that prototypes should have been produced in London. The lack of prototypes led to long delays in delivery, and continued modification of machines as they were being produced. Further problems were created because of arguments about who should design the drum memory. London and Manchester squabbled about this endlessly, but ended up with neither the Moston nor the London operations having a drum ready to incorporate into the system when it was finished, leading to further delay and cost.[48]

However, in the eyes of the NRDC, it was the London centre where costs were running riot. In February 1956, Pollard assured the NRDC that he had £9000 currently in the development account.[49] The truth was that he was already well over budget and later had to apologise to the NRDC for his misleading optimism on the funds he still had, telling them that he had been misinformed by the accounts department.

One problem was that the Portland Place operation had decided to set up an extremely expensive sales promotion centre, and to generally increase its sales activities. This was on top of the increasingly over-spent design operation. They were not keeping any account of work in progress in London, and rather than route bills via Moston they sent them directly to the NRDC, as Moston were doing on their own behalf for the elements they were working on. The NRDC seem to have agreed that Pollard was, in fact, not being given the full picture. Eventually the design cost of the machine was £170,000 and all other costs had also rocketed.

The London operation in Portland Place continued to sell machines at the original asking price of £35,000, despite costs having doubled. Ferranti stuck to this price to the bitter end and the NRDC was left with a massive loss on the machines it had bought for resale. What they had thought was a commitment of £220,000 became close to half a million with only a proportion recovered through sales.

Eventually, after a good deal of arm-twisting by Halsbury and the new NRDC chairman W.R. Black, the company agreed to pay back £75,000, but not until early 1958. The Corporation eventually suffered a loss of £140,145.[50]

*Pegasus second wind – nearly a success*

Ferranti nearly benefited greatly from the NRDC's misfortune. The NRDC systems absorbed much of the costs and the production difficulties were resolved building these early systems. Later machines were therefore expected to be cheaper.[51] Given this fortunate situation the Computer Department continued selling the system. The company installed 26 Pegasus 1s between 1956 and 1960, and 12 updated Pegasus 2s between 1959 and 1962.[52] The only cost to Ferranti of developing the systems and building a larger sales department would be the £75,000 settlement it later made with the NRDC, a fairly small development cost.

During the life of the Pegasus it was becoming obvious that computers were going to be increasingly used in commercial environments. Potential applications included: calculating payroll, preparing accounts, and calculating statistical data. According to Swann,[53] Ferranti had a different attitude to this market compared to the business machine firms. Ferranti was interested in doing calculations that, in the past, had been too large to tackle. Business machines companies wanted the computer to improve efficiency. The tabulating machines firms had experience of selling machines in this commercial market and recognised the needs of these customers.

To sell to commercial users, better peripherals were needed; British Tabulating Machine punched cards were the most common data storage medium in the UK, because BTM used IBM standard cards. Just as important, the selling of small machines to the commercial market needed a national sales force, and a large service organisation. This would be very expensive to build up:

> selling of small computers would [require] many customers to get a reasonable turnover and these would be widely scattered. This would mean a large sales and service organisation, which we were sure the Chairman would not agree to
>
> (Swann 1975)[54]

Ferranti had no national sales network: all selling was done at its London office. While this was adequate for selling to engineers (advanced users were more willing to travel to find the best equipment), it was not a good enough method for selling to commercial users. The business machines firms had these networks and had built up close relationships with commercial users using their punched card systems.

Encouraged by the NRDC, Ferranti began talking to BTM regarding joint sales of the Pegasus system. However BTM wanted the sole right to market any machines to come out of a joint venture; all that would eventually be achieved from these discussions was an agreement allowing the connection of BTM systems as input and output devices for the Pegasus.

However, Swann believed Pollard favoured a link up with BTM's rival Powers-Samas, the number two in the UK market. Discussions with Powers-Samas started after BTM negotiations came to nothing. As far back as July 1952 the two firms had discussed jointly designing a small commercial computer and Power-Samas selling Ferranti computers in the commercial market, but little practical output came from these discussions.

In March 1954, the sales staff of the two companies presented a joint paper, proposing close collaboration leading to an 'integrated data processing system'.[55] Despite these talks, the first 10 Pegasus were going to use BTM, rather than Powers, punched card peripherals. The reason for this was straightforward; The IBM/BTM standard punched card was the one usually used by engineering customers as well as commercial customers. This was because they used an electronic device to read the cards rather than the pin mechanism used by Powers, based on the rival Remington Rand standard cards. Additionally, the IBM/BTM machines also had a plug board 'reprogramming' system, which made them more flexible, especially useful in scientific calculations where parameters change frequently.

Nevertheless, it was hoped that Ferranti and Powers could work together and the Pluto was developed as a version of the Pegasus using the Powers punched cards and which Powers-Samas was to sell. The effective outcome was that Ferranti was selling the Pegasus to technical users primarily with BTM peripherals, while the Powers were meant to sell Pluto to commercial customers.

However, things were very different on the ground. In reality, Powers staff were not actively selling Pluto. By 1955, Powers was selling its own much smaller PCC calculating device, which, while not a fully functional computer, got preferential treatment from the Powers staff as it was seen as more appropriate for the type of customers Powers had. A further problem was that Ferranti would only offer a 15 per cent discount on the price of the machines it sold to Powers; Powers wanted 25 per cent. This further discouraged Powers from actively selling the system.

By the time BTM and Power-Samas merged to form ICT in 1959, Powers had not created a single order for Ferranti. All the arrangement achieved was to reduce the market to which Ferranti could actively sell its systems. The Pegasus sold well enough to technical users, and many of these machines were used in a secondary administration role, proving that it could well have sold in the commercial market - very much the market that Swann and the other sales staff in London wished to see the Pegasus aimed at.

In the early 1960s, Ferranti produced the updated Pegasus 2. Free from the Powers arrangement, many were sold into the commercial market. But by this stage it was too late; this first-generation computer was outdated. Figures 5.3 and 5.4 show a breakdown of the users of Pegasus computers.

### Perseus

In addition to the Pegasus, Ferranti produced another purely 'commercial' rather than scientific system, the Perseus. This was designed specifically for the insurance industry – a sector which was a big user of punched card systems and a likely early adopter of computers for information processing and storage. The scheme to target this sector was devised by the first Ferranti sales manager, Bowden, after he had visited the US to study advances in

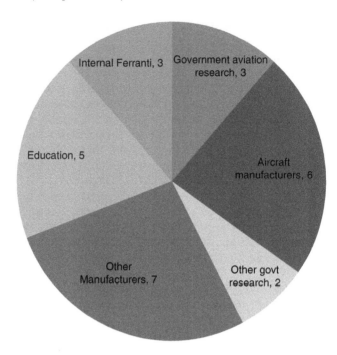

*Figure 5.3*   Ferranti Pegasus 1 sales
*Source*: Data from NAHC Swann 1975. Reproduced by courtesy of the University Librarian and Director, The John Rylands Library, The University of Manchester.

commercial computing. After this trip he had discussed user needs with the Royal Insurance Company.[56] The project consisted of a small number of Ferranti engineers and an actuary from Royal Insurance. Unfortunately for this project, it too became a victim of the agreement with Powers.

Perseus was a large machine constructed out of the same packages that made up the Pegasus. However, its development was held up for a number of years because there was some concern that it overlapped with Powers' interests too much. Powers was the leading supplier of punched card equipment to the insurance industry, and it was concerned that Perseus could damage this market. Perseus used magnetic tape memory and Powers punched cards. Magnetic tapes were particularly useful to the insurance companies as they had huge databases to access. While one would have expected Powers to have grabbed the opportunity to partner in this development to exploit its position in the insurance sector, it instead feared magnetic tapes because they would replace its traditional electro-mechanical punched card systems.

Eventually two machines were built, this time at Ferranti's Bracknell facility, which became the home to the London operations of the Computer Department; a facility which was modern, larger and capable of production work. The first was produced for South African Mutual Life, and the second

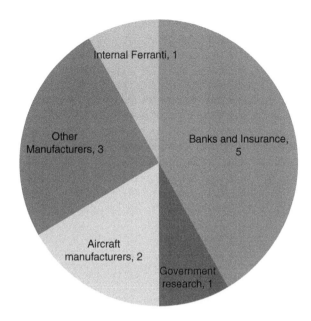

*Figure 5.4*   Ferranti Pegasus 2 sales
*Source*: Data from NAHC Swann 1975. Reproduced by courtesy of the University Librarian and Director, The John Rylands Library, The University of Manchester.

for a Swedish insurance company. Both were completed in the second half of 1959, far too late for a first-generation machine to become popular.

### The Manchester development – the Mark II/Mercury

With the sales department pursuing the future of the Pegasus, the Moston operation was busying itself with the larger Mercury computer. The Mercury was based on another computer developed at Manchester University, the 'Meg' developed by Tom Kilburn (Lavington 1975: 25). It was a machine designed for the same environment as the Mark 1 – a fast computer for scientific calculation.

Kilburn had the basic machine working from October 1952 and in its final floating point version by May 1954[57] – floating point arithmetic eases the programming task for mathematical calculations. In the Meg it was a hardware feature, whereas previously it had to be done slowly with software.

The first production machine was not installed until August 1957. Again blame for the slow time to market was placed on the lengthy negotiations taking place between the NRDC, the Department of Scientific and Industrial Research (DSIR) and Ferranti on the future of the system.

Swann states that Ferranti requested a sum of £25,000 from the DSIR to develop a saleable version of Meg.[58] However, minutes of a meeting held in

1954 show that, in fact, Ferranti had requested £400,000 from the DSIR to fund general computer developments.[59] This was part of Sir Vincent's aim to 'launch' the Ferranti Computer Department through initial state support (see his diagram – Figure 5.4 on page 147). The DSIR turned this plan down on the advice of the Brunt Committee, which did not see industrial support as a DSIR responsibility. On the other hand, Halsbury was interested in supporting the floating point technology. However, to make another cash advance of this nature the NRDC needed certain concessions. They wanted the investment to be recovered over ten years as a flat rate levy on all Ferranti's computer and computer sub-system sales.[60] Second, it wanted the right to vet any sub-contracts that Ferranti wanted to make.

Predictably, such long-term arrangements were onerous to the company. However, this was not the only reason the company rejected the scheme. Pollard argued that the system would be comparatively cheap to produce, having been partially developed by the University and that it would be a profitable offering. Sir Vincent was persuaded to produce the system with company resources. This was a significant moment for Ferranti, for the first time it was making computers not as one off capital electronics contracts, but as a self-sustaining product line.

*Selling the Mercury*

Not surprisingly Swann, as Manager of Sales, did not share Pollard's view of the machine:

> After a meeting in the office of [the] NRDC I wrote that I could not see sales of more than four of the projected big computers.[61]

In fact, 19 were installed between 1957 and 1961. Swann dismisses most of these sales as chance:

> Some years later one of my programmers, John Davidson, told me he had come across this memorandum [see above]; we had by then sold about a dozen Mercury. I said it only showed how difficult market prophecies could be, but John said that apart from the sales to nuclear establishments we had, in fact, sold four.[62]

Swann believed that there was an anti-sales atmosphere in Manchester, with the engineers more interested in the finesse of their technology. They liked the powerful, academically inspired Mercury, but did not like the popular, Elliott-designed, Pegasus. Equally it appears that there was little enthusiasm in London for selling the big machines, which sold at an average price of £120,000 (Hendy 1989:183 at 1963 prices).

Nevertheless, the Mercury was a larger seller than the sales department predicted. If the Pegasus had become the workhorse of the British aerospace industry, then the Mercury did the same for the atomic research establishments, not just in the UK but across Europe. This is not surprising; it was described by Datamation (Nov/Dec 1958:17) as the first computer outside of the USA designed especially for large scale scientific work.[63] Of the 19 sold, 10 were used for atomic energy and power research, 6 of these abroad, 5 in Europe and 1 in Brazil.

This period was the peak of Ferranti's computer operations. The Pegasus was selling well for medium scale technical applications and the Mercury was a standard system for nuclear calculations.

However, there were problems. Ferranti failed to secure any orders in the US, by far the largest market of scientific computers. In some respects this is not surprising. There were a number of US firms supplying such systems, including IBM. There was also a strong tendency for buyers of such machines to look for domestic supply. Breaking into the US market was further undermined by IBM's policy of offering large discounts to scientific users, especially universities. IBM offered discounts of up to 60 per cent to educational buyers, and a lesser amount to some other purchasers, encouraged by US tax policy allowing write-offs against such subsidies. IBM was enthusiastic to tie up this market, so future users would be trained on IBM systems. Ferranti found it completely impossible to compete on these terms in the US.

The final factor preventing Ferranti from selling systems in the US was the need to establish comprehensive sales and service facilities throughout the US. It has already been seen that the company was averse to such risks.

## Part 3: Consolidation phase

It may be a slight exaggeration to say Ferranti reached the consolidation phase – the phase where a structure family of computers was developed to build on the success of the entry into the computer sector – however, because of its early start in computing it did manage to create a number of what were third-generation computers in terms of its own output (clearly the technology was second generation).

By the end of the first generation of computers, Ferranti had the most successful range of computers in Europe and had, despite its infighting, a working Computer Department. By 1957, the Pegasus and Mercury systems were being delivered to customers. However, the sales department was concerned that at the Computer Exhibition of November 1958, Ferranti would have no new system to talk about.[64] It was clear that the company needed to start work on solid state computers; firms such as EMI were already advanced in their development of solid state computers.

A second factor taxing the mind of the company was that commercial and scientific computing systems were beginning to merge into common ranges. In the first generation of computers, it was assumed that scientific machines needed a fast processor, but that peripherals were less important.

In commercial data processing, input-output peripherals were given high priority. However, change was occurring. New scientific applications, such as statistical analysis and meteorology, also required high speed input-output. On the commercial side, the introduction of random access disk drives meant that commercial systems would benefit from faster central processor units.

The company needed a second generation solid state system – this became known as the Orion, aimed at fulfilling the needs of both the scientific and the commercial markets.

Orion was based on a logical unit contained on a standardised circuit board. These boards made use of transistors, magnetic amplifiers (similar to magnetic cores) and transformers; it was called the Neuron circuit.[65] The concept for this type of circuit started in 1953. By 1955, Ferranti's Manchester operation (which in 1956 moved to specialist plant in West Gorton) had started Neuron circuit development[66] and by May 1958, the NEWT test-bed machine was completed. While a non-standard design – Ferranti had a launch pad into second generation solid state computing.

However, the sales team in London and the West Gorton design and manufacturing operation once again started arguing about the direction the company should go. The Neuron circuit was designed at a time when the cost of transistors was very high. The Neuron design was aimed at minimising the number of transistors used. This was done at the expense of making timing extremely critical, requiring the circuits to achieve very tight tolerances because the magnetic amplifiers had to work in conjunction with the transistors to work as logic units. Pegasus engineers told Swann that the older Pegasus circuit packages had a good margin of safety built in to them. Orion did not: the Neuron circuit was highly reliant on near perfect operation.[67] The sales operation argued that the transistor would improve due to better engineering and larger production runs and thus prices would dramatically fall – if this did not happen the transistor would hardly be worth using, especially for commercial applications, as it would be too expensive.

While the NEWT allayed some of the fears that the system would not work at all, there was also some concern as to the suitability of the machine for the market. Pollard was thinking in terms of an expandable machine. It was expected to start at £120,000 and be configured into a system costing hundreds of thousands. It fulfilled the need for a machine that could be sold for commercial data processing: it had very advanced input-output handling routines, as will be discussed later. However, it was only 3-4 times faster than the Mercury, which was less than the ten-fold increase that the sales department would have liked.

The sales department argued that a transistorised Pegasus would be a better strategy, enabling current customers to migrate to better technology with their investments in software protected. Nevertheless, the Orion was advanced and more suitable for commercial use than the Pegasus had been because of its advanced input-output capabilities. Pollard argued that a transistorised Pegasus would have been too expensive to produce while a large Orion configuration was an ideal replacement for the Mercury.

The first saleable machine to come out of the Neuron work was, however, not the Orion, but the small scale Sirius computer, based on the original NEWT.[68] This was a stripped-down system, designed for the very small systems end of the engineering market.

It was easy to program, small, had a fast paper-tape input-output device and offered some punched card peripherals.[69] One extra feature was a simple digital display which showed a representation of the program as it ran; associated with it was a keyboard for direct input, an excellent configuration for educational institutions. The Elliott Automation (née Brothers) 803 was already widely used in British Universities, as it was a small, simple system costing just £29000 in 1960 – over 200 of the series would be sold. Between 1960 and 1963, 16 Sirius computers were installed. Of these, 4 were used for Ferranti's own computer service, while 8 went to manufacturing companies, 2 were used for teaching at universities, 1 was used by the Admiralty and another was exported to Czechoslovakia for unspecified uses (a handful more may have been sold after 1963). However, according to Swann,[70] most of these systems ended up being sold on to colleges for teaching use.

Much more important for Ferranti was the Orion, which was the second generation replacement for its established lines. Ferranti provided a number of features on the Orion which were very advanced. To increase throughput of data, the Orion adopted a technique referred to by the company as time-sharing, though it was of a more limited nature than the later concept of time-shared computers more akin to modern multitasking.[71] The design team realised that there was a lot of wasted time when using a computer. For example, even the fastest contemporary paper tape system could only input 1000 characters per second. The machine was running much faster than this, so it was always waiting for input and output devices to catch up. Therefore, they gave the Orion the ability to perform a number of tasks simultaneously using one of the first comprehensive control programs [operating system], the Orion Monitor Program (OMP). The Orion could control a number of peripherals simultaneously and could handle a number of programs at the same time. Therefore, if the machine was working on a large and time-consuming problem using data from the magnetic tape drive, it could input smaller programs and data from the other devices and process the smaller program during the input-output cycles of the large job. This better utilised the expensive peripherals, and increased throughput.

The second great advantage offered by the Orion was the Nebula high level programming language. This meant the machine could be programed using plain English, which was then translated into machine code, like the computer languages used today.

However, problems with the strict tolerances required by the Neuron circuits soon grew. The problem was caused by the increased size of the Orion over the simpler Sirius. Engineers found that the wave form of an electrical pulse at one end of a wire was different at the other end: this was known as the Ferranti Effect after its discoverers.[72] This difficulty was less obvious in the smaller NEWT and Sirius.

Solving this problem had knock on consequences. It had been intended that the machine be expandable, allowing extra processing equipment to be added to handle more programs at once, and extra peripherals to increase input-output capacity. However, to overcome the timing problem each computer was constructed to meet the exact specification ordered, making future expansion of the machines very difficult. According to Swann, neither the management nor the sales staff were informed of this important change.

The Orion had also grown to be a larger system than originally intended and was by no means a Pegasus replacement. In 1963 prices, the average Orion sold for £300,000 (Hendry 1989: 183). 12 systems were installed. 2 were used for Ferranti's own computer service, and 2 were used by government research establishments; the other 8 were all used for commercial data processing in industry and commerce.

*Efforts to save the second generation strategy*

The Sirius was small and cheap; the Orion was mid-scale but had costly technical problems and was being severely delayed. The sales department therefore resurrected the transistorised Pegasus idea. A set of specifications was created by a study group led by Harry Johnson. However, on his return from holiday in 1961, Swann found that engineering manager, Peter Hall, had cancelled the idea in favour of the Orion 2 scheme.

The Orion 2 replaced the Neuron circuits with the Griblon or Gripple circuit named after the engineer who developed an alternative circuit, and re-launched the system as the Orion 2. It is uncertain how many of the machines sold used the Gripple. Swann only refers to one in his sales figures, the rest being the original Orion 1 design.[73]

However, Ferranti's Canadian organisation, Ferranti-Packard, took up the challenge to develop a mid-size system using more proven technologies, together with some techniques learnt from the Orion and the Gripple circuit. Ferranti-Packard, which had developed on-line ticketing systems based on a real-time computer design, created the FP 6000 (Vardalas 1994). This machine was developed as a medium-size computer for specialist on-line computer activities. When ICT took over Ferranti's Computer Department, this design was also included. It became the base of the ICT/L 1900 family of mainframes which were to be developed and sold from the mid-1960s competing against the IBM /360. Campbell-Kelly (1989: 121) claims that Johnson's specification led to the development of the FP 6000; Vardalas (1994), claims it was inspired by the Canadian business with little support from Ferranti – whatever the case, the FP 6000 proved much more successful than the Orion 2.

By the early 1960s, Ferranti had only two second generation machines on offer in the UK, the Sirius and the Orion; both used a dead-end technology and Ferranti had few resources available to rectify the situation. The Orion 2 was not selling; Ferranti had failed to deliver second generation computers that a burgeoning market wanted. Meanwhile, the FP 6000 in Canada was seen as a marginal niche system.

*Final effort – the ATLAS*

Orion and Sirius were built and developed to sell in numbers; while they failed, Ferranti was still the leading computer technology company in the UK and it had one other contemporaneous project on its books which preserved this preeminent position. Ferranti was working on a UK government contract for a super scale computer (Hendry, J. 1984 covers this project in-depth).

The ATLAS project started after a group of experts from Cambridge University, the United Kingdom Atomic Energy Authority Harwell laboratory and the National Physical Laboratories visited the US in the summer of 1956. Their report concentrated on the potential of the IBM STRETCH. This was a giant-scale computer being constructed to fulfil the mathematical needs of the largest US scientific laboratories.

IBM was backing this project with a team of 300 graduate-level staff, and was reported to be spending $28m a year on computer research.[74] This was probably an underestimate.

The French had already started to develop their own supercomputer project, in the form of the failed Bull 60 project. Supercomputers were becoming items of national pride in Europe, based on the assumption that it was strategically important to be able to produce the computers needed to carry out advanced nuclear calculations, especially as atmospheric testing was ending (a ban was being negotiated in the later 1950s and was finally signed in 1963) creating a need for more modelling and simulation. It was also thought that such a project was important in ensuring the technological competitiveness of any domestic computer industry, a view supported by the Royal Radar Establishment (RRE):

> RRE adhered to the opinion expressed by NRDC that it was broadly in the national interest to engage in a high-speed computer project and that the financing of such a project would have to be regarded as, in large part, support for the computer industry.
>
> (NRDC Crawley 30/8/57)[75]

Hendry (1984) describes the complicated negotiations that went on throughout the late 1950s to start such a programme.

The situation was confused by the different visions held by the NRDC and the United Kingdom Atomic Energy Authority, which were expected to be the largest customer for such machines. The UKAEA wished to be directly involved in the development of the computer they needed and to use the resources of the RRE in the design. The NRDC could make £1m available for a fast computer project[76] but wanted to set up a subsidiary department which would place orders for the overall system with outside contractors. It did not believe that such a development was within the abilities of a single firm: the NRDC would order the components from industry for final assembly by a lead contractor.

Eventually it was decided to create two initiatives. First, the NRDC was to commence a project to produce a supercomputer within a relatively short period.[77] This was to be based on a machine being developed by the Kilburn team at Manchester University, a system called MUSE. It was reckoned that such a machine would be two to three times slower than STRETCH, but still 50 times faster than the Ferranti Mercury.[78] The second project was to be a long-term development programme based at the RRE, which was to leap-frog current technology. Nothing would come of the latter idea.

Being a Manchester development, Ferranti had a growing interest in the MUSE project. The Orion was not going to be a credible replacement for the Mercury so Ferranti needed to do something to safeguard its place in the university and scientific market. The coincidence of Ferranti and NRDC interests in the MUSE project brought the two parties into negotiation yet again. However, there was some reluctance at the NRDC to commit itself to supporting Ferranti, given past problems (many partially caused by the NRDC). A second cause for reticence on the NRDC's part was its feeling that Ferranti was too small to carry out such a large project. It was the NRDC's original contention that the national fast computer project was so large that no single organisation could take it on.[79]

In 1959, the situation became easier when Harwell decided that they no longer wanted to diversify into computer design and the longer term RRE project was taken over by the DSIR. This cleared the decks for the NRDC. They decided to simplify the project and requested proposals from three companies. EMI and Ferranti bid for the development project, English Electric did not.

EMI had been working on a large commercial data processing system, the 2400, with the backing of the NRDC (see Chapter 6). EMI's bid proposed a development loan to be paid back based on a flat levy on all EMI's computer sales. Ferranti accepted that its bid had to comply with this structure – one it had rejected in the past. Halsbury believed the Ferranti change of heart about this form of contract was because it desperately needed a large contract to keep its Computer Department going.[80]

The NRDC Board Meeting of 22nd April 1959 had two potential projects to choose from.[81] The first was Ferranti's bid based on MUSE and was expected to cost £850,000 to develop and build. Ferranti were asking the NRDC to fund 60 per cent of this, a sum of £510,000.

EMI's bid was to produce a computer called the 3400, a scientific version of their large scale 2400 system. EMI expected this to cost £375,000 and was looking for 75 per cent of the costs from the NRDC.[82]

Halsbury and the Electronic Computer Sub-Committee recommended the EMI proposal. Though the 3400 was not expected to be as powerful as the ATLAS, it would be available quicker, and, up to this stage, it was thought that EMI had worked well with the NRDC.

However, the deputy managing director of the NRDC, Hennessey proposed that both projects be supported, but to a lesser degree than was being asked for. He won approval for this plan, allowing £240,000 for the 3400 and £300,000 for the ATLAS. The 3400 failed to materialise, indeed Hendry suggests that the 3400 project may have been a bargaining counter created by Halsbury to get a better deal from Ferranti.

*Building and selling ATLAS 1*

Neither making nor selling the ATLAS was to prove easy, though it was no less successful than some other supercomputer projects.

It was at about this time that Pollard, the Ferranti Computer Department manager, left Ferranti to join the American business machines company Burroughs. Just after he joined Burroughs, he wrote an article in the leading US computer industry journal *'Datamation'*, contrasting the UK and US industries (Pollard 1960).[83] This gives us some insight into the problems Ferranti had at this time, and the weaknesses it had when developing ATLAS.

He saw computers as being a sideline for companies in the UK: UK firms were more interested in other businesses. This was different in the US' business machines firms where the commitment to computers was wholehearted. Pollard noted that British firms, despite their lack of commitment to computing, nevertheless wanted to produce the whole systems; American firms, such as Burroughs, were much more willing to sub-contract to specialists. Finally, he noted a massive skills shortage. UK computer systems were often being developed by teams of as few as twelve; in the US, the R&D and engineering operations were an order of magnitude larger.[84]

Some of these weaknesses surfaced in the ATLAS. Despite the sheer scale of the project, most of the machine was constructed by Ferranti. Only a few, admittedly significant, sub-systems were bought in, such as communications sub-systems and magnetic core stores bought from Plessey and Mullard, and the magnetic tape units bought from Ampex.[85] The rest was Ferranti's.

The ATLAS was a very advanced machine. If STRETCH was about speed, which the machine finally failed to deliver, ATLAS was more about advanced computing techniques. Like the Orion, ATLAS allowed for the running of multiple programs, and could handle a large number of very fast input-output devices, making up for one of Mercury's shortcomings.[86] ATLAS also introduced the concept of virtual memory. This is a technique where active data can be transferred into a secondary store. The user does not know that this has occurred and the system acts as if it had an unlimited fast store. This is an essential capability of modern computers for delivering real-time multi-tasking operations.

These advanced features were the responsibility of 10 programmers writing the operating system, 15 programmers working on user languages, and a similar number of engineers working on the hardware.[87] STRETCH had a team of 300 developing it, and 200 programmers alone worked on the Bull 60.

The original MUSE project had been partly paid for from the small amount of money accruing to the Department of Electrical Engineering from Mark 1 and 1* sales (Lavington 1975:32). To build ATLAS, the NRDC provided just £300,000 while by mid-1960, Ferranti had spent £1m of its own money on the project (Hendry 1984). By comparison to the effort in other countries, this was all very modest. Nevertheless, it seems odd that Ferranti were willing to invest even this sum into a system which could only ever have low volume sales, and yet was parsimonious in its investment in mainstream systems.

It was just too much work for such a small group. Swann highlighted a four-year lag between the installation of the first computer hardware and the full availability of software to run it. Delays to the ATLAS became very long, leading to lost sales and increasing costs. While the company could install ATLAS hardware by 1963, a system capable of supporting end-users would not be available for some time after that, by which time third-generation computing was becoming available and increasing the speed of non-specialist systems.

Another, more immediate, problem was that Ferranti had a great deal of difficulty getting orders. In the early 1960s, ATLAS was the only 'giant-scale computer' available for commercial sale (Datamation, 4/1964: 19).[88] STRETCH had gone awry: it had cost much more than intended to develop and had not proved as fast as required. IBM had offered them for sale at $10m each, but this was at a huge loss, so it had withdrawn the machine from the market. Likewise the Bull 60 was a failure and that company was buckling under great financial strain and General Electric would take its opportunity to take greater control over the Bull operations.

Perversely the failure of other systems actually damaged Ferranti. Many potential ATLAS users, especially in the US, became sceptical that Ferranti could actually deliver.

Sebastian de Ferranti, Vincent's successor, became directly involved in the UK sales effort. For Ferranti, a lot of money was at risk, and yet by 1961 there were no firm orders. In 1960 the UKAEA had ordered an IBM STRETCH for the Atomic Weapons Research Establishment (AWRE), this was despite them initiating the whole fast computer project.

The AWRE opted for the STRETCH because it was slated for delivery earlier than ATLAS and was also expected to be faster. In addition, it could use software developed by nuclear scientists in America. However, as it became clear that STRETCH was not living up to expectations, the UKAEA realised it would need a separate giant computer for civil research as the STRETCH was not going to be fast enough to handle both workloads (Hendry, 1989 Chapter 10). Harwell, the UKAEA's civil establishment, was sympathetic to Ferranti's plight and the UKAEA bought a system in 1961 for delivery in 1964. Sebastian de Ferranti wanted a prestigious order like this to give other users faith in the system, but it was too late: by this time other developments were on the horizon and other potential users were willing to wait and see which system could actually do the job. By the time ATLAS was truly available, the CDC 6600 was near production in the US and this would become the most successful super computer of the age. It was designed by Seymour Cray who, it is claimed, used the academic papers on the ATLAS system to help design the 6600.

The largest single market for this type of computer was in the US. However, Ferranti did not sell any ATLAS machines in the US. Ferranti had identified potential sales opportunities in the US for 6–12 machines. Of these, the closest to a firm order was from Westinghouse, a company with large nuclear interests. However, each ATLAS would cost millions of pounds, and each contract would have had large penalty clauses for late installation. Ferranti decided that this was too great a risk to take. If it had taken half a dozen orders in the US, any hold-up in delivery would have led to large losses, sums larger than Ferranti was willing to lose on computers.

The ATLAS was a commercial failure: by 1963, the machine was already looking obsolete. In 1964, IBM announced its third-generation systems and CDC was winning the scientific market with the CDC 6600.

Like the Pegasus and Orion, ATLAS had a short second wind. The ATLAS 2 project started when Ferranti offered Professor Wilkes of Cambridge University some of the ATLAS sub-units. This was in exchange for Wilkes working on an updated and cheaper machine which Ferranti might be able to sell. By 1963, this work was well in hand.

However, by 1963 Ferranti was negotiating the sale of the Computer Department to ICT, and it seems that it talked up the prospects for the Atlas 2 to be in a stronger negotiating position. At this point, Ferranti benefited from the failure of STRETCH; the AWRE was concerned that it would be left with the only STRETCH in Europe, making it very expensive to get support. Ferranti offered to sell it a replacement, the ATLAS 2, at an extremely low price with severe penalty clauses, an offer that was accepted.

Once ICT had acquired the Ferranti Computer Department, it was left with an order, at an uneconomic price, for a one-off machine. The ATLAS 2 was delivered in 1966, 14 months late.

Overall, the ATLAS was an expensive failure, and Ferranti was no longer interested in this risky and expensive market. Only 3 Atlas 1s were sold, and one of these, the one sold to Manchester University, was far from a commercial sale, while only 1 Atlas 2 was built.

### Ferranti's other electronics businesses

Ferranti's Computer Department cannot be viewed in isolation – the firm had many other areas of interest in digital electronics, all of which required resources. At heart it concentrated on business for which it had a known order before it produced a product, and often concentrated on markets where the contract was cost plus – the buyer paid for development.

In capital electronics it maintained a successful range of military-based computer used for both military and industrial control systems. The Bloodhound anti-aircraft missile was vital in this development. Ferranti was responsible for the electronic systems of the missile. Bristol Siddeley produced the engines and the Bristol Aircraft Company made the fuselage. The whole system was controlled by a Ferranti digital computer, the Argus, developed under the contract.

By 1961, Ferranti had started to install this computer for industrial control purposes. By 1979, 1263 Argus systems and derivatives had been delivered, excluding the many embedded into weapon systems such as Bloodhound (though including stand-alone military computer installations). It is one of the few areas in which Ferranti seemed to develop and maintain a strong sales and service operation in a commercial electronics sector.

Bloodhound also provided cash. In fact, it provided too much cash. Originally the development contract for the system was to be £1m-1.5m. It turned out to be £32m, of which £8m was for the Ferranti control system.[89] The production contract for the missile was worth £44.5m. Of this £13.5m was a fixed price contract for Ferranti's contribution. However, it seems that Ferranti managed to produce the system at a much lower cost. The House of Commons established a committee to examine allegations of excess profit. The outcome of this was the Lang Report which estimated that Ferranti made a profit of £5.77m from Bloodhound, an 82 per cent margin on costs. Eventually the firm was forced to pay back £4.25m.[90]

Ferranti also had a spin-off computer operation from its Bracknell department. This concentrated on very complex command and control systems for navies based on its F1600 range of computers.

As well as making digital electronics for commercial scientific, military and industrial customers, the other key development was electronic components. The company seems to have displayed a similar attitude to this business as it did to its computer ventures, abandoning harsh commercial markets for a more specialised approach.

In 1953, the Valve Department set up a team of three researchers to work on semiconductors. The wise decision was made to investigate the use of silicon devices, rather than the more expensive germanium devices, which were more common in the early stages of solid state electronics. Ferranti produce a number of advanced devices, mostly for the military. In 1962, it became the first developer of commercial integrated circuits outside of the US (Sciberras, 1977:175). Initially, it developed its own architecture using

Diode-Transistor Logic. Its first devices were multi-chip packages called Microlin. It then developed the Micronor chip and the Micronor II, the latter being developed from RCA technology. The last two families of chips were licensed to Marconi, which used them in the military Myriad and Priam computers and in the English Electric System 4 computers – as we will see, this was a commercial disaster for the UK computer industry

Integrated Circuits have to be made available in large compatible families so that they can be used for all possible purposes. Ferranti did not have the financial resources to develop a broad enough range of Micronor chips (Golding, A., 1971). This meant that the Micronor failed to become widely used. A major blow was the failure of ICT to adopt Ferranti chips in the 1900 series, despite a large Ferranti representation on the ICT board after it had taken over the Computer Department.

Ferranti switched from its own designs to producing standard Transistor-Transistor Logic (TTL) devices; Texas Instruments had made this the standard technology worldwide. ICT/L bought large quantities of TTL chips from Ferranti, which cushioned the blow from the commercial failure of the Micronor-based English Electric System 4.

Initially, Texas Instruments was simply too busy supplying the burgeoning US market to compete for orders in the UK (Malerba 1985: 116). However, during the 1970s 'TTL Wars', Texas Instruments slashed prices in an effort to increase volume on these commodity devices. Ferranti, not willing to do the same, became marginalised in the market.

The firm retrenched into specialised, high value devices. This culminated in Ferranti leading the world in the production of semi-custom devices (ASIC devices), where it could produce special devices to order, but avoid the cost of the mass market.

Ferranti sold this successful technologically advanced business to Plessey in the late 1980s, to partially pay for the disastrous acquisition of the US defence business, International Signal. However, by this stage the whole of the UK semiconductor was marginalised to the point of disappearance.

## Leaving the commercial computer market

Ferranti was not at heart a player in any market for which it did not have a known customer order. The firm would concentrate on capital electronics projects based on fairly short production runs and develop new technologies on a rapid basis. However, when these new technology markets became large, it was not willing to build on its early starts and develop a leadership position. Government were happy to fund development of new electronics techniques which its military needed, but Ferranti was not able to convert many of these businesses into functioning commercial businesses able to achieve the minimum economic scale required. Ferranti was technologically advanced, but business conservative. If a market became too competitive the company would abandon it. Given this pattern, it is not surprising that the Computer Department was offloaded. The company did not dispose of activities unless there was an underlying economic reason to do so – however, in the case of the Computer Department, it is clear that these reasons existed.

The Computer Department's ability to compete was hampered by the limited resources of Ferranti. The company was essentially family owned, was unwilling to make long-term cooperative arrangements, was worried about past indebtedness, and yet it still had a policy of continued high technology expansion. Such a combination was always going to make cash flow a problem. Further, Vincent de Ferranti doubted the ability of the firm to sell in commercial markets.

By 1963, Ferranti was perceived as having the most advanced computer team in Europe, yet it had no product that was truly successful. The Sirius and Orion had not matched the sales of Mercury and Pegasus despite the total market having grown ten-fold. The ATLAS machine had been marginalised. Engineers who could have worked on successor machines had been pinned down sorting out problems on the old systems. All this was at a time when it was becoming obvious that IBM would be delivering third-generation equipment by the mid-1960s. This meant Ferranti had to start planning to cope with another leap forward in technology.

It is not surprising that Ferranti decided to negotiate a way out. It did this through exploring the sale of the Computer Department to International Computers and Tabulators, which had been created through the merger of BTM and Powers-Samas. They had merged to prepare themselves to better compete in the market where their old punched card systems were rapidly being replaced by computers.

In fact, the NRDC had been suggesting such a move for a number of years. As we saw at the very beginning of the NRDC's relationship with Ferranti, a merger of the computer interests of Ferranti with BTM had been informally mooted. Though it was not involved in the negotiations, the NRDC had continued to suggest such a move. Duckworth, the new MD of the NRDC, suggested at a 1961 board meeting that it would be wise for EMI, ICT and Ferranti to consider a rationalisation of the industry.[91] In April 1963, in preparation for the sale to ICT, Ferranti repaid the £300,000 ATLAS loan to the NRDC[92] and the sale of the Computer Department was announced on the 7th of August 1963.[93]

ICT was in a position to negotiate reasonably hard with Ferranti. It was doubtful about the saleability of Ferranti machines, especially ATLAS. However, within the Department were the designs for the Ferranti-Packard 6000 and this was just the computer ICT needed on which to base its next generation of systems. The Ferranti Computer Department provided ICT with internal design capability way beyond what ICT already had. It provided a way for the company to build its own systems and not rely on licensing other companies' designs (as it did from RCA) or outsourcing design and development (as it did from GEC). Ferranti provided a huge technical capability which ICT, closer to the needs of business users, could direct.

The Ferranti Computer Department offered the capability that ICT needed, if it could be mastered to ICT's requirements. This culminated in the fortuitous availability of the FP 6000 design which would lead to an integrated range of third-generation systems, engineered and developed by the Ferranti teams inside ICT.

ICT paid for the Ferranti Computer Department in cash and shares which valued it at £5.3m (Campbell-Kelly, 1989:223 – other sources suggest the valuation was £8.4m). Grundy became Ferranti's representative on the ICT board, Basil de Ferranti (Sebastian's Brother) became deputy managing director for R&D (though his only prior experience had been as a Conservative M.P.) and then became joint managing director of ICT. Finally, the last manager of the Ferranti Computer Department, Peter Hall, became a deputy director at ICT and the FP 6000 became the core product of ICT and then ICL for over 20 years.

## Conclusions

While Ferranti is an unusual case, due to its ownership, it still seems to have suffered from the same problems faced by the other electronics firms that tried to enter the computer industry.

*M-form structure – but not quite decentralised:*

It is interesting that a family company should so overtly operate a financially decentralised business. Its business units were meant to be self-supporting. It was even ahead of the big three electrical manufacturers in the UK – GEC, English Electric and AEI – who would not adopt this decentralised, m-form structure until the 1950s and 1960s, while at this earlier stage in the 1940s they were still using a functional organisation (Jones, R., Marriott, O. 1970).

Despite this formal structure, there is stronger evidence that the nature of the entrepreneurial structure was hampered both by interference from senior management who micro-managed many decisions, and by organisational rifts at the business unit level.

It is interesting to note that financial autonomy was in the main maintained, but rather than allow managers to deploy resources themselves within the confines of their financial autonomy, operational interference from the senior management was endemic. Financially, the business departments were left to their own devices, but their decisions, such as offering different funding solutions to the NRDC, were still subject to veto by the family members. Also, the central management had little regard for the capabilities of these divisions, especially in the field of sales and would force on them strategies to mitigate their perceived problems in selling to commercial customers.

The seemingly integrated, pseudo-autonomous business departments were far from unified. The Computer Department was riddled with internal feuds and competition for resources. While Grundy's Instruments Department was having a great deal of success in many fields of digital capital electronics, the Computer Division was bickering about the types of machines to produce and the way they should be sold. Worse still, a complex structure of separating manufacture from development meant Ferranti struggled with initial reliability of its second wave of first-generation computers. It was a department riddled with infighting. Arguably, it should have been left in the hands of the Instrument Division which could have allocated resources as appropriate, but this was not the case.

*Concentric diversification:*

The structure adopted by Ferranti could be found in any company. What added to the pressure at Ferranti was the concentric diversification of the firm which meant that many areas of the business were all experiencing large-scale demands for R&D resources all at the same time. Ferranti was a high technology firm, and every business unit was hungry for resources - as digital technology advanced, so did demand for resources – Ferranti probably had little recourse but to limit investment in those businesses trying to enter commercial markets because it could not afford the pace of change.

Producing mainframe computers is a cash-hungry business. The high demands of R&D mean a continued drain on capital resources. Ferranti took a number of steps which were designed to restrict the capital drain of establishing its computer enterprise. However, these restrictions ensured that it would not achieve a large enough market share to justify even this limited expenditure – the combined effect was to maintain investment in technology, much of it paid for by the government, while restricting marketing and sales efforts. The firm tried to limit commercial costs in four key ways:

Searching for outside sponsorship
Finding a sales partner
Sales not leases
Limiting market reach

Each of these policies had knock on effects. Most important it relied on government support for technology rather than developing a way to address the burgeoning commercial market. The firm's conservative investment policies and stand-alone attitude to departments meant it was never going to have the resources to fund leases nor to develop the peripherals needed for the commercial market. Ferranti's focus on the electronics and not the electro-mechanical systems used in peripherals was obvious to the NRDC where an internal report noted; 'Ferranti themselves were held up by the lack of adequate mechanical engineers'.[94] On the development of high-speed tape input, Ferranti's Carter noted they had 'a man and a boy thinking about the problem at the moment'.[95]

It was not just input output which was an issue, so too was the commitment to helping customers run useful applications. Ferranti were effectively engineers selling to scientists. Again the NRDC saw this philosophy affecting commercial sales because of lack of investment in software. At the 5th meeting of the computer subcommittee, it was noted that despite all the money the NRDC had put into Ferranti, the 'Computer Group' within Ferranti had just 21 staff, of which only 12 were programmers. The NRDC believed that adequate progress on software development could need up to 50 staff.[96]

Above all Ferranti was never, by itself, going to find the funds necessary to compete with IBM and ICT in the commercial market – funding leases was never on its 'to do' list, as such it would always have needed to find willing partners or realise the investment it had made in the core technology through selling the operation – a strategy often used by the company.

## Postscript

Ferranti would continually struggle with its high technology concentric diversification and limited resources. It would be one of its older businesses, the transformer business which, in 1974, would stretch its banking covenants too far, but rather than see this technological powerhouse fail the government would intervene. The National Enterprise Board injected £15 million into Ferranti in return for a 50 per cent share, at the cost of the family losing operational control.

It would remain an important technology player; it would launch the first range of European microprocessors and would provide components for systems ranging from high technology military systems all the way to the Sinclair ZX81 home computer. In 1982, the government stake was sold and it continued to develop strengths in military systems, application-specific integrated circuits (ASIC), and computer networking, among other areas. In 1987, it would finally tackle its lack of US presence and purchase International Signal and Control. The earlier generations of Ferranti were then proved right about avoiding that market. International Signal had, somewhat bizarrely, been valued partially based on a number of contracts it claimed to hold with the US military to provide radio kit. This would prove to be false. The founder of ISG, James H. Guerin, became Ferranti deputy Chairman but would soon face numerous charges for money laundering, illegal technology sales and, critically for Ferranti, defrauding them of $1.1bn charges he was found guilty of, but by which time Ferranti had failed and been broken up.

It was a sad end for a company that was a centre of excellence for so many technologies. The Ferranti conservatism of the 1950s may well not have been misplaced.

# 6
# Electrical and Musical Industries – Computing on a Shoestring

Electrical and Musical Industries (EMI) and Ferranti were very different firms but in essentially many of the same markets. Ferranti was dominated by a large family shareholding and family control, while EMI was a more conventional, listed company without those influences. However, while Ferranti was wedded to electronic capital goods, EMI, while a leader in this field, also had larger consumer electronics and, more importantly, software interests for these devices – i.e., it was the UK's major integrated producer, making the tape decks which recorded, then played the music of their artists, such as the Beatles. Despite these differences, EMI succumbed to essentially the same pressures that led to Ferranti leaving the computer industry. It too lacked the ability to provide the resources to exploit the technology it had developed. As another concentrically diversified firm, it had problems in supporting multiple growth paths and could not justify the resources for the commercial mainframe computer industry – although this was clearly going to be the major source of demand for civilian capital electronics.

## EMI's formation

EMI was formed in 1931, effectively by the American company Radio Corporation of America (RCA).[1] RCA, as already noted, was formed when the US government forced the sale of the American Marconi Company into a new company which also pooled some of the key electronics assets of GE and Westinghouse to form a new electronics and radio company free from British ownership. RCA quickly became both horizontally and vertically integrated. It produced the software that people wanted (music and film), it provided the service which delivered this software (radio stations, cinema equipment and later TV stations), developed the capital equipment used by these services (recoding and broadcast equipment) and mass produced the consumer goods used to listen and view the software provided by these service operations (Chandler 2005 and Sobel 1986 outline this history).

One of these assets was the UK-based Gramophone Company, which RCA merged with Columbia Records to form one of the giants of the recording industry. Coupled with this, RCA included its main UK electronics operations which it had acquired earlier from the British side of Marconi. These were the Marconiphone consumer electronics business, and its holding in electronic components company M.O. Valve (the other partner was GEC).

Initially, RCA had a large stake in EMI with RCA chief, David Sarnoff, sitting on the board. RCA disposed of its interests in EMI when RCA began disposing of all its overseas assets to free funds for its domestic operations to cope with the burst in the bubble for electronics and the new media during the Great Depression (Sobel 1986).

EMI was the world's largest record producer and music publisher and had the rights to RCA's HMV label, and the names Marconiphone and G. Marconi.[2] The largest operation was the record business; records would always remain EMI's largest division. However, it also produced the phonograms and radio sets on which the music was played and made many of the major components that were used to build these sets. Like RCA it was an integrated operation of software and hardware.

## The growth of electronics at EMI

It is worth pausing to consider the role EMI played in the development of television, as it was this activity which really confirmed EMI as one of the most advanced systems engineering houses in the world. This would be essential to the UK in the Second World War and would later give EMI the capability to enter the computer industry – indeed we have seen that F. C. Williams at Manchester University would have preferred to work with EMI than Ferranti (see Chapter 5).

In the mid-1930s, a team of 30 EMI engineers, led by Isaac Shoenberg, produced the world's first all-electronic television system. Baird's much vaunted system was mechanical and clearly little more than a technological curio.

EMI's ability to produce the first practical television owed much to its, by then informal, links with RCA. This work was a development of the work carried out by Vladimir Zworykin at RCA who created the Iconoscope which was the first practical camera tube. EMI improved on this and produced the EMITRON tube (Leggatt 1988), on which it could build a broadcast quality TV system.

EMI worked with the Marconi company which provided transmitter technology, and the two companies formed a joint company to market television equipment, Marconi-EMI Television Co. (see Baker 1970: 324 and Sturmey 1958: 203). The BBC encouraged this development by opening the world's first full television station at the Alexandra Palace in 1936 (Layton, Harlow and de Hoghton 1972: Chapter 8). Following a period of dual broadcasting, EMI's system was selected to be the BBC standard, beating the inferior Baird system.

EMI's knowledge of building complex electronic systems meant that it had a leading role in developing electronic systems for the war effort. One of the most important products was the high-powered Klystron tube which was vital to radar. EMI would stay a leader in this technology after the War. Clearly, this put EMI in a strong position in capital electronics in the post-war period. However, we have already seen Ferranti's problems with contracts in the post-war environment as well as Marconi's dire forecasts for sales in beyond 1945–46 (see Figure 5.1)

Layton (1972) argued that British firms, such as EMI, did not benefit from the Second World War as much as US companies (including RCA). He argued that during the Second World War the UK failed to foster close relationships between companies, government and universities. This meant that much of the military development taking place was outside of the control of the companies; they did not control key elements of the intellectual property developed and were not paid for those elements. American firms had much more control over all elements of development and production and benefited from that.

This of course was one of the reasons the NRDC existed, to exploit these developments and get them back into industry.

Layton notes that, in the 1930s, EMI's £2–3m research expenditure on television was more than a match for RCA's $9m R&D spend. However, after the War, the RCA Sarnoff Laboratory had become a huge and powerful centre of technical innovation, an order of magnitude larger than EMI's Central Research Laboratory. EMI would become dominated by music and film interests: capital electronics counted for only 20–25 per cent of EMI's post-war activities; at RCA electronics was the main activity. RCA had taken a leap over the UK company.

Nevertheless, when preparing its post-war strategy, Marconi identified EMI as one of its main competitors.[3] It expected EMI to broaden its broadcasting activities, a particular concern for Marconi as this represented 25 per cent of its pre-war business. EMI had developed enormous knowledge of radar, telemetry and special valves. This, coupled to the end of the Marconi-EMI Television agreement scheduled for 1949, led Marconi to believe that EMI would start competing with its core transmitter business and that EMI could offer an end-to-end television package – which it did.

In fact, EMI's ambitions were even greater; it made an attempt to take Marconi over. This bid was made possible by the Labour Government's decision to follow the recommendation of the 1945 Commonwealth Telecommunications Conference and nationalise the Cable and Wireless telecoms business which was a part of the Marconi empire (Baker 1970: 233).

However, the manufacturing arm of the firm, Marconi itself, was not to be nationalised. EMI was one of the companies that bid for this rump operation. There certainly seems to have been a good case for arguing that the two firms were complementary: Marconi-EMI Television had already shown the possibilities. However, English Electric was the winner; Marconi adding greatly to EE's much smaller electronics stable. Marconi and EMI's partnership in television ended and they started to compete against each other.

There was opportunity in capital electronics for both EMI and Marconi was television, but the BBC was slow to expand its television activities due to post-war austerity (Layton 1972). EMI had invested large amounts of capital to become a turn-key supplier of television stations. It had also decided to increase its capacity to produce domestic television sets, in preparation for the spread of new transmitters. However, when the Sutton Coldfield transmitter was built in 1949 (by EMI using AEI transmitter gear) the Chancellor increased purchase tax on television sets from 66 2/3 per cent to 100 per cent, which dramatically impacted EMI's sales and margin on sets sold.

## Changing structure

In the early 1950s, EMI was in an unsatisfactory position, primarily because of the slowness of television developments. In 1949–50, trading profits fell substantially, all of which was attributable to poor results from the UK electronics operations.

In time-honoured tradition, later management teams would blame this period of failure on the leadership of Chairman Sir Alexander Aikeman, and Managing Director Sir Ernest Fisk. Aikeman and Fisk introduced a new managerial structure, a strict functional structure:[4] the exact opposite of the 'M' form structure nominally adopted by Ferranti. The functional operations are set out in Table 6.1.

J.E. Wall, (who would become) managing director of EMI, commented that this functional system had proved inefficient, especially in the consumer products field, as it adversely affected the policy-making process:

> The fragmentation of the process of making and selling a product reacted against the formulation of an effective and coherent policy to the market position.
>
> (Wall 1964)[5]

Fisk, the architect of this structure, was later unceremoniously sacked and, as Figure 6.1 shows, EMI's poor returns on capital employed and turnover began to improve.

The company saw rapid improvement in the mid-1950s. A number of steps were taken to sustain this improvement. A new managing director, L. J. Brown, was appointed in 1952, and a new chairman, J. F. Lockwood (the

*Table 6.1*    EMI functional structure of the early 1950s

EMI ENGINEERING DEVELOPMENT LTD
EMI FACTORIES LTD
EMI INSTITUTES LTD
EMI RESEARCH LABS LTD
EMI SALES AND SERVICE LTD
EMI SUPPLIES LTD
EMI STUDIOS LTD
EMI RELAYS (Hayes) LTD
EMI RELAYS (Uxbridge) LTD
EMITRON TELEVISION LTD
ELECTRONIC TUBES LTD
ALPHA ACCESSORIES LTD

*Source*: EMI Annual Reports.

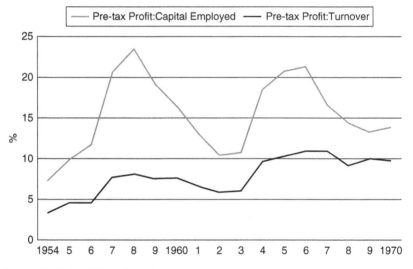

*Figure 6.1*    Basic EMI profit ratios
*Source*: EMI annual reports.

same Lockwood who was a member of the NRDC board and featured in the early stages of the Ferranti computer story. Appointed in 1955, Lockwood would be a power in the company for 15 years. They set about restructuring the company. This time it was based on product divisions. This allowed clearer lines of communication and better accountability and control. The electronics activities were combined into EMI Electronics. The structure of the board gives an outline of how activities were divided (see Table 6.2):

*Table 6.2*  EMI Electronics new board structure and director responsibilities

Board structure of EMI Electronics:
Managing Director: controlled the Military Division.
Deputy Managing Director: controlled the Commercial Division.
Director A: Sales of Military Product.

> B: Valve Division.
>
> C: Technical.
>
> D: Financial.
>
> E: Works.

*Source*: LSE Archive: Wall 19/5/64.

Wall noted that the new structure was arranged so that

> Operating subsidiary companies have authority, as well as responsibility, to an extent that enables them to run their own day- to-day affairs.[6]

The new management decided that the company should be more focused and identified five key product lines: records, military electronics, civil capital electronics, magnetic tape and domestic appliances. This allowed the company to dispose of the troublesome consumer electronics operation. In 1950–51, EMI was producing 2000 television sets per week,[7] around 20 per cent of the British market. In 1953, despite a rocketing TV set market, EMI sales actually fell.[8]

In 1957, EMI and Thorn announced that they were to merge their consumer electronics operations.[9] The stated objective was to concentrate both companies' production of television and audio products at Thorn's two 'flow-line' production plants: it was in reality a takeover of EMI's brands (HMV and Marconiphone) by a company that was specialising in lower-cost, smaller TVs aimed at the mass market. In the 1980s, Thorn would acquire the whole of EMI to become Thorn-EMI.

However, the firm would take steps to build the businesses it had decided to retain. It purchased the US company Capitol Records. This increased record sales to over 50 per cent of group sales.[10] In domestic appliances, it bought Morphy Richards.[11] This would prove a poor decision as EMI would continually struggle with this low-technology, high output business and would have to enter into various joint ventures with other electrical companies to rationalise the British domestic appliances industry.

In the 1960 annual report, Lockwood reported that the firm was concerned that all these changes had adversely affected the company's product mix and it was now over-reliant on consumer expenditure. One solution was to re-emphasise its operations in civil and military capital electronics. In the late 1950s and early 1960s, EMI started a major programme of extending its electronics activities; computers would be one of these expansions.

## EMI and the early computer industry

### Rejecting the opportunity to be in the first wave

The late 1940s, a time when EMI was clearly a leading innovator yet struggling to achieve economic returns, was when computers and the NRDC would first appear on its corporate radar. Again, it was based on the early NRDC hope that an alliance could be formed between an electronics firm and a business machines firm in the area of computing. The first electronics company it approached about this concept was EMI (Hendry 1989: 55). F.C. Williams, designer of the Mark 1, recommended EMI as the technically most competent electronics company. EMI attended the NRDC's one and only meeting of the Advisory Panel on Digital Computers in 1949.[12]

EMI rejected the idea of joining a partnership with a business machines firm focused on computing, as did Ferranti. In any case, EMI already had its hands full with other capital electronics projects. At this early stage the only active connection it had with computers was an agreement to provide engineering support to the Telecommunications Research Establishment in some of its internal computer developments – for five more years EMI would be a background player in computing.

### Part 1: The experimental phase

Computers would resurface again at EMI as the firm strove to reorientate its electronics business towards non-consumer electronics. Following the difficulties of the early 1950s, it could not even rely on records to be constantly profitable as they were subject to a punitive 60 per cent sales tax,[13] although they did remain profitable and would become even more profitable as these taxes fell and the signings of the 1960s made EMI the most important record label.

In one area of computing (if one could call it that) EMI was already a major player. EMI was the UK's largest producer of the highly specialist machines known as analogue computers (as opposed to digital computers). Its main products were the modular EMIAC I and II. Analogue computing took a different approach from digital computing in the study of the physical attributes of engineering problems.

Analogue computers were an electrical model of the subject of study. Effectively they looked to create an electrical model of the problem being researched, emulating the physical world within this model and then seeing how changes to parameters would affect other parts of the model. Most were purely electrical/electronic, but hydraulic and mechanical devices have been used, and the simplest, yet most elegant analogue computer is the slide rule.

They were enormously important devices in the Second World War used for predictive gun laying and for bombsights (such as the British Mark XIV and the American Norden bombsights). When dedicated to modelling industrial flows or other engineering applications, analogue computers could become very large and were superb to look at; they looked like something from the TV series 'Lost in Space'. However, with the development of the digital computer, analogue solutions to technical problems became progressively less economic as the power of digital machines increased, and their prices fell. However, the commercial digital computer operation had little relationship to this analogue activity.

Analogue computers were clearly not the future, but EMI already had connections with individuals that were involved in sponsoring development of the digital computer market. Chief among these links were

- Sir Edward de Stein, who was on the board of both EMI and the NRDC in the early 1950s.
- EMI chairman Lockwood, who was on the NRDC board before he joined EMI and, most influentially, had chaired the NRDC's Computer Sub-Committee during the 1950s.
- Sir Percy Mills, who had been the NRDC chairman, 1949–55 – he joined the EMI board when he retired from the Corporation.

Few other companies had connections like this. Few other companies had people like F. C. Williams saying that they would be their first choice to work with in the early development of computers.

However, EMI had rejected the original opportunity to join an NRDC-sponsored, first-generation, computer project. EMI had little enthusiasm for removing its technical staff from projects which were directed at less uncertain markets. It is not surprising that EMI decided it had better, and more immediate, opportunities to exploit: after all, in the late 1940s, there was no computer market and, until the slow rollout and new taxes took their toll, the development of televisions was a clear priority.

Given the influences on the firm and their clear goal of trying to diversify away from consumer spending, one may have expected a structured approach to this new venture. However, EMI, as is common with so many of the electronics firms, would create rival developments within the same organisation. EMI's somewhat confused structure and strategy in computing reflected in its desire to limit the resources available for developing its computer business; a common situation in electronics firms – they thought being able to build computers would be enough; it wasn't.

By the mid-1950s there were multiple computer initiatives within EMI. Two independent projects existed. One was a completely internal effort by a department to develop commercial digital computing to diversify into a growing part of the electronics market. The second was a project supported by the NRDC – hardly surprising given the connections between the organisations. Both developments started inside EMI Engineering Development Ltd before the restructuring of the company along profit centre lines.

Despite originating out of the same organisation and having similar names implying there was a relationship between the two EMI Systems, in fact, the links were rather distant. These systems were the medium scale EMIDEC 1100 and large scale EMIDEC 2400, both of which were marketed in the late 1950s and early 1960s. It was the team which developed the EMIDEC 1100 which would lead the experimental phase of EMI's development, however, the other team were continuously asked to take part, but would be instead working on an altogether grander computer project. The key to EMI's entry into the market was that, while they did produce a one-off first-generation machine (produced by the team that would later make the 1100 computer), their real push came with second generation computers, offering for sale the first solid state computers in Europe.

*The BMC computer – a starting point*[14]

It was this stream of development which became the main thrust of EMI's computer diversification. It was started when Clifford Metcalfe took over from C. S. Agate as Managing Director of EMI Engineering Development, and became the first Managing Director of EMI Electronics when the 'M' form structure was adopted.

One of Metcalfe's first acts was to try to understand what type of business he had taken over. He commissioned a report from EMI employee R. E. Spencer on the future of electronic business machines with the idea that this would prove a potential market for EMI's capabilities.[15] In this report, Spencer foresaw a system which would consist of many small computers and workstations linked to a large central computer storage unit. Spencer's vision was years ahead of its time. EMI was not about to make this scheme a reality; it would be another ten years before relatively cheap minicomputers were produced, let alone microcomputers. Nevertheless, it did confirm Metcalfe's belief that there was a growing market for computers in the commercial office environment. Spencer was described as the technical guru to Metcalfe and Godfrey Hounsfield (Hounsfield will feature heavily in this story).[16]

Metcalfe had a practical reason for wanting to understand this market because he already had a potential customer for a computer system. ICI Fertilizers were interested in acquiring a computer for invoicing customers. Metcalfe seems to have had a close relationship with ICI: they sent him a bag of fertilizer each Christmas.[17]

A project was started to develop a machine that could fulfill this requirement. To lead this group R. T. Clayden was recruited from English Electric.[18] He had previously worked on EE's Pilot ACE and DEUCE computers, and before this had worked for EMI Central Research Laboratories. Clayden's group produced a Pilot Machine which was a skeleton of a larger system which could perform the task ICI wanted. However, it was decided that this machine would be too expensive to produce as a stand-alone one-off system, and was lacking a number of key components and subsystems.[19]

The decision not to produce a computer based on this Pilot Machine was not the end of the story. Metcalfe's personal interest in developing computers and exploiting his networking capability led to him winning a contract to build a computer for the British Motor Corporation (BMC).

One senior manager at EMI recalls that the BMC system began as a research initiative by Metcalfe to 'Look at Rootes'.[20] This was an exercise to see where process improvements could be made at a large-scale mass-production car company using EMI's technology, especially how computer technology could be applied to that company. The Special Products Unit joined in this 'look', however, that unit soon lost interest as they believed that the problems found in BMC's Longbridge factory were the province of dedicated machine control systems rather than computers. Of course, Rootes was a rival car company to BMC and did not own the Longbridge factory, Austin/BMC did. It does suggest these recollections from a member of the SPU are not totally accurate which may be down to the preference of the Special Products Unit for much larger systems and the unit would later go on to develop the large-scale 2400 system.

Team members from EMI's other computer team (which would go on to build the EMIDEC 1100) recall that Austin/BMC approached EMI after it had approached other computer manufacturers about improving their opera-tions.[21] Metcalfe had persuaded BMC's Sir Leonard Lord that a computerised payroll system was needed for the Longbridge factory. Metcalfe's efforts were so successful that BMC was telling EMI why it was the best firm for the job. BMC's preference for EMI was partly driven by the fact that EMI was large enough to absorb a loss on a fixed priced contract; clearly they had doubts about the outcomes.[22]

It was hoped that the machine developed for BMC could be sold to other customers. Clayden and his team set to work on producing the central proc-essor unit (CPU), which followed similar lines to the Pilot Machine, and was a first-generation valve computer.

The peripherals were subcontracted to EMI's Scophony Baird factory at Wells, which EMI had purchased as a pre-production factory, mostly for gov-ernment contracts. Over the years, much of EMI's magnetic tape and special-ist recording work was transferred to this site. Wells provided the magnetic drum fast store and the magnetic tape system for the BMC machine. It was decided that the tape drive should be tailored to the specific role played by the BMC machine. It therefore produced a modified domestic tape deck, which was of little use as a saleable product to other manufactures and would also mean the BMC machine itself was of little third-party interest. This was a deep shame as EMI was one of the few UK companies to have in-depth knowledge of magnetic tape and mechanics around these important peripherals.

There was another sub-assembly that Clayden wanted to subcontract within the company. This was the peripheral control equipment, the means by which the CPU communicated with the outside world. Two groups were initially interested: the Special Products Unit and a small engineering group led by Godfrey Hounsfield.

The senior management of the Special Products Unit had little interest in this work. Indeed, senior managers of that group viewed the whole BMC/1100 development as a diversion of resources from investment in more useful larger systems. The senior manager of that team claimed that he was surprised when he discovered the existence of the 1100 development team (which the BMC system team eventually became). This is surprising, as one of his senior engineers was seconded to the BMC development team for six months.[23] Indeed, this senior engineer was the only one to have any experience of computer before the Special Products Unit started to build the 2400.

The Special Products Unit's lack of interest in producing the peripheral control side of the BMC machine left Hounsfield to develop this equipment, which proved very fortuitous. Hounsfield took a different approach to Clayden and designed a solid state controller rather than the vacuum tubes being used in the CPU.

Transistors were still expensive in 1955–56, and production in Europe was very limited. Hounsfield therefore used magnetic core logic. Magnetic cores are tiny ferrite loops which are threaded together on wire matrices and can act as on-off switches. Magnetic cores were just becoming the favoured type of computer memory and would be dominant until well into the 1970s as main memory, but their ability to hold binary data also meant that they could be used to build computer logic.

Further help was recruited by employing Derek Hemy from LEO Computers, who took charge of programming the BMC machine. LEO was the most experienced company in the application of computers to commercial problems. LEO I was already being used (on a bureau basis) to prepare Ford's UK payroll; perfect experience from preparing for the BMC work. Hemy and another LEO programmer, John Graver, would become the core of EMI's sales team.[24] The BMC computer was delivered in early 1956. Financially it was not a success: 18 months of debugging was needed at Longbridge before it was acceptable for customer use.

## Part 2: Structured entry

*Second generation EMIDEC 1100*

As the engineering teams worked on the BMC machine in 1956, the logic designers started to work on a machine that could be sold on a commercial basis.[25]

However, rather than building on Clayden's work, they started to develop an architecture based on Hounsfield's magnetic core technology. A senior manager of the Special Product Unit/2400 team recalled that when, in 1958, he found out about the 1100 computer, he was surprised that this technology had been implemented.[26] Magnetic core logic is inherently slow, especially compared to transistors. Indeed, their incorporation into the logic of the Ferranti Orion has already been discussed and it was a real problem for that machine. If the 1100 development team had realised that such a massive fall in transistor prices would take place during 1957–59, they would not have used cores.[27] However, the target market was the commercial sector, where speed was only one consideration, though it ruled the machine out of playing any useful secondary role as a scientific system.

The code name for the system was the OXO 4. In October 1956, Metcalfe expressed support for the system, and in early 1957 EMI set up a formal Computer Division within EMI Electronics Ltd. Norman Hill was appointed as its head. He immediately 'firmed up' the OXO 4's specification[28] and appointed Hounsfield as the project leader. Hounsfield received the full support of the Electronics Group senior management.

The computer was given a 1000-word magnetic core fast memory, and had a magnetic drum supporting this, an extension of the peripheral developed in Wells. However, they decided to buy Ampex magnetic tape decks from the US. They rejected the idea of going back to EMI's Wells operation for tapes, even though it was already developing (at enormous expense) the tape drives for the other EMI computer, the 2400 – the management structures and communications within the Electronics Group seem to have broken down and the opportunity to work together was lost. The slightly updated EMIDEC 1101 would swap Ampex drives for Potter tape drives, a strange move as Ampex was well established as the market leader for third-party drives.

Other peripherals included the Samastronic printer from Power-Samas (later ICT). While this was the fastest printer in the UK, its reliance on bicycle chains was a source of some concern to the EMI engineers.[29] This printer was never as successful as the excellent machines made by IBM. One of the advantages of IBM systems was the good rate of output that they had. When dealing with commercial problems, it is the overall ability of the machine that is important, not just the technical specification of the central processor itself. Electronics firms seem to have had difficulty in appreciating that computers were not just an exercise in circuit board design. Business machines firms took a much broader view of what was required of a commercial computer system.

*The 1100's market performance*

The 1100 was configured as a medium-scale computer: its average price was £180,000.[30] It was the first of the second generation computers built in Europe, and apart from some much smaller BTM/ICT models, the Ferranti Perseus and the LEO II, it was the first production machine to be targeted at the commercial user.

By 1960, analysts Computer Consultants (1960)[31] believed that the UK computer market was in a 'wait and see' mode. Users were looking at, and sizing up, the new second generation of machines as they were being introduced. However, two firms were beginning to take substantial orders in 1960, EMI and IBM. The IBM orders were for the 1401, at an average price of £120,000: it was in the same medium-scale category as EMI. However, outside the US, the 1401 was not delivered in quantity until 1962. EMI was installing the 1100 from 1959 (see Table 6.3).

*Table 6.3*   Annual installations of EMI 1100 and 1101 computers

| 1959 | 1960 | 1961 | 1962 | 1963 | 1964 |
|------|------|------|------|------|------|
| 1    | 5    | 7    | 6    | 2    | 3    |

*Source*: Charles Babbage Institute, University of Minnesota, Collection 62. Computer Consultants 1965 'British Commercial Computer Digest'.

These numbers were not large. However, as a large medium-sized system, by value EMIDEC 1100 sales represented 12 per cent of the value of new UK installations in 1960 and 1961. Combining these sales with the sales from the other team producing the 2400, at its peak EMI had a 27 per cent share (Drath 1973) of UK new installations by value.

While, in 1960–61, the 1100 computer seemed fairly successful (at least in British terms), the commencement of delivery of the IBM 1401 was a watershed moment in the make up of the UK computer market. IBM installed almost 300 1401's in the UK alone, and around 10,000 worldwide (see Chapter 8).

EMI's sales pale compared to this performance. Worse still, EMI quickly fell behind its major British competitor, though to EMI that rival hardly figured in its early thinking. The ICT 1301 medium-scale computer, designed by electrical giant GEC, was marketed at an average price of £120,000 (a third less than the EMIDEC 1100). From 1962, its sales would outstrip the EMIDEC 1100 and eventually over 150 were sold. The 1301 was late for a second generation machine, roughly four years behind the EMI system, however, not only was it more affordable, it had superior input-output capability because of ICT's background as a business machines firm which also gave it large sales and service capabilities. ICT knew that its old product line was dying and the future had to be the computer.

The momentum behind the 1100 seems to have ceased once the second generation machines from the business machine firms became available.

*EMIDEC 2400 – the rival sibling*

The addition of the large-scale EMIDEC 2400 machine to the medium-sized 1100 gave EMI the sort of comprehensive range of computers which many other firms would not be able to offer until the mid-1960s. However, the 2400 did not enjoy the confidence of the divisional or group managements and proved to be an unsuccessful development.

The decision to build this machine was the result of two factors: one emanated from the Special Products Unit of EMI, and the other came from the NRDC which figures so heavily in the Ferranti story. The head of the SPU, Charles Kramskoy, joined EMI in 1949 and headed the team designing the Blue Boar television guided 'smart' bomb.[32] In 1952, he was put in charge of a small engineering group, the Special Products Unit. This group had an across-the-board engineering capability, designing large military electronics systems. As has been seen, RCA had a similar (though much larger) team, called the Advanced Development Group. In 1954–55 the Special Products Unit began to broaden its scope and to take on some large civilian projects in order to secure its position.[33]

At the same time, the NRDC was going through one of its periods of anxiety about the slow development of the British computer industry. NRDC managing director Halsbury had visited the US in the autumn of 1954 (Hendry 1989). He returned concerned that the UK was behind on magnetic tape storage techniques, magnetic core storage and in planning for the use of transistorised circuits. What worried him most was the potential entry of IBM into the UK market.

Halsbury wanted to see the UK industry respond. However, most of the companies which were already producing computers were fully occupied. Ferranti was already fully absorbed with its own developments. BTM and GEC had just agreed to build a machine of the nature Halsbury envisaged, but given the starting point of these two firms, the project was a long-term plan with no machine likely until the early 1960s. No other company had the ability, or will, to bring a commercial computer to the market more quickly. On the other hand, the NRDC and EMI were becoming increasingly close, Lockwood who sat on NRDC committees was now the EMI chairman. Halsbury agreed that EMI Electronics Ltd should put forward a proposal to produce a fully transistorised computer.

Two groups in EMI were interested in this contract: the Clayden/Hounsfield team and the Special Products Unit. The first group was fully occupied on the BMC computer and decided against making a bid for the contract.

However, it was the Special Products Unit which was free to carry out this work, for the Unit it was an opportunity they needed to get away from purely military work.

There were two initial phases to the project. First, they needed to get some computer experience. Therefore, they packed one engineer, Norman

Brown, to the BMC team gather some experience.[34] Brown worked in this group for a period of five–six months in 1954–55. However, the Special Products Unit was not going to follow the same architecture – the large system being developed by SPU was to have no real family relationship with the BMC machine or the 1100 which followed it. The unit instead opted to work on a design philosophy from Christopher Strachey, the NRDC's own logic expert. The Special Products Unit were comfortable that, with NRDC backing both financial and technical, it could build a large-scale solid state computer.

The second phase in preparing the ground for the 2400 was to establish whether users would want such a system. To this end, the EMI Special Products Unit and Strachey studied the needs of the mail order company Freeman's, which was considering how to automate its large clerical operations. Though it was decided that this was not a suitable business in which to utilise the type of computer EMI was planning, it did lead to the notional specification for the 2400, even if this was a system which clearly the test subject did not want.

The proposal from the Special Products Unit was for a large system, utilising transistors, magnetic cores and magnetic tape, all the areas Halbury wished to see developed. It was to fulfil the needs of the largest commercial office. Kramskoy, head of the Unit, put forward a proposal for a three-year project, divided into two 18-month stages.[35] Phase A of the plan was for the design and prototype production of components. Phase B was to produce a machine and perform commercial demonstrations on it. Total cost was estimated at £320,000. One unknown factor was the progress which would be made by the Mullard company which would be developing and supplying its new transistors and diodes to the market and to the 2400 computer. Mullard was the leading component supplier in the UK and EMI was expecting to purchase new solid state components from it.

However, it was EMI's Metcalfe who was praised for winning substantial NRDC backing at reasonable interest rates.[36] Even before Kramskoy had sorted out the specifications, the NRDC had agreed to finance three quarters of an EMI project costing £300,000.[37] In October 1956, this was extended to three-quarters of Kramskoy's final £320,000 plan. EMI accepted the NRDC's view that the best way to recover this finance was a small levy on all EMI's computer output. This safeguarded the NRDC from the risk that the specific machine it supported would not make it to the market, and that EMI would instead utilise the developments made under the NRDC contract in another computer. It is interesting that this form of arrangement was unacceptable to Ferranti until the Atlas super computer contract (see Chapter 5).

In 1959, the contract was again renegotiated to take into account a further extension to the project to cover the related 3400 computer – which will be discussed later. Together, these two contracts would reach over £600,000, with a repayment rate of 2 per cent on all EMI's computer equipment sales and a simple interest rate of 5 per cent on the loan.[38] The effects of these arrangements on various turnover levels are shown in Table 6.4.

*Table 6.4*   EMI NRDC repayment structure

| If EMI computer turnover stabilised at | Profit to the NRDC |
|---|---|
| £2m after 3 years | –£550,000 |
| £3 after 3 years | –£245,000 |
| £4m after 4 years | £60,000 |
| £5m after 5 years | £190,000* |

*\*The account would be cleared after 12 years.*
*Source:* National Archive for the History of Computing, NRDC 86/7/8. 118th NRDC Board Meeting. Reproduced by courtesy of the University Librarian and Director, The John Rylands Library, The University of Manchester.

The contract offered EMI large amounts of cheap cash with which to establish the 2400 computer. The documentation and the quality of the associated business plan seem quite ludicrous now. In addition, the interwoven relationship between the NRDC and EMI seems to have more than a hint of conflict of interest among those influencing the contract.

However, the NRDC now had a firm doing what it wanted, a firm producing or ordering all the components it believed were essential for the British computer industry and that firm was willing to structure repayment of the funding across all of its products. This is what the NRDC wanted – though the supporting business case was based on wafer-thin financial predictions.

*Reorganising the computer business*

By 1956–57, EMI had two quite separate computer operations in the 1100 and 2400 teams, though Metcalfe had been fundamental in getting funding for both these operations. In 1957, Metcalfe decided to rationalise and appointed Norman Hill from Elliott Brothers to bring its computer operations together. Fundamentally, Hill's sympathies were with the medium-sized, lower-cost, less-risky 1100 as the right-sized machine for the market (Hendry 1990: 116) – this may reflect business managers not really understanding the limitations of the core technology being used. The 2400 was treated as a simple cost-plus contract on behalf of the NRDC, just another capital electronics contract. It is likely that the senior management of EMI, sitting on the board of the NRDC as they were, would have found this a worrying decision.

In 1958, EMI finally formed a unified Computer Division, at least on paper. The reality was very different. The 2400 and 1100 projects were not integrated in any practical way. The machines used different technologies and the two teams had a different attitude to the procurement of peripherals: the 2400 group preferring internal sources, while the 1100 team was buying externally. EMI had what seemed like a very powerful market line-up of second generation systems, but there was little opportunity for economies of scale between the two machines.

The 2400 project was marginalised in a world of its own. It was a forgotten project.[39] It was treated very much like any other government contract, with EMI seemingly unwilling to back it beyond what was necessary to fulfil the contract. EMI made little effort to actively market such a large machine without some proof that it would be successful. This isolation also led to a lack of cost control, and a lacklustre attitude to providing any customer programming support for the system.

Costs on the project rose rapidly. By 1962, the NRDC had invested £593,528 in EMI computer projects, of which £500,000 was for the 2400.[40] It was proving expensive to develop and took longer to produce than had been originally planned. The peripherals also presented a major problem. Initially Kramskoy asked the Domestic Electronics Division to consider developing a magnetic tape storage system for the team. However, it was eventually decided to contract EMI's Wells factory to produce a follow-on to the systems it had developed for the Pilot Machine.[41] Members of the EMIDEC 1100 criticised these peripherals as 'battleship' type construction and completely uneconomic to produce[42] – though probably a predictable approach from a team more used to projects for battleships. When a member of the 2400 team was transferred from the large-scale 2400 project to head the development of the 1100 follow-up (ICT eventually marketed it as the 1101), he saw a Potter tape drive advertised in a US journal. He ordered one, having read that it was one-third of the cost of the tape system used on the 2400, with only a 20 per cent performance shortfall. When it arrived, it worked straight away after unpacking: this greatly impressed him.[43] The Potter tape deck was adopted, and EMI stopped making tape drives. At one time EMI had considered using Decca tape drives on the 2400[44] in a project to be funded by the NRDC, of course, but dropped this when the Decca project did not go ahead.

The isolation of the 2400 project and the divisional management's lack of interest in it is not only reveled in retrospective commentaries but also in contemporary reviews by NRDC auditing. In 1960, the NRDC commissioned reports from two computer experts to examine the 2400 development (Francis reporting on 30/11/60 and Morton 25/11/60), with emphasis placed on the programming, customer service and sales activities.[45] Both agreed that the computer itself was well designed. However, both had reservations about the software work that was going on, the low morale in the operation and an apparent lack of sales activity.

For one of the consultants, Francis[46], it was his second report on the programming effort on the 2400 project and he did believe the situation had improved somewhat and there were now some programmers employed. However, he found that the majority of the staff were very junior; he was told that experienced programmers were too expensive to employ. With orders for new systems imminent at this time, both experts found that a number of key sub-routines (these are small sub-programs which were written to allow programmers to avoid having to recode simple, often called-upon activities in a program) still had not been written. Further, EMI had not considered the need for some form of language compiler for the machine and seemed to have expected the programmers employed by them, and more worryingly, by their customers, to rely on laborious machine code rather than one of the higher-level languages then coming to market. Overall, there was a lack of discipline in programming. Staff were allowed to work on anything that interested them. They did not carry out any formal writing up of their software projects. The result was that some items were lost and others were duplicated, resulting in delays and increasing costs. Anyone ever involved in such a project will know how chaotic this situation was, especially for a system not being sold for scientific curiosity, but intended to be used in a production environment – it seems EMI was expecting all their customers to have mathematicians on hand to write their programs!

At the time of these reports, there were two orders for the 2400, one from the Royal Army Ordnance Corps (RAOC) and one from the Ministry of Pensions and National Insurance.[47] Merton noted that there was a completely unrealistic attitude to the amount of work that was involved in programming the huge applications these organisations would need. One of EMI's programming team told Merton that he and one colleague could program the whole of the RAOC system in four months, and that the team working on it was over large. Merton had the opposite point of view, and believed that the programming operation was not large enough. Francis summed up the problems:

> [There was] little sales effort and some feeling of management neglect ... There seems to be little direction and I feel a lot of time is wasted.[48]

The EMIDEC 2400 system was put on sale in 1959–60 at a price of £500,000 per system. Three were sold in the UK and one to the USSR. All the UK contracts were with the government, one for pensions, with the RAOC taking two.[49] However, it appears that EMI had not actually wanted to even bid for the Ministry of Pensions system (Hendry 1989); the NRDC had to force EMI to tender for this contract. EMI had no wish to tie down working capital and cash-flow on selling an expensive computer it had no interest in. EMI seems to have only been interested in the money that the NRDC provided for the project. It is interesting to note that the few systems finally sold were to government departments, and it is hard not to believe that they may have been sympathetic to the NRDC's plight. Both the RAOC and the Ministry of Pensions computers failed their initial acceptance tests when installed and took a long time to debug.[50]

The one bright spot was the sale of a system to the USSR, where the business orientation of the machine meant that it could get around export restrictions. The importance of this contract was that the price included £100,000 for a service contingency. However, the Russian authorities did not require EMI servicing. This £100,000 windfall paid for much of EMI's own costs, though did not greatly help the NRDC.[51] This was the only export order for an EMI commercial mainframe computer, reflecting the unwillingness to back the Computer Department with adequate marketing resources.

### EMIDEC 3400

Before the lack of commitment to the EMIDEC 2400 was clear, EMI became involved in the bid to win the NRDC's contract for a British supercomputer. This was EMI's rival proposal to the Ferranti Atlas.

The 3400 was an extension of the 2400 project and was looked on favourably by the NRDC because it extended and built on what they were already funding. The NRDC had actively explored the possibilities of such a computer from the mid-1950s but with little success. By 1958–59, only two companies were proposing projects for a super-scale scientific computer. One of these was the Manchester University/Ferranti MUSE/ATLAS machine, the other was EMI's 3400. Kramskoy and Metcalfe proposed a project costing £374,000 of which the NRDC was again expected to contribute 75 per cent – £280,000.[52] The system would directly build upon the experience gained with the 2400, and would continue to be guided by the Strachey team of logisticians. Halsbury supported this project wholeheartedly. He took credit for the commencement of the 2400 project and believed that this extension, which again he initiated, would exploit the close relationship between the 2400 team and the NRDC. He also believed that EMI's greater experience with transistorised computers would be of benefit in producing such a large computer system.

Given these factors, Halsbury and the Computer Sub-Committee recommended the 3400 proposal.[53] However, as has been noted in Chapter 3, the NRDC's deputy managing director, Hennessey, made a counterproposal which suggested backing both projects, but to a lesser degree than either had asked for. The Board agreed to this idea, spreading the risk associated with building such complex systems. Thus, £240,000 was initially provided for the 3400 – not far short of the requested amount.

However, Metcalfe, who, as the head of EMI Electronics, was still intimately involved with funding for the two computer teams within the Computer Division, soon got cold feet about the project.[54] This is not surprising given the decision to sideline the 2400. EMI Electronics proposed that the contract be altered to a joint 2400/3400 project which would allow more funding to cover the over running costs of the 2400 while still enabling a pathway to the 3400.[55] The new plan was to increase the 2400 funding by £63,000 to allow for the extra costs that were being incurred. In return, the overall cost of the 3400 was to be decreased: to £190,000 with the NRDC providing £142,500. To allow this, the 3400 project would be downgraded to a general study of new computer techniques for a future computer system. Instead of being a short-term project leading to a scientific fast computer, it became a long-term one, and the 3400 development was drastically slowed.[56]

The 3400 team did remain in existence; slowly carrying out the NRDC-sponsored development work. When ICT took over EMI's computer development operation in 1961, the 3400 team and the rest of EMI's design engineers transferred to ICT's Stevenage centre.[57] The development continued as Project PF172. It was thought that it could provide ICT with a top-of-the-range scientific system. However, the decision by ICT to drop all its previous computer projects in favour of the FP6000/ICT1900 architecture, to counter the IBM 360 family, meant the end of the PF172. ICT needed every engineer to work on the new line. The 3400/PF172 engineers were redeployed to develop the small-scale members of the ICT 1900 range.[58]

## Exit from the computer industry

EMI's Computer Division never really reached the 'consolidation phase' identified in this research – that stage where the firm tried to build on its product coverage and customer base developed from its structured entry into the market.

Instead in 1961, EMI sold its computer operation to ICT. The NRDC was pleased to see further concentration of the industry.[59] However, there were a number of contractual problems to be sorted out between EMI, ICT and the NRDC. The new head of EMI Electronics, P. A. Alloway, wrote to the NRDC's then managing director, Duckworth, to inform him of the details of the merger.[60] ICT had purchased EMI's development and sales operations. ICT were to sell the EMIDEC range of computers, while EMI were to build them and, to this extent, EMI Electronics had reserved production capacity for 20x1100 and 4x2400 computers per annum. The deal was paid for by the transfer of 275,000 ICT shares to EMI,[61] worth £1,250,000.[62]

This deal gave ICT a larger market share, and the right to sell what appeared at the time to be the fairly successful 1100, as well as the 2400. More importantly, it gave ICT the opportunity to capture some of the engineering skills that it desperately needed if it was going to develop future machines in-house. Up to this point, most of ICT's design work had been done by RCA (the ICT1500 was a rebadged RCA 301) and GEC (ICT 1301) – see Chapter 8.

EMI had defensive reasons for this partial disposal. The company's profit ratios had become stagnant, both as a percentage of turnover and of capital employed (see Figure 6.1). In 1961, the company was reporting lower liquidity ratios because of increased working capital requirements and the cost of purchasing Morphy-Richards. Faced with a lacklustre performance, EMI set about cutting some costs. Chief among these moves was the sale of the computer operation. While it would continue to make already designed machines in the short-run, it was freed from the burden of developing and selling these computers.

There were also longer-term problems to be faced if EMI was to stay in the computer business. With the increasing scale of the computer market and falling prices, EMI had to achieve significant sales to cover the spiralling development costs associated with computers. However, EMI was trying to minimise its commitment to the market. It limited its marketing effort to cut costs, especially on the 2400. This meant that it could not reach the sales that were necessary to achieve a long-term, self-sustaining scale in this market. One example of minimising costs was its lack of overseas marketing. It also seems likely that EMI computers were being sold rather than leased to users. This is definitely true of the 2400 computer, which was sold outright to government users. This was not a good approach to securing a large market share for the 2400. Many commercial users were used to leasing data processing equipment, such as tabulators, from the business machines firms. This was particularly good for computer users, as the rapidly advancing technology made outright purchase a risky decision to make. However, it meant that the manufacturer was faced with the initial capital costs of the leased computers. It would not be able to fully recoup the cost of these machines for a number of years. ICT was more used to this situation, having had a long history in the business machines industry. EMI was trying to minimise such costs, even at the expense of not producing enough machines to recoup development expenditures.

Moreover, cost savings reduced the firm's ability to sell these machines to mainstream customers. In the case of the 2400 project, customer support, software development and sales and marketing were all minimal efforts, indeed, according to NRDC experts, well below the minimum level required. EMI was trying to limit the amount spent on the non-NRDC financed aspects of this project. The NRDC was effectively covering the cost of development; the rest was down to EMI. However, EMI was involved in many other activities that demanded company cash, these alternatives seemed more appealing for its limited resources.

These efforts to minimise costs sat uneasily with the fact that EMI's range of computers was targeted at the most competitive sectors of the industry: medium-scale commercial data processing. The dominant companies in the UK, ICT and IBM, were committing their full corporate weight to these types of machine (in ICT's case, primarily targeting small and medium systems). The 1100 was pitched directly at IBM's and ICT's main data processing machines. The 2400 was larger than anything that ICT had to offer and larger than anything that IBM was then offering in the UK. However, because of the great risk associated with producing such large machines, and because of the large support commitment that they would require, EMI failed to market the system actively. Therefore, the 1100 was seen as the main product, despite the fact it was up against the stiffest competition and despite the fact that it had been developed using a dead-end technology – magnetic core logic.

It should be noted that the sale to ICT was not the first time EMI considered getting out of the computer sector. In 1958, the senior manager of the Special Products Unit/2400 team suggested to Metcalfe that he should consider a merger with Ferranti's Computer Department.[63] This would have been reasonably logical as work on the two supercomputer projects could have been rationalised. In addition, Ferranti could have added a range of scientific computers to EMI's business-orientated systems – though the technical limitations of the 1100 and the Orion (though at least the 1100 did work, albeit slowly) and the lack of market for the 2400 and Atlas would have soon created a crisis. At this time, neither the problems with the EMI computer operation nor the rapidly growing scale of the commitment needed to be in the computer market were so evident, and senior management saw no need to pursue the idea. Metcalfe had also rejected an opportunity to set up a joint company with a computer consultancy company. There was even some discussion of the good relationships that EMI had built with Honeywell and with Olivetti, both of which led to nothing.

The ultimate problem was that, by 1963–64, firms such as IBM and ICT were working on their third-generation machines. These would be large families of batch-produced machines, requiring very large teams of engineers to design them, and significant marketing commitments to sell the various members of the range across the whole scope of the computer market. This was not the kind of commitment EMI was looking for.

Following the sale to ICT, a long period of discussion started between EMI and the NRDC about how the Corporation could continue to recoup its investment. ICT had refused to accept the NRDC debt in the deal.[64] EMI tried to persuade the NRDC that the sales of the 1100 and 2400 computers that it was to make for ICT would cover the debt. However, the NRDC believed that, as EMI was unlikely to produce further machines after the 1100 and 2400 and that these systems clearly had only a short, if any, shelf life, it was unlikely that EMI's computer building operations would generate the revenues needed to cover the loan. The NRDC was in a difficult position, as while it was pleased by the consolidation between business machine and electronics firms, the loan had been made to establish EMI in the computer market and in the belief that EMI had an ongoing commitment to that market.

A number of solutions were considered. The final agreement led to EMI repaying the NRDC money over 15 years and signing over 10 per cent of the dividend earned on its ICT shares to the NRDC in lieu of interest payments which seems a very generous compromise toward EMI.

## EMI post computers

EMI was more interested in pursuing other opportunities in the 1960s. According to one EMIDEC 1100 insider,[65] Metcalfe was the main force behind the company's efforts to establish a larger commercial electronics activity. The 1100 team believed that Lockwood, the chairman, preferred investment in the record business, though this contradicts Lockwood's statement in 1960 that the group was over-reliant on records (EMI Annual Report 1960) and the evidence of Lockwood's work with the NRDC. The argument made by the 1100 team members was that they believed that the electronics group was too caught up in the military cost-plus mentality. The firm preferred this safe haven to more competitive scenarios. The latter statement may well have been close to the truth. In many highly competitive electronic markets EMI was disposing of its activities or, at least, merging them into joint companies so as to mitigate the risk. By 1965, 52 per cent of electronics sales were in the form of military products.[66] Furthermore, by the latter half of the 1960s, electronics only accounted for about 20 per cent of company sales (Annual Report 1968) – though, of course, this was in the period of rapid record sales given its success with the Beatles and many other bands and the growing significance of album-based sales.

Outside the capital electronics arena, EMI took a number of initiatives to further reduce its exposure to risky consumer electronics operations while trying to maintain a stake in the market which, in many areas of technology, it had created in the first place. In the early 1960s, EMI merged its magnetic tape manufacturing operation with Philips. EMI held 51 per cent of the operation and Philips 49 per cent; together they invested in a new manufacturing plant to share costs. To further reduce its exposure to the commercial market, EMI merged its French TV manufacturing operation into a joint company with Thomson-Houston (Annual Report 1960). Later, EMI sold its stake to the French partner.

However, EMI did make some major investments in electronics as well. EMI diversified into areas of industrial control and electronics. One step was to purchase licences from Cincinnati Milling Machines, Canadian General Electric, Fairbanks Whitney, Saab and others (various annual reports); most of these licences were for industrial control systems). This gave the firm a stake in the market while reducing upfront development costs. It also entered the market for semiconductors by purchasing a 49 per cent stake in the Hughes Corporation's Scottish operation (Sciberras 1977). However, in 1974–75, EMI sold its stake in this highly competitive sector back to Hughes.

In 1966, it bought the medical electronics company, S. E. Labs and tried to secure a large market for its very expensive medical scanners. Godfrey Hounsfield, of the EMIDEC 1100 team, won a Nobel Prize for his work on developing the CT Scanner while at EMI's Central Research Laboratories. However, despite having installed nearly all the CT scanners in the world in the early 1970s, the market grew slower than expected and EMI saw the investment going idle as demand grew slowly (Bartlett 1983).[67] Worse, when demand did start to grow, the market became dominated by GE, and later firms such as Hitachi joined a market in which their greater sales and service muscle could dominate. EMI's investment in medical scanners was of great social benefit, but of little financial benefit to the company.

Capital equipment for television continued to be an important source of revenue throughout the 1960s. In 1961, EMI was able to report that it was supplying large amounts of equipment to a number of the new ITV companies, and had supplied the BBC with 30 FM radio transmitters and five satellite stations (1961 Annual Report), as well as winning a number of overseas contracts. Later it was to become the UK custodian of the Telefunken PAL licence, further boosting its profit from this area (Layton 1972). PAL was the colour television standard chosen for use in the UK. Kemp-Gee estimated that EMI received £1 for every PAL colour set sold in the UK – £650,000 per annum in the early 1970s.

Outside electronics, EMI was also dynamic. The success of the 45 and 33 1/3 r.p.m. records, combined with the worldwide clamour for Beatles records, saw the record operation becoming highly profitable. Many of the large profits of the 1960s went into diversifying the company's activities. Much of the company's expansion was in a new division: Leisure and Entertainment. For this division, it purchased the Blackpool Tower Company, the Grade Organisation and various theatres. It also purchased Warner Brothers' 25 per cent stake in the television and film company ABPC (Associated British Picture Corporation), which it fully acquired in 1969. This gave EMI a chain of cinemas, a film studio, a production company and a controlling stake in Thames Television.

EMI might have limited its investment in computers, but elsewhere it had plenty of opportunities to deploy its resources.

## Conclusions

Overall, there seems to have been a dual problem for the EMI Computer Division. Its involvement in computers began as it was coming out of a period of poor performance and would end when it was again in a dip in performance. At this stage, it was keen to control costs and while Metcalfe was superb at getting funding for the development of computers, commercialising the offering was more problematic. Given the conservative attitude to resourcing, it seems to have been a mistake to try to take the market head-on by developing medium-to-large-scale commercial systems, IBM's and ICT's favoured territory. Like other electronics firms, despite wishing to limit its commitment to the computer sector, it did not adopt a niche and careful product strategy – it ploughed right into the middle of the fray.

Taking on this sector of the market needed the full support of a long-term programme. As will be seen later, ICT and the US business machines firms were totally orientated to achieving a significant market share; they realised market share was essential to cover the high development costs of computers. EMI wanted to make the operation self-financing at a very early stage and restricted spending on marketing software development and other core essentials for commercial market share. Operating in the small UK market, with a large number of competitors, such a policy was impossible. It would take more than one generation of machines to establish a large enough base to cover future development costs. If EMI was not willing to sink funds into developing a big market presence with the 1100 and 2400, and at the same time invest heavily in the next generation of machines, it could not hope to maintain its place in the heart of the computer market. The situation was not helped by the fact that the 2400 was developed by a team more used to capital electronics projects almost built to order, while the smaller, and potential bigger seller, the 1100, employed a dead-end technology.

In many ways, its weaknesses were similar to Ferranti's: lack of corporate commitment to computing, combined with a preference for less risky and shorter-term diversifications than computers represented. To add to this, both companies seemed over-reliant on the divisional structure. They used it to protect the parent company from failure of any single product, rather than as a method of improving day-to-day running of the company. Meanwhile, the actual operations of the divisions were woefully managed.

At the strategic level, there was a mismatch between the desired level of corporate commitment to computers and the product plan chosen. At the tactical level there was an inability to coordinate operational activities, especially with the divide between the 1100 and 2400 teams.

This chapter has shown that EMI clearly had poor structure and also suffered from competition for resources, an all too familiar scenario for electronics firms trying to enter the commercial mainframe computer market. However, in EMI's case the competition for resources could have been better managed if the computer department could have acted as a single business.

# 7
# English Electric – A Failure of Strategy

English Electric can be seen as a direct equivalent of General Electric (GE) with its combination of heavy electrical and electronics technologies.

With the exits of EMI and Ferranti, English Electric one of two major, domestically owned, commercial computer manufacturers. English Electric's history in computing brings together many separate developments. Its major domestic rival of the mid-1960s was ICT, which brought together the operations of business machines firms BTM, Powers Samas and the computer operations of Ferranti and EMI. English Electric was an established producer of early scientific computers, but had also absorbed the commerce-orientated computer operations of LEO and would also eventually take over the commercial and industrial control computers made by Elliot Automation. It also owned Marconi, giving it both advanced electronic engineering capability and a range of military-orientated systems.

With all of these strands within the English Electric story, this chapter only covers a high-level overview of English Electric in computing. Sadly the depth of information available is nowhere near the level available for GE and RCA.

However, what is fascinating is that English Electric was the only British electronics company which emulated the 'big push' strategies of US firms by developing an advanced (too advanced) third-generation computer strategy. It opted out of the computer market ostensibly for the same reasons as the American firms – the pressures on resources caused by a concentric diversification strategy – however, this was coupled to a hugely flawed third-generation strategy. English Electric's decision to develop systems based on the RCA Spectra 70, and then to delay the launch of these systems while it tried to introduce newer components based on developments at its Marconi division was an enormous mistake and shows the dangers of concentric diversification not only leading to competition for capital, but also to poor technical solutions through trying to exploit in-house capabilities. This strategy would live on when English Electric's computer operations were absorbed by ICT to form ICL. Government sponsorship of this deal weighed heavily on ICL as it was forced to continue support for this failed strategy.

## The company

### Centralised control

English Electric was formed in 1918 with the merger of five established electrical.[1] It merged medium sized companies such as Dick, Kerr and Co, Phoenix Dynamo Manufacturing Co and the Siemens Brothers Dynamo Works to create a firm able to compete with electrical majors such as GEC, BTH and Metro-Vick.

Putting this new company together was not easy and the firm was financially weak in the 1920s. The firm needed support which came from American firm Westinghouse as the major shareholder, though control stayed in the UK. In 1930, George Horatio Nelson (in 1960 made 1st Baron Nelson of Stafford) became the managing director. Nelson was a powerful figure and tackled the company's problems with a highly centralised decision making process. It consisted of functional departments, such as accounts, development, home sales and exports, coupled to a geographically based manufacturing organisation, based on the original pre-English Electric companies.

However, the most important aspect of the company's organisation was the routing of decision making up to Lord Nelson. Until 1948, the firm had no executive members to the board other than Nelson (Jones, R., Marriott, O., 1970:175). When an executive committee was formed, his son the 2nd Baron Nelson of Stratford was appointed to the post of deputy managing director, making him the only natural successor. These were very different days to the modern corporate governance conventions.

### Decentralisation

The organisation of the company only started to change during the Second World War, by which time it was fully independent of the Westinghouse company. However, the structure was only fully reformed in the 1960s with the formation of a complete product group system. This was forced on the company by a crisis caused by over-reliance on centralised control and trying to manage a large portfolio of technically related, but market unrelated products. A new organisational structure was formed.

Before this period, only new acquisitions and new product diversifications had profit centre status.[2] In 1965, following the advice of management consultants McKinsey (Channon 1973: 135–6), the 2nd Lord Nelson (now in charge) adopted a product line organisation across the whole company. He introduced this reorganisation to senior management very professionally with lectures and pamphlets. The remaining functional and central staffs were meant to take on a consultancy and planning role, acting as an internal management consultancy service.[3] This is similar to the GE system of control.

However, it was clearly not just McKinsey which influenced this structural change. Lord Nelson's willingness the year before to openly and honestly address an LSE seminar[4] shows that he was exploring the challenges of managing a multi-divisional company, although perhaps the concentric nature of the diversifications were still seen as an advantage, not a challenge.

## Post-war expansion

Immediately after the war, English Electric underwent a period of growth and profit, fuelled by high demand for its core heavy electrical products. It extended these heavy electrical activities by starting to produce diesel-electric locomotive engines and joined in the development of nuclear power.

It also expanded into three major new markets: aerospace (and aero engines), electronics (led by Marconi, which initially faced the same post-War challenges as Ferranti and EMI) and computers. However, of the three major electrical companies, English Electric remained the most reliant on heavy electrical engineering – a boon as the National Grid expanded and many new power stations were built.

At the non-traditional end of its operations, one of its most important new commitments was to aircraft and aero engines.[5] There were two main underpinnings to this expansion, but not based on the aircraft it made for a short time in early 1920 through its ownership of the Phoenix Dynamo Manufacturing Company. First, English Electric became a large operator of "shadow factories" producing RAF bombers, building up its aircraft capability. Second, during the Second World War, English Electric acquired the aircraft engine maker Napiers (Wilson and Reader 1958). This was a business would provide technology for a number of different areas of activity in the firm, many of which would outlast its aero engine manufacturing days.

After the War, the First Lord Nelson decided English Electric should exploit these assets to establish the firm as a major aircraft company. English Electric developed a number of military aircraft and missile systems. The most successful of these was the Canberra medium bomber which was produced in large numbers and used worldwide; indeed, many hundreds were produced in the US under licence for the US forces. This was the product that enabled the company to stay in this international industry into the 1960s. They also produced the Lightening interceptor (for which Ferranti produced the radar, at the time the world's most advanced) and the Thunderbird medium and long range anti-aircraft missile for the British Army – a rival to the Ferranti Bloodhound produced for the RAF.

The second major diversification after the war was into electronics. English Electric acquired Marconi following the nationalisation of Cable & Wireless in 1946 (Baker, W.J, 1970). It won the bid for Marconi in the face of competition from EMI. Both firms put forward arguments that they would dovetail well with Marconi's product mix. For English Electric, it was an opportunity to acquire one of the most advanced capital electronics organisation in the country. English Electric absorbed an organisation strong in military systems, communication equipment and broadcast transmitters.

English Electric also expanded its scope by ending Marconi's collaboration with EMI on television, and moved Marconi into the production of a full line of television studio equipment as well as transmitters, in competition with EMI. This was done by utilising the technical links Marconi had with RCA, which had been formed from Marconi's US operations.[6] The downside of this move was that English Electric ended its close relationship with its traditional US partner, Westinghouse, which was a rival to RCA in the area of television (Jones, R. Marriott, O. 1970:183). That is not to say that English Electric was reliant on US technology. By 1951, it had a research and development work force of 6000, spending £6.25m per annum, most employed at the Nelson and Marconi Laboratories. For a British firm, this was a very large commitment. Jones and Marriott (1970) argued that this figure, and the fact that the company had 2000 trainees at any one time, was due to the first Lord Nelson's willingness to think in the long term. He was prepared to forego short-term profits for long-term projects.

English Electric acquired Marconi at a very good price. It paid £3.75m, but £1.6m of government stock owned by Marconi was disposed of, making the net price £2.1m (Jones and Marriott 1970: 180).

In 1967, the firm would also purchase acquisition of Elliott Automation. This added to the military command, control and communication activities that Marconi already operated, as well as increasing market share in electronic instruments and adding to the English Electric's industrial automation business. Elliott was also a key player in the computer sector making small-scale systems for university research, industrial control and military application and had been a manufacturer of commercial mainframes in its own right and in partnership with NCR (See Lavington 2011). Elliott's industrial/military mini computers would prove an important acquisition for English Electric and later GEC and would last within the firm until nearly the end of its existence.

### Over extension

Many of the expansions in the post-war period would strain the managerial, operational and financial capability of the company, not least among these expansions was computing.

By the early 1960s, English Electric was faced with a number of problems. It was forced to reshape its operational structure introducing greater management autonomy and to take steps to improve its financial health. At this time a number of its new operations were disposed of.

Napiers was sold to Rolls-Royce following a failed attempt to develop a market for new turbo-prop engines, whose time had passed. In addition, 1960 the aircraft manufacturing operation was merged with Bristol to form the British Aircraft Company (Jones and Marriott, 1970: 190). Eventually the firm would also dispose of its computer division. The reason for the poor performance was in part caused by the cost of supporting so many high cost technologies.

After the war, English Electric had also entered the production of domestic appliances and consumer electronics. However, like the aircraft operation these products were sidelined or dropped as the financial statistics failed to improve. English Electric did not want to bear the cost of developing the marketing network that goes with such products, and was up against stiff competition from Jules Thorn (Thorn Electrical) and Arnold Weinstock (GEC).

However, this story of over extension and retrenchment is best studied through reviewing the history of English Electric's commercial computer operations.

## English Electric and the computer market

The firm's third major non-heavy electrical diversification was in commercial computers. English Electric was one of the first British companies to become involved in computer technology and, after an incubation period which was longer than Ferranti's, it offered an early marketable computer to the scientific market. The company's computer scope increased steadily until the mid-1960s, when it attempted to offer a significant new range of machines to compete head on with both ICT and IBM. Indeed, English Electric's computer strategy of the mid/late 1960s was viewed in some quarters as the only viable way of competing with IBM – they were wrong.

### Part 1: The experimental phase

*DEUCE (Digital Electronic Universal Computing Engine) Computer*

This case study primarily covers the 'mainstream' commercial computer operations of English Electric, with some description of the LEO developments (the full story of which can be read in Hendry 1988 and Caminer 2003). There is also limited coverage of the Elliott Automation story which was important to the end of the English Electric in the commercial mainframe market (the full story of this operation can be read in Lavington 2011), but which played little role in the mainstream of English Electric's history in this market. What should be read, almost in conjunction with this chapter, is the earlier chapter on RCA as. English Electric's strategy became interwoven with RCA's.

English Electric first became involved in computing when the National Physical Laboratories at Teddington started a project to build a computer. In 1944, the Treasury had given permission to the NPL to set up a centralised Mathematical Division (Croarken 1985: 129–31), to provide calculation services both within the NPL and to other research laboratories.

Among its staff was the leading mathematician and computer theorist, Alan M. Turing (Wilkinson, J.H. 1980:101–144. Wilkinson was one of the ACE project leaders.), who designed the Automatic Computing Engine (ACE) for high-speed mathematical calculation. This was the first detailed design for a stored programme computer and was based on Turing's pivotal development at the Bletchley Park code breaking centre in the Second World War.

However, none of Turing's Division at the NPL had an electronics background, so outside support was needed to construct the system. In 1948, the NPL Electronics Section began collaborating with English Electric to develop a fully engineered version the ACE (Croarken 1985: 160–1).

In 1949, Turing's development was fully transferred to the new Electronics Section of the NPL, a section with more appropriate skills (Wilkinson, 1980). The Electronics Section decided not to continue with efforts to build the very large and complex ACE and instead to concentrate efforts on a cut-down model, the Pilot ACE, to prove the technology know-how. The ACE would be constructed once the Pilot had been made to work. This was not to Turing's liking: disillusioned with the NPL's lack of commitment to his original idea to build a machine for immense mathematical experimentation, Turing left the NPL and pursued his own developments, first at King's College and then at Manchester University (Wilkinson 1980).

The Pilot Ace was fully operational in 1952, roughly two years behind the first Manchester/Ferranti Mark 1 computer. The first fully engineered version, known as DEUCE, was delivered to the NPL in 1955. English Electric went on to install two for its own use. The firm had a large demand for scientific calculation as it had a big interest in science-based industries, such as aerospace, conventional power generation, and, later, nuclear power. The firm would also market this machine, which was substantially cheaper than the Ferranti Mark 1* at £50,000. Production ended in 1961, with 30 being delivered (see Table 7.1).[7] This seems impressive compared to the first Ferranti systems, the Mark 1 and 1*'s, of which eight were installed commercially. However, this success was to some degree a symptom of DEUCE being later and longer in the market. By 1955, when production of the Mark 1* was ending, DEUCE was only just being delivered. By 1961, Ferranti had produced the Mercury, Pegasus, Perseus and the second generation Sirius machines, with Orion and Atlas nearing production, all of which, added together, greatly outstripped the sales performance of DEUCE. However, English Electric had established themselves in the market and had based their design on an iconic system. They found major success in areas such as the aircraft industry, and atomic research laboratories, activities closely related to English Electric's own businesses.

### Part 2: Structured entry

During the second generation of computing, English Electric extended the scope of its computer range, especially after it acquired LEO computers.

With LEO (described later) under its wing, English Electric started to become a major force in the UK computer market.

The NRDC estimated that joint English Electric and LEO computer turnover at the turn of the 1950s was £.5m-£1m per annum; by the mid-1960s this had reached £12m, a substantial advance; however, this represented only one quarter of ICT's turnover.[8]

During the early and mid-stages of the second generation of computing, English Electric's strategy was something of a hotchpotch, made up of a series of unrelated and incompatible families of computers, some aimed at scientific work, some at commercial work plus some smaller systems for process control and small-scale data processing. However, it was during this generation that it would make a big drive into computing, first by acquiring one of the most experienced teams of commercial data processing experts in the UK and then by developing a plan for entering the third-generation of computing with the most ambitious strategy outside the US.

*In-house developments: Second generation scientific and control systems*

Of the second generation machines produced, it was the KDF9 which was the natural successor to the DEUCE. This machine was orientated towards the scientific market, and had an advanced architecture. It was marketed in the early 1960s and first installed in 1963. It was more expensive than the DEUCE, at an average price of £120,000. However, research users had a growing demand

*Table 7.1*  Computer Consultants Ltd, 1965. 'British Commercial Computer Digest'

| | |
|---|---|
| DEUCE I customers | |
| AWRE | 1 |
| British Aircraft Corp. | 6 |
| Other Aircraft Designers | 4 |
| inc. Royal Aircraft Establishment | |
| Other Govt. Research | 2 |
| Universities | 3 |
| Other commercial | 2 |
| English Electric internal | 2 |
| DEUCE II customers | |
| English Electric Atomic Power Div | 1 |
| English Electric Nelson Laboratory | 1 |
| Marconi | 1 |
| RAE | 1 |
| United Kingdom Atomic Energy Authority | 1 |
| DEUCE IIA customers | |
| English Electric internal | 2 |
| Ministry of Agriculture | 3 |

for larger scale computing. The US Office of Naval Research (ONR) when looking a the capability of the UK computer industry[9] noted that the machine became available at the same time that British universities were about to purchase a large number of computer systems, as those already with computers needed to replace first-generation systems. In addition, a major expansion in the number of universities with computer departments was expected.

However, university installations tended to be fairly bare. Limited funds meant that universities were primarily interested in the acquisition of the central processor unit but with only limited memory and peripheral options. The universities were hoping to add extra facilities as funds became available.[10] With such a large number of KDF9's users buying fairly basic systems, English Electric seems to have given a low priority to peripherals for the machine. Eventually English Electric did provide disk packs supplied by US company CDC to add to its own tape drives, which were themselves manufactured under licence from RCA.[11] Despite offering these US sourced subsystems, the ONR characterised English Electric as being weak in peripherals. English Electric also only offered limited software support, hoping that the advanced users who tended to buy these systems could do their own programming, a tactic also adopted by DEC and CDC which made systems for US universities. The only language provided by English Electric was ALGOL and was seen as very inefficient.[12]

The NRDC considered that the KDF9, as a machine, represented a flawed strategy,[13] though it did see it as a useful addition to the UK's stock of scientific systems, with the potential to be improved on over time. It sold about 30 units in the five years of production, primarily to universities and research laboratories in government and aerospace[14] (see Table 7.2).

English Electric was also producing small computers to rival Elliotts and Ferranti in the area of process control computer systems. The KDN2/KDF7 sold for about £20,000.[15] By 1965, 12 had been installed, fairly small sales for a system in this market, but clearly widely used in controlling the new steel factories being built at the time (see Table 7.2).

The steel producers using the KDF7 (the later name for the machine) included the Czechoslovakian state producer, which purchased a large package of computers from English Electric in the mid-1960s, including two large English Electric LEO machines.[16]

*Outside technology – second generation business machines*

However, for English Electric the real assault on the computer market came with its decision to target commercial markets. This would require it to develop new types of systems and acquire more resources and new routes to market.

The most significant second generation computer produced by English Electric was the KDP10/KDF8 (the original name was the KDP10, which was re-designated in 1964 to the KDF8). It was significant because it showed the technical and commercial direction in which English Electric planned to go.

The crux of English Electric's plan was to utilise Marconi's traditional licensing and technological links with RCA. English Electric made the decision to broaden its coverage of the computer market by adopting the RCA 501 data processing computer and selling it to the office-based commercial data processing market. It took this design and 'Anglicised' it.[17] The 501 computer was one of the earliest US second generation data processing machines and was sold from the late 1950s to the early 1960s; in total about 99 were installed by RCA – we cover its history in-depth in the RCA chapter.

The English Electric version of the machine was available for installation from 1961 to 1965. However, its sales performance was weak. Only 13 were sold at an average price of £400,000.[18]

One reason for this poor performance was the inevitable lag built into the strategy. RCA had to develop, design and engineer the 501, which English Electric then needed to take, anglicise and develop production techniques to make. The KDP10/KDF8 was not dramatically late into the market, but it was late enough to have alerted English Electric to the potential weakness in the strategy – it did not learn.

The customers for the KDP10/KDF8 are not completely known; Table 7.2 identifies 9 of the thirteen sales:

*Table 7.2* Sales of English Electric KDF 9, KDN2/KDF7 and KDP10/KDF8 systems

| User | KDF 9 | KDN2/KDF7 | KDP10/KDF8 |
| --- | --- | --- | --- |
| Universities | 7 | | |
| Aerospace | 5 | | |
| Gov. Lab. | 3 | | |
| Internal use | 2 | | 1 |
| ICI | 1 | | |
| Steel producers | | 8 | |
| Electrical utilities | | 4 | |
| Banks | | | 6 |
| Other commercial | | | 2 |
| | (other customers unknown) | | |

*Source*: Computer Consultants Ltd, 1965. 'British Commercial Computer Digest'.

At this time English Electric was also selling the smaller KDF6. This sold for £60,000, and appears to have been sold to both commercial and industrial users, 12 being delivered.

Certainly, English Electric in this period did not suffer from a common weakness of the electronics companies by shunning equipment not built by in-house, a weakness pointed out by Ferranti's Computer Department veterans when they left that firm (Pollard 1960).[19] This lack of willingness by some firms to contract out was also noted by the NRDC.[20] Indeed, the NRDC was probably somewhat jealous of this English Electric trait and probably wished it had occurred elsewhere. Not only did English Electric build anglicised RCA 501s, which the NRDC certainly would not have approved of, but they also used its technical links with RCA to get hold of peripheral equipment, building such things as RCA tape drives. However, like RCA, they had to look elsewhere for certain other devices, for example buying discs drives from CDC, though English Electric probably would have bought discs from RCA had they been available. However, the NRDC noted that English Electric planned to produce more equipment in-house as the computer operation grew and indeed, English Electric did have greater plans for the future.

*Expanding the commercial line – acquiring LEO, and Elliot Automation*

An interesting feature of the relationship with RCA was that less than one year after the KDP10/KDF8 was first installed, ICT was installing the later and more sophisticated RCA 301 (marketed by ICT as the 1500). During this period there were some vague discussions about the three firms working together on a new system, but nothing came of it.[21]

English Electric no longer needed RCA for second generation computers. It was fully occupied with the various KDF ranges and had secured a second route into commercial computing by acquiring LEO Computers.

By 1963, English Electric was in the throws of Nelson's restructuring programme which has been outlined. Compared to its international competitors, English Electric's performance looked distinctly weak. Lord Nelson noted that the very high R&D and capital outlays involved in the computer industry made consolidation a natural course of action.[22] This was very much in line with what was happening in the rest of the UK industry, with ICT acquiring EMI and Ferranti. Abroad, US firm Philco left the industry, Bendix sold its computer operation to CDC, and GE took over Bull of France.

While ICT was actively looking to acquire technical electronics skills from the electronics companies, English Electric was going in the opposite direction. English Electric had a sound base in electronic technology, what it wanted was greater access to the skills needed to market computer systems in the commercial environment.

It seems reasonable to speculate about the reasons for its expansion into the commercial environment. The separate arts of scientific and business computing had rapidly merged during the second generation of computing. Scientific tasks required better input-output facilities for such things as statistical work, while improved peripherals meant that the commercial user could benefit from greater processor speed. With the scientific and commercial markets for mainframe computers rapidly coming together, English Electric needed greater capability to sell future machines into both markets.

It needed to do this so it could get the largest possible return from its R&D investment, and ensure that it could achieve scale economies to compete with other general purpose computer producers.

English Electric tried to achieve this greater coverage by forming a joint computer operation with the Lyons Electronic Office (LEO) subsidiary of J.Lyons Ltd. In 1963, English Electric and Lyons formed English Electric-LEO Computer Ltd.[23] In 1964, Lyons sold its shares in the business to English Electric and English Electric thus acquired one of the UK's most progressive, and commercially orientated, computer operations.

LEO has been widely written about and for good reason. A teashop company became one of the pioneers of modern computer – a truly amazing leap which was not driven by random conglomerate diversification but by the desire to manage complex business processes. Today, some of the world's largest software companies specialise in Enterprise Resource Planning software – and it was for planning and logistical control that Lyons became a computer company (see Hendry 1988 and Caminer 2003).

Lyons had prided itself on having one of the most advanced office systems, organised by mathematicians from Cambridge who worked on early operational research techniques. In the late 1940s and early 1950s, it decided to further improve its systems by developing the Lyons Electronic Office (LEO), a one-off computer based on the work Maurice Wilkes and the Cambridge University EDSAC project (Hendry 1988, Crammer 2003). The LEO I was used for a number of roles in Lyons, including managing logistic functions. It was, however, also used for third party functions, performing such tasks as the payroll for Ford's giant Dagenham factory.

In 1954, Lyons, which ran tea shops around the UK, started to develop and market the LEO II and set up a subsidiary to produce it; thus becoming a computer company. From 1957 to 1961, 11 of these first-generation systems were delivered, at an average price of £95,000.[24]

They did not stop there, in the early 1960s they announced the LEO III, a transistorised second generation system.

It was quite an incredible story, which has been well covered by others. However, computer systems were becoming increasingly expensive to develop and were being produced in ever larger numbers. It was clear that the next generation of systems, the third generation, were going to be large integrated families of machines produced in very large numbers. The development costs, especially the software libraries needed for commercial data processing work, were going to cost the same whether you made 10 or 10000 of them. Lyons' small operation was not large enough to justify the expense of developing a third-generation family.

By the NRDC's estimates,[25] both the English Electric and the LEO computer operations had each been operating on a financial shoestring: development costs were very high compared to turnover in both companies and this meant they were cutting back on software development (for example, the appalling availability of high-level programming languages and sub-routine libraries at English Electric). It was hoped that combining the computer interests of the two firms into one range of third generation computers would reduce this problem.

The LEO III and its upgrades, the 326 and the 360, sold reasonably well for English Electric. From 1962 to 1967, 43 of the systems were sold at an average price of £200,000. LEO was English Electric's most important second generation system but sales were comparatively low, and yet the firm still imagined itself to being a potential powerhouse in the industry.

After the takeover of LEO, English Electric decided to consolidate in-house operations as well. It added the real-time computer activities which the Marconi division had developed into a merged operation to form English Electric-LEO-Marconi Computers (EELM).

The main Marconi computer contribution was the Myriad computer. Marconi's computer activities started with a contract to design and produce an air traffic control/air defence environment for Sweden, a project called Fur Hat.[26] Marconi had developed the Transistorised Automatic Computer, TAC (meaning 'thank you' in Swedish) to control the system. The firm developed this into the Myriad computer, which Marconi claimed was the world's first third-generation system. Myriad was sold widely for processing radar information and communication switching.

Marconi's integrated circuit capability was based on a licence to manufacture from Ferranti. The ability to produce third generation components would later prove critical in the future story of EELM as it made a bid to become a major player in the rapidly growing industry. The Myriad used Ferranti's Microlin chips, a kind of multi-chip integration, which was later superseded by higher density Ferranti chips, the Micronor I and II circuits, the latter itself based on RCA technology (Scibberas 1977 and Layton 1972). Such capability would naturally be viewed as beneficial for the push into the next generation of computing – however, the strategy proved flawed as it seriously delayed the launch of the next generation of English Electric mainframes.

The final addition to the English Electric stable was the acquisition of Elliott Automation (previously Elliott Brothers). English Electric took over Elliott Automation in 1967 and with it came a successful, if not quite mainstream, computer business. They had identified niches, and built some success.

After this merger the final name for computer operations at English Electric became English Electric Computers (EEC).

Elliotts had particular strengths in military, control and small scale scientific computers. However, its main general purpose mainstream, the 4100, was out of line with English Electric's strategy and abandoned in 1970 (Campbell-Kelly 1989: 269).

The purchase of Elliott Automation gave English Electric a much stronger presence in the field of process and military control computers, expanding the share given it by the KDN2. Elliotts had over 200 installations in process control, with its leading product being the ARCH system.[27] This gave English Electric an estimated 50 per cent share of the UK market. Additionally, Elliotts and Marconi systems gave English Electric an estimated 80 per cent of the UK dedicated military computer market.[28] In both markets Ferranti was the main rival, and indeed it is difficult to see how IDC concluded that English Electric could have had 80 per cent of the military market given the range of military computers made by Ferranti and other producers.

These control and military assets of English Electric remained with English Electric after it merged the computer division with ICT, and eventually became GEC Computers.

## Part 3:   Consolidation phase

*System 4 and the big push*

In 1965, EELM informed the government's Treasury Support Unit (which was in charge of government purchasing and general computer matters) that it intended to compete head-on with IBM and ICT.[29] EELM was given a high status within English Electric to achieve this goals and the division became one of the eleven trading groups within a new company structure.[30] With this higher station in the company, EELM was expected to grow to become a significant part of the firm, and large enough to survive in the competitive computer industry. To do this, it took radical steps to produce a range of machines that could exploit LEO's commercial connections, English Electric's scientific market, Marconi's integrated circuit technology, and the link to RCA.

In the mid-1960s, it was clear that the second generation of computers needed to be replaced. IBM was making great strides with the announcement of the System/360 family of compatible computers, offering a completely integrated range of machines with massive support and marketing organisations and the best peripheral collection on the market.

EELM took advantage of a decision by ICT that it was not interested in making use of RCA's rival to the 360 series, the RCA Spectra 70. EELM dropped plans to produce its own system and decided to licence the RCA technology.

RCA's strategy, already studied in great detail, was to become the second source for IBM compatible equipment. The Spectra series was made program-compatible with the IBM 360, though it was architecturally different. Initially, the Spectra 70 series consisted of four machines, pitched between members of the IBM family. One of the advantages of RCA being an IBM follower was that it could offer competitive advantage by using third-generation components, integrated circuits (ICs). IBM had to use a hybrid technology as ICs were not readily available at the time the 360 was developed. It was more important within IBM to have the product released at the right time and to capture the market first; the finesse of the component used was not so important. At RCA, the two largest Spectra machines used ICs while the two smaller ones used transistors, as found in second generation machines.

In 1965, EELM announced its third-generation machines, the System 4 family.[31] It was the most significant launch ever of English Electric computers, as the fate of System 4 would determine the ability of English Electric to survive in the industry, would determine the need for future UK computer consolidation and would become a millstone around the neck of the successor firm.

The mainstream members of the System 4 family were the 4/10, 4/30, 4/50 and 4/70. The basic 4/10 cost (in US dollars) $185000; the 4/70 could be configured to cost over $2,800,000.[32]

As at RCA, the largest pair of machines used monolithic chips to make them complete third-generation systems. However, unlike RCA machines, the smaller members of the family used the same multi-chip integration as the Marconi Myriad[33] and Marconi was put in charge of developing the two smaller systems.[34]

Another development member of the family was the 4/75, which was a timesharing system sponsored by the UK's Ministry of Technology (MinTech) and was to be developed at Edinburgh University.[35] The 4/75 was meant to allow up to 200 users to access the computer at the same time. This called for delivery of a prototype 4/70 to the University in July 1968, conversion to the 4/75 by October 1968 and acceptance for use in December 1968. It was significant that EELM beat ICT and IBM for this contract, showing its relative strength in real-time systems. However, as will be seen there may have been other reasons for the selection – English Electric was being sponsored as a national champion, ICT and of course IBM, were not.

Neither ICT's 1900 nor IBM's 360 series would adopt such advanced components. They used simpler components so they could get their third-generation families quickly into the market initially using second generation and hybrid technology. RCA and EELM seemed to be trying to win the market through the use of advanced components.

There were a number of disadvantages with such a policy. English Electric was undertaking a major reworking of the RCA Spectra 70 system, as it had with the RCA501-KDP10/KDF8. However, this meant English Electric was lagging behind not only RCA in the production of third-generation computers, but even further behind IBM as the RCA system itself was an emulation of the IBM 360. IBM was EELM's competitor, not RCA. RCA's strategy meant that it inevitably lagged behind IBM in the introduction of new technologies as it had to wait to copy IBM protocols when they were published. RCA's decision to use transistors for the logic of the smaller members of the Spectra 70 series was an attempt to mitigate this problem; using second generation components meant the smaller machines could be produced quickly, and at a lower cost.

EELM had opted to follow RCA, another step removed from the originators of the concept, IBM. Not only did it follow RCA, but it also decided to redesign the system, another extension to the time period needed to get the System 4 into the field. It also meant that the System 4 would eventually be released comparatively close to the announcement of the next family of IBM systems, the IBM System/370.

The combined effect was that EELM could only expect to maintain its one advantage – more advanced components – for a very short time.

Another problem with this strategy was that it was putting EELM into direct competition with IBM. EELM's main UK rival, ICT, used a unique architecture for its 1900 family of third generation computers, thus locking the customer in. To change from an ICT to an IBM system was relatively expensive and disruptive because of the change in software required. EELM's System 4 and IBM's 360 series were relatively easy for customers to swap between, and price:performance comparisons were easy to make. RCA intended to tackle the market by offering machines set, on average, at a performance level 15 per cent above IBM's comparative machines, but with a price set at 15 per cent below that of IBM. It wanted a 30 per cent price: performance advantage.

RCA aimed to do this by using more integrated components to reduce the cost of building machines where these made most economic sense, and by foregoing some of the very high profit margin with which IBM was operating. It was also aiming to do this within the large US market which could absorb greater numbers of systems. To improve income while containing costs it had decided that it would licence its technology to key partners across the world letting them fulfil demand while supplying royalties to RCA. This was the role English Electric played. However, RCA was something of a tramp, it also licenced its system to Siemens and Hitachi.[36] EELM had a much smaller market in which to achieve the scale economies needed to match this plan and faced competitors in export markets with exactly the same strategy.

A further problem was that at the time, integrated circuits were still comparatively expensive, the second reason for RCA using older technology in its smaller Spectra computers. However, EELM was trying to use the advanced components that Marconi had used to produce the Myriad, a system that had only been built on a very limited scale for a few government contracts. Adopting the same technology for small commercial systems proved expensive and the smallest computer in the range, the 4/10, was never delivered due to its impractical costs.

Potentially the main cost advantage of copying RCA's strategy was in avoiding the cost of design work. Yet English Electric did not exploit this saving as it redesigned the RCA system so much. RCA never managed to make a profit from its policy of building IBM-compatible machines that were more powerful yet cheaper than IBM's own machines, indeed, that seems somewhat of a naive concept, and it would only be in the 1970s that the plug compatible firms would succeed in this (Takahashi 2005). In the limited UK market, English Electric had little chance.

EELM announced the System 4 some twelve months later than ICT announced its 1900 series. The delivery times were to be even longer: ICT delivered the 1905 in January 1965, but the first System 4 was not delivered until March 1967.[37] While EELM redesigned RCA machines, ICT simply produced a range based on existing Ferranti technology, and whether ICs were used was secondary – indeed, once prices had fallen, ICT quickly released the IC-based 1900A series which improved the range's price:performance ratio.

At English Electric delivery dates became longer and costs increased. By 1967, only 60 systems were on order and, as the problems increased, a number of these orders were lost.

### Exiting the computer industry

In 1966 only 2 KDF9's, 8 Myriads and 6 LEO machines were delivered; the other EELM systems were obsolete, indeed these late deliveries probably had their new owners regretting their purchase decision as computing radically improved with the third-generation systems. In 1967 only ten System 4s were delivered.

In 1969, IBM rated the systems it believed were its top ten major rivals for international sales. Surprisingly, the LEO 326 was the only representative from the English Electric Computers' (EEC) half of International Computer Limited (the firm had merged by this stage with ICT to create ICL) which made the top ten. This was due to the installation of a large number of LEO 326's by the General Post Office. Table 7.3 lists the computers that IBM's World Trade Corporation (1969b)[38] rated in the top ten outside the US:

*Table 7.3*   IBM World Trade Corporation competitor ranking

| Manufacturer and system | 1st Half 1969 rank | 1968 rank |
|---|---|---|
| RCA 70/45 | 1 | 2 |
| RCA 70/35 | 2 | 7 |
| Univac 1109 | 3 | 1 |
| ICL LEO 326 | 4 | 0 |
| ICL 1902 | 5 | 0 |
| GE 115 | 6 | 3 |
| CDC 6500 | 7 | 0 |
| Univac 9300 | 8 | 4 |
| ICL 1901 | 9 | 8 |
| Burroughs 3500 | 10 | 6 |

*Source*: Charles Babbage Institute, University of Minnesota, Collection 13. US vs IBM, px2482: IBM World Trade Corporation, Sept 1969b.

According to IBM, ICL was the leading international competitor, but the System 4 was not leading this effort. Yet sales of the RCA 70/45 and 70/35, by Siemens, Hitachi, and RCA in Canada, had made them the biggest individual system competitors in this list. Overall, IBM WTC rated the 1900 series as the most competitive full range of systems it then faced.[39] System 4 had not met the challenge of the market, especially compared to other licensees of RCA technology. Sales were poor compared to the ICT 1900. A year after the merger of English Electric Computers and ICT, the machines from the English Electric part of ICL represented only a small proportion of ICL's installed base and had few new orders (see Table 7.4).

*Table 7.4*  ICT computer sales vs. English Electric Computers by July 1969

|  | First Installed. | Installed by July 1969 | On order |
| --- | --- | --- | --- |
| ICT Systems | | | |
| 1900 Series | Jan-65 | 1033 | 1 |
| 1900A/E/F Series | Sep-67 | 116 | 473 |
| EEC Systems | | | |
| System 4 | Mar-67 | 111 | 20 |

*Source*: International Data Corporation, 21/11/69. 'EDP Europa Report'.

These figures show just how successful was ICT's policy of getting a family of machines that at least looked like a third-generation system into the market rapidly. As time went by the 1900 series was upgraded. The 1900A Series used IC components and the later S series used monolithic chips. The System 4 was marginalised into a system sold only to large users who especially wanted IBM compatibility and good real-time capabilities, even if the systems themselves were, in fact, only emulations of the IBM system and not truly plug compatible.

## A forced wedding – take over by ICT

Cooperation between ICT and English Electric had a number of false starts. These included tri-lateral discussions in the early 1960s between RCA, ICT and EELM to produce a new line of small scale systems, which came to nothing,[40] and a brief plan for a joint EELM-ICT-CITEC supercomputer project (CITEC was a French government sponsored firm tasked with developing a supercomputer protect).[41] This latter plan was akin to the Concorde project and was aimed at underpinning British and French computer technology, but, given the difficulty of developing supercomputer, the Government did not support it. However, a later ICT proposal for a supercomputer, called the 1908, did attract government support; but it was never built (Campbell-Kelly 1989: 245–9).

The first major move towards merger was taken in 1965. At this time, ICT was in the depths of a financial crisis caused by the launch of the 1900 series. Cash flow and profits were in a critical situation, not only due to development and marketing costs, but also because of the success of the 1900 series. The cost of placing large numbers of systems into lease arrangements was very high. Frank Cousin's Ministry of Technology believed that ICT should be acquired by English Electric. The MinTech was elated with the announcement of the System 4 strategy (Campbell-Kelly: 255–7).

Cecil Mead, ICT's chairman, and Arthur Humphreys', ICT's managing director, were told by a government official that

> the Government has made up its mind that ICT should be merged and should be a part of English Electric, because the Government feels that English Electric management is far superior.
>
> (Humphreys)[42]

This bizarre conclusion was not acceptable to ICT, which recognised its stronger long-term position and the potential weakness of EELM's strategy. It also showed a lack of understanding in the MinTech. While it may have been possible to argue that a merger of English Electric, ICT and Elliotts might produce a single British firm which could achieve economies of scale in the limited British market, it is obvious that MinTech had little concept of the long term repercussions of introducing new computer ranges. It was obvious that, at least on a product and marketing basis, ICT was the leading UK company, not English Electric. It seems that the government was making a decision based on shorter term criteria than even the capital markets were making: it saw the cash flow problems at ICT and judged it to have failed, while English Electric, which had not yet even begun to build System 4 machines, was considered successful. ICT could find funding – its problem was as much to do with success as anything else.

By 1966, ICT had recovered, with the 1900 being delivered in large numbers. MinTech still supported a merger, but now with ICT as the leading partner, though there was concern that the two companies' strategies were incompatible.[43] ICT was still not interested.

By 1967, the mood had changed substantially mainly because English Electric's computer strategy was becoming a significant burden on the parent corporation. English Electric was posting poor results in the mid and late 1960s. The company had done well in the early 1950s due to large demand for heavy electrical products. The 2nd Lord Nelson characterised the early period as when there was no shortage of orders, only limited capacity to fulfil them.[44] However, by the late 1950s and early 1960s, the heavy end of the industry had slowed down as new infrastructure was completed. At the same time, English Electric's major investments in new fields, aerospace, nuclear power, and computers, had not shown through in profits.

Worse still for Lord Nelson, he had set a tough benchmark to compare English Electric to other firms – this was to achieve a return on funds invested of 17.5 per cent. This would have made English Electric as successful as all its peers bar the US firm General Electric. The reality was that English Electric was far from achieving this goal as its many high cost developments robbed it off sorely needed profits. Figure 7.1 shows that in the key ratio of profit to funds employed, English Electric lagged behind all its rivals except AEI, and was far from achieving its target of 17.5 per cent return on funds employed:

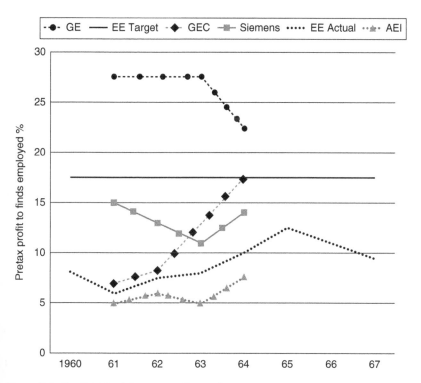

*Figure. 7.1* English Electric comparative performance
*Source:* Nelson 1966 and English Electric Annual Report 1967.

As has been explored in both the GE and RCA case studies, American rivals made similar calculations before they abandoned the expensive computer market. Both were concerned that their profit to capital ratio was too low to attract the capital needed to fund all their operations. During the mid-1960s, English Electric abandoned the expensive and risky field of aerospace partly because of this. However, this did not greatly improve English Electric's profitability ratios and further action was needed.

As English Electric questioned the rate of return it was getting, ICT was starting to accept that if it wanted to receive greater government support it would have to go along with the merger. It might not have believed that English Electric was in a strong position, but it had to take over its computer operation if it wanted further subsidies. The government pressure to acquire English Electric's computer operations was intense.

In 1967, the two companies formed a joint committee to plan a single successor to the 1900 and System 4. The hope was to produce a machine which both sets of users could upgrade to. The initiative for this committee came from MinTech, now under the control of Tony Benn.[45]

It was quickly clear that it was not possible to structure such an upgrade pathway to a new common system; these were totally incompatible systems and creating a system that could support the different word lengths of the machines would be economically impractical. The only arrangement that was possible was to develop software to aid the conversion of data from System 4 to ICT 1900 systems.

Despite the technical incompatibility, it was apparent that merger was inevitable. There was a clear mutuality of interests: ICT wanted Government support for a replacement of the 1900 series, and English Electric wanted to get out of a cash-draining business.

Efforts towards merger were finally galvanised by the Plessey Company, which let it be known that it wanted to take over ICT. To ICT, these approaches were as unwelcome as the 1965 plans for English Electric to take control of ICT.[46] However, with Plessey's approach it meant that there were two sources of finance on the table if ICT and EEC merged their operations: The Government and cash-rich Plessey. Negotiations started to revolve around how much capital the Government and Plessey were willing to commit to a merged company, and for what stake.

For English Electric, the delays suffered during the exploration of a joint system and then the negotiations with government and Plessey was a disaster. The longer time went on the more obvious became the flaws in the System 4 strategy.

English Electric did have some real strength in the computer industry. It could offer expertise in real-time computer operations. The IBM-type architecture was seen as more advanced than the 1900s design as it used 32-character word length as compared to ICT's 24-character architecture. However, ICT was already updating its range to give it the longer word length. Another advantage that English Electric could offer was a fairly strong presence in the Eastern European market.[47] These countries were unable to deal with IBM, but were interested in having the technology: English Electric could provide systems at least able to run most IBM software.

As well as an increasingly obvious flaw in the System 4 strategy, English Electric could not offer capital for further investment: ICT's management saw the availability of finance as the key to making a merged company more successful than the separate firms. Ensuring that the firm obtained a large market share meant it had to be able to finance an increased number of leased and rented computers. ICT saw this as crucial to achieving a minimum efficient scale.[48] Plessey and MinTech were willing to supply finance to a merged company.

The outcome was that English Electric only received equal status to Plessey in the merged firm: money was as important as technical resource, because these technical resources were aligned to a failed strategy (see Table 7.5).

*Table 7.5* ICL ownership structure

| Shareholder | Initial ownership of ICL: Percentage of Ordinary Shares | Form of commitment |
| --- | --- | --- |
| ICT shareholders: including Ferranti and Vickers | 53.5 | ICT operations and assets |
| English Electric | 18 | EEC business computer operations and assets |
| Plessey | 18 | £18 million |
| MinTech | 10.5 | £ 3.5 million direct investment +£13.5 million grant for development of future large computers and a new computer range. |

*Source*: Kelly. T, 1987:45 and Maxwell and Humphreys Interviews 1980/1.

International Computers Limited (ICL), the firm formed by the merger of English Electric Computers and ICT continued to support the System 4 into the early 1970s, but dropped the smaller members of the family because of their lack of competitiveness compared to smaller members of the IBM 370 family – by the time some of the members of the System 4 series were available, IBM had already replaced the 360 range with the 370.

ICL mainly sold the System 4 to large users who required IBM compatibility or strong real-time capability. Eventually, the 1900 was replaced by the 2900 and the System 4 ended, though in the mid-1980s ICL did sell a few large Fujitsu, IBM-compatible, systems as part of a technology and production agreement. However, the management, dominated as it was by ICT personnel, rejected English Electric's policy of IBM-compatibility and the later Fujitsu systems did little better.

## Conclusions

It is clear that in the period 1965–67, English Electric was attempting to become a major player in the UK computer market. It attempted this by following RCA's strategy, itself one of the most ambitious efforts to establish a firm as number two to IBM. By doing so English Electric might have expected to cut the high R&D cost of developing computers. Yet by trying to re-invent the range it pushed back the time when it could put machines on the market, by which time IBM had sold hundreds of 360 systems in the UK, and thousands worldwide.

It is also apparent that such a grandiose scheme was out of kilter with English Electric's overall financial position. As has been seen, RCA and GE both came to the conclusion that they were under-performing in the market because they were trying to support too many high cost projects at the same time, but this reality was not reflected in their computer product strategies. Like RCA and GE, English Electric was supporting a number of high cost expansion paths, such as electronics through the acquisition of Marconi and Elliotts, and the expansion into aircraft, locomotion engines, and nuclear power. All these cost a lot to develop.

Given lacklustre financial returns, the computer product strategy in the 1960s was not appropriate to the company's situation. English Electric wanted to develop a major new group within the company producing computers. However, this meant that it had to spend large amounts of money on building up its production and marketing capacity, and had to reach a scale large enough to compete with IBM. The company was not able to fund such a programme because it had too many other projects. English Electric might have done better, and put the resources of the company under less strain, if it had adopted a niche strategy similar to that of the smaller US business machines firms or the US producers of scientific computers. An alternative was to drop other development programmes and concentrate more resources on the computer diversification.

It seems that English Electric opted to support its other activities before the new computer operation. English Electric concentrated on areas which were less risky and more familiar to the firm, not surprising given its poor performance compared to rivals. While it was willing to continue to build computers for industrial and military control systems, it would not further support the commercial computer operation. Commercial computers were too far away from its traditional areas of activity and had too great an impact on the company's cash balances.

The same problems occurred in the American firms of RCA and GE, where large quantities of internal decision making documents are available. It seems likely that the process of failure in the computer industry was similar across all three firms and it is through the study of these US companies that real understanding of the challenges faced by concentrically diversified enterprises can be seen.

# Part IV
# The Business Machines Firms –
# What Did They Do Differently?

# 8
# Strategies and Organisations of IBM and ICT

The case studies covering the concentrically diversified, multiproduct electronics firms have been used to suggest that vertically and horizontally integrated companies failed to take full advantage of the economies that they should have been able to exploit. However, that statement is clearly unsatisfactory if those firms which did survive in the sector had similar structures, exhibited similar forms of conduct and produced similar product strategies.

This chapter develops two cases which explore companies with significantly different corporate structures based on significantly different corporate histories. Predominantly these firms had a corporate history in business machines rather than capital electronics:

(1)  International Business Machines (IBM) in detail – the primary focus of this chapter is IBM, the dominant manufacturer, distributor and service provider for large and small-scale business machines based on the punched card tabulator technology which it developed (its only significant rival in this technology being Remington Rand, a firm which in 1955 merged with Sperry to form Sperry Rand)
(2)  International Computers and Tabulators (ICT) – the UK's predominant business machines firm based on the same historical roots, and indeed one major constituent being the main licensee for IBM technology in the UK, the other half of the firm having been the main licensee of Remington technology.

There were, of course, a number of significant players in the market. For example, there were in the US a number of second-tier competitors which managed to succeed where the electronics forms had not. Sperry Rand (which acquired Remington) was effectively IBM's main competitor, which, like Radio Corporation of America (RCA) and General Electric (GE), took on IBM in its core computer market. It was a conglomerate, but with computing making up a hugely significant part of the business, unlike the likes of RCA and GE.

Two accounting machines firms also survived in the computer market, National Cash Register Company (NCR) and Burroughs both with something of a niche marketing strategy – again computers became their main product, and significant part of the investment and resources went into the new market.

The other major player by the end of the 1960s was Honeywell which, like Sperry, was something of a focused conglomerate which chose to make computers its key business area. Finally, there were also two major start-ups which became highly significant; Control Data Corporation (CDC) and Digital Equipment Corporation (DEC). Both initially focused on the science market. CDC made giant supercomputers; DEC went the other way producing small systems which individual science labs could use for running calculations of managing experiments at the local level.

However, for this book the benchmark firm has to be IBM: it was the firm which all others had to compete against; which provides a similar scale to the big electronics firms; and whose structure and organisation can most shed light on what the electronics firms were doing wrong. Big Blue was the 'Black Box' that rivals were peering into to determine which strategies they needed to adopt and which products to market so as to compete against it.

ICT in the UK plays a similar role as the dominant business machine firms. It represented a firm which came to the computer industry not through technological push, but really through customer pull. It had the customers who could use computers, what it needed was a way to deliver them.

Some initial data may help indicate the overall position of the business machines and start-up companies compared to the electronics firms in the computer market. Figures 8.1–8.2 show the share of the installed base of computers that the major US companies had. Figure 8.1 illustrates IBM's lead over the rest of the industry, with a consistent 70 per cent share. Figure 8.2 shows the market share of the other major companies. These figures show the fall of Sperry-Rand from its position as IBM's major competitor. They also show that, in the 1960s, while Sperry and Honeywell tended to have a larger market share than GE and RCA, the electronics firms had a user base as large as such firms as Burroughs and NCR. By this measure, RCA and GE were not completely 'out of the game', indeed, these two firms did have much greater resources of all types than their business machine firm rivals – though of course these resources were deployed across many more product lines. These figures also show the boost provided to Honeywell and Sperry when they purchased the computer divisions of the two major case-study firms (GE and RCA), they also indicate the success of CDC in the 1960s, and the success of Burroughs and DEC in the 1970s. ICT is not included as its domestic market was firmly in the UK.

Figure 8.3 shows a significant difference between GE, RCA and the rest of the industry. By 1969, computers made up at least 10 per cent of corporate revenue in every company bar GE and RCA where computers remained significantly less than a tenth of corporate activity. Another company with

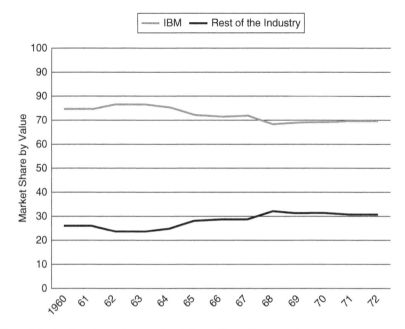

*Figure 8.1*  Market share of categories A-G, small, medium and large computer systems
*Source*: Charles Babbage Institute, University of Minnesota Collection 13. US vs IBM px5448 – data produced by the Justice Department to illustrate IBM's market dominance US Electronic Data Processing Market Share by value

a relatively low commitment to computing appears to be NCR, however it should be noted that computers and Information Technology were important to its success in its other business activities, supporting its sales of accounting equipment to the banking and retail industries.

## IBM

### Dominance of the pre-War business and scientific machine market: the right strategic history

> You never saw another company quite like International Business Machines Corp. Where all men dress well, every office boy is a potential Leader, and the Leader gets $442,500 in one year ... It's marvellous.
>
> *(Fortune* Jan 1940)

Evidently *Fortune* magazine was impressed by the sense of corporate success within Thomas J. Watson's company. IBM's prosperity was founded on its dominance of the market for punched card and tabulating systems. The forerunner of IBM, the Computing, Tabulating and Recording Company, was an amalgam of a time clock producer, a weighing machine company and the company

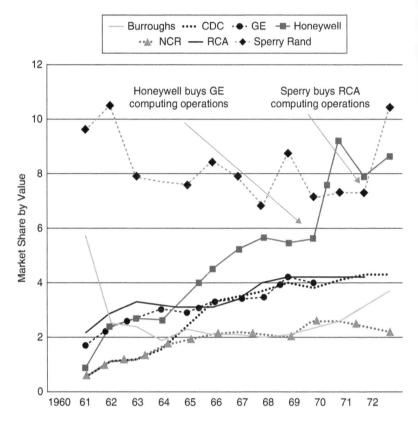

*Figure 8.2*    Computer market share of smaller computer manufacturers by value
*Source:* Charles Babbage Institute, University of Minnesota, Collection 13. <u>US vs IBM</u> px5448 – data produced by the Justice Department to illustrate IBM's market dominance US Electronic Data Processing

that produced the statistical tabulating equipment invented by Dr Herman Hollerith (Malik 1975: 36). In 1914, Thomas J. Watson Senior was appointed to head the company and made it a huge success by exploiting demand for tabulating equipment following the First World War (Rodgers 1969).

During the inter-war years, IBM was operating in a rapidly growing market. Private corporations were increasingly turning to tabulating techniques to automate their administration systems. This was reflected in the adoption of a new name to describe IBM's main products: Electric Accounting Machines (Campbell-Kelly 1989: 91). The expanding role of government bureaucracy also proved a significant market for IBM; as the government developed a hunger for data, so IBM grew (Malik 1975: 36–7). Note, for the early history of IBM, Pugh 1995 and Yost 2011 cover the firm in excellent detail.

IBM saw itself as a complete service operation: its machines were viewed as too complex for users to purchase and service themselves. Therefore, IBM

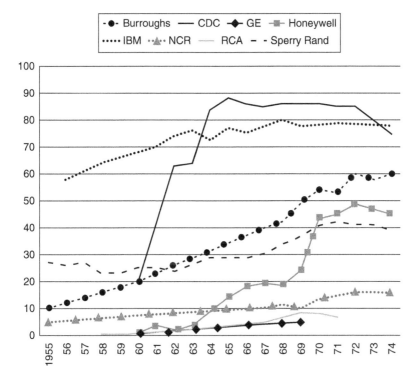

*Figure 8.3* General purpose (excluding mini computers and services) computing manufacture and leasing as a percentage of corporate revenues
*Source*: M. Phister (1979: 291)

only leased machines to users, providing its own service and maintenance staff. This provided good, steady income. It also meant IBM could force users to buy its own supplies for the machines it leased (Malik 1975).

Leasing and IBM's use of 'bundled' services would later become a substantial topic of debate and analysis. Leases were expensive for customers, but it meant that machines were serviced and maintained and customers had a way of cutting costs when they needed to. If a customer wished to terminate a lease, they would pay the leasor the 'net unamortized balance of the purchase price'.[1] However, after five years or so this would normally be less than the rental paid and could also be offset against investment tax credit. In addition leases offered some flexibility to upgrade to updated equipment, usually after eight year,s or to terminate with a reduced capital impact than would have been felt from writing off a fixed asset. IBM would eventually introduce a radical reform when, in June 1969, it announced 'unbundling'.[2] However, this was precipitated, at least in the eye of Auerbach and CDC by its law suit (going to trial in 1972–73) and the US Justice Department's antitrust suit against IBM (commencing January 1969) – unbundling was forced on IBM.

In Watson's first year with IBM there were 1400 employees, and the firm had sales of $4m and profits of $1.3m. Employment reached 10,000 in 1930 and by 1945 turnover was over $140m (Malik 1975: 36–9). This rate of growth was impressive, as were profits, but it was not one of the world's largest corporations, not in the league of firms such as GE, Ford and RCA, though Watson ensured IBM received as much publicity as these larger firms. What is notable is that growth was almost solely internally generated, and most of this was based on the tabulating operation rather than any of the other businesses, such as weighing machines and time clocks. The only merger was with a typewriter company. This move was fairly common to business machines firms: rival tabulator manufacturer Powers merged with the typewriter company Remington, forming Remington Rand, which would be IBM's main competitor in the pre and early computer era. One can speculate that, for these firms, economies of scope through cross-selling to a common customer base was a strategic goal.

Under Watson Senior's guidance IBM managed to achieve an 80 per cent share of the tabulator market. There were many factors behind this success. Watson ploughed back much of the profit into improving the product and established a competitive research and development environment within the corporation. Campbell-Kelly (1989) gives an example of how this worked. One weakness in IBM's range during the First World War was lack of a tabulator that printed: under IBM's competitive research environment four were developed, all competing for the right to go into production.

IBM knew its business and understood the management of a leasing franchise. Even once a winner for the printer competition was found, it was held back so that old leased machines were not returned until fully depreciated. This is an early example of IBM being very conscious of how its policy of renting systems required some competitive practices to be modified. The printing tabulator was not introduced because the model it replaced had not been in service for the minimum time required – five years. An awareness of this problem was not evident within RCA when it replaced the Spectra 70 with the RCA Series years before the older machines had recouped their investment, and of course RCA's depreciation period was longer than the IBM target. During the computer period, with the potential damage to market share of not presenting new technology quickly, IBM again modified its behaviour. During this later period, it used its lower cost base to depreciate its machines faster than other firms, which allowed it to introduce new generations more quickly.

Vital to the policy of leasing machines, rather than selling them, was the availability of capital to finance the cost of putting new machines on to the market. Watson had much greater levels of profit to plough back into building its future strength (see Table 8.6). Shareholders benefited both from predictable dividends (which could have been greater) and from capital growth, as funded R&D led to ever rising numbers of leases thereby ensuring future rental income. If you wanted to find an equity that had the long-term predictable cash flows of a bond, it was IBM.

However, it wasn't simply a story of a rapidly growing high-technology company; underpinning the business strategy was a low-cost base. Low costs allowed IBM to depreciate equipment more quickly than other firms, allowing it to turn over computer generations faster, while maintaining profitability and therefore generating the capital for leases. Efficiency and strategy were therefore linked: low costs made possible a market strategy which kept competitors off-balance with IBM creating a rapid advance in computer generations. This strategy was most pronounced during the 1960s, when the 360 family of computers was introduced even while second generation computers were selling well. The 360 was then replaced in the early 1970s by the 370, well before firms like GE and RCA could cope with a new generation.

If the way IBM operated in the business machines industry led to a business model which would prove successful in the computer era, IBM's significant share of the marketplace for scientific and statistical calculation punched card machinery led to technical advancement which would reinforce its lead.

Initially for the scientific market, Remington tabulating machines seemed more appropriate as they could be more rapidly altered to carry out new calculation tasks. However, IBM reacted by introducing a 'plug board' control panel which enabled its system to be rapidly 'reprogrammed' (Campbell-Kelly 1989: 160). The 600 series of electronic calculators which IBM started to produce in the early 1940s was the right product at the right time as war increased demand for flexible calculators. The flexibility of the plug board was a boon to research establishments that often had a number of different calculations to perform. Therefore, IBM had a foothold in the scientific and engineering markets, and this proved an early incentive for the firm to enter the computer industry.

In addition to plug boards, IBM had also introduced a new larger card format of 80 columns: however, IBM ensured the new machines could also read the cards produced by the old 45 column system. Powers' attempt to introduce a 90-line system was not a great success because it failed to be backward compatible with its old cards (Campbell-Kelly 1989: 82).

Above all, early IBM was a marketing organisation, both internally and externally. Within the company slogans were bandied about to encourage activity, such as 'Make things happen' and the single word, that appeared throughout the company and for which Watson was renowned, 'Think'. Watson developed his management technique in NCR. He emphasised marketing: the salesman was king. It seems that feedback and consultation between development teams, manufacturing and marketing staff was strong. At some electronics firms there was discord between these teams, Ferranti being a prime example.

This brief outline of early IBM has highlighted a crucial phase in its history. Many of the factors that were to be important in the computer industry were tackled by IBM in this earlier period: the link between a solid capital base and the ability to grow with a leased product line; ensuring that new technology was compatible with old (though it would famously and impressively break this creed); ensuring that new technology did not conflict with the financial discipline required to profit from leased products; the importance of marketing; the prominence of information within the organisation; and strong leadership. These policies were made possible by large-scale production and low costs, its ultimate competitive advantage.

## IBM and computing

### Part 1: The experimental phase

On the entry of the US into the Second World War, Watson Senior wrote to the President offering the services of IBM to the country (Fishman 1981: 34–5). However, in essence IBM's activities did not change greatly. It did build a new plant to produce mechanisms such as gun sights; a product which IBM was very appropriate to produce given the intricate electro-mechanical instruments it was used to making. However, the majority of IBM factories were simply told to produce more tabulators. The War necessitated a greatly increased government bureaucracy and even more engineering calculations. IBM machines were in big demand in Washington; thousands of machines were conscripted into military and government service. On the other hand, Remington Rand, IBM's chief rival, had a number of other businesses which were of immediate importance to the War including munitions factories; much of Remington's effort was diverted to this vital production (Fisherman 1981).

IBM machines were not just needed for the running of the bureaucratic war, they also formed the backbone of cryptography, the art of code breaking. The flexibility of IBM machines, and their larger card sizes, made them best suited to this task. IBM also found that one of the developments it was sponsoring in scientific calculators was useful in this role. In 1937, IBM started to fund the development of the Harvard Mark l/Automatic Sequence Controlled Calculator (ASCC) which was completed in 1944. This was an electro-mechanical calculator system, in the main produced from existing IBM components (Ivall 1960: 9–11).

As the leading calculating device, the ASSC was soon overhauled by the very early computers coming from such groups as Eckert and Mauchly at the University of Pennsylvania's Moore School (Fishman 1981: chapter 2). IBM improved on the ASCC, and in 1948 produced the SSEC, Selective Sequence Electronic Calculator. This was still essentially an electro-mechanical calculator, and still not in the league of the first real computers then under construction and soon to be running.

However, during the War and the immediate post-War period IBM was increasingly capable in electronics technology, using electronics to improve the speed of its traditional punched card and tabulator systems. By this stage the key product was the 600 series of electronic tabulators. In 1948, the 604 calculating punch was introduced, of which 5600 were produced (Campbell-Kelly 1989: 160) and which further increased IBM's stake in the engineering calculator market.

Therefore, IBM was moving towards capabilities along two tracks: through its involvement in one-off scientific systems, and in increasingly sophisticated electronic tabulators. Significantly, both trends involved IBM employing more professional electronics engineers and scientists: after the War, IBM had significantly expanded its skill base.

Many of the computer enthusiasts in IBM crowded around Thomas Watson Junior, who after the War was made president of the company, with his father as chairman and CEO. One of the new employees with an academic and research leaning was Ralph Palmer (Fishman 1981: 38). In response to the concerns of Metropolitan Life, a major IBM customer, that it was being swamped by punched cards, Palmer proposed the Tape Processing Machine (TPM) (Fishman 1981: 39). This was to be one of the first machines to work with magnetic tape storage mechanisms, connected to a modified 604 (Malik 1975: 55).

Initially, IBM was cool on this development as the sales staff concluded that such tape-based systems would never sell (Fishman 1981: 39). Their claim was that users preferred the ability to pick out punched cards in any order rather than the sequential storage of magnetic tape. On the other hand, IBM salesmen were increasingly speaking to customers who had been thoroughly enthralled with the new technology of universal automatic computer (UNIVAC), the commercial offspring of Eckert and Mauchly's computer developments, which had been acquired by rival Remington Rand.

The Korean War intervened in the debate by pushing IBM into computers via its interests in systems for scientific and defence calculations. Watson Senior ordered James Birkenstock, Watson Junior's executive assistant (Fishman 1981: 39), to support government contracts in the war effort. Birkenstock was a champion of computers. He started talking to a number of different government departments about developing systems for their unique needs. Birkenstock and a colleague, Hurd, approached Watson Junior and put forward a submission that most of these proposals could be adequately covered by a single type of machine: the instinct of IBMers was to build replicable product, not to rely on one-off capital electronics. They asked for $3m to start the production of the 'Defense Calculator' (Fishman 1981: 41). Before Watson would agree he told them to go out and find specific orders. They came back with around 30 orders for a machine that rented for $8000 per month.

At this stage, the Defense Calculator consisted of only a block diagram drawn by Palmer. It was not the TPM, as this was designed for commercial use and was not fast enough. As development advanced, it became apparent that, to cover costs, a rental of $22,000 per month would be needed. Unwilling to triple the price, a $15,000 tag was chosen as a compromise. Nineteen were eventually produced (Fishman 1981: 39–43). In IBM, nomenclature the Defense Calculator became the 701. It was based on the Williams Tube memory system used in the Ferranti Mark 1 computer, indeed IBM was the first licensee of the Williams technology, though it lagged behind Ferranti in the introduction of computers. The first 701 was not delivered until 1953, well behind UNIVAC and Ferranti.

While the cost overrun on the system was of some concern, the machine was built on the basis of 'build it and see': IBM was building it for the national good, and for the benefit of learning about the new technology. The 701 was extremely reliable for its time, an IBM trait which would prove significant in winning other important military contracts (Jacobs 1986: 47).

The idea of not charging full economic costs of the 701 so as to develop capability and to keep customers happy was a very different attitude to the attitude displayed by some companies, notably Ferranti which while beating IBM to becoming the first producer of commercial computers would never have dreamt of doing so if there was not a contract in place based on a cost-plus arrangement. At this early experimental stage, IBM was already capable of envisaging a market for computers and had customers in the right space and with whom it had relationships it did not want to damage. Often IBM's early days in computing are viewed as halting and sometimes negative. However, while IBM may have been a year or two behind the likes of Ferranti and UNIVAC to the delivery of its first real computers, the result was reliable and it was priced to gain a foothold in what it clearly identified to be a real market, not a series of one-off capital electronics companies – which the early developments at some of the big electronics firms can be likened to.

IBM would continue to develop its first generation scientific machines: the 701 was replaced by the 704, and then the last in the line of first generation computers, the 709. The 704 greatly outsold the 701. However, the 709, while being a big technical advance, was quickly superseded by a transistorised version of its architecture, the highly successful 7090 which was first installed in 1959. The 704 introduced magnetic core memory to IBM's range of scientific computers, though this was some two years after UNIVAC's scientific 1103A (developed by ERA, Dorfman 1987: 54). Nevertheless, the 704 came to dominate the market as it was fast and had a larger memory capacity, allowing it to be the first machine to utilise the IBM scientific computer language, FORTRAN (Dorfman 1987). The combination of the 704's hardware and software, and IBM's prior presence in the scientific market, allowed it to dominate the sector. It is notable that the 709 was compatible with the older 704, showing IBM's early realisation that it should be careful about making users' software obsolete, though it would later manage a successful transformation which did indeed require major rewriting of software and data.

The development of commercial processors took two separate routes. The first of these shared its tools and some key personnel with the developments going on in the scientific and military stream of development and would be targeted at large-scale commercial systems. Confidence in computer technology was increased by the 701 experience, and Palmer returned to the development of the TPM, which became known as the 702 (Malik 1975: 55). However, the 702 was immediately outclassed by new Remington Rand UNIVAC technology (Fishman 1981: 45). The 702 was quickly replaced by the 705 which was a great success. It used buffered input-output, peripherals that were interchangeable with the scientific line of machines, and the new magnetic core memory technology. This was two years before UNIVAC could offer this memory technology to civilian users (Dorfman 1987: 55).

IBM's second route into commercial computing was through the production of small, cheap computers, of a type more easily usable by punched card customers. In 1954, the same year that the 702 was fully developed, the IBM 650 was completed. This was a simple punched card input-output machine that used a drum memory for holding programs and active data. Over a thousand were installed, mainly in the business environment. This was an amazing success in a completely different league to the other first-generation systems developed by other companies. It may have been simple and low cost, but a thousand sites were established as IBM computer leaseholders. The first generation of data-processor managers would build their skills using the 650. However, this was not always IBM's first intent; it was envisaged as a machine appropriate for small scientific calculations (Dorfman 1987: 55). The fact that it was small, simple and used punched cards made it ideal for IBM's established commercial customers.

IBM had rapidly become the biggest computer manufacturer, with the large-scale scientific 704 and 709, the large commercial 705 and the small 650. But what drove the transfer from the unremarkable sales of the 701 to mass production? The process is fairly obvious for the 650. There was simply no alternative to it. Users in the commercial market were used to leasing from IBM, and IBM was offering a machine with more advanced specifications than the old tabulator systems. IBM had far more experience with electronics than any of the other business machines firms. It also offered a degree of backward compatibility for data, as the main input-output media was the 80-hole punched card.

However, IBM had no special advantage in the area of large-scale systems: indeed, initially Remington Ran's stable of computers made it initially a larger producer. It seems that much of IBM's ability in the area of large-scale computers came from the winning of a contract to build the computers for the Semi-Automatic Ground Environment (SAGE). SAGE was to be the backbone of North America's air defences, sorting information and helping to control air warfare (there are a number of descriptions of the SAGE project, see, for example, Jacobs 1986; and of its impact on the technical and production capabilities of IBM, see Redmond and Smith 1980 and Usselman 2011).

SAGE was developed in the Lincoln Air Defence Laboratory of MIT, with the computer side of the project being led by Jay Forrester and the Digital Computer Laboratory (Jacobs 1986: 39–42). The MITRE Corporation was appointed to manage the whole project. To unify the system a number of computers were needed. The main machines were FSQ-7s, one of the first real-time computers, able to process information as soon as it was presented to the computer. In October 1952, IBM was awarded an engineering development subcontract for the FSQ-7 (Jacobs 1986: xvi). IBM beat a number of competitors for this contract, including UNIVAC and Raytheon. IBM won the project because it showed management commitment to the project, availability of skills within the company and production and service organisations able to build and maintain the system (Jacobs 1986: 42).

The SAGE contract proved to be important to IBM. FSQ-7s were big, 110–250 tons, with 49,000–60,000 vacuum tubes, needing three megawatts of power and massive air-conditioning. It also introduced Jay Forrester's magnetic core memory system to IBM. The fast memory on these machines was (for those times) a massive 64K. IBM would use similar memory on the 704 scientific and the 705 commercial computers, giving both systems significant advantages over other competitors. IBM built up mass production of core memory and offered large memory capacities on its machines. The FSQ-7 introduced many other innovations. It also emphasised reliability: FSQ-7 down time was expected to be four hours per year (Jacobs 1986: 74). This is quite incredible for a first-generation technology.

For IBM the deal was clearly worth winning. There were 24 SAGE direction sites constructed, each with two $20m FSQ-7s, and in total 52 machines were built. The scale of the project enabled IBM to build up its ability to mass produce computers:

> A lot had to be done before we could go into electronics in a big way. We did not know how to mass-manufacture circuit boards, for example. We learned by landing a contract to build huge computers for the first North American early-warning system against bomber attacks, known as SAGE. The entire field of computer science was as new to us as it was to everyone else.
>
> (Thomas J. Watson Junior, interviewed in *Fortune* 31/8/87: 27)

SAGE AN/FSQ-7 development was undertaken at IBM's Poughkeepsie labs and was important not only because of the value and scale of the contract, but also because it became a place where IBM's top talent could work on computing and which could be used to attract other top talent.[3]

The 650 and SAGE gave IBM a scale of production well beyond that of other firms. SAGE also gave IBM a number of technical advances with which to underline its lead. It seems from Watson's comment that the SAGE contract was as valuable in terms of moving IBM further along the learning curve as it was in simple sales and profit terms.

## Part 2: Structured entry

Clearly the standard format for these chapters does not fit IBM well, they already seemed to have something of a structured relationship with the computer market even with their very first general purpose computers, whether aimed at the commercial or the scientific market. Nevertheless, IBM's strategy during the latter part of the first generation of computing and into the second generation of computing consolidated its lead in the market at every level.

### (a) Small-medium scale commercial processors

The 650 had put IBM well ahead in transferring tabulator users to computers. One of the first IBM machines to build on this tactic was the 305 RAMAC, announced in 1955,[4] with installations commencing in 1957. This first-generation computer was based around a disk memory system, RAMAC, which had first appeared as an option on the so-called 650 RAMAC (of which 300 were sold) (Dorfman 1987: 142). This allowed users to access relatively large amounts of information in any order required, at two hundred times the speed of magnetic tape. This was a significant feature for a number of users as it gave them their first access to random, rather than sequential, data, improving speeds and allowing for some near real-time interactions with datasets. Over 1000 of these systems were installed on lease at around $3200 per month, and around a thousand 305 RAMACs were installed.

It is notable that IBM spent $10m on developing the disk system, a technology that it would continue to dominate. The 305 RAMAC's disk and magnetic core storage put it well ahead of the competition and, with these features, it was one of the first computers to be used for commercial online applications. Such investment in the future of a peripheral is in some contrast to the less-than-enthusiastic attitudes of the electronics firms to this end of computer hardware.

Even greater success was achieved with the second generation 1401, first delivered in 1960. The 1401 was developed using IBM's competitive research system, with IBM France making the successful proposal for the new processor (Bashe et al. 1986: 465–74). However, the process of decision making was not based on infighting, but organised competition; it did not mean that one division would then become dominant; indeed the 1401 system was initially known as the Worldwide Accounting Machine (WWAC) because of the global team working on it. France developed the processor, Germany the printers and some other peripherals and the US the core electronics. Production was equally global with the 1401 central processor units simultaneously built in the US and West Germany, with printers being built by IBM France as production expertise in these areas were based in these locations.

The 1401 was designed to be an improvement on the 650 and better able to work with magnetic tape rather than punched cards as the primary input method. It was also larger than the 650; it could be configured up to the medium scale of computing.

The 1401, and its cousins the 1410 and 1440, were a great success, outselling the 650 ten-fold, even to IBM's surprise (Campbell-Kelly 1989: 201). Not surprisingly, one of its great advantages was in peripherals: not only did it offer good magnetic tape drives, but also the best printer on the market, the IBM France-built 1403 (Campbell-Kelly 1989: 201). IBM also improved the disk drives that were available for the 1401, a field in which IBM was already the leader. In 1962, IBM was offering the new 1301 disk file with the 1401. This new disk device made obsolete many of the systems other companies were developing to tackle the older RAMAC and 1405 disk files – by the time firms had managed to deliver a system competitive with the old IBM kit, IBM had already moved forward.

With the success of the 305, the 10,000 sales of the 1401 and the best range of peripherals, IBM had secured its place as market leader.

*(b) Scientific systems and larger commercial systems*

IBM's first foray into second generation computing was the very ambitious STRETCH/7030 (Fisher, McKie and Mancke 1983: 47–50). This was IBM's attempt to enter, indeed create, the supercomputer market and was one of the key projects which spurred the UK government to sponsor the Ferranti Atlas. The lead machine was ordered under a development contract by the Atomic Energy Commission's Los Alamos Laboratory in 1956. The aim was to produce a computer a hundred times faster than the 704 computer, utilising solid state, second generation components.

The Los Alamos contract was worth $3.5m, although IBM realised it would cost $15m to develop and $4.5m to deliver the first machine: again IBM was investing in the future. This was not out of generosity; the company expected orders for another 20–30 such systems. However, these orders did not materialise due to the cost problems of developing and building the new components and the complexity of developing a new eight-bit architecture. The first STRETCH was not delivered until 1961 and then IBM decided to stop taking orders for the machines as they proved uneconomic to build. Only nine were built, two of which were used internally by IBM.

However, there were a number of spin-offs from the project which pushed IBM even further beyond the reaches of its larger rivals. Its architecture of four or eight bit bytes and 32-bit instructions (64-bit floating point) was to be found in the third generation 360 range. The packaging techniques were used on other members of the 7000 series of computers, as were many other aspects of the computer. In that respect, it helped IBM to advance its technology.

While STRETCH was an ambitious curio of computing history, IBM's mainstream large-scale and scientific systems were highly successful. The approach was straightforward: take the 700 series and bring them into the second generation of computing. The major systems were the 7010, 7040, 7044s, 7070/2/4, 7080 and the highly successful 7090/94. This policy meant that the various machines were compatible with their old first-generation parent, but were not necessarily compatible with each other. However, a number of peripherals were common between the second generation machines, and the adoption of the new FORTRAN language helped with some data transfer. Nearly a thousand of the various 7000 series machines were produced.

Probably the most significant of the machines was the 7090 and the improved 7094 1/11 models. As outlined ealier, these were transistorised 709s and compatible with it, the 709 itself had been compatible with the earlier successful 704. The original 7090 was developed for the ballistic missile early warning system, DEWLINE – four 7090s being delivered for this purpose in 1959 (Fisher, McKie and Mancke 1983: 51). The civil versions of the 7090/94 range became the workhorses of scientific computing, but they were also used for some of the first truly large-scale real-time applications, in no small part helped by IBM's capability in random access disk technology. One of the most significant uses of the 7090 was in the SABRE aircraft seat reservation system for American Airlines.

The most notable of the business environment machines was the 7070 series, based on the old 705. The 7070/2/4 was most successful when it was coupled to a 1401, which was used to control peripheral and communications functions, freeing the main processor for calculation tasks. This meant 7070 installations were very large systems indeed, generating large incomes for IBM. The 7040/44 was a new system, designed for scientific work, though the provision of a COBOL business language compiler made it popular in the commercial market.

The final computer of this period was the 1620–22 which was at the other end of the spectrum. This was a small scientific computer, designed for departmental research, 1700 of which were produced.[5] This was a very respectable performance compared to many competitors; though, in general, IBM was seen as weak in the small scientific market. The line would stay in production until 1970 and could be configured from simple paper-tape input output to systems using 1311 disks and advanced printers and plotters. It was also the basis for the 1700 series of industrial control computers.

Much of IBM's success in this period was due to its computer peripheral products. The best disk and tape drives and printers all came from IBM. These significantly improved the functionality of the computers, and their rental value. IBM's implementations of its own FORTRAN engineering language, its own business language PL/1 as well as the COBOL business language, also enhanced the IBM reputation.

During this period IBM was functioning with three domestic divisions plus the World Trade Corporation. World Trade's function was to carry out IBM's business on an international basis. However, it was not run along the lines of GE's international venture, nor the lines of RCA's licensing model, though this had been IBM's model before the Second World War in advanced economies such as the UK where BTM benefited from IBM patents. World Trade produced computers, initially in Germany and France and then in the UK and Japan. However, the machines produced were standardised with the US ones. As the European operations gained in strength, they contributed to IBM's development cycle. IBM Germany and France worked on the 1401, and France developed a specialism in printer manufacture. When IBM turned its attention to the third-generation System/360, a number of the components, peripherals and even some CPUs were designed in Europe.

IBM ensured that foreign operations were fully integrated with the rest of IBM: compatibility was worldwide.

The other three components of the company were the Data Systems Division (DSD), General Processing Division (GPD) and the Federal Systems Division (FSD). DSD was responsible for the scientific-orientated machines, and the larger end of the commercial data-processing market. Since the early days of IBM's computer operation, the Poughkeepsie group had developed the 700 series and up.[6] Figure 8.4 shows the first and second generation computers managed by DSD, a table derived from one of IBM's most significant internal planning reports, the 'Final Report of the SPREAD Taskforce'.[7] The SPREAD task group was one of the most significant planning exercises at IBM and it will be seen as a significant step towards its dominance of the third-generation of computing:

*Table 8.1* IBM DSD processors (each bullet represents a family relationship)

---

- Commercial Processors:
  - 1410, 1410X
  - 705, 705 III, 7080
- Scientific Processors:
  - 7070, 7072, 7074
  - 704, 709, 7040/44, 7090/94
  - 7030/34

---

*Source:* Charles Babbage Institute, University of Minnesota, Collection 13. US vs IBM, dx1404. IBM, 28/12/61. 'Final Report of SPREAD Task Group'.

GPD covered the smaller end of the market, together with the punched card business, consumables and peripherals operations (see Table 8.2). It was built on the development of the 650 series which had taken place at the Endicott.[8] The following table shows the main processors:

FSD covered sales to the US government, including applications of IBM technology for military purposes. Notably, despite the importance of military contracts to IBM, it had a smaller proportion of the government market than other markets, though it was still the largest supplier.

*Table 8.2*   IBM GPD processors

| |
|---|
| Commercial: |
| 14LC, 1401 |
| 650 |
| 305 |
| Scientific: |
| 1620 |

*Source:* Charles Babbage Institute, University of Minnesota, Collection 13. US vs. IBM, dx1404. IBM, 28/12/61. 'Final Report of SPREAD Task Group'.

Simple aggregated financial statistics do not give a good indication of the real profitability of IBM machines. However, IBM's own internal figures reveal just how profitable IBM's core products, the 1400 and 7000 computers and their peripherals were (see Table 8.3).

**Part 3: Consolidation phase**

IBM had the bulk of the computer market sewn up. However, there were weaknesses in the IBM line:

> In the low performance end of our present product line, we are strong commercially with the 1401-10, but weak scientifically, with a gap between the 1620 and 7040/44. At the high performance end of our present product line, we are strongest scientifically, with the 7090/94, and relatively weak commercially with the 7074, 7080. Throughout the line there is insufficient capability for real-time, multiprogramming systems.
> (IBM SPREAD Report 1961)[9]

The conclusion must be that GPD's emphasis was on the commercial sector, while DSD was more interested in the scientific market, so arguably showed less interest in what could be seen as the other division's natural market. However, during the second generation of computers commercial and scientific computing had begun to merge; they were after all both classes of general purpose processors. Only in the areas of very large supercomputers and very small mini-type computers had scientific computing maintained a separate identity. It was becoming evident that improved peripherals meant commercial computers could make use of faster processor speed, while new scientific and statistical applications needed much greater input-output support. A general-purpose computer should have been able to perform both tasks. Specialist computers were increasingly the realm of industrial and military control systems with functions geared to very specific input and output devices.

These factors led to radical product reform at IBM. The SPREAD Task Group is renowned in the history of IBM. It was a planning group established to consider how IBM should approach the third generation of computing.

*Table 8.3*   Profitability of IBM's second generation hardware

| Machine | Revenue $'m | Profit $'m | Profit as % of Revenue |
| --- | --- | --- | --- |
| Intermediate systems: | | | |
| 1401 | 1613 | 705 | 49.3 |
| 1440 | 277 | 133 | 48.1 |
| 1460 | 187 | 81 | 43.5 |
| 1410–7010 | 328 | 155 | 47.2 |
| 7070–7074 | 309 | 34 | 10.9 |
| 7080 | 145 | 57 | 39.3 |
| Total | 2859 | 1255 | 43.9 |
| Large systems | | | |
| 7040–7044 | 158 | 36 | 23.1 |
| 7090/94 | 540 | 227 | 42.12 |
| Total | 698 | 263 | 37.7* |
| Memory systems | | | |
| 1406 | 174.9 | 107.7 | 61.6 |
| 7301 | 106.4 | 56.7 | 53.2 |
| 7302 | 224.4 | 107.2 | 47.8 |
| Total | 505.7 | 271.6 | 53.7 |
| Storage products (Disk, tape and other drives) | | | |
| Total | 2149.5 | 913.3 | 42.5 |
| Punched card input output | | | |
| Total | 387.8 | 94.9 | 24.5 |
| Printers | | | |
| Total | 505.7 | 271.6 | 53.7 |
| Communication products | | | |
| Total | 51.5 | 3.8 | 7.4 |
| Grand total | 7157.2 | 3073.2 | 42.93 |

*Note: *, in the original IBM report this was inadvertently calculated at 27.7 per cent.*
Also note many second generation products remained in production at this stage. This, coupled with the large number of leases still in place, means that this table only captures some of the profitability of the second generation IBM systems.
*Source*: Charles Babbage Institute, University of Minnesota, Collection 13. US vs. IBM, px1888 – internal IBM report 27/9/66, Manager Program Profit Evaluation, Program profit evaluation on selected 1400/7000 series systems and component machine types'.

At the end of 1961, the Task Group recommended establishing a new product line which was an expandable range of compatible machines, from the small-scale mainframe to supercomputer systems;[10] a plan that was adopted in early 1962 and systems announced in 1964. The twenty or so engineering groups involved in processor design were to be made subservient to Corporate Processor Control (CPC) which laid down the new logical architecture across GPD, DSD and WTC operations.[11] Not only was architecture to be standardized, but also was programming, testing and even marketing. As firms such as GE and RCA, and the UK industry planned their second generation compatible family approach, most of which never came to fruition, IBM was laying down the requirements for third-generation families even though the expected core componentry, the integrated circuit (IC), was far from economically viable.

CPC and WTC were to work in tandem to ensure worldwide standards. A third organisation, the new Component Division, was to ensure that the 'Design Automation Procedure' was a standard maintained throughout the company. The Component Division was important to the plan as it was responsible for the supply of Solid Logic Technology, SLT.[12] This was a kind of hybrid technology, transistors being automatically inserted on a ceramic block which had passive components, such as resistors, integrated into the block. It was hoped that this technique would not only increase computational speed, but also lower prices. IBM, by standardising the computers in its range, could mass produce huge quantities of standard circuits, and SLT technology allowed component assembly to be fully automated. Though not fully third-generation components, SLT was quite fast enough and offered potentially cheaper circuits for a considerable length of time. In the English Electric and RCA chapters, it was shown that early ICs proved too expensive for small-scale systems, while GE was still stuck with developing its incompatible second generation systems. ICT, which followed IBM in understanding the value of compatible families, would launch its 1900 family based on second generation components and not update them to ICs until the end of the 1960s.

Developing the Component Division was another major commitment by IBM into the future of its computer family. In its first year, 1961, it cost IBM $7.2m and in 1962, $30m (Usselman 2011: 34). However, the combined effect of using reliable technology which was highly replicable was enormous for IBM. It was estimated that IBM's new range would offer systems half the cost of their old 1400 or 7000 equivalents.[13]

However, it was not just improved performance and cost that was to attract new customers; it was the whole system concept which represented a complete update of computer standards, though few of the ideas were new. The 360 Series offered the following advantages:

- a fully compatible range of computers,
- interchangeable peripherals,
- better disk storage,
- very large memory,
- better communication and peripheral handling facilities, 32-bit data paths (first seen in STRETCH),
- facilities for multi-programming (though this proved to be one of the system' major failings),

- a full operating system (this too was a problem, especially the multi-tasking operating system),
- the COBOL business language, and IBM's own PL/1 and FORTRAN languages.

The system was expected to make all other computer systems obsolete. This was the barb in the tail of the plan. Not only would IBM bear the cost of developing the system, tooling up for the production of the new technology, preparing new software, accepting the returns of old leased machines for new 360 machines, but it also ran the risk that users would resist changing to a new system that was incompatible with the old. The SPREAD Task Group took the attitude that to provide greater functionality of the 360, backward compatibility with the 1400 and 7000 could not be offered. The preferred view was that users who required new functions, such as the ability to use large random access stores, would in any case have to reprogram their old applications: therefore getting users to upgrade would not present an additional problem.

There were other views on why IBM decided to provide new functionality. In 1972, CDC commissioned a report from the Auerbach Corporation to investigate IBM's pricing and product announcements.[14] They believed that IBM's massive growth faced a threat in 1964 (the 360 being launched in April of that year). New medium-large-scale systems were impacting IBM in both the scientific and commercial space. Systems such as the RCA 3301, the GE 200 and 400, UNIVAC's 400 and the Honeywell 200 were major competitors in the business space. The GE 600 and CDC 3600 were serious rivals in the large-scale scientific market. They believed that both the 1400 and 7000 families (if the 7000 series can, in fact, be seen as a single family as they were not all compatible with each other) were under threat.[15]

Auerbach believed one of IBM's key goals was to protect the $3.5bn installed base they had, which generated rental income of $700m a year.[16] They believed most of the equipment was fully depreciated and was therefore highly profitable. By making the 360 incompatible with previous families, they would make it more likely to keep current systems in the field and yet be able to offer a much more powerful environment for those firms deciding to upgrade. Auerbach was consistent in its belief that profit maximisation for IBM would be from maintaining its equipment in the field as long as possible. For example, they believed that IBM would try to maximise its investment in the 360 by not rushing to a fourth-generation family.[17]

In fact, we have seen the huge investment that went into the 360 began in 1961, when many of the second generation systems were still in their infancy and that IBM was perfectly willing to take the best technologies and architectures they had developed for second generation systems and repackage them in such a way as to move early into third-generation computing. In addition, IBM would eventually act to make upgrading easier, especially as there were real competitors offering alternative paths to IBM customers, even if the alternatives were still second generation systems.

Two companies tried to exploit IBM's lack of backward compatibility, though their strategies were decided before the 360 announcement. Honeywell's main 1960s strategy was to offer a machine that was program-compatible with the IBM 1401. With IBM abandoning the 1401 for the 360, Honeywell picked up extra orders for this machine. It was seen by Auerbach as a highly competitive system.[18] For Honeywell, IBM's strategy was a windfall, though it only impacted the smaller scale systems in the 360 range.

IBM responded to the Honeywell success by repackaging returned 1400 machines and offered them as cheap alternatives to the Honeywell systems. It also took steps to produce conversion programs to transfer 1400 data to 360 machines. Finally, it would also produce software emulators of the 1400, which, due to the increased speed of the 360, performed reasonably well. The System/360 Model 25 was introduced in 1968 and would use the 360's microcode capabilities to run either 1400 or 360 software, which was a better solution than an emulator on the Model 20 which had limitations because of the small size of that system.[19]

GE was in a similar position. Its 600 series was closely program-compatible with the 7090/94. It also hoped to benefit from the 7090/94's incompatibility with the 360, though most of GE's advantages came in the area of multi-programming operations. The 600 was less successful than the Honeywell H200, mainly due to the system's unreliability – it simply did not work when the market opportunity existed. There were rumours that IBM would be forced to develop a specific challenger to the 600 – an SLT version of the 7090[20] but it did not appear; the GE600 was hardly a mainstream competitor.

In reality, IBM's greater scale and full line concept of compatibility coped adequately with the threat posed by others competing for its old customers. The 360 concept and architecture were well ahead of the opposition: there was no other family that could offer all the 360's features. Yes, some would use ICs in their machines, but that hardly mattered to customers. System/360 was modern computing backed by vast libraries of software – and that, in reality, was what customers wanted.

Nevertheless, the 360 programme did have problems. A major difficulty, and one that became a common feature in the computer industry, was the failure to deliver the operating system on time. The 360 family was to offer a comprehensive control program called OS 360 (Malik 1975: 141), one of the first major operating systems. However, it proved much more expensive and time-consuming than expected. Eventually only the larger machines in the family had this comprehensive operating system, the rest having a simplified system known as the Disk Operating System, an obvious reference to the preferred peripheral. These problems led to some delays in 360 delivery times.

However, the 360 was a great success; indeed it had to be. There are various estimates of how risky and expensive the worldwide implementation of the

360 was. An R&D budget of $750m and a total cost for development, tooling, marketing and other items in the region of $4.5bn is quoted by Thomas J. Watson (Watson Junior, T. J. and Peter, P. 1990: 347). Whatever the true cost, it was a huge risk, but it was a managed risk. IBM was very professional in its market analysis, and carefully evaluated the likely reactions of the competition. IBM made the considered judgement that by offering this type of family ahead of competitors, even before IC components were an option, IBM was striking well before any competitor could afford to make obsolete their entire ranges. IBM's lower cost base and large user base allowed it to depreciate its machines faster than competitors, so it could tackle such a radical change.

The sheer scale of the System/360 announcement was immense. IBM announced:

> the System 360/ consisting of six programme compatible central processors (Models 30,40,50,60,62 and 70), 44 peripheral devices and comprehensive software packages.[21]

IBM would have problems delivering both the large-scale model 70 and the multi-tasking 62 as these both needed advanced operating systems and 'hardwire logic' rather than microcode logic to achieve the performance needed. IBM would announce further additions both at the high end as it tried to compete with the firms establishing their position in the multi-tasking market. It would also announce smaller units. The Model 20 was only a partial implementation of 360 aimed at very small users, but often used as a communication and input-output device for larger 360s, and the already noted Model 25 which was a fully capable member of the family, effectively it was a much smaller version of the 30 and aimed specifically at 1400 upgraders and competing against the Honeywell 200.[22]

While it is not possible to find out the individual profitability of the various System 360 computers, it is possible to observe just how profitable IBM was compared to its competitors. It managed to maintain the profit ratios it had achieved with the earlier second generation systems (see Table 8.4).

The figures suggest two things. First, by the 1960s, only the broad-based electric/electronic/conglomerate corporations were in the same league as IBM in terms of size. Second, IBM's high ratios of profit to turnover and employees were unchallenged by its competitors. In pre-tax terms, IBM's profit to turnover amounted to a massive 26.1 per cent. Return on investment was at 17 per cent, approximately 3 times most of the opposition.[23]

However, the most remarkable thing to consider was that during the time in which IBM was developing and initially delivering the 360 series, there were periods when it was more profitable than the rest of the industry combined – indeed, in 1966 the rest of the industry combined was losing money and IBM represented more than 100 per cent of profitability in the sector (see Table 8.5).

*Table 8.4* IBM profitability compared to major competitors

|  | Gross income | Net earnings after tax | Net earnings: gross income | Net earnings per employee |
|---|---|---|---|---|
| $'000 |  |  |  |  |
| IBM | 3,572,825 | 476,902 | 13.3 | 2,706 |
| Burroughs | 456,667 | 17,528 | 3.8 | 498 |
| CDC | 158,651 | 4,763 | 3 | 489 |
| GE | 6,213,595 | 355,122 | 5.7 | 1,134 |
| Honeywell | 700,357 | 37,500 | 5.3 | 686 |
| HCR | 736,849 | 24,725 | 3.3 | 339 |
| RCA | 2,042,001 | 101,161 | 4.9 | 1,012 |
| SDS | 43,999 | 3,372 | 7.7 | 1,421 |
| Sperry | 1,243,319 | 20,055 | 1.6 | 219 |

*Source*: Charles Babbage Institute, University of Minnesota, Collection 13. US vs. IBM, px3446, IBM internal report 19/5/1966. 'Analysis of Major Computer Manufacturers'.

*Table 8.5* IBM's share of worldwide EDP revenues and profits

| Year | 1966 | 1967 | 1968 | 1969 | 1970 | 1971 |
|---|---|---|---|---|---|---|
| IBM's % of worldwide EDP revenues | 63.5 | 65.5 | 67.5 | 62 | 61 | 60.5 |
| IBM's % of pre-tax income | 116 | 99 | 92 | 89 | 98 | 95 |

*Source*: Charles Babbage Institute, University of Minnesota, Collection 13. Data from, IDC, 31/12/71 'EDP Industry Report': 5.

This ties in with the evidence from the RCA and GE case studies which show that, for most years, their computer operations were running at a loss, pulling down the profit for the non-IBM part of the industry. No one turned in profits like IBM, but given IBM's huge scale in the industry, and its low costs, competitors had to forego IBM's high profit ratios to compete adequately against it.

It was stated earlier that Tom Watson Senior had a policy of ploughing back as much profit as possible to fund internal expansion. Internal figures show that on average this was still IBM's policy. Very high profits gave the company great scope for investment, including the phenomenal investment in the 360. Even such a large expenditure could be funded without substantial debt. Notably as the 360 investment decreased, IBM increased profit distribution (see Table 8.6).

Both Sperry and CDC were experiencing unusual circumstances at this time. Sperry was suffering from low profits as it struggled to change its structure and introduce new products. CDC, being a star of the stock markets,

*Table 8.6*    Percentage of earnings distributed by US Computer Producers 1960–65

|           | 1960 | 1961 | 1962 | 1963 | 1964 | 1965 |
|-----------|------|------|------|------|------|------|
| IBM       | 27   | 25   | 27   | 32   | 38   | 44   |
| Burroughs | 72   | 63   | 70   | 83   | 73   | 42   |
| CDC       | 4    | 3    | 1    | 1    | 0    | 1    |
| GE        | 80   | 74   | 69   | 67   | 90   | 61   |
| Honeywell | 53   | 59   | 55   | 43   | 37   | 43   |
| NCR       | 48   | 44   | 48   | 50   | 42   | 38   |
| RCA       | 53   | 56   | 34   | 44   | 42   | 38   |
| Sperry    | 63   | 2    | 3    | 2    | 2    | 2    |

*Source:* Charles Babbage Institute, University of Minnesota, Collection 13. US vs. IBM, px 3446. IBM, 1966.

was utilising all its resources in a meteoric rise developing supercomputers which even IBM could not match – its shareholders were happy with capital growth alone.

As was shown in the RCA chapter in Table 3.12, by 1970 IBM's debt/equity ratio was 10 per cent, RCA's was 88 per cent and GE's 22 per cent.

Overall, the mix with which IBM dominated the market consisted of

- Pre-established market penetration, both in the commercial and scientific markets;
- Strong marketing and sales with a strong feedback loop into product development;
- Strong leadership willing to direct the company into radical reform;
- Integration of corporate effort and control;
- Large-scale production;
- Strong financial base.

Maybe, above all, there was a willingness to do the opposite of what Auerbach believed its best strategy to be. When IBM had a stock of depreciated kit, while it was clearly happy for this to stay in the field servicing customers and bringing in very high profits, it also invested in the future by launching new systems earlier than rivals with the impact, if not by design then by good fortune, of preventing rivals from fully exploiting their own investments. IBM's strategy, the 'black box' into which everyone peered to gain insight into what to do next, was moving faster than its large mainstream rivals wanted it to do.

## Forcing out the electronics companies – the System/370

In 1969, the threat of fourth-generation computing to the then current third-generation systems seemed small. The Auerbach Corporation, in a report for the Computer Leasing Company outlined a number of mitigating factors which made them believe (1) delivery of fourth-generation systems would be delayed and (2) would have less of an impact than previous generation changes, the first three were:

> [T]he fourth generation of computers will not have the catastrophic effect on third-generation computers as was the case with previous generations
>
> new equipment being marketed is similar to present gear. This sustains the posture of the third-generation equipment.
>
> IBM has invested 1 billion dollars in the System/360 and, apparently intends to prolong the life of this system in order to make a substantial return. Also, it is being reported that IBM's fourth-generation computers are being designed to be compatible with the System/360.[24]
>
> (Auerbach)

Auerbach believed that these and other factors would not have the impact other commentators believed they would have and that it was unlikely that even a conceptual specification for fourth-generation computing would be available until the early 1970s, let alone anything deliverable. They accepted that IBM could produce an IC version of the 360 very soon, but estimated the impact would be minimal.

On 30 June 1970, Tom Watson Junior announced the first members of the 370 family, the medium to large batch-processors, the Models 155 and 165.[25] These could indeed be seen as straightforward performance upgrades of the 360. IBM quickly announced smaller members of the family, the 145 (September 1970) and the 135 (February 1971), other additions would follow later.

The biggest enhancement, however, was the 2nd August 1972 announcement of the 158 and 168, bringing to the family virtual memory, which at last gave IBM easy-to-implement, multitasking capability. The 370 was now both the system of choice for batch processing, a mode which built on IBM's dominance of the old tabulating market, and real-time computing, the computing mode of the future. Arguably, the many failures in delivering multitasking was IBM's major technical failure. However, it had corrected the problem by the time affordable video terminals became available – which was the moment multitasking became truly essential. IBM's intelligent, green screen terminal, the 3270 was also launched in 1972; many a bank loan has been processed through these or the PC terminal emulation of these screens.

Most importantly, the 370 came with a suite of both batch and multitasking/real-time operating systems to which over time would be added advanced transaction processing systems and database management systems. The 370 was the model for mainframe computing for decades to come, even adapting (in later forms) to the client-server world, acting as giant data servers to the low-cost computing environments developed in the 1990s and 2000s.

Auerbach's commentary on the likely impact of fourth-generation computing, that it would not be until the early 1970s before it would have a major impact unless firms reacted in the wrong way, was true. GE, seeing the threat and the cost of staying in the market had already opted out of the sector having failed to build a convincing third-generation strategy, let alone a fourth-generation one. Of the electronics firms, only RCA was in the game; and it reacted in the wrong way to the 370. As we have seen, it accelerated the release of its next generation of systems, despite the limited nature of the IBM initial announcement and so saw a flood of unamortized leased hardware back into its warehouses. RCA threw itself out of the computer market.

## Anti-competitive?

Before moving on, one question remains: was IBM using its market position to compete unfairly with its opponents? During this period, IBM has been accused of a number of anti-competitive acts, some against major hardware producers, and others against smaller producers and service companies. In the following section, a number of these anti-competitive practices will be touched upon, especially those which were aimed at the major hardware producers, GE, RCA and the new entrant/start-up CDC. However, the evidence on these anti-competitive actions is less than clear. While some actions can be framed in such a way as to appear as exploitation of monopolistic power, equally they can be seen as IBM wishing to maintain competitiveness by establishing themselves in two areas which were widely perceived as the future technologies of computing. It is one of the oddities of capitalism, the idealised version is often seen as perfect competition, however, the economic entities operating in capitalist markets are always striving to gain competitive advantage and, ideally, building and then exploiting capabilities which give them an economic rent.

IBM was subject to many cases, both in the tabulating machines era and the computing era. On 21 January 1952, IBM was alleged to have monopolised the control of the electronic tabulation industry through not allowing firms to buy its equipment outright and only allowing leasing – a case which meant that for over 40 years IBM became required to sell as well as lease equipment. IBM's unbundling decision in the late 1960s was seen as an attempt to deflect further similar court actions.

IBM failed in this deflection and the US Justice Department started the decade long US. v. IBM, filed in US District Court, Southern District of New York on 17 January 1969 by the Justice Department, a case which was finally dismissed in 1982 after costing millions of dollars. IBM was accused of using anti-competitive behaviours to monopolise one of the most important businesses of the period, the general purpose computer market; a market which represented a significant contribution to economic growth both as an important new source of economic activity in its own right, and as a tool for efficiency in so many other sectors. Undeniably, economic and business historians, and indeed all theorists looking at company strategy should be grateful the case was filed, not because IBM did or didn't do anything wrong – but because it provides a superb repository of company archives and working strategy papers.

The Justice Department case was joined by a number of private suits. Major among these was CDC vs. IBM 1972–73, there were also cases bought by Telex and Greyhound Computer Corporation. IBM is still subject to such cases. On 26 July 2010, the EU Commission launched two separate cases of 'alleged infringements of EU antitrust rules related to the abuse of a dominant market position' in mainframe hardware/operating systems and mainframe maintenance services (EU Commission, 26/7/2010. Europa. IP/10/1006).

The biggest case of all would dissolve (US vs IBM), but it would lose some of the smaller ones, including settling with CDC for the sum of $80m for the use of tactics deemed to create 'fear, uncertainty and doubt' in the supercomputer market by announcing high-end supercomputers which it failed to deliver or delivered very late, so undermining CDCs efforts to lead in that market.

CDC had a big stake in the market for large scientific computers with the 1604 and the later 3000 series, but the major problem for IBM was the dominance of the 1960s supercomputer market by the CDC 6600. The Auerbach Corporation worked with IBM to identify its major rivals in the large-scale systems sector.[26] It identified the CDC range, especially the 6600 and 6800 as the real competitors to the IBM System/360 Model 75. The 6600 and 6800 had the huge advantage of allowing multiple programs and compilations to run – rather like modern CPUs which have multithreading capabilities. The Model 75 could only run one process at a time.[27]

It has been argued that IBM tried to undermine CDC in two ways. The 360 model 44 has been described as a 360/50 at 360/30 prices. It has been suggested that its role was to undermine the CDC 3000 range of medium-scale scientific computers (Malik 1975: 99). Unusually, it was not fully compatible with the rest of the range, being 'tweaked' for scientific processing and did not sell in great numbers due to this incompatibility with the rest of the family. To fight off the larger CDC 3600 computers, IBM announced larger members of the 360 range (Malik 1975: 109), the /75/85 and the /195, for sale to the scientific market.

To head off the CDC 6600 supercomputer, IBM had a project for a family of machines larger than the 360 series, called the Series 90. Malik (1975) among others, argues that the Series 90 was a phantom product aimed at undermining CDC sales. It is argued that its main role was to encourage users to wait for an IBM product rather than buy CDC. The Series 90 was to be based on the so-called Advanced SLT components. IBM worked on the project with the help of the National Security Agency who required large computers for code breaking. According to one study, the Series 90 was announced in August 1964 (Fisher, McKie and Mancke 1983: 157). This was a number of years before machines could be delivered, and it was quickly found that Advanced SLT (ASLT) was flawed and that the component design had to be reworked. Yet the marketing staff continued to discuss it with users. Its specifications seem to have shifted continuously: Series 90 announcements were cancelled and replaced by new models on a number of occasions. It seems to have been a difficult if not a chaotic project, and finally only eleven machines were produced: far from covering the investment, an overall loss of $114.1m was made (Fisher, McKie and Mancke: 103).

The main problem presented by GE was the dominance it had in the area of multiaccess, time-shared computers. GE was perceived as a technology leader due to its involvement in the Project MAC, MULTICS development project at MIT. This perceived technological leadership had rubbed off on GE's simpler and smaller solution, based on the Dartmouth BASIC time-sharing systems. While the use of time sharing at the time was limited, and except for military applications and specialist functions such as air traffic control, was primarily used simply to allow multiple customers to simultaneously batch process data via bureau services, time sharing was clearly the future of computer.

IBM's reaction was to start offering extensions to the 360 range. The initial announcements were the /64 and /66. Like the Series 90, it was the sales force's concern that sales were being lost which led to the pressure to announce such a system. This again led to the multiplication of specifications (Malik 1975, 101–3). Eventually the various promises were brought together. The first step was to minimise any potential advantage the GE 600 was trying to deploy in the non-time-sharing space (though as has been noted, it was not much of a threat). The conventional, batch process /60 and /62 were replaced by the successful 360/65 in April 1965.[28] This system introduced an optional compatibility with the 7000 series, to compete with the GE 600 machines.

Linked to this new system was the extended time-share version called the /67. While the hardware modification was comparatively easy and the first installation of /67 machines was in August 1966,[29] the software proved next to impossible to develop. The problem was the Time-Share System (TSS) operating system. The sales staff had promised so many users different specifications that the TSS could not hope to fulfil them all.[30] Only a few of the systems were delivered, mostly to universities. Again, this was portrayed as a phantom product and was seen as merely an attempt to undermine the sales of a rival – the internal documents seem to tell a different story of project failure and the problems associated with trying to implement the feedback/wishes of the all-powerful sales staff; some things were simply not possible. As has been described, it is also true that a failure to develop true multitasking would have been a disaster in the 1970s, IBM needed to develop such technology. Also, GE's own Project MAC showed the difficulties of overcoming the complexity of large time-sharing implementations.

Another possibly anti-competitive practice was IBM's policy of giving huge discounts to colleges and government laboratories. The educational market was seen as important, due to the fact that those that learnt on university machines would be the customers of the future, and it was the major market for scientific and time-sharing systems. Some of the discount was paid for, and justified by, the high level of tax concession available on sales to educational and non-profit research organisations. However, a hidden agenda may have been that IBM was covering up its lacklustre performance in areas such as supercomputing and time sharing, by offering low prices for its standard scientific installations to attract noteworthy customers.

However, as noted by Barney Oldfield of the GE computer division, IBM had a strategy of selling to itself (Oldfield 1996: 126), it sold cheap system to the education systems so the next generation of data processing managers would be most familiar with IBM systems. Thus, IBM was willing to accept losses on the systems it sold to the education system not because of weaknesses in its current line-up of scientific and time-sharing systems, but instead to ensure future data-processing managers would be trained on IBM systems.

Malik estimates that the loss incurred on the phantom and anti-competition machines, the Models 360/44, /67, /75, /85, /90 /195, which represented over 500 delivered machines in total, was nearly $235m (Malik 1975: 103–4). This was comparatively small fry to IBM: less than 10 per cent of a single year's revenue.

There are obvious defences for IBM's behaviour. A number of companies in the industry were working on time-shared computers. Time-sharing was seen as the next wave of computing: it was the 'buzz' concept of the 1960s, and IBM needed to get into this area to maintain future capability. It was far from the only organisation to have problems in producing what it promised. IBM's next generation, the 370, would become a complete range of time-shared systems, IBM having learnt much from the TSS. Supercomputers were also seen as an important technology. IBM may well have viewed supercomputers in the same way.

Whether the projects mentioned above simply show that IBM was capable of expensive failure, or had deliberately tried to undermine opponents' sales, it did bring anti-trust scrutiny. It certainly prevented IBM continuing to target CDC, clearing the way for that company's dominance with the 7000 series and the later Cyber series of super computers, but CDC would eventually lose dominance in the supercomputer market to specialist firms (including Cray, which was led by the famous Seymour Cray, developer of all of CDC's most iconic machines) and by overseas firms making national champion systems, firms such as Japan's NEC. The more fundamental challenge to supercomputing was the simple increase in power of 'normal' mainframes and clusters of small-scale systems based on PCs and even game console technology – a technology in which IBM would lead. The market for vector supercomputers is now tiny.

In another area, peripherals, IBM may well have tried to limit competition. There were two targets, RCA and the so-called Plug Compatible Manufacturers (PCMs). PCMs were small firms that emerged in the late 1960s and produced low priced peripherals for attachment to the standard 360 input-output interface. PCMs achieved this by 'reverse engineering' IBM products, often employing ex-IBM engineers to do this (Dorfman 1987: Chapter 10). Therefore, development costs were minimised. In IBM's view, PCMs were parasites (Ibid.).

The problem with RCA was that it was in direct conflict with IBM machinery; to compete adequately, RCA needed to keep up with IBM in all its nuances. As was seen in the RCA chapter, IBM filibustered about supplying it with the details of the new 3330 Merlin disk drives, preventing RCA from making an early start on copying it. The argument IBM offered was that it could not have been expected to release detailed technical data before the system was even on the market.

It seems that this was not the first example of IBM hostility towards RCA. It has been recorded that Thomas Watson Junior was incensed when RCA entered the commercial computer industry; General Sarnoff had previously assured him that RCA's only interest was the BIZMAC logistics systems and other military computers (Rodgers 1969: 247). With this assurance, IBM continued to use the management consultant, Booz Allen, who were also RCA's advisers. Two years later RCA hired J. L. Burns from Booz Allen as president. He had been the consultant who had advised IBM on management organisation (Ibid.). IBM sales staff were informed that they could undercut RCA by any means.

IBM's reaction to PCMs became apparent in the early 1970s. It offered a new rental deal on its peripherals, called the Fixed Term Lease Plan. This gave a small discount on the first year of rental, which steadily increased over the subsequent years, the idea being that the price would be declining as rival PCM products appeared in the peripheral market (Dorfman 1987: 91). IBM saw the peripheral as vital: peripherals were becoming an increasing percentage of hardware value and it was clear that IBM understood their critical importance to the user. IBM's Fixed Term Lease Plan was the major cause of the Telex vs IBM anti-trust case.

IBM took similar action against another group of companies that threatened its role as the supplier of complete computer services: these were the leasing companies. These firms bought a manufacturer's machines and then leased them to users on their own terms, often with peripherals from the PCMs. IBM's actions against leasing firms led to <u>Greyhound vs IBM</u>, another case overlapping the main <u>US vs IBM</u>.

However, IBM's underlying competitive advantage was the company's conventional computer ranges and its associated selling tactics, advantages that have already been considered. IBM's ability to progress from one generation to the next, before the opposition could adequately recoup expenditure from the last generation, was much more vital to ensuring the IBM lead. Underpinning all its strategies were its large-scale, low-cost production and its subsequent high profits.

Clearly IBM was an aggressive company, in the strongest position in the market, a position which had been built on its historic strength in the business machines market. No other large firm could match IBM's vision or its focused attention on the sole market of data processing: this was certainly the case with the electronics firms. While other business machines firms and some start-up companies did match IBM's commitment to the computer market, they only had limited resources compared to IBM. Though more successful than the electronics firms, they could not muster enough resources to make a significant impact on the leading company.

IBM was the dominant supplier. This, in turn, meant that it had the longest production runs, lowest costs and highest profits, thus ensuring that it remained number one in the mainframe market. Using its market and production advantages, IBM was able to maintain a significant competitive advantage over the smaller business machines firms. This forced these firms to adopt strategies aimed at surviving in a market dominated by a single large supplier.

Unlike the electronics giants, IBM's traditional competitors (business machines firms) and newer computer-focused start-ups adopted niche tactics to enable them to survive in this environment – they understood IBM better and either built on the same advantages as IBM and/or developed niche capabilities which even IBM could not, or would not, match as it focused on its mass market activities.

Clearly the failure of the electronics companies was not the problem of being small firms taking on a large monopolist. The electronics corporations were larger than IBM and had a much greater technological base from which to draw skills, at least at the beginning of the computer industry. The failure of these firms to establish themselves in the EDP market has been discussed in those case studies. The core to the story is their failure to marshal their large resources to tackle IBM, and their reliance on technical economies of scope, as opposed to IBM's focus on market and productive economies of scope. They also failed to match IBM in understanding customers. IBM made reliable peripherals and built vast libraries of reusable code – that was what customers wanted, as much, if not more, than fast processors.

If one could sum up IBM's strength, it may well be that it knew better how to exploit the economies of scope. The economies of scope it was exploiting were inter-temporal. Helfat and Eisenhart (2004) note that these are economies of scope which some firms are able to carry over from operations over time as those operations change their nature as the market changes:

> [I]nter-temporal economies of scope derived from the redeployment of firm resources between businesses over time, as firms exit some product-markets while entering others. Inter-temporal economies of scope have implications for the evolution of related diversified corporations over time, particularly in markets where technologies and demand are in flux.
>
> (Helfat and Eisenhart 2004: 1217–32)

The industry was well aware of this entrenched advantage. Key to IBM's inter-temporal economics of scope was the punched-card business. Auerbach Corporation in 1960 described it as such:

> IBM's 'Punch-Card-foot-in-the-door': of major importance to IBM's Marketing Success, and a factor which can hardly be overlooked, is the tremendous advantage represented by IBM's punch-card accounting business. Electronic data processing is a natural extension of punch-card techniques, and IBM, with its full line of EAM [Electronic Accounting Machines] equipment in a well-entrenched position in this market, and with an established and well-trained marketing organization, had, in effect, its foot in virtually every data processing door.[31]
>
> (Auerbach Corporation)

However, it was not just marketing it provided. Auerbach believed it was 'in-tune'[32] with the market like no other company. It also provided technical capability overlooked by the electronics giants – electro-mechanical expertise giving it the ability to produce technical advantage in the area of peripherals. This is reflected elsewhere. This story has concentrated on IBM's mainstream mainframes. However, early systems such as 650 were of modest scale. IBM understood this end of the market as well. In 1969, it introduced the System/3 aimed at those firms which had not converted to computers from punched card systems and at the smaller end of the 1401 user base. System/3 was the genesis of a three-decade long success story for IBM in the area of 'business appliances'. The System/3 was built around the Report Program Generator (RPG) computer language and would eventually develop into the AS/400 of the 1990s which was marketed as a database in a box and around which hundreds of industry-specific applications would be built. If you wanted to set up a bank, you could buy the operations side in a box – the AS/400 running its database under an application from one of a dozen companies.

IBM was indeed a concentrically diversified firm looking to develop economies of scope: however, it had the advantage of inter-temporal economies to exploit in the market and had built up feedback mechanisms to benefit from these. Yes, of course, like any other firm developing systems in a complex environment, project failures occurred, and indeed, its own competitiveness may have led it to take actions which could be deemed anticompetitive because of the structure of the market. However, the large electronics firms it competed with had the technical and financial resources to compete. What they did not have was the history to build the right type of competitive stance against IBM.

## ICT

The UK's 'IBM' was ICT, though while it had a shared history and many of the same advantages as IBM, it was far from a complete success story. However, unlike the UK's electronics firms, it would survive the early computer industry and was a survivor into the 1990s.

In 1968, ICT was at the heart of the creation of a British national computer champion, International Computers Limited (ICL), which was the largest computer company in Europe, similar in size to a number of the mid-tier US computer rivals to IBM. It combined both the strength of technologically advanced electronics companies and the market relevancy of the UK's largest business machines firms. This sounds like a winning combination, but it was not able to mould this into success. The firm had real strengths, however, the legacy it inherited from some of the firms it absorbed (primarily the poor strategy of English Electric Leo Marconi, a merger caused in the main by government inference) destroyed what chance this interesting firm had to develop a successful strategy against the IBM.

The roots of the firm were in British Tabulating Machines (BTM) and Powers-Samas: punched card tabulator manufactures in the UK which licenced US technology. Before the Second World War, these firms effectively operated a competitive duopoly for punched card systems in the UK and the British Empire. However, their reliance on licenced technology would greatly affect their entrance into the computer era.

BTM was formed in 1907 (Kelly 1987: 41) as an independent company to market and then to manufacture the tabulating products designed by Herman Hollerith in the US.[33] Hollerith's US operation, the Tabulating Machine Company, evolved into IBM, and BTM remained IBM's licensee until after the Second World War. The second, smaller, British supplier of tabulating equipment was Powers-Samas. This company produced punched card machines designed by James Powers, whose American company became a part of Remington Rand, the second largest US business machines firm. In the UK, Powers was set up as a British source of tabulating equipment by the Prudential Assurance Company, a major user of this equipment.[34] Powers later took over the French distributor of Powers machines, Samas, forming Powers-Samas.[35]

During the War, both companies were allowed to keep a large percentage of their output in the form of tabulators; tabulators were necessary for the administration of the war effort (Campbell-Kelly 1989: 106). The major effect of the War on these firms was to engender an increasing independence. Both undertook some independent development work during the War. BTM also became involved with the ENIGMA code-breaking operation at Bletchley Park (Campbell-Kelly 1989: Chapter 5). This offered BTM a chance to get involved in innovative work, demanding advanced tabulating techniques.

Partially emboldened by this work but more driven by IBM's 25 per cent royalty on equipment sold in the UK,[36] the firms agreed to part company. However, Campbell-Kelly (1989: 90–4) believed IBM was more than happy with this because it believed BTM could not match the growth rate it could achieve by itself in the UK market.

After the War, the Prudential sold Powers-Samas to the Vickers Company, which was desperate for opportunities to diversify from its military engineering activities:

> The problem which, for the second time in this century, had been placed before the Vickers Board, was to turn swords into ploughshares after the Second World War. The large armament factories and plants had almost at once to stop production and we were faced with the major task of finding new products, techniques and new employment for the thousands of people who were then in the plants. One of those opportunities for going into refined engineering appeared to be the punch card systems.[37]
>
> (Puckey)

## ICT in the computer era

### Part 1: The experimental phase

After the War, both BTM and Powers-Samas faced a major problem. They were separating from their usual source of technology and had to build up their capability in their traditional electromechanical systems base. Yet, they also faced a new challenge – the replacement of these older systems with new generation electronic and computing devices. BTM's directors recognised the problem:

> [T]he extent to which a pure computer, specifically designed for office use, is likely to be of widespread commercial appeal.[38]
>
> (Puckey)

This line of thought was also found at Powers, with the same questions being asked:

> [T]he big problem facing the punch card industry [was] when and how they were expected to get into some form of electric or electronic data processing and computing.[39]
>
> (Maxwell)

BTM approached Prof. A. D. Booth of Birkbeck College to develop its first computers (Booth 1980). His early computer work led to the Hollerith Electronic Computer, later called the BTM 1200 (HEC II),[40] and a second machine, the BTM 1201 (HEC IV). The HEC II was a simple drum memory accounting machine, the HEC IV was a full computer.

Unlike the electronics firms, BTM had a user base in commercial data processing, through its punched card customers. It was to this user base which BTM concentrated sales of HEC machines. The sales organisation had a computer department added to it. This was a stop-gap while information on computers was being disseminated to the district sales organisation.[41] This comprehensive sales organisation and the established market links were something that the electronics firms needed to develop to be serious competitors in the commercial market.

By 1955, there were 20 HEC IVs and 7 HEC IIs on order, with another three earmarked for internal use.[42] Fifty per cent of orders were for payroll, with the balance to be used for a number of accounting, production, and administrative functions.

Powers was also able to offer electronic systems. First, there was the Electronic Multiplying Punch, which was an electronic calculating device sold by the 250-strong general sales force. However, the second machine, the Powers Card Programme Calculator, PCC, was much closer to a computer, offering drum storage and a memory of 160 words. To sell these, the sales force would call in members of the Computer Department.[43] They managed to sell some 110 EMPs and 140 PCCs, half to overseas markets.

However, while the numbers sound good, they were little more than calculators. The firm needed access to more advanced machine, not ones which would be a calculator enhancement to the current punched cards, but full-scale data processors.

One initial effort to achieve this has already been covered in the Ferranti chapter. Both firms were courted by the NRDC which recognised the power of matching the electronic and digital computing capability of the Manchester University and Ferranti team with the distribution capability of a BTM (initially) or a Powers-Samas (which partially occurred.)

This thinking showed incredible foresight; the NRDC was, at this stage, further advanced in its thinking on the likely development of the computer market than any of the major firms involved. On 14 December 1949, the Corporation hosted the first and only meeting of its Advisory Panel on Digital Computers at which representatives from all interested firms were present.[44] The NRDC wanted the two sets of companies to come to some arrangement to safeguard the UK's leading position in computers, a position given to it by the work at Manchester University and the National Physical Laboratory (the Turing ACE development). The NRDC was concerned that IBM was going to use its huge sales network and market knowledge to bring the computer into its own, and establish itself as the dominant company. The NRDC posed three opening questions:

(1) Is there in the UK any firm with the manufacturing, selling and servicing facilities of the International Business Machine Corporation, with particular reference to the manufacture of electronic equipment?
(2) If not:
   (a) Would it be an economic proposition for Powers-Samas or the British Tabulating Machine Co., or both, [to] build up a large-scale electronic manufacturing organization, and could they in effect do so other than by taking staff away from the electronic manufacturers?
   (b) Would it be economic for any of the electronic manufacturers to set up a separate selling, servicing and advisory organization in competition with the Powers-Samas and British Tabulating Machine organizations?
(3) If the answer to the above two questions are negative, does the Panel consider that there is no practicable alternative to a joint effort between Powers-Samas and the British Tabulating Machine Co. on the one hand and one or more of the electronic firms on the other.[45]

Such far-sighted thinking is really rather impressive – however, it led to nothing as the firms were not willing to countenance such radical integration in a sector which had barely produced its first product. Ferranti failed to form a meaningful relationship with BTM, the sector leader, while the work it would do with Power-Samas, leading to the Perseus, was frankly ignored by the Powers-Samas sales team who did not sell the system and simply stopped Ferranti targeting certain markets for its Pegasus system. As has been argued, the Pegasus sales effort had been partially undermined by the associated division of sales activity between the two firms. The two firms also established some mutual R&D activity, but the outputs were seen as disappointing and the firms agreed to stay in touch but end further immediate collaboration.[46]

## Part 2: Structured entry

### ICT Merger

While all of this was going on, Powers-Samas had been investing in the new Samastronic range of electronic tabulators. This major effort to update its tabulator systems, for the first time independently of Remington Rand, proved to be a technical and commercial failure. Powers managed to get itself into severe financial difficulties. It had placed large numbers of machines into lease arrangements while the required investment costs in Samastronic equipment were astronomic for a system that would soon be replaced by true computers.

Increasing interest rates and new credit restrictions exacerbated Powers' problems. The credit restrictions made leasing even more attractive to customers, while the high-interest rates made it more expensive for the company to finance (*Times*, 13/5/58).

Meanwhile, BTM was still trying to extend its ad-hoc computer development. In 1956, it formed a joint subsidiary, International Computers Corporation Inc, with the small Boston company, Laboratory For Electronics, which was to develop a machine for the Chase Manhattan Bank (*Times* 31/5/56: 19) The project would ultimately fail, but would give BTM access to new magnetic drum technology – though the world was already shifting to disks.

A few days before the announcement of the International Computers Corporation deal, another, more important, deal was struck with General Electric Company (GEC) (*Times* 25/5/56: 19). This led to the formation of a joint company called Computer Developments Limited. This would go on to make the most important early machine for the merged ICT Company. In 1957, it also acquired a 51 per cent holding in the small British company, Data Recording Instruments, to give it access to magnetic tape technology (Campbell-Kelly 1989: 187).

Both BTM and Powers-Samas clearly recognised there was a shift away from traditional business machines, both needed to invest in maintaining their old market and build systems for the future market – all while supporting increasingly less economic leases.

The two firms decided to consolidate the market and merge their activities to take on the big US players. According to Maxwell, negotiations between BTM and Powers-Samas were difficult. Eventually they were merged on a 62/38 basis in favour of BTM.[47] Vickers, as the main Powers shareholder, was willing to take a subordinate role if that meant the mounting problems at Powers were shared with other equity holders.

### Obtaining second generation computer capabilities

*GEC and the 1301*

At the time of the merger, ICT had inherited a number of computer developments, all from BTM. First, there was the established HEC line of small computers. However, this system was becoming dated. In 1959, ICT started to install an improved model with larger drum memory, the 1202.[48] This kept the first-generation technology alive and another 28 units were installed in the UK and approximately 30 abroad. However, it was only a stop-gap until a second generation machine was ready.

ICT was also planning a medium-sized, first-generation computer, called the 1400. Development of this machine had been delayed in the hope that it could be based on the system being developed in the joint operation for Chase Manhattan (Campbell-Kelly 1989: 186). Chase scrapped the contract and only a prototype was produced. Development of the 1400 accelerated in 1958 when it was realized that the joint venture had achieved little. In

1958–59, the company publicised the machine heavily, but it was withdrawn following the advice of US consultants – it could not hope to win orders in the face of the new transistorised competition.

The more successful project was a joint venture with British GEC. The two firms worked together to produce a second generation replacement for the 1200 HEC series. Like the 1400, the 1300 was intended to be available in a magnetic tape and a random access configuration. The project went well:

> In November 1959, International Computers and Tabulators Limited and the General Electric Company Ltd. formed Computer Developments Ltd. as a jointly owned design and coordinating group. The 1301 computer, the first outgrowth of this united effort, is a file processor for medium size companies. ICT will manufacture the peripheral equipment and market it through its world-wide channels. General Electric [Company] will manufacture the electronics. At present there are two production prototypes of the 1301 in construction, with a backlog of 17 orders.[49]
>
> (Auerbach Corporation)

The one problem was that the random access version was dropped, and only magnetic tape was available for mass storage. This was because the BTM drum system, which it had got from the US joint development, was not competitive with newer IBM disk systems (Campbell-Kelly 1989: 200). It appears that ICT decided not to offer this facility to avoid unfavourable comparison. This meant data could only be accessed from magnetic tape or punched card peripherals, greatly limiting its flexibility. GEC constructed the computers at its Coventry telecommunications plant.[50] ICT provided the peripherals and sold it.

The 1300 was up against stiff competition. ICT was forced to announce the system in May 1960 because of the large sales IBM was achieving with its second generation IBM 1401. This was two years ahead of delivery, which somewhat undermined confidence in delivery. There were also a number of other competitive machines, such as the EMI 1100 and the successful NCR 315.

Despite the competition, and the lack of random access stores, the system was a success, at least in the context of the UK market which was smaller than that of the US. By 1965, 102 1301s had been installed, with another 27 on order; there were also 24 smaller 1300s delivered and orders for 51, plus 1 larger 1302 on the order books.

This meant the firms had delivered £13,320,000 worth of these systems and had another £5,685,000 worth were on order.[51] In the same price category, only the IBM 1401 outsold it in the UK. None of the other British manufacturers' machines approached it: Ferranti and English Electric were concentrating on scientific or large-scale systems, both much smaller markets, while Electrical and Musical Industries (EMI) had problems coping with its chosen commercial market.

In 1961, ICT absorbed the team that developed the 1301. GEC continued to manufacture the system, but this represented the end of GEC's interest in commercial computing.[52]

## ICT 1500 and the UNIVAC 1004

The 1301 did not solve many problems for ICT. The 1301 had a sale price of £120,000[53] which covered only the smaller part of the medium-scale market. There was also a feeling among board members that the company still needed 'additional technical skills'.[54] To try to get the extra skills it needed, it started to negotiate with two American companies, GE and RCA.

Negotiations with GE came to nothing: GE was simultaneously talking to Bull of France and some arrangement between all three companies was being considered. Representatives of GE came to the UK and discussed the possibility of purchasing a 25 per cent stake in ICT. However, these negotiations petered out. GE was already about to acquire large stakes in Bull and Olivetti and so may well have completed its European ambitions.

In 1961, Arthur Humphreys was placed in charge of the planning role at ICT, and took charge of negotiations with another potential partner, RCA.[55] RCA already had English Electric as a licensee of the medium scale RCA 501 sold as the English Electric KDP10 computer. Briefly all the three firms considered some joint arrangement, but again this came to nothing.

Talks between RCA and ICT were more successful. ICT (and Bull) was given the right to sell the RCA 301.[56] This seems to have been a good arrangement for both firms. RCA was able to make a large number of cash sales to its European partners, increasing its cash flow and helping to increase its economies of scale. ICT marketed the system under the name of the ICT 1500 and in British terms it sold well. By 1965, 89 of the machines were installed, at a value of £6,408,000, and another 52, worth £3,744,000 were on order (though many of the latter may not have been delivered as newer systems were developed); about 40 of the orders were abroad.[57]

While RCA link only provided a computer for ICT to resell, and gave it few new technical skills, ICT 1500 enabled ICT to gain a larger market share than would otherwise have been the case and must be counted as a successful short-term project.

ICT also agreed to resell UNIVAC's successful small calculating tabulator, the UNIVAC 1004. Between 1963 and 1966, ICT sold nearly 500 of these units, enabling ICT to cancel an internal project for such a machine.

## Building internal capability: acquisition of EMI and Ferranti computer capabilities

The absorption of GEC's computer capability and the deal with RCA gave ICT two reasonably successful second generation machines, but they covered only the small and medium-scale computer markets, though this represented the largest part of the European market. In addition, manufacturing capability was outside of its control. ICT wanted to decrease reliance on outside technology and improve its market coverage. In the early 1960s, Humphreys started talking to EMI,[58] whose medium scale 1100 and large scale 2400 were both aimed at the commercial data processing market. EMI's range was advanced, but it had many problems (see the EMI chapter).

ICT bought the EMI operation for shares. Although in terms of product the purchase was of little value, it gave ICT EMI's design team. They were experienced in the use of solid state electronics in computers. This team proved important when ICT was faced with the task of designing a whole family of third-generation computers, and it was the ex-EMI team that developed the smaller members of the range.

However, EMI did not give the firm access to the advanced architectures and integrated family of systems which was needed to compete in the future. The 1100 and 2400 were being offered for sale, but they were being marginalised in the market as more advanced second generation systems were on offer.

It could be argued that ICT was the country's premier computer seller;[59] however, Ferranti was the UK's technology leader. As has already been seen, there had been efforts earlier to bring about some coordination of these skills. These plans had floundered due to the two companies' conservative attitude to the market, and Ferranti's unwillingness to see BTM have complete control of sales. In the early 1960s, no such problem occurred, as Ferranti was more than willing to give up its stake in computers.

Ferranti had a number of major problems. While it was true to say it probably had the best design operation, in the early 1960s it only had a limited number of machines to offer to the market. It had achieved its best success with scientific machines, but the only major machine that it had available for mass production, the Orion, while dual-purpose, was not really fast enough for scientific operations, and had a number of technical problems. Even if Ferranti had decided to continue in the computer market, it had to compete with the marketing and leasing capabilities of US and UK business machine firms. Apart from the Orion and the small scientific Sirius computers, all efforts had been directed towards the super-scale ATLAS development. ATLAS had two negative effects, first it worsened the profit and loss situation of the Computer Departments, second, it had distracted the department from other work.

The real problem for Ferranti was that the third generation of computers would be families of mass-produced and mass-marketed systems, not a scale of financing that the Ferranti company was willing to consider. Therefore, Ferranti was willing to cut its losses and merge its commercial computer activities into ICT.

Ferranti did, however, have one commercial EDP design on the 'back-burner': this was the FP6000 developed by its Canadian operation, Ferranti-Packard.

Initially, ICT identified the FP6000 as a machine suitable for the mid to large-scale sector, and would join a range of systems, some internally developed, some imported, the majority of the proposed range was to offer upgrade paths to current customers.

- Small: Enhanced UNIVAC 1004.
- Small/medium: PF182 to replace the EMI 1100 and ICT 1300 and being designed by the EMI team.
- Small/medium: 2201 being designed with RCA
- Medium/large: FP6000 sold as ICT 1900.
- Large: RCA 3301 to be sold as the ICT 1600, Orion replacement.
- Giant: Atlas replacement

Clearly this was a chaotic plan, but investigation of the FP6000/ICT1900 showed it was suitable to form the base of a third-generation-like computer family.

Purchasing the computer department from Ferranti was to prove key to ICT's survival. ICT obtained a strong design team with expertise in the area of scientific computing. This team, together with the FP6000 design, was vital to ICT. The alternative was to go in with another supplier and become subservient to that supplier's technology, an option EE-LEO-Marconi chose by following RCA.

**Part 3: Consolidation phase**

After all the mergers, a member of the NRDC staff wrote that ICT 'represents the major component of the UK industry as far as computers and data processing are concerned'.[60]

This left ICT with a mixed bag of incompatible machines, some of which were competitive with each other.

> One of the things that pleased me very much is that after having acquired the Ferranti Computer Division and EMI's computer activities and because of the arrangement with RCA, [ICT] had a large mixed bag of computers to offer to the market place, we were able to put all the expertise and techniques together and come out with an entirely new range of computers which was the 1900 series.[61]
>
> (Humphreys)

By the time of the 1963 merger with Ferranti, the computer industry was starting to turn its attention to developing the next generation of machines. These were the third-generation systems which emphasised compatibility, improved peripherals, comprehensive operating systems, and the move towards ICs as the core component. During the third generation the many different computers made by a company were replaced by members of a common family. The difference between scientific computers and those for commercial data processing, a distinction which was already being blurred, became insignificant in all but the realm of supercomputing and the new small engineering machines appearing from such firms as DEC and Elliotts (a smaller UK electronics firm with a number of small-scale commercial, scientific, military and process control computers which was absorbed by English Electric). IBM's reaction to these changes in the market was to replace its whole product line with the 360 family of computers: this allowed IBM to achieve significant scale economies on common subsystems, and gave users greater flexibility.

ICT made a decision to produce its own compatible family, based on the Ferranti FP6000. Ferranti's Canadian subsidiary had taken on this development as the British operation had its hands full with the Orion and Atlas. The specification was devised by a Ferranti salesman, Harry Johnson, for a system based loosely on the Pegasus computer and as a follow-up to it (Campbell-Kelly 1989: 221). It used component technology from the Ferranti-Packard airline reservation system, Gemini, and some of the systems philosophy of the Orion. It was a very flexible design and could be configured to cover a large spectrum of the market. Its components were transistors, not ICs – but, like IBM, the fundamentals were an integrated family and a commitment to software development.

All this closely fitted ICT's needs. It was a much more advanced system than ICT's own developments, and it was possible to produce it quickly as the circuitry had already been proved by Ferranti-Packard. Officially, Ferranti did not sell its operation to ICT until September 1963, but it is obvious that the merger was accepted well before this. ICT dropped all its other options (including building a new system of its own or adopting the RCA 'Poplar' concept) in favour of an expanded FP6000/ICT1900 project to cover almost the whole range of the computer market. The initial announcements were made in September 1964 and by 1967 the range, consisted of the 1901, 1902, 1903, 1904-5, 1906-7 and 1909. There was also a proposal for a large-scale scientific system, the 1908.[62] The -5 and -7 were scientific versions of their commercial siblings.

The smallest member of the family, the 1901, was launched in 1965. Its launch was delayed for two reasons: first to spread out R&D costs, second to protect the 'cash cow' 1004 sales. The 1901 seems to have been singled out for special attention and was especially successful. It was a small system, with a starting price of £60,000 only.[63] In its larger configuration (costing around £120,000) it came with magnetic tape drives. It was also provided with the NICOL programming language which was designed to emulate tabulator techniques, making it easy for punched card users to switch, and was fully compatible with the rest of the line. These kinds of facilities were unusual in the smallest member of a computer family: even IBM could not offer such a cheap magnetic tape machine. In its first year, there were 228 orders for the 1901, a third from overseas.

The US Office of Naval Research, ONR, saw the whole 1900 family as a successful product, and an updated series with 8-bit data paths promised more success:

> The other machines have also sold successfully with over $200m in value and over 650 total sales. More than a third are for export, notably to Australia, New Zealand, Africa, France (over 30 sales), Germany (to scientific universities among others), and Eastern Europe. About 300 have been delivered. Lower cost 1900s have been promised before the end of 1967 by direct updating with microcircuits. It is also intended to make the 6-bit character structure of the series (24-bit words) compatible with the 8-bit extended BCD set adopted by IBM and English Electric.[64]

IBM also recognised the range as a major competitor in the overseas market. IBM was conscious that it did not offer magnetic tape facilities on its smallest system, the 360-20. IBM rated ICL (T) and the 1900 as its largest overseas competitor.[65]

There were a number of reasons for the success of the 1900. It was, in some ways, not as advanced as other systems announced at that time. It did not use the IC components of RCA and English Electric, or hybrid technology as used by IBM, instead relying on the tried and tested transistor. However, this gave one great advantage: it meant that the medium-sized 1900s (the ones closes to the original FP6000) could be delivered four months after announcement. The ICT 1900 family was available in Europe before the IBM 360, mainly due to production delays in IBM's SLT components, and way ahead of EE's IC-based System 4. The 1900 was available and it had the philosophy of the third-generation machines: it was a family of compatible moderately advanced machines, with some good commercial software. In the late 1960s, the 1900s were given a new lease of life when the integrated circuit versions were released and later developments offered a 32-bit architecture.

However, before the success of the 1900 could show through in profits, the company had some bad financial results. It had high development costs while it also had to fund new leases on its successful 1900 range. In 1965, the trading profit collapsed and did not cover ICT's increasing interest burden: pre-tax loss was £509,000 on a reduced turnover of £55,250,000.[66] Much of the reason for the profit down turn was the cost of growth, as outlined by the chairman, Sir Cecil Mead.

> '[F]irstly, the expensive preparation needed for the successful marketing of the company's new 1900 Series computer; secondly a significant loss in the planned output of punch card and ancillary equipment, due to difficulties encountered in the change-over of production facilities to computer manufacture; and thirdly, the considerable fall in revenue (the UK total was down from £43.9m to £36.7m) that resulted both from the falling

away of deliveries of earlier types of computers, and from the inevitable lag in getting started an adequate flow of deliveries of the 1900 Series.'[67]

However, ICT also suffered from a familiar problem in the industry – tabulators were being sent back. Customers were ordering computers to replace punched cards. Leased tabulators, which had been giving a steady stream of income, came back to the factory to be replaced by leased computers, with all the initial capital costs of the computer being borne by the supplier. It then took a number of years for the income from the leases to match the capital outlay for the growing number of machines. It was this problem that led to the formation of Computer Leasing Ltd, a leasing finance company backed by financial interests. This company bought ICT computers, leased them out and repaid investors at a few per cent above base rate; ICT received the remainder (Campbell-Kelly 1989: 220–1). The aim was to reduce the financial strain of leasing computers on ICT itself.

### Staying in the sector – turning to government support

The 1900 was being accepted in the market place. The real problem was coping with the cost of this success and ensuring that future growth was not curtailed by the expense of introducing the 1900 series. ICT took a number of steps to improve cash flow, such as raising rental prices, selling assets and even cutting staff and other costs (Campbell-Kelly 1989: 252–5). The present growth was putting future growth at risk.

However, ICT had learnt much from the computer departments which it had acquired from Ferranti and EMI – they turned to government for support for their R&D activities. This is not surprising, Basil de Ferranti was Managing Director, while Peter Hall, also from Ferranti, was in charge of the Computer Equipment Group which was based on the Ferranti operations and produced ICT's large systems. Clearly leadership was given to the technology providers not the sales, marketing and service capabilities of the firm.

In the period 1963–65, there was considerable debate within the NRDC as to how to support the computer industry. This debate was sparked by the announcement of the IBM 360. One of the first items to be filed in the NRDC folder marked 'the UK computer debate' was an article from the *Financial Times*.[68] This noted that while ICT had previously been neck and neck with IBM in terms of in new orders, in the seven to eight weeks following the launch of the 360, IBM orders had rocketed, with over 100 on the books.

The NRDC viewed ICT as the most important part of the UK industry, but was concerned about whether it could compete with IBM.[69] There were three main factors in ICT's situation:

- The £10m tabulator business had grown in the 1950s but was expected to decline, becoming insignificant by 1970.

- The Electronic Data Processing market had been zero in 1950, but was growing rapidly.
- The data capture/peripheral sector, while not well defined at the time, was expected to grow to replace the tabulator business in size.

Crucial to ICT's future was the expected growth in the computer business. This market was expected to grow between 15 to 20 per cent per annum.[70] This was the crux of the problem; ICT estimated that, at most, it could only fund 10 per cent growth. It was predicting that its market share would fall from 40 per cent in 1964 to 28 per cent in 1974, allowing IBM and other US companies to become even more powerful.

ICT was having problems in giving an adequate return to its investors. The argument was that, as ICT was earning only 6 per cent on capital,[71] this was not high enough to attract new investors. Therefore, it had to grow using only the £65m of capital it already had. All new finance would have to be generated internally. This limited the speed at which it could bring new machines to the market.

The NRDC's view was that ICT had to achieve growth rates of over 15 per cent to ensure that it could reach a minimum efficient scale to maintain long term R&D. The NRDC was coming to the view that ICT was too small to match IBM's R&D expenditures. ICT's cost cutting was an attempt to compete with the lower IBM cost base, but this was at the expense of abandoning future developments.

To increase the projected growth rate, the NRDC believed that ICT needed to have a larger R&D budget. ICT's spending on R&D was roughly £3m per annum,[72] about £2m at Stevenage and the remaining £1m in Manchester, where the old Ferranti operation was based. However, in 1965, ICT proposed cutting long-term research to save £300,000 a year. It abandoned long-range development of systems for the early 1970s.

Following discussions between ICT's Basil de Ferranti, and NRDC representatives,[73] the organisations came up with a scheme for the NRDC to support ICT's R&D work.[74] The scheme envisaged R&D expenditure of £20m, spread over four years (financial year 64/5 to 67/8), the NRDC was to provide one quarter of this.[75]

ICT had a list of projects it was carrying out, some of which were expected to use NRDC money, focusing on smaller and larger members of the 1900 family and on developing improved peripherals, in which it considered itself as moderately successful, primarily because it could provide IBM 80 column card systems to other manufacturers. ICT had previously made a commitment to updating the 1900 to the 1900a which used ICs.

NRDC support was earmarked for developing a range to replace the 1900 in the 1970s. Repayment of the £5m loan was to start in 1969–70 and was to be linked to ICT's profit on funds employed ratio. If ICT maintained a 10 per cent profit on funds employed for four years, the NRDC would receive £5.1m.[76]

Therefore, to give the NRDC a reasonable return, it was looking for a substantial improvement in ICT's profit ratios.

The NRDC money was essentially a method of supplying cheap long-term debt to ICT.

The company also received help from other government departments. Some £700,000 was provided for long-term work from the Ministry of Technology's Advanced Computer Technology Project.[77] This money was used to fund the Basic Language Machine (BLM) concept developed by ICT's J. K. Iliffe. The BLM concept, combined with Professor Tom Kilburn's Manchester University MU5 development, was to form the basis of ICL's 1970s and 1980s systems, the ICL 2900 (Campbell-Kelly, 1989: 247). In the 1970s, ICL received a further £40m from the government to develop the 2900.[78]

Further support was given or asked for in terms of funding supercomputer developments, although none of the various supercomputer projects came to anything, except a proposal for a National Computer Centre (together with a number of regional centres) which created a bureau service offering very large systems outside of the traditional higher educational facilities. The National Computer Centre was established in 1965,[79] providing a service for scientific computer users, helping to disseminate computer use and to act as a source of demand.

Indeed, the final support sought and discussed was that of government providing demand for the computer industry – as had proved so successful in the US. Professor Blackett, an NRDC board member, prepared a report on the use of computers by various governments.[80] He found that by 1964, 1565 computers were being used by the US government, and the French state used 111. The UK lagged behind: in a House of Lords debate on 8 April 1963, Lord Blakenham stated that the British authorities used 88 computers, 81 of which were domestically produced.[81] However, the list of machines included some very limited systems such as the Powers PCC calculator.

Professor Gill, came to the conclusion that a 'National Computer Authority' was needed. It would have a dual role, first to direct and supply R&D support, and second to act as an information source and purchasing agency for government departments. While this did not come about, a Computer Advisory Unit was set up to help government departments to adopt computer techniques. The agency actually in charge of purchasing computers, the Treasury Support Unit, also started to favour British systems.[82]

The final piecemeal method of supporting the data processing industry was the provision of tax breaks on the purchase of equipment. This amounted to an extra 20 per cent tax rebate on computer equipment. Purchasers of computers received a 40 per cent grant, rather than the normal investment grant of 20 per cent (Moonman 1971: 1).

However, the tradition of support in the sector had become firmly based on providing support for development – the British state supported the development of technology – it is an interesting contrast to the US state.

What is notable is how many business machines firms in the US benefited from a level of government purchasing – hugely greater than the what UK government undertook. Indeed, we can identify a number of contracts where a single firm effectively gets a contract equivalent to the whole stock of the UK government computers, and more. Some notable contracts included

- The US Air Force purchased 175 NCR 390 computers for the simple process of payroll calculations at air bases.[83]
- By 1959, Burroughs' revenue from SAGE had reached $155m and it had received another $35m thereafter for an airborne version of the AN/FST-2 for the Airborne extension to SAGE, ALRI (Airborne Long Range Inputs).[84]
- Burroughs was awarded a contract to build the navigation computers for the ATLAS ballistic missiles. This led to Burroughs' first solid state military computer; by 1959 this contract had earned $77m for the company. IBM believed this was the first large-scale solid state computer ever built, and gave Burroughs real prestige.[85]
- Then Burroughs B200 sold 500 systems by 1967. Its sales were helped by the winning of the US Air Force Base Level Program, Phase 1A which took around 150 of the systems.[86]

ICT was supported, eventually, by government like the electronics firms before it, however this was in no way as valuable as the way the US government employed its purchasing power to support the sector. Government support was vital in allowing ICT to continue long-range development while maintaining a reasonable earnings-to-equity ratio. It must also be said that the support was targeted at long-term projects which did actually lead to commercial products. MinTech backing for the Advanced Computer Technology Project (ACTP) led to ICT's BLM development, and this, together with Manchester University's MU 5, was used as the base for the ICL 2900 series. After the merger with EE-Leo-Marconi, ICL continued to need government assistance: at the time it received £17m of government funds for further development work. The government's involvement in the merger also enabled ICL to get £18m from the Plessey Company. These funds were essential to ICL.[87] To maintain growth the firm needed funds to place more leased machines onto the market and to pay for further developments. Eventually, another £40m of government funding was found for the launch of the 2900 series of computers in the 1970s.

Ultimately, when ICL was formed in 1968 – as outlined in the English Electric chapter, the government would pour more money into ICL, taking a stake in the newly created firm and sponsoring development of future systems. It would encounter a number of crises, receiving state loan guarantees and other financial bailouts. Unlike IBM and the other US business machines firms, ICL would be permanently drawing on government aid for development and financing until eventually the remnants of ICL were acquired by Fujitsu, having previously been acquired by telecommunications equipment manufacturer Standard Telephones and Cables (STC) in yet another failed effort to exploit 'synergies' between mainframe computing and communications systems. Under Fujitsu subsidies stopped, but by this time the company was a shadow of its former self, with its hardware lines now ended and it primarily acting as a second-tier IT services company.

## ICT compared to the British electronics companies

### Structure of ICT

Not surprisingly, ICT's organisation differed from that of the multiproduct electronics companies that are the main focus of this study. ICT's structure reflected the single market place in which it operated, with an organisation based on functional divisions. It did, however, toy with the IBM formula of partial decentralisation by splitting the product line in half, according to system sizes, and using this to create separate profit centres. This was a short-lived exercise. Of the 11 companies and divisions that went into the formation of ICL, BTM seems to have been the dominant one, in terms of structure, if not in terms of senior management. BTM had been organised into functional divisions and with a geographically arranged sales operation. There was, however, some division between the tabulator and computer operations.[88]

With the takeover of the Ferranti, GEC and EMI computer operations, the firm made an effort to decentralise its operations, forming two design and production groups. The Data Processing Equipment Group was based in Stevenage. This division

> deals with the development and production of the smaller computers, of tabulators and all punched card ancillary equipment, and of peripheral equipment for all computers.[89]
>
> (ICT Annual Report, 1964)

The second unit was the Computer Equipment Group:

> Our Computer Equipment Group, at West Gorton, Manchester, and also at Bracknell, Berkshire, deals with the development and production of the larger computer systems, such as Atlas, Orion and the bigger systems in the 1900 Series.[90]

The latter was basically the old Ferranti division. Though this represented a major decentralisation, it was done with the 1900 architecture as the chosen design for both operations. This resembled IBM's structure with the General Processing Division producing smaller 360s and peripherals, and Computer Systems Division producing larger-scale computers.

The marketing operation was maintained as a separate functional unit as outlined in Figure 8.4.

Ferranti's influence was large, with both Basil Z. de Ferranti and P. D. Hall having come from Ferranti. Hall had been the last general manager of Ferranti's computer department, so was a natural choice as the head of CEG. Ferranti was also the second largest shareholder with 10.3 per cent of ordinary shares. Basil was Ferranti's representative on the board of ICT. The largest shareholder was Vickers with 23.6 per cent.

However, decentralisation was not a success for the company. During the financial crisis of the mid-1960s, one of the non-executive directors, Sir Anthony Burney of accountants Binder Hamlyn, was asked to make recommendations (Campbell-Kelly, 1989: 251–2). He recommended the cutting of R&D and selling assets. He also criticised Basil Ferranti for allowing decentralisation to go so far as to lose control of expenditure. As previously seen, this was something that the Ferranti computer operation (now the substantial part of ICT's CEG division) had been accused of previously when its expenditures had been investigated by the NRDC. This led to the re-establishment of a single control over the R&D and production operations. Basil left and long-time ICT company employee E. C. H. 'Echo' Organ was placed in charge.[91]

The experiment with reorganisation was a failure. While it aped the successful IBM structure, it was incongruous given ICT's smaller scale. IBM's partially decentralised divisions were huge compared to the whole of ICT, and in any case they were strictly controlled. Rather like the situation at Ferranti when there were computer operations in both Manchester and London, coordination seems to have been incomplete and costs were not kept under control.

### Strategy

The main focus of this case study is to show the reasons why ICT, rather than an electronics firm, came to dominate the British industry (the ICL merger is covered in the English Electric chapter).

The business machines firms started from a different point from any of the British or American electronics companies. The drive into computers

*Figure 8.4* ICT structure
*Source*: ICT annual report 1964.

was led by changing demand within its usual market place: it was a matter of survival rather than diversification. In some respects, the ICT history is similar to the experience of US business machines companies, especially at the point of entering the manufacture of computers. Like its US counterparts, acquiring the right skills was all-important; ICT did this by taking over the computer departments of the electronics companies. In the US, business machines companies acquired the small entrepreneurial firms that started building computers in the 1950s. For example, Remington Rand purchased UNIVAC and ERA to start its computer operations and would initially lead the market ahead of even IBM. Burroughs purchased ElectroData, while NCR bought Computer Research Corporation. The only exception to this was IBM, which grew internally by building on its experience of incorporating electronics into its tabulating machines.

What is different is the higher level of direct government intervention surrounding the ICT history. In the US, the government's role was focused on purchasing systems on a vast scale. In the UK, it was deemed necessary to intervene directly in the fastest growing industry in the world to ensure that the UK maintained a foothold in this strategically important technology. ICT received an important contribution from the state.

ICT's R&D figures seem small compared to the figures that are bandied about for IBM. Clearly, ICT could not match the $4.5bn spent by IBM on the introduction of the 360 family. However, when comparing ICT's spending on the 1900 with, say, RCA's expenditure on the Spectra 70, it does not seem to have been so far out of line. During the development of the Spectra, in the mid-1960s, RCA was spending around $15m per annum on engineering,[92] in some years it was much less than this. ICT, supported by the government, could at least match these kinds of expenditures. ICT had also taken steps to reduce the number of areas in which it had to spend development money, so it did not have to spread its development funds as thinly as the electronics companies did.

ICT's major problems were financial rather than technical; indeed it has been seen that ICT was willing to buy technology elsewhere if it considered itself not up to the task. The time of crisis was the period when a new generation of systems was introduced. ICT/L seems to have always needed financial assistance to cope with the financial strain of introducing new ranges. The government deemed it necessary to step in as it thought that ICT was unable to find enough funds to cope with the cash flow problems of carrying out R&D and marketing a new system, as well as funding leases. Likewise, in the US, it was this problem that forced the electronics firms out of the market.

One great advantage ICT/L had was that it was seen as the UK's premier computer company. As such it was to some degree protected. For many buyers, especially in government, ICT/L received sympathetic treatment when buying machines. Other business machines firms such as Burroughs and NCR exploited their established user bases in niche markets to build their computer businesses. For ICT, the UK was its niche, since around 40 per cent of the UK market would stay loyal to the British producer, a base from which ICL could compete with American producers.

ICT had to make the transition from punched card technology to computers as the latter superseded the former. ICT was more capable of dealing with the vagaries of the commercial computer market than the electronics companies. ICT had long dealt with the needs of commercial data-processing customers. ICT also had an established user base, a group of clients which it was able to upgrade to computers. It also meant that ICT had an established sales force, an expensive organisation for the electronics firms to build up in an area in which they had little experience.

The concentration of the firm on a single market was the major difference from the electronics corporations. Apart from some partial attempts at decentralisation, the company was focused from top to bottom on a single function. ICT was not tempted to go too far down the path of vertical integration, even when it was directly relevant to manufacturing computers. All the funds were focused on producing systems and their software. Components were bought from outside: Ferranti and later others supplied ICT's basic components, Plessey provided memory in the 1960s and early 1970s and CDC made ICT's disk drives. ICT thus did not have the expense of developing the full paraphernalia of electronic systems and could concentrate resources on developing computers. Electronics firms had the opposite attitude. They would develop new components, such as ICs, and then exploit them in end products. Electronics firms tried to develop and supply as much as possible from internal sources, bearing multiple costs at once. The conflict this could cause within the electronics company is best described in the RCA and GE chapters. ICT recognised that technology was only part of the competitive mix in the computer industry. Unlike English Electric, when it came to the third generation of computing, ICT recognised that component technology was much less important than having a well thought-out product that it could produce rapidly. ICT did not hold back its third-generation systems to wait for ICs to become available, it wanted to offer an intra-compatible range of systems as soon as it could. English Electric, and its American counterpart RCA, put a great emphasis on the core component technology and less on the system and software design.

The different approaches of the electronics and business machines firms had, we have seen, been noted by the manager of Ferranti's Computer Department soon after he left Ferranti and joined Burroughs. Writing in *Datamation*,[93] he noted the focus of business machines firms on computers, as compared to the side line that they were in Ferranti and other electronics firms. He also noted that the US business machine firms were not over-worried about producing every nut and bolt of the machine. They supplied a system, but many components and subsystems were supplied from outside, if they were better and cheaper. It appears that these lessons had been learnt by ICT, and it benefited from the focus of effort in a similar way to the US firms. ICT certainly seemed more market-aware, and had a greater desire to remain in the industry, than the British electronics firms. Looking at both the UK and the US case studies in this book, it is far from surprising that it was the business machine firm that ended up dominating the one British mainframe computer manufacturer to survive in the 1970s' market.

Yet ICT/L failed to survive without government support. It may have suffered from a certain burden imposed on it by its role as the state-supported computer flagship. There seems to have been an expectation that the UK's flagship should cover the whole market for computers (a common mistake made by British policymakers: when they intervened to ensure mass production was retained when the Phoenix Consortium took over car manufacturer Rover in 2000, rejecting other offers which foresaw a future for Rover as a niche manufacturer). While it has been said that ICT was concentrating on computers, this was still a broader market than many of the smaller American companies tackled. Similar-sized US firms concentrated on even smaller niches than just the computer industry. NCR concentrated on the retail and banking industries, Burroughs' main market was its traditional banking clientele. Both firms used this strategy to control growth, as one of the biggest challenges was funding leases – of course outright sales to the state certainly helped reduce this challenge.

Having portrayed the British business machines industry as more in-tune with, and better able to cope with, the complex EDP market, it could be argued that Lord Halsbury was correct in the early 1950s to try to get business machines firms to take a leading role in the computer industry. However, this would have been at the expense of the UK foregoing, even more than was the case, one of the great advantages the US had: the innovation driven by having a number of competitive domestic companies feeding from each other's ideas. Michael Porter (Porter 1989) has pointed to the benefits of such a hot-bed environment in the makeup of a country's competitive advantage.

BTM and Power-Samas were clearly technologically weak. Licencing technology meant they were not advanced R&D houses nor did they have much experience of electronics. The alterative direction for the UK would have been to continue supporting computer developments at the big electronics firms. The potential success of such a strategy would appear unlikely. These firms were, in many cases, doing little more than producing capital electronics and were not really productising their output nor investing in marketing and leases. The one company which did try to make the leap was English Electric and it had chosen an incredibly poor strategy which would continue to be a burden on the merged ICL. Taking this point of view, it seems that the industrial assets that the UK entered the computer industry with were considerably less suited to exploiting the computer innovation than the US industrial base.

# 9
# The Nimble Survivors: Sperry Rand, NCR, Burroughs, CDC and Honeywell

In the 1960s, it was IBM and the Seven Dwarfs, those firms which competed against Big Blue. These were RCA, GE, Sperry Rand (UNIVAC), NCR, CDC, Honeywell and Burroughs. In addition, in Europe, there were electronics and business machines firms targeting their domestic markets. By the 1970s, it was IBM and the BUNCH: Burroughs, Sperry Rand (UNIVAC), NCR, CDC and Honeywell, and a few survivors in Europe, or at least that was the stereotype of the market. In reality it was more complex. In the Dwarf period, a number of firms tried to enter the burgeoning market. Some were major companies, such as the Ford-owned Philco and the large electrical company, often associated with connectors and avionics, Bendix, which both had short forays into the sector. More importantly, CDC established itself as the leading supercomputer maker and Digital Equipment and SDS established the minicomputer markets.

In the 1970s, BUNCH period, new competitors entered the mainframe market, led by plug-compatible manufacturers, those who took the RCA strategy of IBM compatibility to new heights. Amdahl (established by one of IBM's leading designers), Fujitsu, Hitachi and other firms produced CPUs directly emulating IBM while firms such as Memorex and many others produced rival peripherals (Takahashi 2005). Again, the newer firms and those firms which tried to redefine what computing was had the most impact. Chief among these redefinitions was the rapid growth of minicomputers led by Digital and then Hewlett Packard which became a real force in open source minicomputing. In the desktop space, the PC would revolutionise people's use of computing both in the professional and consumer space with software companies and chip manufactures Microsoft and Intel coming to the fore.

Finally, the minicomputer, the PC and even the mainframe would be interwoven in seamless network technology where the complexity of computing became hidden behind a standardised interface which could be accessed by new and increasingly mobile information devices which would have been little short of science fiction even a few years before.

IBM remained one of the standard setters, on occasion fighting the migration to open systems and client server computing but quickly becoming a leader in these technologies. IBM is still an incredibly successful firm, with services, middleware and systems capabilities which any major purchaser will have at the top of their list of likely options. Its return on capital for an old firm is still very respectable. Hewlett Packard may make more hardware, but that is not where the margins now lie.

A few firms did manage to bridge the period between first-generation and second generation computing and the beginning of the fourth generation of computing in the 1970s.

So far, except for IBM and ICT/L, this book has been about the failures of large scale concentrically diversified electrical and electronics companies in the US and the UK. It has been an exploration of the limitations of the concentrically diversified business model where those firms operate in a number of interlinked highly dynamic changing technologies. But were the survivors of the early computer industry different?

Here we very briefly consider these survivors to see what advantages they may have had compared to the concentrically diversified electronics firms. In general, we find a series of firms, some highly focused, some more conglomerate in nature, which tend to have fewer other demands on their resources than the electronics firms. Even where a company clearly had a character closer to a conglomerate in nature, their commitment to computing was substantial and in some cases it would become total. In addition, many of these firms may have had some element of the advantages IBM had, with a strong inter-temporal carry over between different generations of product and customers. Finally, there were also start-up firms which aimed for niches which the bigger firms were either not attracted to or not nimble enough to tackle.

## Punched card rivals – Sperry Rand

Along with ICT covered in the previous chapter, Sperry Rand represented a mainstream rival to IBM competing as it did both in the tabulator market and the computer market. Both ICT and Sperry shared many of the features of IBM as major business machines groups. However, in the case of Sperry there is also some commonality with the major electronics groups in that there is certainly an element of corporate diversification, though maybe in more of a conglomerate form than a concentric form. Sperry's operations in computers were primarily based on the acquisition of the Remington Rand business, which itself had been the first major firm to acquire and sell computer technology in the US.

Remington Rand was the second largest business machines firm, and the only true rival to IBM in tabulating systems. Not only that, but during the genesis of computing in the US, it was the major player, its stable of computer operations produced all the commercially delivered US computers up to 1954, at least according to one source (see Table 9.1). Until the launch of the IBM 700 and 650 families of computers, it was the dominant force in computing.

*Table 9.1*  Delivery of early large-scale computers in the US

|  | Total computer deliveries in the US | Of which built buy Remington Rand companies |
| --- | --- | --- |
| 1950 | 1 | 1 |
| 1951 | 4 | 4 |
| 1952 | 5 | 5 |
| 1953 | 7 | 7 |
| 1954 | 9 | 8 |
| 1955 | 32 | 9 |

*Source*: Charles Babbage Institute, University of Minnesota, Auerbach Collection 4/10. Auerbach Corporation for RCA 6/1960. 'A Corporate Business Strategy for Information Processing' 1–10, Chapter 2 'Sperry Corporation'.

Sperry Rand was formed in 1955 when Sperry the defense electronics, controls, hydraulics and farm equipment company, acquired Remington Rand.[1] For Sperry, Remington represented both a diversification for what was already something of a varied enterprise, but also offered a strong combination of government related connections and electronics knowhow. The firm struggled to build on these connections.

## Computing – the experimental phase

Remington was the number two punched card and tabulating machine company, but it was potentially weak in the post-war environment. Its punched-card system made less use of electronics and its war work was less involved in advanced computational methods than IBM. It made vital war equipment from the Norden gun sight for bombers and increasing its armaments manufacturing, a business for which it had been famous and which had some operational overlap with its large typewriter business. Electronics, however, were far from its core competence, though they government contracts were becoming vital.

It tackled this weakness by moving quickly to acquire the skills it needed when it purchased two of America's leading computer enterprises, both start-up companies developing computers for government sponsored computing work. These were the Eckert and Mauchly Computer Corporation, developers of the early ENIAC and BINAC military computers and the commercial UNIVAC (see Stern, N., 1981), and Engineering Research Associates, developers of the 1101 system used by the US Navy and the National Security Agency.[2]

Remington partially absorbed ERA into UNIVAC, leading to an uncomfortable atmosphere within ERA whose leading staff wished to pursue their own path.

After Sperry purchased Remington Rand in 1955, the position of the computer operation was complex. James Rand, the powerful and controversial leader of Remington, was allowed to run Remington as a self-governing operation, so the computer operation was in effect the UNIVAC division of the Remington Rand group of Sperry Rand.[3] Even within UNIVAC, the ERA and UNIVAC teams were not always on talking terms.

This structure led to real operational and product problems. The purchase of UNIVAC and ERA gave Remington-Rand control of two of the most significant early computer systems, the UNIVAC I and the ERA 1100 series.[4] The former tended to be used by commercial clients, while the 1100 range was favoured for scientific calculation. Together it was a powerful lined up, but replacement models were slow to emerge. The UNIVAC successor was the UNIVAC II, engineered by the ERA team in Minnesota, which had basically the same logic, but added magnetic core storage and improved tape speeds. However, problems seem to have occurred in coordinating the two halves of the UNIVAC division and the first-generation UNIVAC II was not released until 1957, when other firms were starting to offer second generation computers. By 1960, only 33 had been sold.[5]

On the ERA product side, the 1101 was replaced by the 1102 which was widely used for air traffic control. This was then replaced by the 1103-A and the upgraded 1105, which, while similar, were not compatible with the older machines.

The UNIVAC operation was also slow to capitalize on its early start in computing by producing a smaller computer; one which might have appealed to the large Remington Rand tabulator user base. In other words, it was slow to exploit the most powerful inter-temporal economy of scope which it had.

The first offering aimed at the Remington Rand user base was the UNIVAC File Computer in 1956. This machine again came from the Minnesota side of the operation. The File Computer had to compete with the IBM 650 and 305 RAMAC, but it was not the success that might have been expected: it did not match the sales of IBM machines, and only 130 were made.[6]

### Structured market entry – second generation computing

*Entering the small-scale systems market*

The firm's first really successful small-medium scale computer was the UNIVAC Solid State. This was a semi-second generation machine from the Philadelphia half of UNIVAC, which, surprisingly, initially used IBM standard 80 hole punched cards for input-output. This strategy did, of course, give that system access to a much larger user base – except it was a user base to which Remington sales staff had little access. The Solid State drew on technology developed for a US Air Force-sponsored computer for its Cambridge Research Center. It used transistor-magentic logic, a dead-end technology but one which other firms were exploring at the time, and presumably had IBM punched cards because these were standard at that research facility.

Initially, it was only marketed in Europe; all sales enquiries in the US were refused until 1959. There appears to have been two reasons for this: first, it would have undermined sales of the delayed File Computer and, second, it would also have undermined the core Remington product line, the 90 hole card punches and tabulators (Fisher et al 1983:59). Eventually a respectable 600 of these machines were installed, including both 80 (IBM cards) and 90 (Remington cards) hole version and including the updated Solid State II (Fisher et al 1983:60). This was good, certainly when compared to companies from an electronics heritage. However, the Solid State only had sales amounting to almost 6 per cent of the IBM 1401 and was based on a technology that would not be continued. Also, compared to the 1401, it was a basic system, not only did it use slow magnetic logic, its memory was an old fashion drum system, which, although it was fast, had very small capacity compared to the advanced disk systems and magnetic core direct access memory offered by IBM.

The system the firm made which sold in large numbers was the 1004. This was a small punched card based calculator/computer released in 1962 and was programmed using a plug board. This was ideal for the large Remington tabulator user base that wanted to have improved functions, but did not desire a larger computer; it was computing at its smallest in those days. Many thousands of these were sold, and it became a vital product to Sperry-Rand. The company extended this range to give customers upgrade routes. The updated 1005 (at last adding internal memory to replace the plug board) and the 1963 medium scale 1050 were added to the range. Eventually, this gave Sperry Rand the low end range it needed in the UNIVAC operation, but all so late compared to the speed at which IBM was moving.

### Large-scale second generation systems

If this product strategy sounded like a hotchpotch of systems, things only got worse; the larger second generation computing systems made by UNIVAC just added to the confusion. The UNIVAC II was replaced by the transistorized UNIVAC III, while the 1107 became the new solid state ERA offering. The confusion was noted by UNIVAC co-founder J.P. Eckert, who stayed in a senior role in Remington Rand, and tried to alert senior management to the chaos.[7]

Effectively, in the second generation, the UNIVAC and ERA lines remained as transistorised versions of the old machines, while these were joined by the two tabulator market-target machines, the Solid State and 1004. However, it did not stop there. There was also the 490, a large-scale real-time computer used for such things as airline booking and reservation systems[8] and finally, larger than all these was the LARC, Sperry's turn to fail in the supercomputer market.

The LARC was ordered under a development contract by the Livermore Atomic Research Laboratory. Sperry is estimated to have over-spent by $10m on the fixed price contract.[9] If Sperry got anything from this effort, it was only one or two sales and some extra circuit know-how. In addition, the component technology it used, surface barrier transistors, was already out of date.

Outside general purpose computing, the UNIVAC Division and the rest of Sperry Rand built many specialist computers. Most of these were military systems: unsurprising given the military connections of both the UNIVAC Division and the rest of Sperry. UNIVAC was the largest producer of specialist military computer systems in the USA. This gave the company both access to military R&D sponsorship and a good market for high-value high-profit systems.

By the end of the second generation, the company was still number two in the market but had still clearly made a hash of a promising combination of an early start in computers through the ownership of the most iconic early computer entrepreneurs coupled to a large tabulator customer base.

The problems seem to have fallen into two categories: first, early products were not delivered on time and were poorly supported; second, there were serious problems with the organisation of the corporation, problems which mirrored the difficulties found in electronics companies.

### Product failure

UNIVAC was undermined by the publicised failure of some of its early products. One of the most discussed installations of the UNIVAC I, was at the GE Appliance Park in Louisville, the first commercial electronic data processing system, at least by US measurement (Osborn 1954: 99–107). However, it took much more than installing the computer to give GE and the other early users an operational data processing system. The Auerbach Corporation believed UNIVAC was delivering computers before the customers were ready, and then not offering the service and programming support needed to make the computers useful to their new owners.[10] It was a new technology being used for a new type of application: users needed help in achieving this.

A second problem was that the UNIVAC II and the File Computer were both promised well before they were delivered. Potential customers lost faith in the ability of the firm to deliver, and when they did finally appear they were too late for the first generation of computing.

### Organisational confusion

Remington, then Sperry, had created a complex organisation. It had some of the best minds in computing to leverage, and perhaps it was the need to keep these pioneers happy (though most of the ERA leaders left very soon after being acquired by Remington as they disliked the role they had, compared to that given to UNIVAC), which led it to allow so much uncoordinated development.

The major failure seems to have been the inability of Remington to integrate the two computer operations with each other or with its business machines operation. At the time of the Sperry purchase of Remington, the company was described thus:

> Washington has a name for it: a 'conglomerate' merger, the union of two non-competitive companies with nothing in common except the desire to face the future together. Sperry-Rand is 1955's biggest conglomerate to date.
>
> (Van Deusen 1955: 88)

It was headed by company CEO Harry F. Vickers, with James Rand in charge of the Remington Division, and with Remington's ex-chairman, General Douglas MacArthur, becoming the chairman of Sperry-Rand – yes that General Douglas MacArthur! The logic for the merger was seen as the combination of UNIVAC with the Sperry military electronics operations, which would have both technical and marketing opportunities to exploit together. However, William Norris, the head of ERA which had been acquired by Remington along with UNIVAC, viewed the real situation differently:

> Harry Vickers [Sperry CEO] didn't understand what he bought. He thought he bought into the computer business. What he bought was a chance to get into the computer business by investing a hell of a lot more in R&D. And he wasn't prepared to spend the money.[11]

Norris was placed in operational charge of the UNIVAC division, but his control seems to have been very limited, with UNIVAC's Eckert acting as the division's president, with Rand above the both of them as the boss of the Remington arm. Despite an early statement by Vickers that he wanted to build up the EDP operation, Sperry management were not pleased by the heavy R&D costs and the losses incurred in this division.

Coordination between sections of the company seem to have been limited. When questioned as to how much cooperation there was between ERA in Minneapolis, UNIVAC in Philadelphia and, most importantly, the punched card operation in Norwalk, Norris gave a long discourse on the bad relationships between different parts of the company, summing up the level of cooperation by saying there was

> Very little. President Eckert took the view that what ERA was doing was not state of the art. Therefore, he didn't want to waste his time with us. Norwalk was less involved in electronics. They were still in the tabulator era.'[12]

Eckert also blamed the failure to exploit its position on the poor structure of the company, but not surprisingly saw Philadelphia as the hard-done-by organisation. Until his retirement, James Rand was running Remington Rand as a separate entity within Sperry Rand (Eckert interviewed in Forbes

15/9/61. 'Post-Mortem': 35–6). This meant that the Sperry management did not have direct control over the computer operation and yet they were expected to find the funding necessary to cover the losses. From 1953 to 1958, Sperry Rand sales had increased by 39 per cent, but profits fell by 19 per cent (Forbes 15/9/61). The cause was the cost of developing and marketing computers.

A further problem was the division of the sales operations from the computer manufacturing units. Sales staff were split between such things as typewriters and office equipment. Initially there were few sales staff dedicated to computers; even by 1962, the computer sales team numbered just 500 (Forbes 15/9/61). The advantage IBM had exploited by marketing to entrenched users was wasted by Sperry Rand and senior management seemed to know it.

It became clear in the second generation of computing that Sperry had made a number of errors:

- It did not establish central control of architectures; therefore, it was producing multiple and incompatible systems, multiplying R&D costs;
- the mergers led to no manufacturing economies;
- programming, support and service costs were multiplied;
- too little was spent on programming and support, especially at an early stage giving the firm a poor reputation in the commercial field;
- it did not utilise the marketing advantage of having a large and well-established tabulator user base.

This internal chaos within the UNIVAC division was perpetuated after Norris had taken his engineers away to form supercomputer leader CDC; effectively showing the firm who was really at the cutting edge of computing. Eckert became a director without portfolio. He fully recognised the problem and tried on many occasions to persuade the company to coordinate its activities better:

> Back when Mr Schnackel was president of UNIVAC, it was proposed that we build a 490, a UNIVAC III and an 1107. I strongly opposed this idea .... Unfortunately, the political nature of UNIVAC prevented a resolution of this problem and we went ahead and built three logically unrelated machines. At that time there were several meetings and discussions on the matter but the situation was never resolved. All this occurred over ten years ago.[13]

## Consolidation phase

Nevertheless, Sperry remained a competitor for the number two position in the industry, and UNIVAC became the largest single component of the conglomerate – computers were not a sideline to Sperry Rand. In 1963, after a major conference (which would also lead to the Product Line Task Force which plotted Sperry's third-generation strategy), Sperry finally decided to reduce the range by deciding not to update the UNIVAC III. The 490 medium scale real-time systems continued. The 1107 scientific computer was replaced in 1964 by the successful third-generation 1108 and time-shared 1108 II. These also had a great deal of real-time capacity, and were used in large scale applications where the 490 was not appropriate. The 490 survived throughout the 1960s and the 1108 architecture remained Sperry's scientific and real-time system well into the 1970s.

However, the main third-generation initiative was the small-medium scale 9000 series, which replaced the 1005, 1050, and Solid State computers, and to some degree, also replaced the 490 for general applications. The 9000 series was recommended by the Product Line Task Force of 1964/5;[14] Sperry Rand was deciding its third-generation strategy four years after IBM's SPREAD committee. It recommended building a machine that was compatible with the IBM 360 which would become the bottom half of the Sperry range while the 490 and 1108 computers would form the upper half of the range.[15]

What emerged was a near-IBM-compatible machine (the 9000), which was not compatible with the other Sperry machines[16] and only competed against the small end of the 360 series, primarily against the /20 and /30. It was a similar strategy to RCA, but RCA was fully committed to the strategy, decided to follow it more quickly and tended to compete at the larger end of the 360 spectrum, while offering systems across the board.

However, while it had a sort of strategy, near IBM compatibility low down and real-time Sperry Architectures for larger systems, it did nothing to deal with other issues, such as a weak line-up of peripherals, especially in mass storage devices. It persisted with drum memories into the 1960s, when others had adopted the disk drive. Drums did give fast access, and were useful for on-line operations, a Sperry specialty, but were not much use for really large data bases.

What probably made all these disparate and less than awe-inspiring offerings successful enough to keep Sperry in the business were two key areas in which it performed rather well; namely sales of computers to the US government and selling to the market for on-line reservation systems. Sperry was a leading supplier of military computer systems, and this seems to have rubbed off on the commercial computer operations, especially those areas needing real-time operations. Sperry had double the share of the government market as it had of the general market. In terms of the numbers of computers installed, Sperry was IBM's only close rival (see Table 9.2).

Like many other American companies, Sperry Rand benefited from the sale of big numbers of computers to the US Armed Forces for what were essentially business-type applications. An example of this was the sale of

*Table 9.2*   IBM and Sperry percentage shares of the US government installations

| % | 1966 | 1967 | 1968 | 1969 |
|---|------|------|------|------|
| IBM | 34.3 | 29.9 | 28.4 | 28.1 |
| Sperry | 19.8 | 21.6 | 21.3 | 20.4 |

*Source*: Charles Babbage Institute, University of Minnesota. General Services Administration Federal Supply Service 1969.

150 1050s and three 1107s for logistics work at air force bases. These represented about half the 1050s sold. The company also developed, under contract, many special purpose military computers which helped to extend its technological base.

The second strong area was in real-time computers, where the 490 and 1108 were highly successful in ticket reservation systems. This included an order for $39m worth of 1108 computers from United Airlines for its reservation system. Sperry claimed this was the largest commercial computer contract ever up to that point.[17] Sperry extended the 1108 capability by adding a time-shared version to the range, the 1108 II, and, in 1969, it also released a smaller scale version called the 1106. During 1966–67, the 1108 represented half of the UNIVAC Division's sales.

Despite the success of the real-time military systems, Sperry had failed to maintain its position in the computer market. Its failure to integrate its operations was more reminiscent of the electronics companies, rather than business machines firms. Eventually Sperry did stabilize its position. In 1971, it bought the computer operation of RCA, which fitted in well. The Spectra/RCA series was a much better implementation of IBM compatibility than the 9000, and offered in the range a number of larger machines. Sperry managed to hold on to the RCA user base, ensuring that it kept up with Honeywell and Burroughs in the 1970s.

The Series 9000 was replaced by the Series 90 giving an upgrade path for the RCA users – it was effectively the RCA pathway rather than Sperry's path. However, the main focus for Sperry Rand was to become the 1100 series. In general, both ranges fared well enough to maintain Sperry's position as one of the leading firms in the so called 'BUNCH', the smaller competitors to IBM. Yet it had failed to make good its early position and had frittered away the opportunity to be the leading player in the world's fastest growing market.

Indeed, in 1986, when Burroughs and Sperry merged to form Unisys, Burroughs was in the better position. However, it seems that some of the lessons that Sperry should have learnt were ignored even during this later merger. The Unisys' product line was a vast array of both companies' systems, including the 1100 (by then called the 2200 and the main focus for Sperry) and 90 architectures, and the A series from Burroughs, to which it added a large range of UNIX systems. Unisys has not fared well, and seems to have suffered from many of the problems inherited from Sperry. It is primarily a services company with specialism in government work and supporting legacy customers. Its remaining mainframe offering, ironically called ClearPath, offers support for both the final Sperry architecture, the 2200, and the final Burroughs architecture, MCP, as well as support for open systems operating systems.

However, while it may be a shadow of its former self, Sperry (and indeed Burroughs), under the Unisys banner, still exists in the computer market (at the time of writing in 2012) – which is more than can be said of any of the US or UK large-scale electronics firms. It was a chaotic firm in many ways, and suffered problems caused by its diversified structure, failing to fully exploit the inter-temporal economies of scope open to it. It did not exploit the opportunities it had, but its focus on the key growth market of computing kept it in the game. Structure is not the only thing that can go wrong for a company: leadership, strategic decision making, capabilities failures and simple chance can all lead to failure. At least Sperry, after a fashion, survived.

## The accounting machines companies – NCR and Burroughs

Tabulator systems were not the only form of business machine. Another group of companies would draw on their established user base to enter the computer sector and would survive longer in it that the electronics companies. These firms had a heritage based on accounting machines. The two firms covered here are NCR and Burroughs (the latter would later acquire Sperry to become Unisys). Both firms still exist in some form and still, to some degree, compete in the computer market, at least as at 2012, although NCR has very much gone back to its roots and not producing conventional general purpose computing devices.

### NCR

The National Cash Register company was one of the two niche business machines firms that competed with IBM. NCR's early success had been built on the cash register business. Despite achieving a 75–85 per cent market share in the interwar cash register business,[18] competition from the likes of Monroe/Sweda had completely wiped out any monopolistic profits and this part of NCR's business was not growing.[19] However, the firm had found a new source of rapid expansion, the manufacture, distribution, servicing and provision of supplies for the adding and accounting machine market.

NCR entered the accounting machine business in the 1920s, and enhanced its market share with the purchase of the Allen-Wales Adding Machine Company in 1943.[20] Within ten years of entering this business, NCR had managed to match and surpass its main rival, Burroughs. NCR's lead was built on the Post-Tronic accounting machine, which was widely seen as the best on the market with a parity-checking system to prevent errors from occurring and advanced paper tape and magnetic card input devices. NCR was particularly successful in the retailing and banking markets, markets in which its cash register and teller systems had opened the market – an example of inter-temporal economies of scope.

By 1960 NCR employed 49,000, of whom 23,000 were employed outside of the US.[21] Of this workforce, IBM believed the main strength was the huge marketing force needed to sell cash registers and accounting machines.[22] NCR employed thousands of salesmen and service engineers. IBM's Watson Snr. himself had been a graduate of the NCR marketing system, and it was clear that NCR was rated highly within IBM.

However, IBM also believed the firm had one weakness. The traditional businesses of cash registers and accounting machines did not generate high profit margins. IBM viewed them as basically financially healthy but not generating the resources to develop and lease a complete line of computers.

Figure 9.1 shows that revenue increased significantly in the 1960s, but that profit fell as a proportion of these earnings:

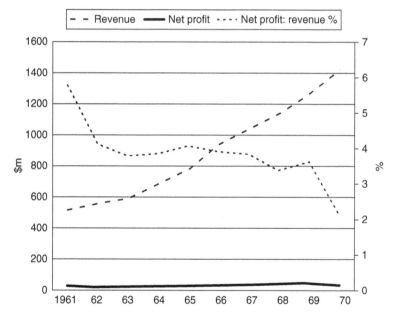

*Figure 9.1*   NCR basic financial data
Source: NCR Annual Report 1971.

A second weakness IBM saw in the company was its conservative management, which was unable to make radical decisions to exploit its very large marketing force. It was clear to IBM that NCR's accounting system product set would be replaced by computers, requiring the management at NCR to react to this challenge, and yet it was a very conservative body without the resources to be a major threat.

*Computing – the experimental phase*

Nevertheless, NCR entered the computer industry in the 1950s. Like other business machine firms it had a number of reasons to do so. The company had started electronics research in the 1930s for use in its accounting products. By the 1950s, some of the applications for NCR's traditional systems were being superseded by computer technology. Of immediate note was that a number of financial institutions were becoming interested in using computers; these were NCR's core clients.

NCR took a slow methodical path in entering the commercial computer business, and took a number of actions to keep down the costs of doing so. The first step it took was to acquire the Computer Research Corporation, CRC.[23] This was a small firm making specialist computers. It consisted of engineers who had left the Northrop Aircraft Corporation when it ceased developing its own computer to guide the SNARK long range missile, instead opting to buy the BINAC computer from Eckert and Mauchly's firm. NCR set this team to work on developing a commercial computer. However, many of the CRC engineers left when NCR announced that the operation was to move away from California to NCR's home town, Dayton, Ohio. By the time this order was reversed, most of the engineers had gone.[24]

For this reason, and to limit the financial impact of producing the computer, NCR turned to GE to engineer and produce its first major system, the NCR 304. As has been seen, GE had already made an impact on the banking market with the production of the ERMA computers for the Bank of America, so it seemed natural that NCR should look to it to produce the 304. However, they clearly did not yet realise the ERMA contract would not be a one-off and that GE would be a major competitor in the NCR banking backyard. The 304 was a fairly substantial computer, costing between $750,000 and $1.25m. It was a transistorised machine, relying on GE's capability in this area. Deliveries began in 1960; 33 were delivered.

By 1960, NCR was developing two further arrangements with other firms to give it additional options in the data processing market. In the UK, NCR went into partnership with the Elliott Automation company to form National-Elliott. By 1960, Elliotts was delivering the 405 computer in numbers, which NCR sold to commercial users in Europe. Later National-Elliott would sell a number of NCR systems in Europe. However, as it built up its own computer operations, NCR started to market directly, and in the mid-1960s the agreement with Elliott ended. NCR had come to a similar arrangement with CDC. CDC had been selling the 160 computer into the scientific market very successfully. In July 1960, a team from NCR visited the CDC operation in Bloomington, Minneapolis.[25] It was arranged that NCR would sell the system to the banking and retail sectors.[26] The system was sold as the NCR 310. However, by second generation standards the sales were not large, 45 being installed by 1964.[27]

*Structured market entry*

Eventually NCR needed to produce and sell its own computers. The first of these was released in 1960. This was a small scale, second generation system, the NCR 390. It had paper tape input-output and optional punched card peripherals, but most important was the provision for input-output via magnetic ledger cards, which the NCR Post-tronic banking calculators used for their input-output.[28] Many hundreds of these computers were sold.

While the 390 had a ready market in the NCR heartland, what is remarkable is how one order really launched NCR in the computer market and gave it scale enough to really justify its new business. The US Air Force purchased 175 NCR 390 computers for the simple process of payroll calculations at air bases.[29]

NCR received none of the industrial and R&D support which the British electronics firms received; it received none of the flagship military contracts for advanced systems which its US rivals achieved. No, all it got from the government was a contract for payroll systems – 175 of them. NCR was in the computer company thanks, in part to this deal, though if it had not shifted to computer devices it would have probably not survived in the new market

In 1962, the NCR 315 was released as a replacement for the 304. The 315, together with the small scale 390, was to remain the standard NCR computer throughout most of the 1960s. The 315 was gradually enhanced, being offered in more sizes and with more peripherals. By March 1968, NCR had 800 315s either installed or on order, and another 120 of the improved 315 RMCs installed or on order.[30]

This level of sales was way ahead of the original plan. On its release, NCR had budgeted for the production of 200 315's, of which 90 per cent were to be leased to customers. By May 1961, with the release of the on-line (real-time) version of the machine, the planned production had been raised to 500 machines.[31] NCR was to double this by the end of the decade.

In 1965, NCR added the NCR 500 to its range. This system was not compatible with any of the other machines in its range. It was specifically aimed at handling the type of data generated by its traditional users (Fisher et al. 1983: 250). Over 1000 of these small machines were being used, many in a core area of NCR business, payroll calculations.[32]

One major failure for NCR was the CRAM memory device. This was a mass storage system similar to the RCA RACE. It used magnetic cards which were stored in a large device which would select a card and read it. It was NCR's rival to the disk drive for mass random-access storage. While it could store large amounts of data, it was slower and less reliable than the disk drive. Its single advantage – large capacity – was quickly matched by new IBM disk drives. NCR stuck to the product for a long time, showing a conservative refusal to accept the failure of the concept.

NCR computers were most successful in its traditional banking and retailing markets. Many of the smaller machines went to mid-sized banks. The 315 had a program for controlling early on-line banking terminals and automatic tellers, a facility which helped it sell to banks. The 315 RMC was given multi-access capability to improve NCR's position in this same market. NCR was most successful in small and medium sized banks, as can be seen from Table 9.3

*Table 9.3*  NCR's computer customers

| | Customer industries for NCR computer and electronic accounting machines % share |
|---|---|
| Banking | 51 |
| Distribution | 14 |
| Manufacturing | 9 |
| Federal government | 5 |
| State and local government | 4 |
| Process | 3 |
| Insurance | 3 |
| Consultants and service bureaus | 3 |
| Medical | 3 |
| Other | 6 |
| Note rounds to 101 | |

*Source*: Charles Babbage Institute, University of Minnesota, Collection 13. US vs. IBM, px2050: IBM Market. Evaluation Department, 1/5/1967. 'A company study of [the] National Cash Register Company'.

*Table 9.4*  NCR's product mix

| Product | 1965 | | 1966 | |
|---|---|---|---|---|
| | Amount $m | % | Amount $m | % |
| Cash Registers | 190 | 26 | 200 | 23 |
| Accounting Machines | 246 | 33 | 319 | 37 |
| Service | 130 | 18 | 157 | 18 |
| Supplies (inc NCR Paper | 113 | 15 | 131 | 15 |
| EDP | 58 | 8 | 63 | 7 |
| Total | 737 | 100 | 871 | 100 |

*Source*: Charles Babbage Institute, University of Minnesota, Collection 13. US vs. IBM, px2050. IBM Market Evaluation Department, 1/5/1967. 'A company study of [the] National Cash Register Company'.

Overall, while it appears computers took a long time to become an important revenue generator for NCR, as Table 9.4 suggests, the spread of computer technology throughout its product range was growing, though it counted the small scale 390 as a part of its accounting machine range, not its EDP product range.

*Consolidation phase*

In 1968, the company released the first members of the Century Series of third-generation computers, a brand it would use for decades. It is significant that, while computers did not form a large part of NCR sales before this, it had been able to keep selling second generation computing well into the third-generation period. NCR had milked as much as possible out of its investment in second generation equipment.

The Century Series changed this, and heralded what IBM had feared in 1966, a more positive attitude towards the computer industry on the part of NCR. NCR continued to emphasise the smaller end of the market, the end where it already had strong customer rapport, a market in which IBM believed NCR had an excellent reputation.[33] Increasingly NCR began selling the Century 100 and 200 computers to a wider audience outside its traditional markets (Fisher et al. 1983: 252). There were probably two reasons for this: the desire to increase market share, and the need to spread costs to maintain competitiveness. Sales of NCR computers rocketed by 98 per cent in one year, but profits fell on the back of the large cost of financing so many new lease agreements.[34] Electronic data processing rapidly rose to well over 25 per cent of the whole business. In the main however, its main sales remained in the banking, retail, payroll and accounting sectors – big markets where NCR was well known.

Computers were only a part of the mix of technology that would maintain NCR's place in the information processing market of the 1970s. The company benefited greatly from on-line applications of technology, such as bank cash machines and automated retail check-out systems and tills. It came to focus on these areas. As computing technology standardised and it had little opportunity to exploit a niche strategy in this segment, it increasingly focused on technology where it could add value - the retail and banking input-output systems which communicated with customers and the big mainframes sitting behind them. Following a dalliance with massively parallel processing (MPP) aimed at the management of online real-time customer management databases through its subsidiary, Teradata (now spun out), and following a few years as the EDP division of AT&T, NCR continues, but without general purpose computers as a part of its line-up.

NCR had a different approach to RCA and GE, and indeed IBM. It took to computers slowly, expanding deliberately on its traditional user base, a base which allowed it to introduce new technology slowly to ensure it maximised returns from the old systems. Yet even by 1964 NCR, despite its slow adoption of computers, its concentration on a few niche markets, and its small size as a corporation, it had already matched GE's market share of the computing market.[35] By this standard, NCR's approach seemed to be successful and allowed NCR to be a profitable player in the new market. It was respected by IBM and seems to have moved at the right pace to bring its accounting machine customers with it into the computer era.

## Burroughs

Before NCR moved into accounting machines, the Detroit-based Burroughs company dominated the market.[36] It supplied a wide array of accounting machines, adding machines and office supplies. Like NCR, the main customers were accounts departments of large- and medium-sized companies, government departments and banks. However, by the 1940s, NCR had stripped it of its lead in this market.

IBM believed that Burroughs' decline was due to the poor management structure of the company. It described Burroughs' management as having been 'casual'[37] for its inability to make the necessary structural changes to maintain its success. The company was split between manufacturing and marketing; this stifled the flow of information between the key operating functions. It also had a weaker field sales force than NCR. Better strategies and tighter control slowly came about in the 1960s. The company was revitalised with the rise of R.W. Macdonald, who cut his teeth selling accounting machines, to the post of Executive Vice President, a role he took in 1964: eventually he became President and CEO. The new management split the company into four groups:

- Business Machines,
- International,
- Defence Space and Special products,
- Business Forms and Supplies.

The following (see over) tables show Burroughs' product and market breakdown (see Tables 9.5 and 9.6). Notably, computers became more important to Burroughs at an earlier stage than at NCR, though overall Burroughs was smaller and therefore the computer revenues were little more than those of NCR.

Like NCR, it was basically a financially sound company, especially after Macdonald shake up. The transformation to computing was, however, a financially stressful time. While not in the league of IBM, it was moving in the right direction, and during the 1960s a number of financial indicators started to look better than NCR's. Figure 9.2 shows Burroughs' revenue, profit, and profit to revenue. The latter showed a healthy improvement as Macdonald programme developed.

*Table 9.5*   Burroughs revenue by product

| Burroughs revenue by product, 1966 | Amount $'m | % |
| --- | --- | --- |
| Accounting machines | 194 | 39 |
| Adding machines | 28 | 6 |
| Data processing | 62 | 13 |
| Service | 73 | 15 |
| Supplies | 76 | 15 |
| Components/misc | 16 | 3 |
| Total commercial | 449 | 91 |
| US Government contract | 45 | 9 |
| Total | 494 | |

*Source*: Charles Babbage Institute, University of Minnesota, Collection 13. US vs. IBM px2082, IBM Market Evaluation Department, 30/6/1967. 'A Company Study of [the] Burroughs Corporation'.

*Table 9.6*   Burroughs revenue by customer

| | |
| --- | --- |
| Banks and other financial institutions | 37% |
| Manufacturing and wholesales | 27% |
| Retail trade and general | 22% |
| Government | 11% |
| Public utilities | 3% |

*Source*: Charles Babbage Institute, University of Minnesota, Collection 13. US vs. IBM px2082, IBM Market Evaluation Department, 30/6/1967. 'A Company Study of [the] Burroughs Corporation'.

Like many other firms going through the transformation into the computer era, the high costs of R&D, and the sheer cost of the systems impacted short-term financial performance, especially because the firms had to finance the building of systems which were then leased. As will be seen, in the case of Burroughs this included some very large systems which needed large amounts of funding upfront. By 1967, the firm had 2,200 research personnel and an annual research budget of $22m.[38] As most of these were committed to some form of data processing work, this was a significant R&D force.

### Computing – the experimental phase

Burroughs developed two routes into computing. First, it took part in a number of high technology military contracts which it used to develop a limited range of scientific and military systems, and, second, it purchased computer technology skills from outside. All business machines firms, except IBM, had to acquire electronics and computer technology from outside when it started to impinge on traditional techniques. At the

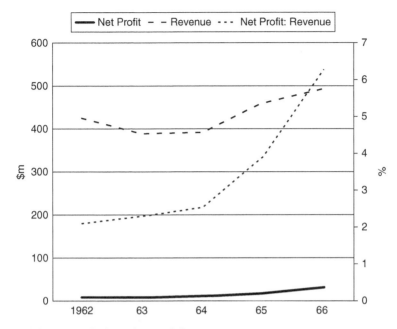

*Figure 9.2*  Burroughs basic financial data
*Source*: Charles Babbage Institute, University of Minnesota, Collection 13. US vs. IBM px2082, IBM
Market Evaluation Department, 30/6/1967. 'A Company Study of [the] Burroughs Corporation'.

end of June 1956, Burroughs bought a small computer company called
ElectroData.[39]

Electrodata was formed in 1954[40] and had developed the Datatron computer, delivering 9 of them in the 1954, and a further 13 in 1955.[41] It also
supplied some of the earliest magnetic tape drives. Under Burroughs' control
the Electrodata machines were branded as the 203 and 204, and were replaced
by the 205 and later the 220 computer. The latter introduced magnetic core
memory instead of the magnetic drum memory used in the earlier systems.[42]

The ElectroData Division absorbed Burroughs' own early computer developments, namely the E-101. The E-101, was aimed at the scientific market[43]
and was basically a simple electronic calculator. Burroughs itself had had a
growing interest in electronics since the Second World War. It had made a
number of specialist components for other firms and had started work on
air defence and communications projects.[44] Like IBM, Burroughs benefited
from the SAGE contract. Burroughs was responsible for the building of the
AN/FST-2, which was the main computer for processing radar information.[45]
This contract led to the growth of the Paoli electronics laboratory, the establishment of a large electronics facility in Detroit, a large defence service
organisation, and the acquisition of computer-literate personnel. By 1959,
Burroughs' revenue from SAGE had reached $155m and it received another

$35m thereafter for an airborne version of the AN/FST-2 system for an Airborne extension to SAGE called ALRI (Airborne Long Range Inputs).[46]

Later in the 1950s, Burroughs was awarded a contract to build the navigation computers for the Atlas ballistic missiles. This led to Burroughs' first solid state military computer; by 1959, this contract had earned $77m for the company. IBM believed that this was the first large-scale solid state computer ever built, and gave Burroughs real prestige.[47]

The merger of ElectroData and Burroughs' own computer operations made a good deal of sense. ElectroData was trying to sell to both the commercial and science market, taking on both the IBM 650 and 704.[48] This was expensive for a small company, especially given the slow returns from leased machines. However, for Burroughs, ElectroData represented an opportunity to break into commercial computing, as ironically, Burroughs itself, despite being an accounting machine manufacturer, had focused its computer attention on these big military projects. Table 9.7 shows how ElectroData systems grew in importance as a proportion of Burroughs' total output.

*Table 9.7*   Burroughs sales of first-generation computers

|       | 1954 | 1955 | 1956 | 1957 | 1958 | 1959 |
|-------|------|------|------|------|------|------|
| E-101 | 65   | 130  | 165  | 180  | 205  | –    |
| 205   | 7    | 20   | 50   | 85   | 100  | 120  |
| 220   |      |      |      |      | 2    | 31   |

*Source*: Charles Babbage Institute, University of Minnesota, Auerbach Collection 4/10. Auerbach Corporation for RCA 6/1960 'A Corporate Business Strategy for Information Processing' 1–10, Chapter 3 'Burroughs Corporation'.

Burroughs developed a computer operation of small size compared to IBM, only selling around 250 computers per year in the mid-1960s, but with an extremely loyal customer base.[49] By the early 1970s, it was a contender for the number two spot in the US market in terms of new sales and by 1977 it had equalled the installed base of Honeywell and Sperry.

*Structured market entry and consolidation phase*

Despite its relative success, Burroughs was a small company compared to the likes of IBM, RCA, GE, and Sperry. It only had a small computer business in the late 1950s and was not greatly profitable in the early 1960s. As has been stated, this changed with Macdonald taking control and recovery was greatly helped by the success of Burroughs' second and third-generation computers.

The machines that developed its position in the market were on the whole larger than NCR's, and they had significant advanced features over the opposition. One area in which Burroughs fared well was in large commercial computers and, more importantly, the concepts that went with them. The basis of this was the continuation of its military work. In 1962, it received an order to supply the military with the D825 large scale computer to control the Back-up Interception Control, BUIC.[50] This was a smaller scale SAGE-type system. It allowed Burroughs to fund the development of a computer with multiple processors, advanced communications and sophisticated memory. This gave it a very advanced real-time computer, which Burroughs utilised in a number of ways. In 1965, as the D830, it was used to supply TWA with a large-scale flight reservation system.

Burroughs updated the second generation D830 in the form of the B8500, announced in 1965. This was third-generation system using integrated circuit technology and advanced thin-film memory. The B8500 was to be a very large time-shared computer system, the largest system of what became the x500 family, though it was not fully compatible with the rest of the Burroughs family.

B8500s were ordered by the University of Wisconsin and US Steel. However, the most significant order was from Barclays Bank in the UK[51] - it was significant as it was seen as one of the first real implementations of real-time computing in a large-banking environment, a market which was expected to be very large. The Barclays plan was for a centrally located 8500 to communicate with Burroughs TC 500 terminals in almost all 2,500 of its branches. This was to be the largest On-Line Transaction Processing (OLTP) banking system in the world, an application firmly based on Burroughs' technology strengths and based in its traditional market; banking. However, the plan was overly ambitious. The 8500 was too complex and never became a standard product. Most of the ordered systems could not be delivered, including the Barclays installation. Indeed the Barclays effort became something of an embarrassment as it was such a widely publicised project. However, the 8500 gave Burroughs the capabilities in communication peripherals and On Line Transaction Processing that was to be the strength of the rest of the x500 range.

The main stream x500 series architecture proved to be a successful range of large scale systems. It was based on the second generation B5000 first delivered in 1961 (predating the 8500). The B5000 was updated in 1964 becoming the B5500, and then in 1966, it was brought into the third generation of computing as the 6500.

The 5500/6500's great advantage was that it could communicate with 15 independent terminals, and consequently sold reasonably well in the real-time market. The 6500 was also a fast and powerful system, equivalent to the IBM 360/65. Burroughs' peripheral systems were geared to support the advantages that the x500 architecture offered. Burroughs' disk drives had a fixed pick-up head on each groove of the disk. While this meant they could not store as much information as competitor's moving head systems, it did make them very fast, which was important when giving simultaneous access to the system to multiple users. Together with good communications facilities, this feature greatly improved the ability of the x500 range to act in the

OLTP role. This was a significant market for which other firms had difficulty in supplying products.

Burroughs quickly introduced smaller systems compatible with the 6500, the additions to the range were the medium scale B2500 and B3500, seen by IBM as the best competition to the 360/30 and /40.[52]

While this strategy meant it was taking on IBM's core medium and large scale products, Burroughs took steps to ensure it did not over-stretch itself. Components came from outside: it purchased the most advanced chips that Fairchild had to offer and, while it provided its own fixed head disk drives, printers were bought in. The 2500/3500 was very successful A.D. Little Inc., saw the 2500/3500 as a large system at moderate prices, utilising advanced components and concepts.[53] It had virtual memory derived from the 6500, giving it advanced multi-user abilities. In 1970, the 6500 and 2/3500 machines were replaced by the x700 series, also described by A.D. Little as the most sophisticated on the market. In large scale, real-time computing, Burroughs was a powerful competitor to IBM

Burroughs offered a separate range of smaller computers. Announced at the same time as the B5000 in 1961, the B200 fared moderately well. By 1967, about 500 had been placed on the market. However, this had been greatly aided by Burroughs winning the contract for the US Air Force Base Level Program, Phase 1A.[54] This single contract accounted for 30 per cent of sales, and put a B200 in most large USAF bases. This is another example of how large US military expenditure on conventional computers was helping to increase the economies of scale of the US industry. However, the B200 also had significant success in the financial services sector which absorbed 40 per cent of the systems produced. The reason the system did well in both sectors was that the B200 was designed with an operating set that allowed direct access by terminal. In banks, this was used for direct on-line access by bank tellers. Though crude, this was an attractive feature for smaller banks. A smaller compatible version, the B100, was added to the range. The B200 was replaced by the B300 in 1965.

Burroughs had two other notable products. First, the traditional accounting machines were superseded by the E and L ranges of calculators which used electronic rather than electro-mechanical components.[55] They were selling 20,000 of these machines per year by 1970, and A.D. Little saw this as a large potential upgrade market for any small third generation computer that Burroughs could turn its attention to. This was a potential market for the B500, a small scale member of the x500.

Second, there was the much vaunted ILLIAC IV. This was Burroughs' supercomputer venture. The project was funded by [D]ARPA, the [Defence] Advanced Research Project Agency, and was being constructed at the University of Illinois, for NASA use. It was to provide large scale interactive supercomputing, to improve the productivity of NASA engineers: in this respect it was similar to MIT/GE's project MAC, which was also funded by [D]ARPA. This project started in the 1960s and lasted well into the 1970s, but was not successful. It was another established enterprise which failed in the supercomputer market.

Burroughs was a growing force in the industry and was outstripping giants like RCA and GE. Despite this, evidence shows that it was not competing for all aspects of the market: instead it concentrated on such areas as banking and military systems, and ignored some peripherals and components. Yet it seems that Burroughs was somewhat less enthusiastic about its traditional user base than NCR. It was not until the latter half of the 1960s that the firm started offering small scale computers for its accounting machine user base. Burroughs was concentrating on two basic product lines: large scale commercial computing, later joined by a range of small scale computers for accounting purposes. It was effectively a mainstream niche player if such a thing can exist: Burroughs made some of the systems which IBM rated as most competitive against the heartland of its systems range and yet it primarily delivered them to specific sectors.

A breakdown of Burroughs' computer sales in 1967 shows that, indeed, the firm had a finance and government emphasis. Figure 9.3 shows a simple breakdown of Burroughs' customers. It should be noted that the figures for 1967 are not representative as they over-emphasise the importance of non-government and non-financial customers due to the inclusion of two large orders for the 8500 systems from manufacturing and educational users.

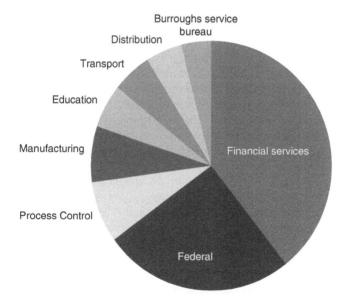

*Figure 9.3*   Breakdown of Burroughs' market share
*Source*: Charles Babbage Institute, University of Minnesota, Collection 13. US vs. IBM px2082, IBM, Market Evaluation Department, 30/6/1967 'A Company Study of [the] Burroughs Corporation'.

In the IBM section it was shown that NCR and Burroughs were fairly highly geared compared to IBM. This underlines the financial burden placed on them when they tried to expand their computer user base. They needed long-term debt to fund high levels of R&D, expensive sales networks, and to cover leases. This seems to have been one of the factors that prevented either firm from being able to tackle IBM head on. The niche strategy was more successful than the broad attack of the electronics companies, but it also showed the trap these firms were in which prevented them challenging the market leader; lack of funds reduced the number of systems which could be placed out on lease in any one time period. However, these were firms which were able to work around the challenges and build successful strategies to build and retain a computer business.

## The start-ups – CDC and DEC

The start-up firms CDC and DEC, though completely different types of organisation and operating in different areas of computing, also followed niche strategies. The details on these firms will be limited: they will merely be contrasted to the electronic/electrical corporations to show their more focused approach, which was certainly technology-led but with a focus on parts of the market for which they knew rivals would struggle to make appropriate products.

Digital Equipment Corp made its reputation building minicomputers for the scientific community. DEC would reach the number two position in the computer market, having extended its machinery into every aspect of small to medium scale computing. DEC was formed by engineers from the Lincoln Laboratories of the Massachusetts Institute of Technology, part of the computer team supporting MIT's air defence developments, working on such famous projects as Whirlwind and SAGE. In the late 1950s, the future head of DEC, Kenneth Olsen (Rifkin and Harrar 1988), worked on developing MIT's TX0 and TX1 computers. While others were starting to develop large, time-shared computers to satisfy the need for interactive computer access for engineers, the TX0 team took the opposite approach. The TX0 provided a small departmental machine for engineers to interact with, decentralised as opposed to centralised computing.

DEC was formed in 1957 to build on the Tx0 ideas. the firm rapidly expanded from making specialist research equipment to producing the PDP series of computers which were small-scale machines for engineers – the aim being to enable interactivity via distributed small systems rather than through interactive terminals to monolithic systems. The first PDP machines did well, selling in large numbers to the scientific and research community. Throughout the 1960s the company grew rapidly, but steadily. There were two notable features of computers of this class: first, they were purchased rather than rented, and second, they were sold to advanced users, therefore requiring only limited programming and service support, a fabulous market to target.

The purchasers of these systems were willing to develop their own programs, as most of the tasks that the machines were used for were highly specific. DEC did not have to find the capital to fund leases or to develop large software and servicing operations. This meant that the firm avoided the cash-flow problems which forced the first-generation of small computer producers to sell-out to the business machines firms.

Another advantage that the company had was the fact that many of its machines were sold on an OEM basis (Original Equipment Manufacturer, effectively the provision of major subsystems or whole systems under a white label arrangement), as a part of another firm's commercial application. Many firms used an embedded DEC computer as the controller device for industrial and military systems, a good source of cash sales.

From this solid base, the company expanded into larger scale systems for the science market, and later it started to support and market its minicomputers for the commercial market. The minicomputer market of the 1970s is where DEC managed to score its major victory, building on the niche base it had developed in the 1960s. The firm's great success was producing a product which tapped a huge pent-up demand from advanced users not satisfied by the larger time-share computers. It did so without encountering crippling cash-flow problems of the type encountered by the more ambitious approach taken by a firm like RCA. With this solid foundation, the firm boomed in the 1970s and then the 1980s and 1990s when its VAX minicomputer led the market, even eclipsing IBM in the minicomputer market.

Unfortunately for them, two developments took place in the 1990s which radically reduced the firm's niche. First, the very users it had originally courted, high technology researchers, including those disillusioned with MULTICS, decided they really had no need for the proprietary operating systems offered by large systems companies and could develop their own. First Unix, developed by Bell Labs technicians when their involvement in the MULTICS development ended, and then the Linux operating system based on Unix, heralded the open source era reducing the link between the operating systems and the hardware, undermining the value of the DEC installed base. Second, IBM had created the even smaller system, the Personal Computer. Coupling PCs to Servers via intelligent networks made even the minicomputer look like a bloated and inflexible environment. Digital struggled to adapt to this world and would be acquired by Hewlett Packard (via Compaq) which had more successfully adapted to the new environment.

Before the minicomputer boom of the 1970s, Control Data Corp had been the most dramatically successful firm in the industry. CDC worked at both ends of the scientific market, but has been most renowned for its 1960s range of supercomputers, though at the time its insatiable desire for acquisitions created as much furore.

CDC was formed by many of the people who had also started Engineering Research Associates (Lundstrom 1987). ERA was a small high technology company in Minneapolis formed by a number of ex-US Navy code breakers, who started to act as the USN's captive computer and electronics firm. Remington bought ERA and merged it into UNIVAC (see Sperry Rand section); this caused some discontent in Minnesota. In general, UNIVAC's Philadelphia operation got the general purpose computer work, while ERA tended to get the specialist military work, though they managed on occasion to pre-empt their colleagues in Philadelphia with well-timed commercial machines and, ironically, they got the job of bringing the original UNIVAC into the second generation era.

William C. Norris, while a senior official with UNIVAC, was one of the most discontented.[56] He led the ERA men into a new firm, CDC, which was backed by local venture capital (Worthy 1987).

The core reason for CDC's meteoric success was its chief designer, Seymour Cray. Discontented with UNIVAC, Cray phoned Norris and told him he would start work at CDC the next morning (Worthy 1987:38). Norris had originally encouraged Cray to stay at UNIVAC as the Minneapolis operation was working on a vital US Navy contract and he didn't wish to disrupt it, expecting the US Navy would become an important customer for CDC, as it had been for ERA. However, Cray was determined and came equipped with a business plan which was

Five-year goal: Build the biggest computer in the world.
One-year goal: Achieve one-fifth of the above.

(Worthy 1987: 39)

CDC's first major product, the 1604, was snapped up by the US Navy; the second was bought by the UK Government for code breaking. CDC was producing a large, powerful machine, cheaply. It avoided the costs of developing huge amounts of applications software and targeted the highly advanced science market. Sperry tried to sue CDC for using knowledge acquired from UNIVAC. However, CDC was moving rapidly beyond its UNIVAC days. It was the next large machine it built which proved the small company's ability, and the genius of Cray. New circuit techniques, cryogenic cooling, the shortest possible connections between circuit boards, led to the 6600 supercomputer, the first really successful super-scale computer. CDC established true leadership in supercomputers. As has been seen, IBM's reaction to this was a mere paper phantom. IBM caused confusion in the market and cost CDC sales. However, the firm took measures to prevent IBM doing the same thing again and before the release of the follow-up 7600 machine in the late 1960s, CDC started anti-trust proceedings against IBM, putting 'Big Blue' off announcing another unbuildable machine. It would be some twenty years before IBM seriously ventured into this market again, and when it did it did so with a completely different technology, massively parallel computing.

The 6600 became a range of supercomputers, the single processor 6400 and the multi-processor 6500 (basically two 6400s coupled together) and the 6700 (two 6600s together).

CDC was able to offer excellent price/performance ratios (Dorfman 1987: 59). As in the case of DEC, this was because, by offering the machines to expert users who had unusual applications, CDC did not have to provide the vast backup and software services needed elsewhere. At the same time, it supplied what were probably the most technically advanced systems then available.

However, CDC did not just build supercomputers. The smaller 160, like the larger 1604, was sold into the science market, though NCR sold a few into the commercial market. These machines were replaced by the 3000 series in the mid-1960s. These were comparable to larger IBM 360 machines, but were mainly sold to scientific users.

CDC was one of the most aggressive companies in the computer market, acquiring dozens of companies. From 1957 to 1973, IBM lawyers calculated CDC had purchased 60 companies at a value of $951.4m.[57] This included the minicomputer arm of Bendix, the scientific computer bureau, CEIR, and the Commercial Credit Corp worth $0.75bn. Bendix gave it a stake in the market for scientific minicomputer, and it was successful in OEM markets.

CDC moved only slowly into the commercial market: it opened up computer data networks, computer bureaux, and became the largest supplier of OEM peripherals to other producers. While firms like Memorex and Telex are famous for offering plug compatible disk and tape drives to end users, CDC was supplying the mainframe producers themselves, including Burroughs, ICL, Honeywell and many others. In the 1970s, it continued to supply supercomputers, replaced the 3000 range with machines of broader appeal, and even started producing IBM-compatible computers.

CDC's fall from grace was equally dramatic. CDC was built on the back of a star rating in the investment market. The loss of its key designer, Seymour Cray who then started to develop his own systems in competition to CDC, and the financial failure of the huge interactive education system, PLUTO, undermined this status as early as the mid-1970s, and by the late 1970s this made supporting its debt an extremely difficult prospect. Barely anything now exists beyond a few small operations, primarily of a service nature, owned by other firms.

These firms only competed in an oblique way with IBM, though IBM reacted forcibly to the threat in the supercomputer business. They both displayed an ability to capture a niche and to build on that niche to enter the more mainstream markets. They had solid cash flows from the tendency of scientific and OEM users to purchase systems. R&D was focused on the hardware. Better software and support came as the companies grew and enough funds became available to provide these extra facilities.

This is not dissimilar to NCR and Burroughs. The accounting machine firms did have the expense of leasing systems, but they were able to concentrate on established niches, giving them a solid base to build on, a major contrast to the electronics firms.

## An outsider: Honeywell

Honeywell, by a combination of a shrewd approach to the market, a slow build-up of its computing operations and the purchase of General Electric's computer division, entered the 1970s as one of the main chasers of IBM. This was a long way from its roots as the Minneapolis-Honeywell Regulator Company, historically a light instruments and control company.

### Computing – the experimental phase

Honeywell's entry into the general purpose computer business was via a joint venture with Raytheon.[58] In the late 1940s and early 1950s, Raytheon had undertaken some early computer developments with military sponsorship. However, once these sources dried up it was not interested in continuing with computers on a speculative basis; Raytheon was and is a firm primarily focused on military contracts. It needed an outlet for these operations where it could realise some value, but did not wish to stay in the general purpose side of computing.

Honeywell was also in the military business, but it was equally involved in civil instrumentation and industrial control. In 1955, Honeywell and Raytheon formed DATAmatic.[59] Raytheon supplied 150 engineers, Honeywell supplying just 12 staff, but Honeywell took 60 per cent of the stock and quickly took full control.[60]

The first product was the D-1000, a very large business machine. Seven were built, two for use by Honeywell and five were leased out at an annual income of $3m.[61] Compared to most of the established firms covered in this book, this was a pretty meagre start to the development of a computer division. Honeywell barely had its toe in the water.

### Structured market entry

Honeywell's real entrance into the sector came in the second generation of computing. The medium scale H400 and large scale H800 were designed to run multiple programs simultaneously, therefore being able to perform such things as input-output functions while a main program was running. They were compatible machines, a fairly advanced feature for the time. They had limited success with over 120 H400's and 12 upgraded H1400 systems installed by late 1966 and 89 H800 and 21 upgraded H1800 systems.[62]

Simultaneously, Honeywell produced the industrial control H290 computer, which was used by Honeywell's Brown Instrument Division. In the mid-1960s, the industrial process control division, the computer department, the computer bureau operation and some other activities were merged into one: Honeywell Information Systems (which later included GE and Bull's computer operations).

In 1960, the Auerbach Corporation had noted that Honeywell was building up a very large marketing force.[63] In 1967, IBM estimated that the size of the field force had rocketed to nearly 5,500; the third largest in the industry.[64] However, a sales force without a product is of little use, the main product was neither the H400 nor the H800. Instead, Honeywell exploited a weakness in the IBM 360 strategy, using its H200 range of small and medium scale mainframes.

In 1962, the company took a radical decision to attack IBM's user base. It got lucky in that it approached the IBM user base in a different way from the strategy adopted by IBM itself. The H200 was introduced a few weeks before the IBM 360.[65]

Honeywell recognised that IBM was likely to merge the commercial 1401 range with the larger 7000 machines, and therefore the new range would not be compatible with the old systems. The H200 was designed so that an IBM 1401 program could be easily run on it, in the hope that this would entice some of the 10,000 1401 users into using Honeywell's implementation of the second generation architecture and to offer upgrade pathways IBM would not. The hope was that many users would not want to change to IBM's new architecture as it entailed large alterations to software, but that firms taking this approach would still need to maintain their computing environment with larger more capable systems which implemented the old 1401 architecture. In many respects the H200 was not as advanced as the Honeywell 400/800 range, but it did have the potential of 10,000 ready-made customers.

This worked. A significant number of IBM 1401 users wanting to upgrade to more capable systems opted for the H200. The scope of the range grew with the additions of the smaller H120, and larger H1200 and H2200 (see Table 9.8).

IDC estimated that by 1966 Honeywell had installed $270.1m[66] worth of systems, 7.4 per cent of the market, putting them a distant second to IBM (at 68.3 per cent).[67]

Honeywell also developed an earlier range of minicomputers, many used in industrial controls and military systems, in part built on its purchase of Computer Control Company. These computers were used throughout Honeywell's operations, being supplied as imbedded controllers in industrial systems, as well as being sold in their own right.

Honeywell had a good reputation among its users. IDC found that most Honeywell users rated its machines and services as excellent.[68] However, it had cut some corners to ensure costs did not mushroom. Users found that Honeywell's training was limited, and some advanced software was not available. More importantly, like other firms, Honeywell was relying on outside sources for some peripherals; CDC was again the disk supplier. Some peripherals, especially Honeywell's punched card reading equipment, were seen as being weak. Honeywell was also targeting its computers at certain

*Table 9.8*   Honeywell 200 Series Sales up to December 1966

| System | Installed base |
|--------|---------------:|
| H120   | 350 |
| H200   | 1014 |
| H1200  | 65 |
| H2200  | 20 |

*Source*: Charles Babbage Institute, University of Minnesota, Collection 13. IDC, 29/12/66, EDP Industry and Market Report.

markets. IDC believed that the emphasis was on: manufacturing, retailing, insurance, state government, transport and finance[69] – though it has to be said, that seems like a reasonable list of markets. In 1966, Honeywell launched on a plan to reinforce its position in these markets by boosting its investment by 50 per cent in software for these markets.

To observers at IDC, Auerbach and IBM, Honeywell was much more market-driven than the larger electronics firms and was making a bigger commitment to the industry – even though, of course, it also had the features of a conglomerate. It was clearly willing to invest in its subsidiary operations so they reached the minimum viable economic scale. It had a large marketing organisation, and was willing to use and update second generation architectures which were still of value to potential customers; it was not a technology-led strategy, but a customer-led strategy. It targeted a certain type of computing and built the scope of the operation steadily, unlike the other electronics firms.

Again, unlike many of the electronics groups, Honeywell's EDP and control computer activities were covered by the same operational group; in other electronics firms they tended to be separate profit centres. As the firm progressed in the industry, Honeywell improved its peripherals and increased software support for its target groups: techniques more in keeping with the business machine firms.

However, the key difference between Honeywell and GE, RCA and the British electronics firms was the greater importance of the computer operation to the company. IDC estimated that, by 1967, EDP sales would represent 26 per cent of Honeywell's revenue.[70] In addition, unlike in many other firms – Honeywell was believed to be making a profit from computer operations from an early stage. IBM estimated that Honeywell's computer group was profitable by the late mid-1960s,[71] something few others could achieve. Computers were much more important to Honeywell than to GE and RCA.

## Consolidation phase

However, by the late 1960s, Honeywell was offering a second generation architecture in the era of the third generation, with the potential of another generational change in the early 1970s. IBM believed that Honeywell's rapid growth would slow down in the 1970s. The H200 range had been a great marketing success but offered little to users wanting more advanced features. Honeywell needed more capability and needed advanced systems.

Fortunately for Honeywell, GE wanted to get out of the business.

By the late 1960s, Honeywell was having problems developing a path forward. The Honeywell 200 was basically a 1950s architecture, and efforts to develop a unified range of systems had proved to be impossible because bringing the H200 and the H400/800 together was not possible. It started developing the very large 8200 computer which would, it hoped, create a unified architecture which could be used in smaller systems as well. However, it was too complex and the system was cancelled.[72]

Thus, Honeywell needed a more advanced offering. It also believed that a wider international base was needed to spread R&D burdens. The firm was concerned that to develop the system it needed to replace its old systems was going to be difficult not only technically, but financially. It needed a bigger user base to adequately spread the R&D costs involved,[73] simply building a system to which most H200 customers would migrate would not be enough to adequately pay back the investment. It needed advanced technology and it needed a bigger user base.

GE could offer all this. In 1970, the successful marketeer Honeywell acquired GE's computer division for an exchange of shares. This not only gave Honeywell the market share it perceived was needed, but it gave it computers based on more advanced concepts. Despite the MULTICS operating system problems, the GE 600 architecture was advanced and Honeywell built upon it. The GE 600 became the H6000, which in turn led to Honeywell's main 1970s products, the Level 66 and Level 68 machines.[74] The company offered an advanced distributed processing concept into which was also tied Honeywell's minicomputer technology and it strengthened its activities in this field. The GECOS operating system became Honeywell's main operating system, but it even managed to deliver some massive scale MULTICS systems as well.

The H200 had proved highly popular, Honeywell was not going to drop that success and it updated it with the H2000 range. The small scale GE 100, developed by the Italian arm also became a mainstay of the company.

Honeywell was more committed to surviving in this market than GE, which had other opportunities/burdens such as a never-ending investment drain from its nuclear power and jet engine developments. Computers represented a large part of Honeywell's business and were tied into many of its other operations. GE's technology added to Honeywell's operations: the H200/IBM 1400 compatibility being a somewhat stale marketing coup by the 1970s. Much of Honeywell's work in the 1970s was spent in ensuring that the users of the various GE and Honeywell systems upgraded to the GE600/Honeywell L66/68 architecture.[75] While the GE 600 may have been the straw which broke GE's commitment to the computer industry – it was, for Honeywell, the means of keeping them in the business for another twenty years.

In 1991, Honeywell left the general computer business, having been slow to manage the transition to smaller-scale computer environments. Ironically it sold out to the shareholders in a related business, Machine Bull, which while partly related to the GE and Honeywell operations had also maintained independence. The era of standalone mainframe manufacturers was over. The mainframe was by this stage becoming a high-powered server with powerful on-line transaction processing and database management capability. Mainframes remain important in this role, but their dominance was over.

## Concluding remarks

This whole chapter is but a brief, rather descriptive run through of the main competitors to IBM to survive the early eras of computing. What is clear from these cases is that:

• While some of the firms exhibit some level of conglomeratisation, namely Sperry and Honeywell, all were more focused on the general purpose computer industry than the big electronics firms.
• All the firms involved tried some form of niche strategy to compete against IBM. While this is clear for Honeywell, Burroughs, NCR, CDC and DEC, it is also true for ICT (having a geographical niche in the UK) and Sperry (which, while the most like IBM, did have a greater focus on government markets).
• All were focused on IBM, how to compete with it and how to mitigate the costs of doing so – in the case of Sperry, CDC and DEC focusing large amounts of activity on areas where computers were bought rather than leased, and in the case of Honeywell exploiting IBM's own abandonment of its 1401 market.
• That where they had them, firms exploited their prior links to their customers to exploit the same inter-temporal economies which IBM exploited, in the case of Burroughs and NCR building on links to accounting machine customers (albeit belatedly!) and in the case of Sperry and ICT exploiting their massive user base in the tabulator data processing business. Honeywell did not have this advantage, but instead invested in a vast sales and marketing effort to emulate these firms.

These firms seemed to have a slightly better understanding of how to develop a strategy for the market. They did not go straight for the IBM jugular by focusing on the development of mid- and high-level CPUs targeted at the mainstream market – though in approaching their niches, they would indeed develop such systems. They also recognised that the computer, to be of value to end users, was more than the central processor unit – customers needed more. They needed software and they needed input-output devices capable of keeping workflows moving. A big firm with access to hugely capable electronics development engineers was not enough.

To a degree, these firms also owed their ability to build a niche in the industry to the government, all had some form of government or military project on which to build their business. The US Air Forces purchase of hundreds of payroll and logistics systems from NCR and Burroughs, purchased through competition, which seems to have been a much more effective route to support than the UK government's policy of supporting development in the wrong firms at the wrong time.

# 10
## Conclusions: Concentric Diversification, Resource Allocation and Government Policy

The case studies provide the raw material for an explanation of the failure of broad-based electronics firms in the new market for commercial computers. We can now analyse more systematically the weaknesses of these firms, bring out their common faults and then contrast these failings with the systems adopted by the more successful firms.

The evidence points to a variety of possible causes for failure.

We will look at five key themes:

- The significant drivers behind the entry into the computer sector and the pre-history and capabilities which this brought to each firm;
- The product policies of the electronics firms compared to those of the business machines firms;
- The place of the computer operations within the corporate structure;
- Competition for resources; and
- The nature of government support.

### Market entry: incentives to innovate and the first phase product strategy

The starting point for this analysis is to consider the incentives that firms had for entering the industry. The main split is between those firms that started building computers as an extension to their existing activities, exploiting technical knowledge in a concentric diversification, and those that were forced to develop commercial computer technology to maintain their current market position. The former case describes the electronics companies and the latter the business machines firms.

The majority of electronics firms did not join the computer industry at its inception; most either joined the industry or made a more structured push into the sector at the cusp of the first and second generations of computers, with Ferranti being the obvious exception.

This cusp between generations was when computers started to become a significant commercial tool and became a batch-produced capital good.

It is possible to speculate on why many of them chose to join the market at this time. These firms had in-depth knowledge of electronic components and used digital technology elsewhere within the company, often in military products. Whether by strategic decision, or through tactical expediency, these skills were put together to develop computers for the rapidly growing commercial computer market.

In general the latter, tactical, pattern was dominant: development of the first general purpose computer was usually undertaken to fulfil a specific contract. Examples of this include the GE ERMA, RCA BIZMAC and the EMI BMC computers. The building of these machines relied on the enthusiasm of a handful of people within an operating division of the company.

Later, a second decision was made to continue to build on this base and to add more resources to the new opportunity. This decision was followed by the setting up of an operating unit to batch produce second generation computers for the rapidly growing commercial market. These firms were exploiting technological skills in what was becoming a major market for electronics. The decision to build computers was facilitated by the large profits being earned in other areas of electronics which helped fund this diversification. Another factor was that these companies already had the technical resources to build computers and, therefore, had a low initial entry barrier to the market.

Ferranti, (and to some degree English Electric through involvement with the Pilot Ace), were early movers partly because they wished to preserve the electronics teams built up during the War, but for which there was little work left. For Ferranti, government development funds given to the company to build computers allowed the division to survive. Self-preservation led the Instruments Department to become an early computer pioneer. It too was exploiting its technical skills, and the whole project relied on the enthusiasm of a handful of managers.

The self-preservation motive was even clearer in the entry of the business machine firms into the computer industry. For these firms, the incentive was the encroachment of digital technology on the punched card market; their main problem in entering the industry was the acquisition of technical knowledge. Two firms, Remington Rand and IBM, entered the industry at a fairly early stage.

IBM was by far the strongest business machines company when it came to the new technology. It had already been working on incorporating electronics into its current punched card product line; it also had an established user base in the science market. By using its established marketing channels for its range of small computers, such as the 650, and exploiting research opportunities in the science space, IBM was both able to build capability and orientate its developments to a very large captive customer base.

In the UK, ICT also adopted computer technology when it became necessary to maintain its place in the business machine market. Unlike IBM, it had to buy in the necessary skills to build computers. ICT's main source of bought-in technology came from buying the computer divisions sold by the British electronics industry.

Most of the electronics companies entered the computer industry as a concentric diversification. They had established technological skills which could be used in the development of commercial computer hardware, reducing the entry barriers to this new and expanding market. For the electronics firms, developing a commercial computer was a relatively cheap exercise. The business machines companies became increasingly involved in the new computer technology as it started to invade their traditional market place. It is therefore not surprising that the attack of the business machines firms on the market for computers was initially slow. It took off with IBM's later first-generation systems, especially the 650 which was the first computer to reach 1000 installations. From this point, all the business machines firms were forced to react.

While the electronics companies had the advantage of having technical resources available, the business machines companies had the advantage of established marketing and service networks. These organisations were large and gave the firms a method of placing equipment on the market and understanding of how this process worked. Electronics firms seemed to lack this understanding of how to market commercial data processing equipment, an issue which is taken up in the next section.

## Product and marketing strategies

The different backgrounds of the firms, and the time at which the firms entered the new industry, affected their product strategies. The electronics firms had certain advantages in entering the computer market by exploiting their great technological experience, in the 'first phase' of their history in the market.

Their 'second phase' product and marketing strategies were not as successful as those adopted by the business machines companies.

To be in the general applications market, a firm needed to be able to offer a number of capabilities:

- Since the mid-1960s they needed to offer an integrated range of computers, from the small to the large scale;
- A wide range of peripherals able to manage high-speed input-output, exploiting the ever more capable central processor units;
- Software support for the mass market which consisted of business and government departments not scientific laboratories;

- Giving customers a cost-effective means of purchasing – in the majority of cases through offering leases;
- Comprehensive field support.

Families of compatible machines were very costly to develop, the provision of a full range of peripherals and software adding significantly to the costs. Scale as well as scope became important as the funding requirements for computer development grew. Firms such as Ferranti and EMI were never likely to make the transition to the third-generation market. They were from a tradition of capital electronics manufacturing where the products were practically handmade to order for a cash buyer – often a government or military service. They had intra-temporal technical capabilities but their structure and history and funding models were never going to support this change in the market – even if they had a customer base to which to sell in the business space, which they did not.

A key weakness for both firms, pointed out a number of times by their state backer, the NRDC, was their woeful provision of software. Success in selling systems to new types of users meant undertaking more software development, and supporting high cost applications design.

A further expense came from the high percentage of commercial machines that were delivered under lease agreements. This meant that firms wanting a large and rapidly expanding user base had to find large amounts of capital funds to finance these leases.

A number of firms felt that the general purpose market was the best route to take. IBM, and later ICT, took this course because they had to fulfil the requirements of their many customers who wanted computer technology to replace their punched card systems. They also wanted to compete for the business of new users attracted to data processing by computer technology.

RCA and GE also adopted such a policy; in both cases because they lacked any niche market to build upon, and thus took IBM on in its core market. They therefore believed that, to gain large enough production runs for their systems, they needed to sell to the widest possible number of users.

EMI and English Electric also targeted the mainstream market when they made their major pushes into the market, EMI with the second generation 1100, though they were never likely to succeed as discussed above, English Electric with the third-generation System 4.

The general-purpose commercial market was the largest part of the computer market and offered the quickest route to large market share. It is interesting that the electronics firms did not explore any alternatives and clearly believed achieving scale quickly was vital.

The alternative was to aim at a niche market. Burroughs and NCR are the best examples of this. Their traditional user bases were already concentrated in specific industries. NCR had an established base in retailing, and, more importantly for computers, in bank branch networks and accounting offices. Burroughs was the established leader in banking systems, though heavily pressed by NCR. NCR's first systems were small and well suited to the kind of clients that it had. Burroughs' larger systems were provided with early time-share facilities, which was particularly useful for online (though not in the modern sense) banking applications.

These firms were, in fact, developing and selling general-purpose computers, but by targeting them at niches and supplying comprehensive software and peripheral support for that niche, they could expand their lease base in a controlled manner – they did not have a rush for growth requiring the writing of lots of new leases at the same time with the crippling costs involved. They aimed to develop a base from which they could more carefully expand.

A second group of niche firms existed: the second generation start-up firms. Prime examples were CDC and DEC. These firms were greatly influenced by their founding entrepreneurs and by some of their key employees, such as Seymour Cray of CDC. They used a number of methods to cut the costs of both entering and then operating in the computer market. They targeted specialist technical users. One significant feature of these users was that their requirements were so specific that they expected to write their own software. Science users also tended to buy the machines they used. This reduced the capital outlay required by the producer, as they did not have to find as much finance to cover leasing deals or develop software. An extra dimension was that there were only a few users in this category and they were a tight-knit community, which kept marketing costs down.

The big electronics firms went for the mainstream – other firms were more successful.

Maybe the most successful firm in building a mainstream rivalry to IBM was Honeywell, which had some of the same characteristics of the big electronics firms. Honeywell's tactic of producing machines based on old IBM computers was very successful and gave it a launch pad into the rest of the market. The strategy for the H200 family was to emulate the IBM 1401, of which 10,000 had been installed, but with which the new 360 family was not compatible (IBM would later add a small system to the range to offer a direct upgrade path for 1401 users following the success of Honeywell). This proved a clever move, giving it a market to target which IBM was, in part, not supporting as well as it might have.

However, while Honeywell, as a producer light engineering products, was in many ways similar to the big electronics firms, there were three key differences:

- Its product strategy targeted a specific market, which, while general purpose in nature, offered a specific capability – i.e. upgrade paths for IBM 1401 customers;
- While a conglomerate, by 1970, computing made up approximately 50 per cent of its activities – ten times the commitment of firms such as RCA and GE;

- In 1967, IBM estimated that the size of Honeywell's field force had rocketed to approximately 5,500; the third largest in the industry.[1]

In contrast, the big electronics firms decided on a broad-based attack on the market in order to gain scale to go with their scope economies. Most chose to do so by exploiting their technical skills to offer an early second generation commercial system, to which larger and smaller scale ranges were added. RCA took this process furthest by moving from its large range of second generation systems to its third-generation Spectra 70 family.

English Electric took the same course. These two firms consciously chose a path of following IBM, imitating its technology to the point of compatibility. Most firms imitated IBM's method of offering inter-compatible families of third-generation computers, but RCA and English Electric opted for full compatibility with the IBM 360 itself. As stated in the relevant chapters, neither RCA nor English Electric managed to achieve much benefit from this policy. The hope was that they would become the second source for the IBM architecture. They also hoped that development cash would be saved by not having to develop so much software.

These firms were adopting a policy which closely resembled a 'fast second strategy' (Baldwin and Childs 1969). This required a fast response to changes made by the market leader. The black box, into which all firms were peering to divine what was going on, was of course IBM. RCA and English Electric had therefore to quickly emulate the advances made by IBM so that their customers had a product equal to IBM's. However, RCA and English Electric, and indeed all the electronics firms, made a number of errors which nullified the advantages that such a policy was meant to give them. The RCA/EE architecture was unique; it was not a matter of reverse engineering. These were high technology companies: they had advanced techniques that they wanted to build into their computers. Therefore, large sums were needed to develop what, to the user, was a machine essentially the same as IBM's. This meant that RCA had to develop a unique operating system which worked in the same manner as IBM DOS, a large development expense. On top of this, the two firms wasted large amounts of development funds on dead-end projects. RCA tried to develop the RACE storage system, wasting a lot of money and putting it a long way behind IBM in the area of disk storage. English Electric spent relatively large sums on trying to use advanced Marconi chips to make the System 4, the first range of computers to use integrated circuits throughout; this was found to be uneconomic.

The RCA/EE strategy would only have succeeded if they had made enough savings from being a follower. They had to have a lower cost strategy in order to compete against IBM's greater scale in this market. They were the most vulnerable to IBM's cost and technology advantages, as their machines were the most directly comparable to IBM's computers. They hoped to make savings on applications costs, exploiting programs developed for the

IBM systems, but they still had to support all the other areas needed to be internationally competitive. They needed to build up large marketing operations, continually to develop new systems and techniques, to build modern plants, and to finance lease contracts on computer installations. They could have achieved some savings through economies of scope, but it seems that this was only a factor when the firms were entering the industry; 'm' form decentralised organisation limited any ongoing economies.

The few, marginal savings that RCA and English Electric made were not enough to outweigh IBM's huge-scale advantage; especially as both firms were wasting large sums on dead-end projects. At least firms like ICT had locked in users, whose costs of moving to another company's architecture would have been high. Another problem was that RCA and English Electric were accepting a follower's role in a rapidly changing technological environment. They had to mimic the advances made by IBM to ensure that their computers could at least perform as well as IBM's. While all the firms faced the problem of keeping up with technological advance, RCA and English Electric had a compounded problem. The fact that their computers were pitched directly against IBM meant they had to respond to changes at IBM quickly, but their unique architecture meant that, like all the other firms, their machines had to be designed from the ground up; they couldn't just copy new IBM equipment. English Electric's position was even worse. It followed RCA, which in turn followed IBM. What was more, it went about redesigning RCA's systems. The consequence was that the System 4 reached the market too late.

While RCA and English Electric made the most direct attack on IBM, most of the other electronics firms also had a policy of producing computers for the largest section of the market. Though the others did not become IBM-compatible (except Honeywell which offered backward compatibility, as too did a small part of the GE range), their product ranges were mirrors of it. EMI tried to enter the largest section of the market, medium-scale commercial systems, abandoning it when it became obvious that the required investment was huge. GE tried to market a diverse range of general purpose systems, though it did develop a time-sharing niche.

As stated earlier, the reason that the electronics firms tried to tackle the largest section of the market was that this was the only way to get a significant market share. This was seen as a pre-requisite for generating enough income to fund future developments. The companies were trying to establish significant new operations. The exploitation of their electronics knowledge in the commercial computer market was the strategy adopted for this expansion. The target that RCA and GE had was to reach the number two position in the market. They both aimed at a 10 per cent market share, which was seen as the long-term minimum efficient scale. Given the size of the electronics firms and their resources, such a policy seemed attainable. However, to achieve the rapid growth needed, it was necessary to tackle as much of the market as possible, at least this was the view within the electronics firms. A second reason for this strategy was that the niche markets were already occupied by firms such as NCR and Burroughs.

The problem with this strategy was that it meant taking on IBM, the established leader in commercial data processing, with the largest marketing operation in the industry, a very profitable line of products, and a very able management. The tactics adopted by the electronics firms evidently failed to combat this giant. However, at the beginning of the period studied, RCA, GE and even English Electric were larger than IBM; if they had been able to turn their full resources against IBM, surely they could have achieved the 10 per cent market stake that was the perceived target.

The electronics companies adopted the wrong 'second phase' product strategy. In the first stage of the industry, computers built were for one-off orders. Once it was established that the computer market was going to be large, firms wanting a big stake in the industry aimed to capture market share quickly, usually with general application second- and third-generation computers. This 'second phase' product strategy was too costly compared to the financial commitment that the electronics firms wanted to make – the computer strategy was not aligned with the corporate capability to support that strategy.

The strategy described above closely paralleled what Porter describes as the 'pure spending' method of attacking a market leader (Porter 1985: 513–36). It was inappropriate because of the many other calls on the electronics firms' capital budgets.

## The position of commercial computer technology within the firm

To understand the choices faced by firms, the place of computers in the corporate structure has to be understood. Most commercial computer developments in the electronics firms started as tactical expedients. This meant that the decision to undertake the development and building of early systems was taken by departmental or divisional level management. GE's ERMA computer was built thanks to the enthusiasm of departmental staff, mainly Barney Oldfield; Ferranti's connection with the Mark 1 was due mostly to the Instruments Department manager, Grundy; and EMI's BMC machine was produced for a one-off contract negotiated by the Electronics Division management. The other developments were equally small compared to the company as a whole, and none appears to have received much attention at corporate level. This includes the RCA BIZMAC and English Electric's involvement in the Pilot ACE.

Given this pattern, it seems likely that, for most electronics firms, the initial product champions were from the operational units of the company. One exception was Honeywell. Its entry into the computer market involved the acquisition of Raytheon's computer operation and the formation of a new division. Such a decision required a high level of authority, implying a strategic move agreed at a senior level in this company.

As computer technology developed and the market started to blossom, the computer operations also grew. These operations soon won divisional status in their own right, and those that survived into the late 1960s became whole groups within the corporations. The computer division was made a decentralised profit making centre and, as the technology became more complicated, it established its own sub-units acting as profit centres. An example of this was RCA's Information Systems Group, which had a number of divisions (five by the end of the 1960s). As the scale of computer activities grew, these divisions started to adopt the m-form structure described by Williamson (1975: 148–54).

However, outside the internal sub-departments of the computer divisions, there was little coordination of effort within the electronics companies. The m-form structure isolated divisions from each other: this made the achievement of economies of scope very difficult. Even if the firm did achieve some horizontal or vertical linkages, they were just as likely to have been a disadvantage as an advantage.

The evidence for this is anecdotal, but, certainly in the cases mentioned, the links between various departments within the company were sometimes a real handicap rather than an advantage. The first example of this comes from the comments of Ferranti's ex-computer manager after he joined Burroughs.[2] He criticised the British industry, and here he must have had Ferranti in mind, for trying to make every part of the computer. He pointed to the fact that American business machines firms bought many sub-assemblies from specialists, thus benefiting from the skills of these specialists. These suppliers could have high production runs by producing for a number of firms. In the RCA chapter, it is seen that the memory products supplied to the Information Systems Group by the Memory Division of the Components Group were not well suited to the computers being produced. One of the great weaknesses of RCA systems was the poor reliability of memory stacks. Another company faced with the inappropriateness of internally sourced components was English Electric, especially when it decided to use advanced chips from Marconi in its System 4 computers. Not only did this greatly slow the development process, but the chips also turned out to be uneconomic to use in smaller computers of the range.

The company that clearly had the most problems with its organisation was GE, which ironically had the most developed organisational strategy. Despite its system of decentralised control within a framework of product departments and groups, coupled to a very large internal management consultancy operation, its computer division was chaotically run. Out of its one computer group (which contained four US development teams, one French team and one Italian team) it managed to create a large range of incompatible systems. This led to multiplied development costs and destroyed any chance of gaining economies of scale on shared sub-systems. GE failed to become a success in the computer market, a great relief to IBM, which feared GE above all others due to its size.

Two points can be deduced from this. First, there was little advantage for the computer department in being linked to a semiconductor division that itself was not a very successful player in the component industry. In general, the broad-based electronics companies were as unsuccessful in maintaining a long-term stake in the components market as they were in the computer industry. The vertical link was a connection between one problem area and another; business machines firms could pick and choose suppliers. A second problem for the electronics firms was that, while they were tied into buying internal components, the decentralised structure meant that the requirements of the computer operations were not always synchronized with the developments being made in the component operations. Electronics firms could lose both ways.

The single-product business machines company tended to have a different structure from that of the multi-product firm. They tended to use a functional structure rather than a separate profit centre structure. The business machines firms had a central electromechanical technology before the digital computer. These firms adopted electronics either to improve the functionality of their systems, like IBM, or as a defensive measure to protect themselves from the encroachment of computer producers on their territory, such as Burroughs. These firms were more likely to be functionally organised, with the computer displacing the tabulator as the core of their manufactured output.

Representation of commercial computer interests was likely to be significantly different between the two types of company. Commercial computers were an adjunct to the rest of the diversified company's product line. Commercial computers, while expected to fit in with the company's portfolio and to benefit from economies of scope within the firm, were not very close to the company's traditional product lines. Firms like RCA and EMI had bases in consumer electronics and professional and defence electronics. GE and English Electric were more familiar with consumer electrical products, electrical power generation, and professional and defence electronics. Computers became important in a number of these activities, especially as they became used in military and industrial control systems. However, commercial computers occupied an unusual position. While the computer market was booming, it was still a very competitive activity. The computer was unlike the consumer products that these firms made; computers were very large, complex and expensive professional products. However, they also differed from the other capital electronics that the electronics firms made; computers had to be mass-produced and supported by vast marketing and development operations in a highly competitive market.

The commercial computer was something of an alien product for the electronics firm. However, for the business machines firms, computers became the core technology. This had a knock-on effect on the status of the computer within each type of company. As the computer was a new product developed on the initiative of low-level people within the electronics firm, computer product champions seem to have been few and far between at the board level. Most board members came from the traditional product divisions. They often favoured investment proposals from these traditional activities, rather than from the new computer diversification. The opposite usually occurred in the business machines firm, where the computer's core place in the business machines market put it at the centre of attention.

The electronics firms opted to take IBM on with a broad attack, a method that implied committing large resources to tackle the established market leader. This was an attempt to rapidly develop a major new product line for the company. Yet the computer operation was not represented at the highest level in the firm, and it seems that most computer divisions suffered from inconsistent support for this 'spending method' of capturing market share. Even in a firm like RCA, where the Sarnoffs were very enthusiastic about having a large computer operation, the funding for this major diversification fluctuated greatly as the firm targeted other growth options. Again it seems that the second phase policy, of trying rapidly to become a major player in the market, was out of line with the nature of the electronics firm and its other commitments.

## Competition for resources

One conclusion of this book is that a concentrically diversified, high technology company faces a major problem in dealing with the many calls on its capital resources. The difference between the multi-product electronics firm of the time and most other innovators was that they had adopted a strategy of supporting multiple high-technology growth paths.

Having a choice of growth paths can be seen as an advantage. It can lead to internal competition for funds, making operational units more efficient and forcing them to develop good plans to win financial backing. A firm can then chose the option which it anticipates will give the highest long-term return. This is the main decision to be made when comparing the relative advantages of the numerous innovations that high technology firms generate.

However, problems do occur when the wrong choices are made. A number of these firms opted to support too many of these innovations in the market place, whereas the efficient course of action would have been to concentrate resources one or two technologies. The pre-war philosophy of many of the electronics firms, that they should be in everything electronic or electrical, was carried over to the post-war period. This led them to support too many products, to the detriment of establishing themselves in any one of the new electronics markets.

Computers were an expensive development and as the market grew they became increasingly costly to bring onto the market. The full cost of selling mainframe computers is multifaceted. In the early stages of the industry, when demand was limited to scientific users, most of the cost was in developing and producing the computer hardware. As the computer market advanced, the cost of producing and selling computers grew. The machines had to offer more features and be much more refined. One-off designs were superseded by programmes to develop whole series of machines that had to be internally consistent, and which had to relate to the outside world in exactly the same way. Computers had to have an ever-wider range of facilities. Improvements included more advanced electronic and electromechanical mass storage systems, communications peripherals, logic improvements to allow online and real-time processing, and ever faster calculation speeds and memory capacities.

As the market developed, other costs grew to outweigh development expenses. The scale of the industry was increasing all the time, requiring the building of specialist plants and an increasing level of mechanisation. The manufacture of one-off or short production run electronic equipment was (and is still) surprisingly unmechanised. With computers becoming mass production items, greater investment in plant was required.

## Software development

An additional cost came from the ever-increasing complexity of software, and the variety of it. One of the most complex, and often most expensive pieces of software to develop, was the operating system. This was the program which enabled the system to communicate with the outside world and which had to allow access to an ever more complex array of features. Many firms had problems with creating operating systems capable of exploiting the advantages of the hardware architecture. Among these were IBM and RCA which both had problems in delivering time-share systems to the market when promised. Costs also increased as the number of applications programs rose, and as the scale of marketing the machines grew. With the growing scale of production, companies had to look increasingly to overseas sales to ensure the production runs that they wanted. That meant replicating all the sales and support facilities overseas.

One significant cost that has been highlighted in some of the case studies was financing leases for rented machines. As the number of installed machines increased, more capital was needed to fund the building of rented computers. Income from these leased systems was spread over a number of years. Some of the electronics firms, especially RCA, had difficulty dealing with this system of operation; for the business machines firms it was already standard practice.

It cost just £220,000 to produce the first four Ferranti Mark 1 computers, but the IBM 360 was estimated to have cost up to $4.5bn to bring to the market. Thus the opportunity cost of staying in the market was growing.

Business machines firms required the computer as the core feature of their product mix. They all had large installed bases of business machines, both new computers and old electro-mechanical systems, which provided steady lease incomes. For IBM, this was more than enough to enable it to be the greatest producer of general purpose commercial computers.

The situation for the electronics firms was very different. The ever-rising costs had a much more profound effect on firms trying to develop a large, across-the-board, computer capability from scratch. Of the firms studied, the first to leave were EMI and Ferranti. They were the two smallest firms in the study, Ferranti being family controlled, and EMI only having an electronics activity equal to roughly 20 per cent of the company. They chose to leave the market before they had to build the third-generation of computers. This is not surprising; their financial resources were limited and the product champions of the computer operations were always low in the company hierarchy. Ferranti had problems with its second generation systems, and was probably not making any profit on them. At the time of entering the industry, Vincent de Ferranti had shown an extremely negative attitude towards commercial systems. The idea of committing the huge resources needed to develop third-generation computers was not contemplated by the firm. Ferranti was a firm that prided itself on being on the edge of technology and its limited resources had to be carefully marshalled to remain in a number of high technology areas.

It is not surprising that the two smaller British firms were forced out first. They were operating in a smaller market than the US firms and were achieving few overseas sales. This small market was not large enough to support many firms bearing the costs of developing third-generation systems. Both firms had other options for their capital and could expand in other directions which were less expensive and less risky, at least in the eyes of the senior management.

The problem of competition for resources becomes clearer when looking at the larger firms that did go into the third-generation. It is possible to follow the decision making process and to see the difficulties in supporting a number of high cost diversifications. All the electronics firms involved in this study had multiple growth paths open to them, and this had a profound effect on the computer divisions. RCA's computer department was invariably dependent on the state of play in the firm's television operation for its funds, as well as being affected by the component and military projects that were going on. GE was also heavily involved with a number of 'venture' projects, namely jet engines and nuclear power. Both these firms went through a period of self-examination during the late 1960s and early 1970s: the main question was whether enough cash could be generated to fund all the developments in hand.

Thus, the concentrically diversified firm, which could have been expected to benefit from economies of scope, instead suffered from having to support multiple high-cost development options.

The case studies of RCA, GE and to a lesser degree English Electric, describe the financial introspection that was going on at the time that the firms left the computer industry. They also show that, even before this point, investment in computers had been subject to developments elsewhere in the company.

The next question to ask is why, given that finance was limited, was the computer operation dropped and not one of the many other equally expensive developments that these firms had in hand?

The schemes adopted by RCA, GE and English Electric were grandiose attempts to take on an established market leader. These firms tried to produce a broad range of computers directly pitched against IBM, with little attempt at product differentiation. While the computer industry was one of the fastest growing industries in the world, it was still risky. The failure to adopt a niche strategy meant that further investment had to be sufficient to keep up with the largest firm in the sector, yet up to this point the electronics firms had not made a profit on their computer operations. Given this fact, it was a reasonable decision to drop this division rather than to continue to support it. The corporate staff had little evidence that the computer division could be profitable.

There were other justifications for the preference for the non-computer investments. The other new activities tended to be either closer to the original core products of the company, or in industries where established market leaders were less dominant. The latter case can be made for GE's interest in commercial jet engines, remembering that it was already an established producer of military jet engines. The core technology argument certainly applies to GE's interest in nuclear power, because of its large stake in the electrical equipment market. In RCA's case, colour television development built on its traditional strength in the field of broadcast equipment.

At least disposal of the computer operation was comparatively easy to carry out, because decentralisation kept it separate from the corporation as a whole. The product centre organisation makes it easier to offload difficult sectors without destabilising the rest of the company.

## Government policy and the British failure

The basic difference between the role of the American and British governments was that the US government's main influence was through purchasing huge quantities of technology and funding the development of new computer concepts. The British government tried a more direct method of influencing the industry through intervention in the market place and supporting hardware developments. The US government bought equipment from market leaders to meet its demand for computer equipment, supporting its industry by buying product. The British government tried to help British firms to compete against the large American industry by underpinning companies which were building computers; until the late 1960s, this meant supporting the electronics firms that were trying to build a stake in the computer sector.

The US computer industry received substantial support from the government, much of it through sales to the armed forces. These sales were of a large magnitude and helped firms establish series production of standard commercial models:

> Another hot government trend – fleet purchases of computers, with the Air Force playing the lead role. Following up the AFLC order for 30 [RCA] 301's, the Air Force has announced plans to install between 160 and 174 NCR 390's for payroll processing at some 105 US and 25 overseas bases. The two orders sandwiched a dinky order for 19 CDC 160A's for an AF Satellite Control Facility tracking network.[3]
>
> (Datamation)

This scale of purchasing was much larger than the output of the whole of the British industry at this time.

What is as important as the scale of the purchase was that these orders were for standard commercial machines. Often military equipment is of little relevance to commercial products because of the very specific nature of the equipment, and because of the very short production runs tend to use components and production techniques many years behind those used in mass produced commercial equipment. This was not the case with these systems. The NCR order was enormous for a second generation system, and they were basically used for a payroll application of directly relevance to the commercial market.

It has to be emphasised that the US government was not concentrating its spending on specialist computers; a large proportion of systems that it bought were standard commercial or scientific machines. This is borne out by looking at the weighting of administrative systems to special purpose machines (see Table 10.1).

*Table 10.1*   Types of computers in use by the US federal government 1967–72

|  | General management classification | Special management classification | Total |
|---|---|---|---|
| 1967 | 2754 | 938 | 3692 |
| 1968 | 2909 | 1323 | 4232 |
| 1969 | 3039 | 1627 | 4666 |
| 1970 | 3404 | 1873 | 5277 |
| 1971 | 3389 | 2545 | 5934 |
| 1972 | 3433 | 3298 | 6731 |

*Source*: Charles Babbage Institute, University of Minnesota, General Services Administration, 'Inventory and summary of federal ADP activities for fiscal year 1972'.

General management systems were used for standard administrative activities and essentially that same as commercial systems. It also has to be remembered that many of the special classifications systems were standard

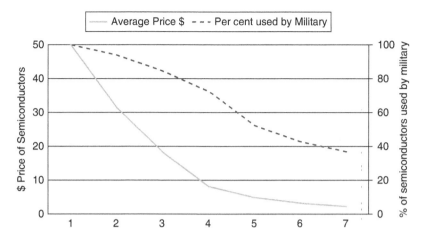

*Figure 10.1* Average price of integrated circuits and the proportion of production purchased by the US military, 1962–68
*Source:* Data from: Tilton, J. 1971 'International Diffusion of Technology. The case of semiconductors': 91.

scientific machines used for such things as real-time strategic control systems.

The importance of standard business applications to the US armed forces also shows through in the type of research that they funded. It is interesting that IBM developed the standard scientific computer language, FORTRAN, while the US armed forces paid for the development of the business language COBOL.

The US government also had a similar effect on the basic component market; government purchasing of such things as integrated circuits allowed prices to fall to a level low enough for commercial use (see Figure 10.1).

The analogy between the role of the US government in the semiconductor and computer industries is striking. In neither case did the government favour its traditional suppliers, the defence electronics companies. Instead it bought chips or computers from the best source; increasingly this meant specialist producers.

In contrast, the British government's role was often reactive. The British policy was based on meeting the challenge of competing with the advancing US industry. The British government purchasing was low, while direct intervention was more common. It is notable that much of the British intervention was aimed at keeping up with technology, rather than in developing new application concepts as in the US.

Professor Blackett, an NRDC board member, prepared a report on the use of computers by various governments. Blackett reported that, by 1964, 1565 computers were being used by the US government and the French state used 111. The British authorities used only 88 computers, 81 of which were domestically produced. However, the list of UK systems included some very small systems, such as the Elliott 153 control computer, and the Powers PCC calculator.

One obvious explanation of the slower British government purchasing of computers was that the UK economy was much smaller than the US economy, and therefore government purchasing was proportionately smaller. However, if the British industry was held back by one general economic problem, it was that the adoption of computers was much slower in the UK than America. In 1958, for each billion of Gross National Product (GNP), the US had 5.7 computers, the UK just 1.8. By 1971, the gap had closed substantially with the US having 84.7 computers per billion of the GNP and the UK 50.4 (Phister 1979: 289).

It was not until the late 1960s that the British government started a programme to increase demand for British computers. At this time it initiated a more active purchasing policy, discriminating in favour of British computers in government purchasing and offering tax rebates to encourage private industry to purchase systems (Campbell-Kelly 1989: 247).

Before this change, the British government's policy was to intervene directly to underpin the firms making computers. Until the end of the 1960s, the main responsibility for carrying out this policy was with the NRDC. The main concern of the NRDC was that the UK was falling behind the US. It was these concerns that led it to support the Ferranti Mark 1, Pegasus and Atlas computers and the EMI 2400. This same concern also led to the government supporting ICT in the mid-1960s, when there was widespread concern that IBM was starting to dominate the industry.

Policy was orientated to keeping the UK industry's hardware up-to-date and, until the mid-1960s, this meant supporting the computer divisions of the electronics firms. There were two reasons for this. First, the British business machines firms were not as interested in the early computer industry as the equivalent firms in the US. They were already busy establishing themselves as independent punched card manufacturers following their separation from their US partners after the war. Second, electronics firms looked on computers as a way of extending their scope in the electronics market and a way of making use of their expertise. They were used to receiving government funds to develop military equipment and were willing to receive it to support their policy of concentric diversification. The fact that computers had a major military role fitted well into this framework.

The NRDC from its earliest inception knew these were not the firms to carry forward the British computer industry, but after their efforts to get them to collaborate with business machines firms failed, the NRDC had little choice but to support Ferranti and EMI.

The consequences of this were twofold. First, attention went on developing hardware rather than on production techniques and commercial applications skills. The government support tended to go on the development of new computers; relatively little support went to peripherals and applications, and what support there was in this area tended to be wasted. This seems inappropriate, as the main weakness of these firms was not in developing electronic systems, but rather was their lack of understanding of the market place: this was where they needed help.

Second, it meant that, in what was already a market that was much slower to develop than the US market, firms that were inherently weak were receiving support to stay in the industry.

British industrial policies were less successful at developing the UK industry than the simple mass purchasing of the US government. This buying of computers not only supported hardware developments, but also led to economies of scale and to conceptual improvements in the use of computers.

## Economies of scope and the concentrically diversified enterprise

The diversified electronics firms failed to gain the benefits from economies scope that might have been expected. They chose over-ambitious product plans, while at the same time limiting the amounts of capital invested in developing their computer operations, so as to marshal resources for other high technology developments. Capital rationing prevented them from fully exploiting all their opportunities.

It was IBM with its inter-temporal economies based on its understanding of customers and an established base of customers wishing to exploit computing techniques which would win. Of course, in 1950, these customers did not know they needed computers, but IBM knew what they actually needed and delivered it to them. Yes, being able to process a problem was critical, so a computer was useful, but so too was getting the problem into the system, getting the answer out and providing software and services to do this cheaply and reliably.

IBM was focused and not pulled in all directions by multiple divisions crying out for resources to exploit what were often more immediately profitable opportunities, but which were fundamentally less profitable than the computer industry in the long term.

Even if the big electronics companies had been able to peer into IBM and understand exactly what its strategy was, it is unlikely that their organisational form would have allowed them to compete with it.

# Notes

## 1 Historiography

1. CBI Auerbach Collection 91/2. J. R. Brandstadter, Project Engineer Auerbach Corporation. 6/12/1968. 'Computer Categorization Study Submitted to Control Data Corporation'.
2. NAHC. B. B. Swann, 1975. 'The Ferranti Computer Department', private paper prepared for the Manchester University Computer Department.
3. As a side note, while in the US I drove past International Signals' main building in Lancaster, Pennsylvania. Being vaguely familiar with the production of military radio equipment, I wondered at the time how a facility like that could possibly have a backlog of orders with billions. It turned out that they did not have these orders at all.
4. London School of Economics. Archival collection, 'Edwards and Townsend Seminars on the Problems in Industrial Administration'.
5. CBI Archive. International Data Publishing Co. EDP Industry (and Market) Report, Newtonville, Mass., published from 1964. The company name was changed in the late 1960s to International Data Corporation, and is now commonly referred to as IDC. The 1960s and early 1970s reports from IDC appear within the US vs. IBM collection.
6. CBI Archive. J. Cowie, J. W. Hemann, P. D. Maycock, 'The British Computer Scene', Office of Naval Research Branch Office London, Technical Report, ONRL 27–67, unpublished, 17/5/67.
7. NAHC. Moody's Investors Service Inc. Moody's Computer Industry Survey. New York.

## 2 Scope, Scale, Concentric Diversification and the Black Box

1. In 2003 Deutsche Bank estimated HSBC spent €3.04bn on technology-related activity, Deutsche Bank, 2004. E-Banking Snapshot Number 10. Deutsche Bank Research P2. This represented about a fifth of all administrative costs of HSBC (€15.7bn – HSBC 2003 Annual Report at 31/12/2003 exchange rate).

## 3 RCA

1. CBI Archive. Warner, J.C. 1957. 'A History of Radio Corporation of America-The Years to 1938'. *RCA Engineer*, August/September 1957: 3–6 – Warner was the Vice President of the Radiotron Division of the RCA Manufacturing Company.
2. Interestingly this was a paper based on a presentation to Harvard postgraduate business students – we will see in the UK cases that a similar series of seminars at the London School of Economics also provides a good record of structure change in the electrical/electronic industry.
3. CBI Archive. Engstrom, E.W. 1958. A history of Radio Corporation of America; the years 1938 to 1958, *RCA Engineer*, June–July 1958: 29–34. Engstrom was a Senior VP at RCA.

4. CBI Archive. Mastran, J.L 1956., How RCA Organization is Planned to Meet Changing Needs, *RCA Engineer*, Feb-March 1956: 32–5 – Administrator Organizational Planning RCA. Mastran was RCA's Administrator, Organizational Planning.
5. Ibid.
6. US vs. IBM, Px344A. RCA press release 1960.'Quarter-Century of Research is behind RCA's EDP systems', 13/4/60.
7. US vs. IBM, transcript (tr) 8652, Beard, A. D. Chief Engineer RCA Computer Systems Division.
8. CBI Archive. Rosen, S. 1969. 'Electronic Computers: A historical survey' Association of Computer Manufacturers Computing Survey. March 1969: 17.
9. US vs. IBM, tr8446, Beard.
10. US vs. IBM, tr8655, Beard.
11. US vs. IBM, tr8653, Beard.
12. CBI Archive. Martin H. Weik, 1957. Second Survey of Domestic Electronic Digital Computing Systems; report No. 1010, Ballistic Research Labs, Aberdeen Proving Ground Dept. of Army.
13. CBI Archive. Leas, J. W., 1956. 'Engineering the RCA BIZMAC System' *RCA Engineer*, Dec/Jan 1955/6: 10–21. Leas was Chief Product Engineer, Computer Engineering, Engineering Products Division, Camden N.J.
14. US vs. IBM, tr8652, Beard.
15. US vs. IBM, tr56507–8, Withington, F.G (Withington was an industry analyst and author of A. D. Little Consultants' reports on the computer industry).
16. Leas, J.W. 1956: 10–21.
17. US vs. IBM, tr8653-4, Beard.
18. US vs. IBM, tr8661, Beard.
19. US VS. IBM, tr8677, Beard.
20. CBI Archive. Segal, R.J, Guerber, H.P. (RCA engineers), 1962 'COmLogNet Automatic Store-and-Forward Message-Switching Centres', *RCA Engineer*, Feb/March 1962: 30–3.
21. US vs. IBM, tr8723, Beard.
22. Elliott, H.M. 1959 'The RCA 501 System', *RCA Engineer*, Feb–March 1959: 39.
23. US vs. IBM, tr9404, McCollister. E.S. (McCollister was the Marketing Vice President of the Computer Systems Division).
24. US vs. IBM, Px114, RCA, 1959. 'Business Review of the Electronic Data Processing Division' 1/12/59.
25. Ibid.
26. US vs. IBM, px244, RCA, 1965. RCA Computer Systems Division 'Five-Year Plan' March 1965.
27. CBI Archive. Bureau of the Budget, Executive Office of the President, July 1966 Inventory of automatic data processing equipment in the Federal Government.
28. US vs. IBM, tr9543, McCollister.
29. CBI Archive. Kranzley, A.S., 1960. 'Planning the RCA 601 System'. *Datamation*. Sept/Oct 1960: 30. Kranzley was RCA Product Planning and EDP Methods Department manager.
30. CBI Archive. Elliott, H.M. 1960. 'RCA and Commercial Computer Systems'. *RCA Engineer*. Dec60–Jan61: 5–7. Elliott was the manager of engineering at RCA.
31. US vs. IBM, tr9599, McCollister.
32. US vs. IBM, tr9009-9010, Beard.
33. Ibid, tr9004.
34. US vs. IBM, tr9404, McCollister.

35. US vs. IBM, tr8945, Beard.
36. US vs. IBM, px4462, IBM, 4/2/66. 'Competitive Environment'.
37. CBI Archive. Bureau of the Budget, Executive Office of the President, July 1966 Inventory of automatic data processing equipment in the Federal Government.
38. Kranzley, 1960: 31.
39. RCA 301 and 601 announcement advert 1960. Datamation, May/June 1960: 14.
40. Kranzley, 1960: 31.
41. US vs. IBM, Px114, RCA, 1/12/59. 'Business Review of the Electronic Data Processing Division'.
42. US vs. IBM, tr9546, McCollister.
43. Ibid., tr9544.
44. US vs. IBM, trS457/S, Beard.
45. Bergstein,H. 1962 'RCA and EDP' *Datamation*, Oct 1962:57, an article based on interviews with McCollister.
46. US vs. IBM, trS722, Beard.
47. Ibid., tr8723-8.
48. US vs. IBM, tr9619, McCollister.
49. US vs. IBM, tr8717, Beard.
50. Ibid., tr8715.
51. Impact of Federal Research and Development Programs, House of Representatives Select Committee on Government Research, 88th Congress, 2nd session, report number 1938, December 28, 1964.
52. CBI Archive. Malearney, A.L. 1961.'The Outlook for DEP'. *RCA Engineer*, August/ Sept 1961: 6–9. Malearney was Executive Vice President, Defence Electronic Products division.
53. US vs. IBM, px242, RCA 'EDP Five-Year Plan 1963–1967'.
54. US vs. IBM, tr8456, Beard.
55. US vs. IBM, tr9623, McCollister.
56. Ibid., tr9623.
57. US vs. IBM, tr8990, Beard.
58. US vs. IBM, 8487-a, Beard.
59. Ibid., tr9046.
60. Ibid., tr9048.
61. US vs. IBM, px242, RCA 'EDP Five-Year Plan 1963–1967'.
62. Ibid.
63. Ibid.
64. Ibid.
65. US vs. IBM, tr9626, McCollister.
66. US vs. IBM, px243, RCA Computer Systems Division June 1964 'Five-Year Plan'.
67. Ibid.
68. US vs. IBM, tr9056, Beard; tr9626, McCollister.
69. US vs. IBM, tr8475, Beard.
70. Ibid.
71. US vs. IBM, tr8518, Beard; px244, RCA March 1965, 'Five-Year Plan'.
72. Ibid.
73. US vs. IBM, px244, RCA CSD March 1965, 'Five-Year Plan'.
74. Ibid.
75. US vs. IBM, tr9269-70, McCollister.
76. US vs. IBM, px245, RCA CSD, March 1966 '1966 Five-Year Plan'.
77. US vs. IBM, px244, RCA CSD, March 1965 'Five-Year Plan'.

78. US vs. IBM, dx621, J.W. Rooney, 26/6/69. 'Administrator Field Engineering', RCA internal memo.
79. US v IBM, tr9913, Beard.
80. Ibid., tr9935.
81. Ibid., tr9914.
82. Ibid., tr9936.
83. US vs. IBM, tr12135, Rooney.
84. US vs. IBM, px840, Memo from Bradburn, J.R. to Sarnoff, R.W. 18/12/68, Bradburn was CSD's general manager.
85. US vs. IBM, px245, 'Five year plan', 1965.
86. US vs. IBM, dx960, Fizzell, C.E. (IBM General Data Processing HQ), memo to Watson T. J. Jr, IBM CEO, 11/12/64.
87. Ibid.
88. US vs. IBM, px4459, IBM Data Processing Group '1967–1968 Operating Plan' 7/11/66 p. 184.
89. US vs. IBM, tr9620-9622, McCollister.
90. US vs. IBM, tr 11156-57, McCollister.
91. Ibid, tr11158.
92. US vs. IBM, tr12217, Rooney, divisional VP for Marketing.
93. US vs. IBM, tr9803, McCollister.
94. US vs. IBM, tr12219, Rooney.
95. US vs. IBM, px245, RCA CSD, March 1966 '1966 Five-Year Plan'.
96. US vs. IBM, 12225/6, Rooney.
97. US vs. IBM, tr9809, McCollister.
98. US vs. IBM, tr11814, Rooney.
99. US vs. IBM, tr9817, McCollister.
100. US vs. IBM, tr12240, Rooney.
101. Ibid., tr12241.
102. US vs. IBM, dx872, Memo from Fazio, A.L. (head of VMOS4 development) to Rooney, J.W. 'Impact of VMOS4 Slippage', 24/12/70.
103. Ibid.
104. US vs. IBM, tr12264, Rooney.
105. Fisher, F.M., McKie, J.W., Mancke, R.B., 1983. IBM and the US Data Processing Industry: An Economic History. Praeger: 367.
106. US vs. IBM, Wright, V.O tr13114: Wright had joined RCA from IBM as head of government marketing.
107. US vs. IBM, dx868, internal RCA memo, Johnson, J. to the head sales Donegan, E. 3/2/71.
108. US vs. IBM, tr11939, Rooney.
109. US vs. IBM, dx936, Birkenstock, J.W. (IBM vice president), replying to RCA's request for information, 22/7/70.
110. US vs. IBM, dx937, RCA correspondence to Birkenstock.
111. US vs. IBM, tr9838, McCollister.
112. Ibid., tr9839.
113. RCA Annual Report, 1970.
114. US vs. IBM, dx872, RCA 'Returns Presentation', 4/8/71.
115. CBI Auerbach Collection 91/6. Auerbach 3/1969. 'An Evaluation of Computer Systems Inventory submitted to General Acceptance Corporation'.
116. ibid.: 5–4.
117. Ibid.: 5–4.

118. US vs. IBM, dx872, RCA 'Returns Presentation', 4/8/71.
119. US vs. IBM, dx952, '1971 Business Plan 11'.
120. US vs. IBM, px347a, Memo from Peterie D.A. (whose role is unknown) to Morsey 26/5/71, which criticised accounting procedures and px955, Memo from Morsey to Donegan 29/6/71, concerning a report by Arthur Young concerning major accounting problems, especially regarding inventories and depreciation.
121. US vs. IBM, tr13580-13600, Wright.
122. US vs. IBM, tr14058, Conrad (who had just become RCA's new President and CEO at the time of the financial debacle in the Information Systems Group).
123. US vs. IBM, px201, Chase Morsey 27/8/71, report to Sarnoff and Conrad.
124. Ibid.
125. US vs. IBM, dx952, '1971 Business Plan II', and Letts' accompanying letter, 16/4/71.
126. Ibid.
127. The language at this stage is very variable, some people calling it the Computer Systems Division, some the Information Systems Group and still others referring all the way back to the EDP division.
128. US vs. IBM, tr13559-61, Wright.
129. US vs. IBM, tr13939-42, Conrad.
130. Ibid., tr13943-4.
131. US vs. IBM, px208.
132. RCA 1971 Annual Report.
133. CBI Auerbach Collection 126/9. Auerbach Corporation for the UNIVAC division of the Sperry Rand Corporation 21/8/1972. 'An Analysis of the Series 70 Customer Base'.
134. CBI Archive. Datamation, 15/10/71. "In Breach of Ten Thousand Promises':7.
135. CBI Archive. Datamation, 1/12/71 'RCA Autopsy: The cause was within':42.
136. Wall Street Journal, 8/11/71, page 26103.
137. CBI Auerbach Collection 3/21. File note, Conference Report Project 540 from Auerbach to E (Evan) Herbert on a meeting with RCA Military Advanced Systems senior managers Dr N.I Korman and Mr A Katz at RCA Princeton.
138. Ibid.

# 4 General Electric

1. CBI Archive, Auerbach Electronics Corporation, 1960 'A corporate business strategy for information processing, 1960–1970, Industry Analysis.' June 1960, chapter IV. This industry survey was prepared for RCA's Advanced Military Systems Division.
2. Ibid.
3. Ibid.
4. Ibid.
5. US vs. IBM, px3222. IBM. 1968 'A corporate study of the General Electric Corporation': this was one of a series report on competitors prepared by planners within IBM.
6. CBI Archive: GE 1957 'The story of the G.E. Electronic Data Processor for bank automation', ERMA Systems Laboratory, Menlo Park, California (A preliminary document for internal circulation telling the history of ERMA).

7. CBI Jacobi Collection, GE February 3 1956. 'Proposal ICB 1100101 ERMA': this was the original GE bid for the ERMA contract. This document was contributed to the CBI by the head of GE's ERMA Laboratory, G.T. Jacobi.
8. CBI Jacobi Collection, Oldfield, B. Undated (probably 1957). GE booklet introducing the ERMA team prepared by Barney Oldfield.
9. CBI Archive , Auerbach Corp, 1960 chapter IV.
10. US vs. IBM, tr6115, Oelman, R.S. NCR Chairman and CEO.
11. CBI Archive, Datamation 1958. 'The New NCR Data Processing System'. May/June 1958: 12–14.
12. US vs. IBM, px320, GE 1964. Computer Department presentation to the GE Executive Office'. This was a presentation to the President's Office as a part of its role of 'needling' operational departments.
13. CBI Jacobi collection; Lasher, C. 1957. 'Marketing presentation – Product Scope Review Meeting', 1957. The Product Scope Review was an important stage in the formation of the computer division.
14. CBI Jacobi collection, GE Computer Department, undated. 'GE 304 Electronic Business Data Processor' brochure.
15. CBI Jacobi collection, Geiser, K.H. 1957. 'engineering presentation', Product Scope Review Meeting.
16. CBI Jacobi collection, Clair Lasher, October 1957. 'marketing presentation', Product Scope Review Meeting.
17. Ibid.
18. CBI Jacobi collection, GE 1957 'Summary – Product Scope Review meeting'.
19. Ibid.
20. GE was heavily involved with government-sponsored research to develop nuclear powered long-range bombers.
21. Ibid.
22. CBI Jacobi collection, 'Barney' Oldfield, 1957 'Opening presentation' Product Scope Review Meeting.
23. CBI Jacobi collection, Geiser, K.H. 1957. 'engineering presentation', Product Scope Review Meeting.
24. CBI Archive, Datamation, 1960. 'In Business and Science'. July/August 1960: 11–12.
25. US vs. IBM, tr7007, Weil.
26. Ibid. tr7262.
27. US vs. IBM, px4462, IBM, 4/2/66. 'Competitive Environment'. This was one of a series of IBM competitor surveys.
28. US vs. IBM, tr7172, Weil.
29. Ibid tr7176.
30. US vs. IBM, px4462, IBM, 'Competitive environment', 1966.
31. US vs. IBM, px321, GE, 20/4/1965. 'Computer Department Presentation to Executive Office' chart 12.
32. US vs. IBM, tr7178, Weil.
33. US vs. IBM, dx490, GE press release 3/12/63. and CBI Burroughs Corporation Records 90/5. GE Computers (yet another name for the division!) Brochure, undated. 'Compatibles/400...a growth-oriented family'.
34. CBI Archive. GE 200 advertisement in Datamation 1/1964:39.
35. US vs. IBM, px3222, IBM Market Evaluation Department. 1968. 'A company study of General Electric' December 1968.
36. US vs. IBM, px4462, IBM, 1966. 'Competitive Environment'.

37. US vs. IBM, tr7182, Weil.
38. US vs. IBM, px4462, IBM, 1966 'Competitive Environment', 1966.
39. Ibid.
40. US vs. IBM, px321, GE, 20/4/65. 'Computer Department Presentation to the Executive Office.
41. US vs. IBM, tr7192, Weil.
42. Ibid., tr7178.
43. US vs. IBM, px1205, IBM, Undated. Internal IBM discussion paper on GE's success in time-sharing.
44. Time-shared computers allow many, interactive users to access a computer at the same time and run multiple applications on the system.
45. US vs. IBM, tr7192, Weil.
46. Ibid., tr7213.
47. Ibid., tr7217.
48. CBI Archive, International Data Publishing Co, 15/7/64. 'EDP Industry and Market Report': 1–5.
49. US vs. IBM, px4829, Arthur D. Little inc. 10/1964, 'The computer industry-the next five years'.
50. US vs. IBM, px3222, IBM. 1968. 'A company study of GE'.
51. Ibid. and Tr7222-6, Weil.
52. IDC, 12/1/67. EDP Industry and Market Report: 4–5.
53. US vs. IBM, tr8339, Ingersoll, financial manager of the GE Computer Department 1967–1969.
54. CBI Archive, Auerbach Collection 79/12. Auerbach Associates 15/10/68 Technical Market Evaluation of the General Electric 600 Series, Phase 1:2–1.
55. IDC. 30/4/64. EDP Industry and Market Report: 3–4.
56. US vs. IBM, px3222, IBM. 1968. 'A company study of GE'.
57. US vs. IBM, tr7107, Weil.
58. US vs. IBM, px3222, IBM. 1968. 'A company study of GE'.
59. Ibid.
60. Ibid.
61. US vs IBM, px1205, IBM internal discussion paper, 18/6/64.
62. US vs. IBM, tr7108, Weil.
63. US vs IBM, px1205, IBM internal discussion paper, 18/6/64.
64. US vs. IBM, px1246, *The Wall Street Journal* 18/11/64.
65. US vs. IBM, tr7234, Weil.
66. US vs. IBM, px3222, IBM. 1968. 'A company study of GE'.
67. US vs. IBM, px321, GE, 20/4/65. 'Computer Department Presentation to the Executive Office'.
68. CBI Archive, Auerbach Collection 79/9. Auerbach Associates 11/12/1968. A Jointly Sponsored Study of Commercial Time-Sharing Services Vol 1:1–2 and 2–6.
69. US vs. IBM, px3222, IBM. 1968. 'A company study of GE'.
70. CBI Archive, Datamation, 1961. 'Bull's rule in Europe', September 1961, 30–3.
71. CBI Archive, IDC, 1965. EDP Industry and Market Report, 18/3/65: 1–3.
72. CBI Archive, Datamation, 1961b 'Bull's 300 Series': November 1961:47.
73. US vs. IBM, px3222, IBM. 1968. 'A company study of GE'.
74. Ibid.
75. US vs. IBM, tr7241, Weil.

76. Ibid. tr7238.
77. Ibid., tr7240.
78. Ibid., tr7240.
79. US vs. IBM, px321, GE, 20/4/65. 'Computer Department Presentation to the Executive Office'.
80. Ibid.
81. US vs. IBM, tr7240, Weil.
82. Ibid., tr7241.
83. CBI Archive, IDC, 1968. EDP Industry Report, 23/12/68: 10.
84. CBI Archive, Auerbach Collection 92/7. Auerbach Associates 20/3/1969. Responses to questions regarding the usage of small disk-oriented computer system. Prepared for Olivetti/GE.
85. CBI Archive, IDC, 1967. EDP Industry and Market Report, 12/1/67: 4–5.
86. US vs. IBM, tr7242, Weil.
87. US vs. IBM, tr7243, Weil; px3222, IBM 1968. 'A company study of G.E.'
88. US vs. IBM, tr7615, R. Bloch. Bloch had been hired by GE from Auerbach Electronics Corp and previously worked for Honeywell and was among a number of external recruits brought in to create change in the ISG operation.
89. CBI Archive, IDC, 1967 EDP Industry and Market Report, 12/1/67:4–5.
90. Ibid.
91. Ibid.
92. US vs. IBM, px3222, IBM. 1968. 'A company study of GE'.
93. Ibid.
94. Ibid.
95. Forbes, 1967. 'GE's Edsel'. 1/4/67:280.
96. US vs. IBM, px353, 'APL Master Plan', 1/1/70.
97. US vs. IBM, tr7636, Bloch.
98. US vs. IBM, px322, GE 15/4/69. 'Alternative Business Strategies, Presentation to Information Systems Strategy Board'.
99. Ibid.
100. US vs. IBM, tr8752, R.H. Jones.
101. US vs. IBM, px371A, GE Venture Task Force 2/2/70 'Preliminary Report on the Computer Business'.
102. US vs. IBM, px371, Ventures Task Force 'preliminary report'.
103. Ibid.
104. US vs. IBM, px3222, IBM. 1968. 'A company study of GE'.
105. Ibid.
106. US vs. IBM, dx555, GE 1970 Annual Report.
107. US vs. IBM, px3222, IBM. 1968. 'A company study of GE'.
108. US vs. IBM, dx555, GE 1970 Annual Report.
109. US vs. IBM, px371A. GE, 2/2/70. Ventures Task Force report to the CEO.
110. Ibid.
111. Ibid.
112. CBI Auerbach Collection 107/4. Auerbach Corporation to Salomon Brothers August 1970 'Economic Study of the Computer Market':57.
113. Ibid.: 57.
114. ibid.: 58.
115. US vs. IBM, px331A, GE 24/4/70. Ventures Task Force, 'Presentation to the Board of Directors'.

116. US vs. IBM, tr8273, Ingersoll.
117. US vs. IBM, tr7646, Bloch.
118. US vs. IBM, px3222, IBM. 1968. 'A company study of GE'.

## 5   The Ferranti Company

1. Ferranti Archive (currently at the Manchester Museum of Science and Industry – originally viewed at Ferranti). Ferranti International Signal, March 1989. Ferranti down the years, Pamphlet prepared for Ferranti's public relations.
2. LSE Archive Collection Vincent de Ferranti, 1955. 'The growth and development of Ferranti Limited', Seminar on the problems in industrial administration. London School of Economics, 22/11/55.
3. Marconi Archive (currently at the Bodleian Library Oxford – originally viewed at GEC Chelmsford) Marconi 1944a 'Post War Policy-Factual Review of Pre-war and Current Positions'.
4. Marconi Archive. Marconi 1944b. Bangay, R.D. (Marconi) 10/5/44. 'Report on post-war problems in relation to sales policy'. Internal Marconi planning paper.
5. National Archive for the History of Computing. Swann, B. 1975. 'The Ferranti Computer Department', 1975. National Archive for the History of Computing.
6. NAHC: Swann, 1975– Bernard Swann was the sales manager for Ferranti's computer department, this paper was prepared for the Computer Science Department of Manchester University.
7. NAHC: Swann, 1975.
8. NAHC: Swann, 1975.
9. Ibid.
10. NAHC, Fer/bl Grundy 1948.
11. NAHC: Swann, 1975.
12. NRDC 86/7/5: NRDC 22/1/51. Concluding minutes of a meeting held.
13. NRDC 86/7/5: NRDC 21/6/51. Halsbury, Managing Director of the NRDC, to W.G. Bass, Ferranti Director with responsibility for the computer operation.
14. NRDC 86/7/5: Bass W.G. (Ferranti) 20/2/51. Letter to the NRDC.
15. NRDC 86/7/5: Hennessey, D. (NRDC) 21/2/51. 'Comments on Ferranti proposals'.
16. NRDC 86/7/5: NRDC 25/4/51. Minutes of meeting between NRDC and Ferranti.
17. NRDC 86/7/5: NRDC 21/6/51. Halsbury.
18. NRDC 86/7/5: Bass, W.G. (Ferranti) 22/11/51. Letter to Halsbury.
19. NRDC 86/7/5: Halsbury 26/11/51 meeting note.
20. NRDC 86/7/5: NRDC, 27/11/51, 27th Board Meeting Minutes.
21. NRDC 86/7/5: NRDC, 19/12/51, 28th Board Meeting Minutes.
22. NRDC 86/7/5: Strachey, C. (undated) Internal NRDC Memo from Strachey (consultant to the NRDC) to John Crawley (secretary to the NRDC).
23. NRDC 86/30/2: Halsbury, (NRDC, Managing Director) 15/2/57. 'Some thoughts on Ferranti'– a briefing note written for the new NRDC Chairman, Sir William Black.
24. NRDC 86/7/5: NRDC, 27/12/51. Unsigned copy of letter to S.A. Dakin (Board of Trade).
25. NRDC 86/9/1: NRDC, 11/3/53. Internal NRDC file note on the meeting between Halsbury and Sir Vincent de Ferranti.
26. NAHC: Swann, 1975.
27. NRDC 86/30/2: Halsbury, 15/2/57. 'Some thoughts on Ferranti'.

28. NRDC 86/29/7: Halsbury, 23/3/54: File Note of meeting (16/3/54) between NRDC and Ferranti Ltd, included in the meeting were Halsbury and Lockwood of the NRDC and Vincent de Ferranti and the senior management of the Instruments and the Computer Departments.
29. NAHC. NRDC 86/29/7.
30. NRDC 86/9/1: Halsbury, 11/3/53: File Note of meeting (9/3/53) between Halsbury and Vincent de Ferranti.
31. NRDC 86/9/1: NRDC 24/7/53. File note on meeting between Halsbury and Messers. Grundy, Bowden, Swann and Welchman.
32. NRDC 86/9/1: NRDC File Note 17/6/52. Notes on a meeting between the NRDC (including advisor Prof P.M.S. Blackett) and Ferranti on 16/6/52.
33. NRDC 86/13/1: NRDC, 23/8/50 14th Board Meeting.
34. NRDC 86/13/1: Johnson, W.E.P, 24/11/50. Letter to Sir Percy Mills on discussion between Halsbury (NRDC) and Bagrit (Elliott Brothers) in Chicago.
35. NRDC box 86/13: Halsbury 10/4/53, letter to Bagrit.
36. NRDC 86/13: Hennessey, D., 31/3/53. Internal memo summarizing the state of the 401 contract.
37. NRDC 86/13: Crawley, J. 17/7/53. Letter to Elliott Bros.
38. NRDC box 86/13: Halsbury, 16/10/53. Letter to Bagrit (Elliott Bros).
39. NRDC 86/13: NRDC, 24/11/53. Minutes of the 13th Electronic Computer Subcommittee.
40. NRDC 86/30/1: Halsbury, 29/9/53. Letter to Grundy (Ferranti).
41. NRDC 86/30/1: NRDC, (probably Hennessey) 26/11/53, to Grundy.
42. NRDC 86/30/1: Swann (Ferranti), 17/12/53. Note to the NRDC.
43. NRDC 86/30/1i: Halsbury, 2/2/54. Letter to Ferranti.
44. NRDC 86/30/2: Halsbury, 15/2/57. 'Some thoughts on Ferranti'.
45. NAHC: Swann, 1975.
46. NRDC 86/30/2: Halsbury, 15/2/57. 'Some thoughts on Ferranti'.
47. NRDC 12/9/56 meeting notes with Ferranti. Attendees, Hennessey Crawley, NRDC and Grndy and Pollard, Ferranti. NRDC 86/30/1.
48. NRDC 86/30/2: Halsbury, 15/2/57. 'Some thoughts on Ferranti'.
49. NRDC 86/30/1: NRDC, undated internal memo.
50. NRDC 86/30/3: NRDC, 26/2/58. Estimates of the loss on the FPC contract presented to the 97th Board Meeting.
51. NRDC 86/30/2: Halsbury, 15/2/57. 'Some thoughts on Ferranti'.
52. NAHC: Swann, 1975.
53. Ibid.
54. Ibid.
55. Ibid.
56. Ibid.
57. NRDC 86/29/4: NRDC 15/3/55, 27th Computer Subcommittee: note of a conversation with Tom Kilburn.
58. NAHC: Swann, 1975.
59. NRDC 86/29/7: Halsbury, 23/3/54: File Note of meeting (16/3/54) between NRDC and Ferranti Ltd.
60. Ibid.
61. NAHC: Swann, 1975.
62. Ibid.
63. Datamation, Nov/Dec 1958: 17.
64. NAHC: Swann, 1975.

65. NAHC: Ferranti brochure 1960, 'Orion'.
66. Ferranti Archive (now at the Museum of Science and Industry): Wilde, A.R. 1960. 'The Sirius Computer'., Ferranti Journal. 18 (1).
67. NAHC: Swann, 1975.
68. Op cit Wilde 1960.
69. Ferranti Archive: Ferranti, 1961, 'Advantage of the Ferranti Sirius Computer', sales brochure.
70. NAHC: Swann, 1975.
71. In this case time sharing meant a system which could simultaneously share resources across a number of independent programmes, allocating resources as they were available – a form of multi-programming. This capability was essential for a further development, multi user computing where many users could interact with the same system, ironically often calling on the same programmes. Later time-sharing systems would effectively be multi-programme multi-user systems.
72. Ibid.
73. Ibid.
74. NAHC: Swann, 1975.
75. NRDC 86/40/6: Crawley, J. 30/8/57. File note on a meeting with RRE representatives.
76. Ibid.
77. NRDC 86/40/6: Wansbrough-Jones, Sir Owen 28/5/58. Draft report of the 'Harwell Working Party', presented to the 100th NRDC board meeting.
78. NAHC: Swann, 1975.
79. NRDC 86/40/6: Halsbury, 17/7/58, Internal memo from to NRDC chairman W.R. Black.
80. Ibid.
81. NRDC 86/40/6: NRDC, 22/4/59. Minutes of the 110th Board Meeting.
82. NRDC 86/42/5: Halsbury, 1959. 'Swan Song': Halsbury wrote this internal report at the time of his retirement summing up the NRDC's role to date for the information of the next managing director.
83. Pollard, B. 1960. 'A comparison of computer industries in the US and the UK', Datamation, May/June 1960: 51–52.
84. Notably, however, these large development teams were no more successful in developing supercomputers than the Ferranti team – the 1960s supercomputer market would become led by CDC. In 1963, Tom Watson Jr, president of IBM, would write to his senior management asking how they had lost the supercomputer market to a firm with a development department of '34 people, including the janitor.' – a note available online at the Computer History Museum.
85. NRDC 86/32/2: NRDC, 30/9/60. Atlas progress report.
86. NAHC: Swann, 1975.
87. Ibid.
88. Datamation, 4/1964:19.
89. The Times, 30/4/64 'Statement by Mr Amery, Minister of Aviation, in reaction to the 2nd report on the Bloodhound missile from the Committee of Public Accounts' pages 6,7 and 14.
90. *The Times*, 29/7/64: 10.
91. NRDC 86/42/1: NRDC 22/11/61. 138th NRDC Board Meeting.
92. NRDC 86/42/2: NRDC, 4/1963. 151st Board meeting.
93. Ferranti Archive: Ferranti Computer World, 1963. Issue 7 September/October.

94. NRDC 86/9/1: NRDC 6/1/53 file note of visit to Ferranti by Halsbury, Lockwood and Stratchey.
95. Ibid.
96. NAHC NRDC 86/41/1 minutes of the 5th Sub Committee on Electric Computers 24/3/1953.

## 6   Electrical and Musical Industries – Computing on a Shoestring

1. LSE Archive: Wall 19/5/64. 'The Development and Organisation of EMI Ltd'. In the Edwards and Townsend LSE seminar series, 'Seminar on the Problems in Industrial Administration'.
2. Ibid.
3. Marconi Archive: Marconi Wireless Telegraph Co. Ltd. 1944. 'Post-War Policy', internal planning document.
4. LSE Archive: Wall 19/5/64.
5. Ibid.
6. Ibid.
7. *The Times*, 19/12/1950, EMI Chairman's Statement.
8. *The Times*, 14/12/53, EMI Chairman's Statement.
9. *The Times*, 29/3/57, EMI Chairman's Statement.
10. *The Times*, 12/12/55, EMI Chairman's Statement.
11. EMI Annual Report 1960.
12. NAHC: NRDC 14/12/49. Outline minutes of the Advisory Panel on Digital Computers meeting.
13. EMI. Company Meeting and Statement 1958. New Scientist 20/11/1958. 4 (105): 1337.
14. In these sections much use is made of original research conducted by Professor John Hendry, author of *Innovating for failure: government policy and the early British computer industry*. MIT Press, 1989. During his studies of the British computer industry he conducts some interviews and received a number of letters regarding EMI's efforts to establish themselves in the computer sector. He has kindly allowed use of these used and unused resources. The interviews and letters have been used in anonymous form due to the time lag between the undertaking of Prof. Hendry's research and the use of that evidence here. The interviews and letters are

   Manager A, EMIDEC 1100 Team, 1987.
   Senior Manager B, EMIDEC 2400 Team, 1985.
   Senior Engineer C, EMIDEC 2400 Team, undated.
   Project Manager D, initially EMIDEC 2400 team then leader of the EMI 1101 Team (an upgrade of the 1100), 1986.

15. Hendry interviews/letters: Manager A, EMI 1100 Team, 1987.
16. Hendry interviews/letters: Senior Manager B, EMI 2400 Team, 1985.
17. Hendry interviews/letters: Manager A, EMI 1100 Team, 1987.
18. Ibid.
19. Ibid.
20. Hendry interviews/letters: Senior Manager B, EMI 2400 Team, 1985.
21. Hendry interviews/letters: Manager A, EMI 1100 Team, 1987.
22. Ibid.

23. Hendry interviews/letters: Senior Engineer C, EMI 2400 Team, undated.
24. Hendry interviews/letters: Project Manager D, EMI 2400/1101 Teams, 1986.
25. Hendry interviews/letters: Manager A, EMI 1100 Team, 1987.
26. Hendry interviews/letters: Senior Manager B, EMI 2400 Team, 1985.
27. Hendry interviews/letters Manager A, EMI 1100 Team, 1987.
28. Ibid.
29. Ibid.
30. CBI Archive: Computer Consultant Ltd. 1963. British Commercial Computer Digest.
31. CBI Archive: Computer Consultants Ltd. 1960. Commentary 1/6/60.
32. Hendry interviews/letters: Senior Manager B, EMI 2400 Team, 1985.
33. Hendry interviews/letters: Senior Engineer C, EMI 2400 Team, undated.
34. Ibid.
35. NRDC 86/37/8: Kramskoy, C. 1/12/1955. Proposal for the 2400 project.
36. Hendry interviews/letters: Hendry interviews/letters: Senior Manager B, EMI 2400 Team, 1985.
37. NRDC 86/37/8: NRDC. 20/9/55. Minutes of the 32nd meeting of the Electronics Computer Sub-Committee.
38. NRDC 86/7/8: NRDC 1959. Notes on a December 1959 meeting between EMI and the NRDC, appearing in the minutes of the 118th NRDC Board Meeting.
39. Hendry interviews/letters: Project Manager D, EMI 2400/1101 Teams, 1986.
40. NRDC 86/37/8: NRDC 14/5/62, Progress Report on the 2400 Programme.
41. Hendry interviews/letters: Project Manager D, EMI 2400/1101 Teams, 1986.
42. Hendry interviews/letters: Manager A, EMI 1100 Team, 1987.
43. Hendry interviews/letters: Project Manager D, EMI 2400/1101 Teams, 1986.
44. NRDC 86/26/6&7: Decca 1960 'Draft Proposal for Support for a Computer Type Magnetic Tape Equipment' submitted by Decca Radar to the NRDC.
45. NRDC 86/37/8: NRDC EMIDEC 2400 reports: Francis 30/11/60; and Morton 25/11/60.
46. NRDC 86/37/8: Francis 30/11/60.
47. NRDC 86/37/8: Morton 25/11/60.
48. Op. Cit. Francis 30/11/60.
49. Computer Consultant Ltd. 1965. British Commercial Computer Digest.
50. NRDC 86/37/8: NRDC 14/5/1962 [EMI] Progress Report.
51. Hendry interviews/letters: Senior Engineer C, EMIDEC 2400 Team, undated.
52. NRDC 86/42/5: Halsbury, 1959. 'Swan Song'.
53. NRDC 86/37/8: NRDC 110th Board meeting 22/4/1959.
54. Hendry interviews/letters: Senior Manager B, EMI 2400 Team, 1985.
55. NRDC 86/37/8: NRDC 118th Board Meeting December 1959.
56. Hendry interviews/letters: Senior Engineer C, EMIDEC 2400 Team, undated.
57. Hendry interviews/letters: Project Manager D, EMI 2400/1101 Teams, 1986.
58. Hendry interviews/letters: Senior Engineer C, EMIDEC 2400 Team, undated.
59. NRDC 86/37/8: NRDC 118th Board Meeting December 1959.
60. NRDC 86/37/8: NRDC 16/8/61 Alloway (EMI) letter to Duckworth (NRDC).
61. EMI 1962 Annual Report.
62. NRDC 86/37/8: Donaldson 22/11/1962. 'Legal Opinion Prepared for the NRDC'.
63. Hendry interviews/letters: Senior Manager B, EMI 2400 Team, 1985.
64. NRDC 86/37/8: Duckworth (NRDC) 22/6/1962. 'Note on a Meeting with EMI's Lockwood'.
65. Hendry interviews/letters: Manager A, EMI 1100 Team, 1987.

66. P.N. Kemp-Gee and Co. 1971 'EMI Ltd' January 1971. Investment Circular on EMI, held in the London Business School library.
67. Bartlett 1983. EMI and the CT Scanner. HBS Premier Case Collection.

## 7  English Electric – A Failure of Strategy

1. Marconi Archive: Second Lord Nelson of Stafford, 2/11/65. 'Address to the meeting of executives and managers of the English Electric Company'. This address summed up the past performance of the company and outlined a major shift in the company's organisation.
2. Ibid.
3. Ibid.
4. LSE archival collection: Second Lord Nelson, 5/5/64. 'The Development and Organisation of the English Electric Company Ltd.', paper given at the London School of Economics in the series, 'Seminars on the Problems in Industrial Administration'.
5. Ibid.
6. Ibid.
7. CBI Archive: Computer Consultants Ltd, 1965. British Commercial Computer Digest.
8. NRDC 86/35/5: NRDC 1965 'Commercial prospects for English-Electric-Marconi', internal NRDC report.
9. CBI Archive: ONR 1967a. United States Office of Naval Research, London Branch 1967. 'The British Computer Scene; Part II, The British Computer Industry'.
10. Ibid.
11. NRDC 86/35/5: NRDC 1965 'Commercial prospects for English-Electric-Marconi'.
12. CBI Archive: ONR. 1967b. 'The British computer scene; part IV, the universities'.
13. NRDC 86/35/5: NRDC 1965 'Commercial prospects for English-Electric-Marconi'.
14. CBI Archive: Computer Consultants Ltd, 1965.
15. Ibid.
16. Op cit CBI Archive: ONR 1967a.
17. Op cit CBI Archive: Computer Consultants Ltd, 1965.
18. CBI Archive: Computer Consultants Ltd, 1965.
19. CBI Archive: Pollard, B. 1960. 'A comparison of computer industries in the U.S. and the U.K.', Datamation, May/June 1960: 51–52.
20. NRDC 86/35/5: NRDC 1965 'Commercial prospects for English-Electric-Marconi'.
21. CBI: oral history collection: Colonel A.T. Maxwell, ICT chairman, interviewed by A.L.C. Humphreys, former managing director and deputy chairman of ICL, 9/1/80.
22. LSE archival collection: Second Lord Nelson, 5/5/64.
23. Ibid.
24. Computer Consultants Ltd, 1965.
25. NRDC 86/35/5: NRDC 1965 'Commercial prospects for English-Electric-Marconi'
26. Marconi Archive: Trafford, Sir, R. 16/10/80. 'From Wireless to Chips-All in a Lifetime', The Third Mountbatten Lecture. Sir Robert ran GEC Computers into the 1980s which included the industrial and military computer operations of English Electric and Marconi, but which was primarily based on Elliott Automation.
27. CBI Archive: International Data Corporation, 21/11/69. EDP Europa Report: 3.
28. Ibid.
29. NRDC 86/35/5: NRDC 1965 'Commercial prospects for English-Electric-Marconi'
30. Marconi Archive: Second Lord Nelson of Stafford, 2/11/65.

31. CBI Archive: ONR 1967.
32. Ibid.
33. Ibid.
34. Marconi Archive: Marconi 1967. 'The Marconi Company. A pamphlet introducing the workings of the Marconi Company'.
35. CBI Archive: ONR 1967.
36. US vs. IBM, px 2482: IBM, Sept 1969a. 'World Trade Corporation: Competitive Manufacturer New Sales, Rentals Installed'. This was a summary paper showing the main competition to IBM's overseas operation.
37. Archive: International Data Corporation, 21/11/69.
38. US vs. IBM, px2482: IBM World Trade Corporation, Sept 1969b. 'Competitive Manufacturer New Sales, Rentals Installed'.
39. Ibid.
40. CBI: oral history collection: Colonel A.T. Maxwell, ICT chairman, interviewed by A.L.C. Humphreys.
41. NRDC 86/35/5: ICT and EELM 1965 'Large computer project: presentation to the Government' September 1965.
42. CBI Oral History Archive, Humphreys, A.C.L., interviewed by Tomash, E., 28/2/81.
43. Ibid.
44. LSE archival collection: Second Lord Nelson, 5/5/64.
45. CBI: oral history collection: Colonel A.T. Maxwell, ICT chairman, interviewed by A.L.C. Humphreys.
46. Ibid.
47. CBI Archive: ONR 1967.
48. CBI: oral history collection: Colonel A.T. Maxwell, ICT chairman, interviewed by A.L.C. Humphreys.

# 8   Strategies and Organisations of IBM and ICT

1. CBI Auerbach Collection 76/5. Auerbach Corporation 1/2/1968. 'An Evaluation of Rental vs. Full Payout Leasing of the IBM 360/40'. Submitted to Converse Rubber Company: 2–2.
2. CBI Auerbach Collection 128/6. Auerbach Associates, 7/7/1972. 'Analysis of IBM Price and Product Announcements for Control Data Corporation': 25.
3. CBI Auerbach Collection 4/10. Auerbach Corporation for RCA 6/1960). 'A Corporate Business Strategy for Information Processing', 1–10 (section analysing IBM).
4. CBI Burroughs Corporation Records 90/6. *Business Week* 14/5/55. 'IBM': 66.
5. US vs. IBM, px1888, internal IBM Manager Program Profit Evaluation, 27/9/66. 'Program Profit Evaluation on Selected 1400/7000 Series Systems and Component Machine Types' – which includes 1620–1622 numbers.
6. Op. cit., CBI Auerbach Collection 4/10. Auerbach Corporation for RCA 6/1960: 1–7.
7. US vs. IBM, dx1404. IBM, 28/12/61. 'Final Report of SPREAD Task Group'.
8. Op. cit., CBI Auerbach Collection 4/10. Auerbach Corporation for RCA 6/1960: 1–7.
9. Op. cit., US vs. IBM, dx1404. IBM, 28/12/61. 'Final Report of SPREAD Task Group'.
10. Ibid.
11. Ibid.

12. Ibid.
13. CBI Archive. International Data Publishing, 23/3/1964. *EDP Industry and Market Report.* 1(1): 1.
14. CBI Auerbach Collection 128/6. Auerbach Corporation, 7/7/1972. 'Analysis of IBM Price and Product Announcements' for the Control Data Corporation.
15. Ibid.: 2–3.
16. Ibid.: 3.
17. CBI Auerbach Collection, 76/6. Auerbach Corporation, 4/1969. 'Economic Justification for the Purchase of Third Generation Computers', submitted to Computer Leasing Company: 1–2.
18. op cit z1 CBI Auerbach Collection 128/6. Auerbach Corporation, 7/7/1972.
19. Auerbach Ibid.: 17.
20. CBI Archive. IDC 15/5/1964 EDP Industry and Market Report: 2.
21. Op. cit. CBI Auerbach Collection 128/6: 1.
22. Ibid.:17.
23. US vs. IBM, px3446, IBM, 19/5/1966. 'Analysis of Major Computer Manufacturers'.
24. CBI Auerbach Collection, 76/6. Auerbach Corporation, 4/1969. Economic Justification for the Purchase of Third Generation Computers, submitted to Computer Leasing Company: 1–2.
25. IBM press release 30/6/1970.
26. CBI Auerbach Collection 51/7. Auerbach Corporation for IBM 12/7/1965. 'Competitive Analysis of Large-Scale Systems'.
27. Ibid.: 1–3.
28. US vs. IBM, px226, IBM, 4/68. 'System 360/65 Financial Analysis'.
29. US vs. IBM, px2227, IBM, 4/68. 'System 360/67 Financial Analysis'.
30. Ibid.
31. Op. cit., CBI Auerbach Collection 4/10. Auerbach Corporation for RCA 6/1960: 1–17.
32. Ibid.: 1–16.
33. National Archive for the History of Computing ICL/A1M, 'Induction Course, Some Notes on ICL History', circa 1968. This document was used in the induction of new employees.
34. Ibid.
35. CBI Oral History Collection, Maxwell, Col A.T., interviewed by A. C. L. Humphreys, 9/1/80. Both men were in ICT then: ICL directors; Maxwell was also chair of Power-Samas before the ICT merger.
36. London School of Economics, archival collection. Sir Walter Puckey, BTM Director, 22/11/55. 'Design, Development and Marketing of Hollerith and Allied Machinery', Seminar on the Problems in Industrial Administration.
37. Ibid.
38. Ibid.
39. CBI Oral History Collection, Maxwell interview.
40. NRDC 86/44/3. NRDC 11/7/55. 'Summary of Digital Computer Production and Development in the UK'.
41. NRDC 86/44/3, NRDC 11/7/55. 'Notes on Sales Promotion and Application Of Computers', appendix to paper no 106, 'Survey of Computer Availability, Application Studies and Training'.
42. Ibid.
43. Ibid.
44. NAHC NRDC 86/35/1, Advisory Panel file.

45. Ibid.
46. Op. cit. CBI Oral History Collection, Maxwell interview.
47. CBI Oral History Collection, comment by interviewer A. L. C. Humphreys, who would become ICL managing director, while interviewing Maxwell.
48. CBI Archive, Nelson M. Blachman, 8/1/1959. 'Commercial Digital Computers in Britain'. Office of Naval Research, US Embassy, London.
49. CBI Archive, Auerbach Electronics Corporation, 15/1/61. 'European Information Technology, a Report on the Industry and the State of the Art'.
50. London School of Economics, archival collection, A. L. G. Lindley, Chair and M. D. of GEC 13/3/1962. 'The Development and Organization of the General Electric Co. Ltd'. Seminar on the Problems in Industrial Administration.
51. Computer Consultants, British Commercial Computer Digest, 1965.
52. Op. cit. Lindley.
53. Computer Consultants, British Commercial Computer Digest 1965.
54. CBI Oral History Collection, Maxwell interview.
55. CBI Oral History Archive, A. C. L. Humphreys, interviewed by E. Tomash, 28/2/81.
56. *Datamation*, December 1961: 53.
57. Computer Consultants, *British Commercial Computer Digest*, 1965.
58. Op. cit. CBI Oral History Collection, Humphreys interview.
59. A. S. Douglas CEIR (UK) Ltd., August 1963, 'The European Computer Scene: 1963', *Datamation*: 24–6.
60. NAHC NRDC 86/35/4. J. Crawley 22/7/64. 'The UK Computer Industry with Particular Reference to ICT'.
61. Op. cit. CBI Oral History Collection, Humphreys interview.
62. CBI Archive, Office of Naval Research 17/5/1967. 'The British Computer Scene'.
63. Ibid.
64. Ibid.
65. US vs. IBM px2482, IBM World Trade Corporation, Sept 1969. 'Competitive Manufacturer New Sales, and Rentals Installed'.
66. ICT annual report, 1965. 'Review by the Chairman': 4 and Group Financial Statistics: 23.
67. Investors Review, 8/1/66. No Swift Recovery for ICT;, report of Cecil Mead, chairman's statement: 11.
68. NAHC NRDC 86/35/4. Michael Shanks, 3/6/64. 'Can IBM's Rivals Stay the Pace'. *Financial Times* 3/6/64: 14.
69. NAHC NRDC 86/35/4, Crawley, NRDC internal report, 22/7/64. 'The UK Computer Industry with Particular Reference to ICT'.
70. Ibid.
71. Ibid.
72. Ibid.
73. NAHC NRDC 86/35/4, internal undated memo probably by Crawley, 'UK Computer Industry-Possible Arrangements between NRDC and ICT'.
74. NAHC NRDC 86/35/4 ICT, 16/2/1965. 'NRDC Support' a paper submitted to the ICT Executive Committee and submitted to the NRDC as a proposal for support.
75. NAHC NRDC 86/35/5. 'NRDC/ICT Draft Agreement'. 13/4/65.
76. NAHC NRDC 86/35/5. 'NRDC/ICT Draft Agreement' 13/4/65.
75. CBI Archive, ONR, 17/5/1967. The British Computer Scene, pt II.
78. Op. cit. CBI Oral History Collection, Humphreys interview.
79. CBI Archive, ONR, 17/5/1967. The British Computer Scene, pt III.

80. NAHC NRDC 86/35/4, Prof. Patrick Blackett, 19/5/64. Blackett prepared this report after receiving a memo on the subject from Prof. Gill, a long-time advisor to the NRDC.
81. NRDC 86/35/5, Prof. Patrick Blackett memo, 19/5/64.
82. NRDC 86/35/5, internal memo by Crawley 29/1/65 on a meeting at the Ministry of Technology.
83. US vs. IBM, px4829, Arthur D. Little Inc, Services to Investors, October 1964. 'The Computer Industry – The Next Five Years'.
84. CBI Auerbach Collection 4/10. Auerbach Corporation for RCA 6/1960. 'A Corporate Business Strategy for Information Processing': 1–10, Chapter 3 'Burroughs Corporation'.
85. US vs. IBM, px2082, IBM, Market Evaluation Department, 30/6/67. 'A Company Study of [the] Burroughs Corporation'.
86. Ibid.
87. CBI oral history collection, Humphreys interview.
88. Op. cit. NAHC NRDC 86/44/3, NRDC 11/7/55. 'Notes on Sales Promotion and Applications of Computers'.
89. ICT Annual Report, 1964: 7.
90. Ibid: 7.
91. ICT annual report, 1967.
92. US vs. IBM, McCollister tr9634, McCollister was RCA's Computer Systems Division's Vice President of Marketing.
93. B. Pollard May/June 1960. 'A Comparison of Computer Industries in the US and the UK', *Datamation*: 51–2.

# 9 The Nimble Survivors: Sperry Rand, NCR, Burroughs, CDC and Honeywell

1. CBI Auerbach Collection 4/10. Auerbach Corporation for RCA 6/1960 'A Corporate Business Strategy for Information Processing' 1–10, Chapter 2 'Sperry Corporation'.
2. CBI Archive, Hakala Associates Inc., undated Engineering Research Associates: The wellspring of Minnesota's computer industry, St Paul Minnesota. This pamphlet was commissioned by the Sperry Corp.
3. Op cit CBI Auerbach Collection 4/10. Auerbach Corporation for RCA 6/1960.
4. Ibid.
5. Ibid.
6. Ibid.
7. US vs. IBM, dx8, J.P. Eckert internal memo to H.B. Horton 7/4/61, outlining the chaotic state of the Sperry computer range and the wasted effort this entailed.
8. Ibid.
9. Op cit CBI Auerbach Collection 4/10. Auerbach Corporation for RCA 6/1960.
10. ibid.
11. CBI Oral History Collection: William Norris Interview.
12. Ibid.
13. US vs. IBM, dx10, Eckert 19/7/71 memo to Sperry CEO R.E.Macdonald.
14. US vs. IBM, dx15, Sperry Rand 9/2/1965. Product Line Task Force: Report No.2.
15. US vs. IBM, tr2882, Macdonald testimony.
16. US vs. IBM, dx10, Eckert 19/7/71 memo to Sperry CEO R.E.Macdonald.

17. US vs. IBM, dx61, Sperry Annual Report 1966.
18. US vs. IBM, px 2050, IBM Market Evaluation Department, Data Processing Group, 1/5/67. 'A company study of [the] National Cash Register Company'.
19. Ibid.
20. CBI Archive. NCR, 1984 Celebrating the Future: NCR 1884–1984, Booklet two, '1923–1951, The Accounting Machine Era'.
21. Ibid.
22. US vs. IBM, px2050. IBM Market Evaluation Department, 1/5/1967. 'A company study of [the] National Cash Register Company'.
23. CBI Auerbach Collection 4/10. Auerbach Corporation for RCA 6/1960 'A Corporate Business Strategy for Information Processing' 1–10, Chapter 9 NCR.
24. Ibid.
25. US vs. IBM, dx330, Correspondents from R.S. Oleman, NCR President, to W.C. Norris, CDC President, 8/7/60.
26. US vs. IBM, dx331. Norris, W.C. 2/3/61 'Address to [the] Twin City Security Analysts'.
27. CBI Archive, IDC, 23/3/64 EDP Industry and Market Report:ll.
28. op cit Auerbach Corproation 1960 Chapter 9.
29. US vs. IBM, px4829, Arthur D. Little Inc, Services to Investors, October 1964. 'The Computer Industry-The Next Five Years'.
30. CBI Archive. IDC, 29/3/1968 EDP Industry Report:7.
31. US vs. IBM,dx746, NCR, 10/6/1963 'Financial report on the 315 program'.
32. Op cit IDC, 29/3/1968 EDP Industry Report:7.
33. US vs. IBM, px2050. IBM Market Evaluation Department, 1/5/1967. 'A company study of [the] National Cash Register Company'.
34. US vs. IBM, dx340A, NCR Annual Report 1968.
35. US vs. IBM, px4829, Arthur D. Little Inc, October 1964 'The Computer Industry-The Next Five Years'.
36. US vs. IBM, px2082, IBM, Market Evaluation Department, 30/6/67 'A Company Study of [the] Burroughs Corporation'.
37. Ibid.
38. Ibid.
39. US vs. IBM, tr9185, McCollister, ElectroData Marketing vice president.
40. US vs. IBMdx698, Electrodata Annual Report 1954.
41. US vs. IBMdx698, Electrodata Annual Report 1954.
42. US vs. IBM, tr9185, McCollister.
43. CBI Auerbach Collection 4/10. Auerbach Corporation for RCA 6/1960 'A Corporate Business Strategy for Information Processing' 1–10, Chapter 3 'Burroughs Corporation'.
44. Ibid.
45. Ibid.
46. Ibid.
47. Op cit. US vs. IBM, px2082, IBM, 30/6/1967.
48. US vs. IBM, tr9180, McCollister.
49. Op cit. US vs. IBM, px2082, IBM, 30/6/1967.
50. Ibid.
51. Ibid.
52. Ibid.
53. US vs. IBM, px4835, A.D.Little Inc, 4/1971 'The computer industry 1970–1975'.
54. Op cit. US vs. IBM, px2082, IBM, 30/6/1967. A company study of Burroughs'.

55. Op cit <u>US vs. IBM</u>, px4835, A.D.Little Inc, 4/1971.
56. CBI Oral History Collection, William C. Norris interviewed by A.L. Norberg, 28/7/86.).
57. <u>US vs. IBM</u>, dx296, IBM attorney's estimates.
58. CBI Auerbach Collection 4/10. Auerbach Corporation for RCA 6/1960 'A Corporate Business Strategy for Information Processing', Chapter 5 'Minneapolis-Honeywell Regulator Company'.
59. Ibid.
60. <u>US vs. IBM</u>, tr7573, R.M. Bloch, at the time of the merger Bloch had been head of the Raytheon Computer Division.
61. Ibid.
62. CBI Archive, IDC, 29/12/66 EDP Industry and Market Report: 2.
63. Op Cit, CBI Auerbach Collection 4/10. Auerbach Corporation for RCA 6/1960.
64. <u>US vs. IBM</u>, px3454, IBM Market Evaluation Department, 29/12/69. 'A company study of Honeywell Inc'.
65. CBI Archive, IDC, 29/12/66 EDP Industry and Market Report: 1–12.
66. Ibid.
67. Ibid.
68. Ibid.
69. Ibid.
70. Ibid.
71. Op cit. <u>US vs. IBM</u>, IBM Market Evaluation Department, 29/12/69.
72. <u>US vs. IBM</u>, tr4989, C.W. Spangle, vice president and general manager of Honeywell's EDP division.
73. Ibid. <u>US vs. IBM</u>, tr4990, C.W. Spangle.
74. Ibid. <u>US vs. IBM</u>, tr4961, C.W. Spangle.
75. <u>US vs. IBM</u>, dx230, internal Honeywell memo from, R.A. Kovak to R.R. Douglas, 20/5/75, This memo discussed methods of ensuring that GE 400 users transferred to the L66, rather than to a rival product.

## 10   Conclusions: Concentric Diversification, Resource Allocation and Government Policy

1. <u>US vs. IBM</u>, px3454, IBM Market Evaluation Department, 29/12/69. 'A company study of Honeywell Inc'.
2. B. Pollard 1960. 'A comparison of computer industries in the U.S. and the U.K.', Datamation, May/June 1960: 51–2.
3. Datamation, July 1963: 19.

# References

Abernathy, W.J. and Utterback, J.M. 1978. 'Patterns of industrial innovation', *Technology Review*, 80: 41–7.

Abernathy, W. J., 1978. *The productivity dilemma: roadblock to innovation in the automobile industry*. Johns Hopkins University Press.

Aguirre, M. S., Lee, T. K.and Pantos, T. D. 2008. 'Universal versus functional banking systems: the structure conduct performance hypothesis revisited', *Journal of Banking Regulation*, 10 (1): 46–67.

Anon, July 1958. 'Ferranti-the family and the organisation', *The Electrical Manufacturer* 22–5. http://archives.li.man.ac.uk/ead/html/gb133nahc-fer-p1.shtml

Arnold, E. 1982. *Competition and technical change in the television industry*. Palgrave Macmillan.

Baldwin, W.L. and Childs, G.L. 1969. 'The fast second and rivalry in research and development', *Southern Economic Journal*, 36: 18–24.

Baker, W.J. 1970. *A history of the Marconi Company*. Routledge.

Bard, B.J.A. 1955. 'The National Research Development Corporation', *Aslib Proceedings*. 7 (2): 84–91.

Barney, J.B. 2001. 'Is the resource-based "view" a useful perspective for strategic management research? Yes', *Academy of Management Review*, 26: 41–56.

Bartlett, C.A. 1983. 'EMI and the CT Scanner'. HBS Premier Case Collection.

Bashe, C.J., Johnson, L.R., Palmer, J.H. and Pugh, E.W. 1986. *IBM's early computers*. MIT Press.

Baumol, W.J., Panzar, J. and Willig, R. 1982. *Contestable markets and the theory of market structure*. Harcourt.

Berger, A.N., Hanweck, G.A. and Humphrey, D.B. 1987. 'Competitive viability in banking : Scale, scope, and product mix economies', *Journal of Monetary Economics*, 20 (3): 501–20.

Bergstein, H. 1962. 'RCA and EDP', *Datamation*, October 1962: 57.

Booth, A. D. 1980. 'Computers in the University of London, 1945–1962', in N. Metropolis, J. Howlett and G-C. Rota (Eds) 1980. *A history of computing in the twentieth century*. Academic Press.

Burgelman, R.A. 1988. 'Managing the internal corporate venturing process: some recommendations for practice', Chapter in: R. A. Burgelman and M. A. Maidique (Eds), 1988. *Strategic management of technology and innovation*. Irwin: 348–62.

*Business Week* 14/5/55. 'IBM':66.

Caminer, D.T. 2003. 'Behind the curtain at LEO: a personal reminiscence. IEEE Annals of the History of Computing', 25 (2): 3–13.

Campbell-Kelly, M. 1989. *ICL: a business and technical history*. Clarendon Press

Campbell-Kelly, M. and Asprey, W. 1996. *Computer: A History of the Information Machine*. Basic Books.

Ceruzzi, P.E. 1983. *Reckoners: the pre-history of the digital computer from relays to the stored program*. Greenwood.

Chalmers, M. 1985. *Paying for defence*. Pluto Press.

Chandler, Alfred D., Jr. 1977. *The visible hand*, Cambridge, MA and London, England: The Belknap Press of Harvard University Press.

Chandler, Alfred D., Jr. 1990. *Scale and scope*. Cambridge, MA. The Belknap Press of Harvard University Press.

Chandler, Alfred D., Jr. 2005, *Inventing the electronic century*. Harvard University Press.

Channon, D.F. 1973. *The strategy and structure of British enterprise*. Macmillan.

Cobbold, R.S., FRSC. 2010. 'Arthur Porter "1910-2010"', Obituaries of deceased Fellows', Royal Society of Canada.

Cohen, A.A. and Tomash, E. 1979. 'The birth of an ERA: Engineering Research Associates Inc',. *Annals of the History of Computing*, 1 (2): 83–100.

Cravens, D.W., Piercy, N.F. and Baldauf, A. 2009. 'Management framework guiding strategic thinking in rapidly changing Markets', *Journal of Marketing Management*, 25 (1–2): 31–49.

Croarken, M.G. 1985. 'The centralisation of scientific computation in Britain 1925–1955'. PhD. University of Warwick.

*Datamation*, 1971. 'RCA Autopsy: The cause was within'. December 1971: 42.

*Datamation*, 1971b. 'In breach of ten thousand promises'. October 1971: 7.

*Datamation*, 1958. '304 the New NCR Data Processing System'. May/June 1958: 12–14.

*Datamation*, 1958. atomic centers order british mercury. Nov/Dec 1958: 17.

*Datamation*, 1960. 'In business and science'. July/August 1960: 11–12.

*Datamation*, 1961. 'Bull's rule in Europe', September 1961: 30–3.

*Datamation*, 1961b. 'Bull's 300 Series': November 1961: 47.

*Datamation*, April 1964: 19.

Department of Business Innovation and Skills. Innovation Survey 2009.

Dorfman, N. 1987. *Innovation and market structure: lessons from the computer and semi-conductor industries*. Harper Business.

Drath, P. 1973. 'The relationship between science and technology: University research and the computer industry, 1945–1962', PhD Thesis, Manchester University.

Dyer, J. H. and Singh, H. 1998. 'The relational view: Cooperative strategy and sources of interorganizational competitive advantage', *Academy of Management Review*, 23: 660–79.

Eckert, J.P. interviewed 15/9/61.'Post-mortem', *Forbes*: 35–6.

*Eurostat*. Science and Technology. 91/2008.

Fisher, F.M., McKie, J.W. and Mancke, R.B. 1983. *IBM and the US data processing industry: an economic history*. Praeger.

Fishman, K.D. 1981. *The computer establishment*. Harper and Row.

Flamm, K. 1988. *Creating the computer: government, industry and high-technology*. Brookings.

*Fortune* 31/8/87. 'The greatest capitalist in history'.

*Fortune* January 1940. 'International Business Machines'.

Fraser, T.C. 1967. 'Economic development committees – a new dimension in Government-industry relations', *Journal Of Management Studies*, 4(2):154–67.

Rifkin, G. and Harrar, G. 1988. *The ultimate entrepreneur: the story of Ken Olsen and Digital Equipment Corporation*. Contemporary Books.

Golding, A. 1971. 'The semiconductor industry in Britain and the United States: a case study in innovation, growth and the diffusion of technology'. PhD. Thesis, University of Sussex.

Graham, M. 1986. *RCA and the video disc; the business of research*. Cambridge University Press.

Gruenberger, F.C. 1979. 'The history of the JOHNNIAC', *Annuals of the History of Computing*, 1 (1): 49–64.

Hamilton, R. 1996. 'Despite best intentions: the evolution of the British minicomputers industry'. *Business History*, 38 (2): 81–104.

Harbord, General, J.G. 1928. 'Radio in the World War and the organisation of an American-owned transoceanic radio service', in *The Radio Industry; the story of its development as told by leaders of the industry to the students of the Graduate School of Business Administration*. A.W. Shaw Company.

Harris, W.B. 1955. 'The overhaul of General Electric'. *Fortune*, 12/55.

Helfat, C.E. and Eisenhart, K.M. 2004. 'Inter-temporal economies of scope, organizational modularity, and the dynamics of diversification', *Strategic Management Journal*, 25: 1217–32.

Helfat, C.E. and Lieberman, M.B. 2002. 'The birth of capabilities: market entry and the importance of pre-history', *Industrial and Corporate Change*, 11 (4): 725–60.

Hendry, J. 1988. 'The teashop computer manufacturer: J. Lyons', *Business History*, 29 (8): 73–102.

Hendry, J. 1984. 'Prolonqed negotiation: the British fast computer project and the early history of the British computer industry', *Business History*, 26: 280–306.

Hendry, J. 1989. *Innovating for failure: Government policy and the early British computer industry*. MIT Press.

Hodges, A. 1983. *Alan Turing: the enigma*. Simon & Schuster.

Ivall, T.E. 1960. *Electronic computers: principles and applications*, 2nd edn. Iliffe.

Jacobs, J.F. 1986. *The SAGE Air Defense System: A personal history*. MITRE Corp.

Jeremy, D.J. (Ed.) 1984. *Dictionary of Business Biography: a biographical dictionary of business leaders active in Britain in the period 1860–1980*. Butterworths.

Jones, G. and Wadhwani, D.R., 2006. 'Schumpeter's plea: rediscovering history and relevance in the study of Entrepreneurship'. Harvard Business School Working Paper 06-036.

Jones, R. Marriott, O. 1970. *the anatomy of a merger: a history of GEC, AEI and English Electric*. Jonathan Cape.

Katz, R. and Allen, T. 1982. 'Investigating the not invented here (NIH) syndrome: A look at the performance, tenure, and communication patterns of 50 R&D project groups', *R&D Management*, 12: 7–19.

Kelly. T. 1987. *The British computer industry: crises and development*. Routledge.

Kranzley, A.S. 1960. 'Planning the RCA 601 System', *Datamation*, Sept/Oct 1960: 30.

Lavington S. 2011. *Moving Targets: Elliott-Automation and the Dawn of the Computer Age in Britain, 1947–67*. Springer.

Lavington, S.H. 1975. *A history of Manchester computers*. NCC Manchester.

Lavington, S.H. 1980. 'Computer development at Manchester University', in N. Metropolis et al. 1980. *A history of computing in the twentieth century: A collection of essays*. Academic Press.

Lavington, S.H. 1980. *Early British computers*. Digital Press.

Lawson, B. and Samson, D. 2001. 'Developing innovation capability in organisations: a dynamic capabilities approach', *International Journal of Innovation Management*, 5 (3): 377–400.

Layton, C., Harlow, C. and de Hoghton, C. 1972. *Ten innovations. An International Study on Technology Development and se of Qualified Scientists and Engineers in Ten Industries*. Allen & Unwin.

Leggatt. P. 1988. 'The evolution of television technology', *Electronic Engineer*, 60 (735).

Lundstrom, D.E. 1987. *A few good men from UNIVAC*. MIT Press.

Malerba, F., 1985. *The semiconductor industry: the economics of rapid growth and decline*. University of Wisconsin Press.

Malik, R. 1975. *And tomorrow the World? Inside IBM*. Millington.

Metropolis, N., Howlett, J. and Rota, G-C. (Eds) 1980. *A history of computing in the twentieth century*. Academic Press.

Moonman, E. 1971. 'British Computers and Industrial Innovation; The implications of the Parliamentary Select Committee'.

Nagata, T., Maeda, Y. and Imahigashi, H. 2004. 'Economies of scope in financial conglomerates: analysis of a revenue Side'. Financial Research and Training Center Discussion Paper.

Oldfield. H.R. 1996. *King of the seven dwarfs: General Electric's ambiguous challenge to the computer industry*. IEEE Computer Society Press.

Osborn, R.F. 1954. 'GE and UNIVAC: Harnessing the high-speed computer', *Harvard Business Review*, July-August 1954: 99–107.

Owen, G. 1999. *From empire to Europe: The decline and revival of British industry since the Second World War*. Harper Collins.

Oxford Economics, 2010. 'Examining sectoral growth in the UK - A report for the national endowment for science', *Technology and the Arts*.

Panzar, J. and Willig, R. 1975. 'Economies of scale and economies of scope in multi-output production', Economic Discussions. Bell Laboratories. 33.

Phister, M. 1979. *Data processing technology and economics*. Digital Press.

Pollard, B. 1960. 'A comparison of computer industries in the US and the UK', *Datamation*, May/June 1960: 51–2.

Porter, M.E. 1985. *Competitive advantage: creating and sustaining superior performance*. Free Press.

Porter, M.E. 1989. *The competitive advantage of nations*. Free Press.

Porter, M.E. 1980. *Competitive strategy: techniques for analyzing industries and competitors*. Free Press.

Pugh, E.W. 1984. *Memories that shaped an industry. Decisions leading to IBM system 360*. MIT Press.

Pugh, E. W. 1995. *Building IBM: Shaping an Industry and Its Technology*. MIT Press.

Rajchman, J. (RCA Engineer) 1980. 'Early Research on Computers at RCA', in N. Metropolis et al. 1980. *A history of computing in the twentieth century: A collection of essays*. Academic Press.

Randell, W.L. 1946. *S.Z. de Ferranti-his influence upon electrical development*, 2nd edn. Longmans, Green & Co.

Redmond, K.C. and Smith, T.M. 1980. *Project whirlwind: the history of a pioneer computer*. Digital Press.

Riordan, M. and Hoddeson, L. 1998. 'The transistor's father knew how to tie basic industrial research to development', *Research Technology Management*, January 1998.

Rodgers, W. 1969. *Think: A biography of the Watsons and IBM*. Stein & Day.

Rosen, S. 2004. 'Recollections of the Philco Transac S-2000. IEEE annals of the history of Computing', 26(2): 34–47.

Rothwell. R. et al. 1974. 'SAPPHO updated – project SAPPHO Phase II'. Research Policy. 3: 258–291.

Sarnoff, D. 1928. 'Radio in the World War and the organisation of an American-owned transoceanic radio service', in *The Radio Industry; the story of its development as told by leaders of the industry to the students of the graduate school of Business*.

Sciberras, E. 1977. *Multinational electronic companies and national economic policy*. JAI Press.

Snively, G. 1988. 'General Electric enters the computer business', *Annals of the History of Computing*, 10(1): 74–8.

Sobel, R. 1986. *RCA*. Stein & Day.

Soete, L., Dosi, G. 1986. *Technology and development in the electronics industry*. Science Policy Research Unit.

Srivastava, M. and Gnyawali, D. 2011, 'When do relational resources matter? leveraging portfolio technological resources for breakthrough innovation', *Academy of Management Journal*. 54 (4): 797–810.

Stern, N. 1981. *From ENIAC to UNIVAC: an appraisal of the Eckert-Mauchly computers*. Digital Press.

Sturmey, S.G. 1958. *The economics development of radio*. Duckworth.

Swann, G.M.P. and Baptista, R. 1999. 'The dynamics of firm growth and entry in industrial clusters: a comparison of the US and UK computer industries', *Journal of Evolutionary Economics*, 9 (3): 373–99.

Takahashi, S. 2005. 'The rise and fall of plug-compatible mainframes', *IEEE Annals of the History of Computing*, 27 (1): 4–16.

Teece, D.J. 1980. 'Economies of Scope and the Scope of the Enterprise', *Journal of Economic Behavior and Organization*, 1 (3): 223–47

Teece, D. and Pisano. G. 1994. 'The dynamic capabilities of firms: an introduction', *Industrial and Corporate Change*, 3 (3): 539.

*The Times* 25/5/56: 19.

*The Times* 31/5/56: 19.

*The Times* 13/5/58, report of A.T. Maxwell's chairman's address to the Powers' annual general meeting: 17.

*The Times* 29/7/64: 10.

*The Times* 30/4/64 'Statement by Mr Amery, Minister of Aviation, in reaction to the 2nd report on the Bloodhound missile from the Committee of Public Accounts' pages 6, 7 and 14.

Tilton, J. 1971. *International Diffusion of Technology. The case of semiconductors*. Brookings.

Usselman, S.W. 2011. *Learning the hard way: IBM and the sources of innovation in early computing*. Stanford. University Seminar in the Social Sciences and Technology, 23 February 2011.

Van Deusen, E.L. August 1955. 'The two-plus-two of Sperry Rand', *Fortune*, August 1955: 88.

Vardalas, J. 1994. 'From DATAR To The FP-6000 Computer: technological change in a Canadian industrial context'. *IEEE Annals of the History of Computing*, 16 (2).

Vennet, R. V. 2002. 'Cost and profit efficiency of financial conglomerates and universal banks in Europe', *Journal of Money, Credit and Banking*, 34 (1): 254–82.

*Wall Street Journal* Transcript, 8/11/71, 26103.

Watson Jnr, T.J. and Peter, P. 1990. *Father Son & Co. – my life at IBM and beyond*. Bantam Doubleday.

Wilkes, M.V. 1985. *Memoirs of a computer pioneer*. MIT Press.

Wilkinson, J.H. 1980. 'Turing's work at the National Physical Laboratory and construction of the Pilot ACE, DEUCE, and ACE', in N. Metropolis et al. 1980. *A history of computing in the twentieth century: A collection of essays*. Academic Press.

Williams, F.C. 1975. 'Early computers at Manchester University', *The Radio and Electrical Engineer*, 45: 327–31.

Williams, K., Dennis, T. and Williams, J. 1983. *Why are the British bad at manufacturing?* Routledge & Kegan Paul.

Williamson, O.E. 1975. *Markets and hierarchies, analysis and antitrust implications*. Free Press.

Wilson, C., Reader, W. 1958. *Men and machines: a history of D. Napier & Son Engineers Ltd 1808–1958*. Weidenfeld & Nicolson.

Wilson, J.F. 1988. *Ferranti and the British electrical industry 1864–1930.* Palgrave Macmillan.

Wilson, J.F. 2007. *Ferranti: A History. Building a family business 1882–1975.* Carnegie.

Worthy, J.W. 1987. *William C. Norris: Portrait of a Maverick.* Ballinger.

Yates, J. 1993. 'Co-evolution of information processing technology and use: interaction between the life insurance and tabulating industries'. Sloan School Working Paper #3575-93 / Center for Coordination Science Working Paper #145.

Yost, J. R. 2011. The IBM Century: Creating the IT Revolution. IEEE Computer Society Press.

Young, P.L. 1958a. Public relations employee of Ferranti Computer Department, 'The growth of a computer department. Part 1', *The Electrical Manufacturer*, March 1958: 18–20.

Young, P.L. 1958b. 'The growth of a computer department, part II', *Electrical Manufacturer*, April 1958, 30–3.

# Index